GEMS AND JEWELRY APPRAISING

2ND EDITION

ANNA M. MILLER, G.G., M.G.A., R.M.V.

FOREWORD BY ANTOINETTE MATLINS, P.G.

GemStone Press
Woodstock, Vermont

To Joanna, for her help,
friendship, and support

To Philip, my colleague in London

Gems & Jewelry Appraising, 2nd Edition:
Techniques of Professional Practice

Copyright © 1999 by Anna M. Miller

Library of Congress Cataloging-in-Publication Data
Miller, Anna M., 1933–
 Gems & jewelry appraising, 2nd edition : techniques of
professional practice / by Anna M. Miller.
  p. cm.
 Includes bibliographical references and index.
 ISBN 0-943763-10-X (hc)
 1. Jewelry—Valuation. 2. New business enterprises—
Management. I. Title. II. Title: Gems & jewelry appraising. III.
Title: Gems and jewelry appraising.
 NK7306.M54
 1999
739.27'029'7—dc21   99–29596
                                   CIP
                                   6910

10 9 8 7 6 5 4 3 2 1
Manufactured in the United States of America

Jacket photo: An exquisite emerald cameo, Colombian emeralds,
diamonds and pearls jewelry from the Granger of Singapore
Collection. Photo by Aw Toke Ghee.

Jacket design: Bronwen Battaglia

Published by GemStone Press
A Division of LongHill Partners, Inc.
Sunset Farm Offices, Route 4
P.O. Box 237
Woodstock, VT 05091
Tel: (802) 457-4000
Fax: (802) 457-4004
www.gemstonepress.com

CONTENTS

FOREWORD

The world of gems and jewelry is endlessly fascinating, endlessly changing, and endlessly challenging. Throughout history, gems have been coveted for their beauty, rarity, and value; throughout history, artists have been inspired to create exquisite jewels; and throughout history, people have attributed high *value* to virtually *all* gems. Today we know that many of the historical gems and jewels treasured by the world's rich and powerful were *not* what they first *appeared* to be. We also know that some of the "gems" in historical collections have little *value*, but these are modern insights.

It has been in relatively recent times—as the young science of gemology matured over the past few decades—that we have come to understand gems and jewelry, identify the vast quantity of gem materials, and recognize differences in beauty, rarity, and overall quality. In terms of determining *value*, "valuation science" is a discipline still in its infancy. New technologies impact on its development every day, and procedures are still in the formative stages.

Of all the appraisal disciplines, none is more demanding than that of appraising gems and jewelry. There are now more gems in the marketplace than ever before. There are gems that were unheard of several decades ago—new colors of known gems, new sources of gems, and more gems in any given color, with widely varying prices. There are new types of synthetics and more varieties of gemstones being synthesized, and new treatments to improve, alter, or conceal.

However, for today's gem and jewelry appraiser, gemological determinations are just the beginning of the appraisal process. Before reaching any conclusion about value, gems and jewelry appraisers must understand many other areas such as production techniques, antique jewelry, design, craftsmanship, legal issues including IRS and FTC rulings, and new technologies for collecting valuation information. As we move into the new millennium, appraising may become the most challenging part of the profession.

There has never been greater opportunity for appraisers. To conduct appraisal services in a professional manner, gems and jewelry appraisers need a comprehensive, reliable, up-to-date guide to appraising, combined with a standard reference work that sets forth procedures and techniques. This new edition of *Gems & Jewelry Appraising: Techniques of Professional Practice* has been published to meet these needs.

The first edition of *Gems & Jewelry Appraising: Techniques of Professional Practice* clearly established its author, Anna M. Miller, as the "First Lady of Appraising." A masterful work that quickly won international acclaim, it was an important addition to the gems and jewelry literature. This new edition has incorporated important changes and new developments since the first edition was published. As we enter the new millennium, the second edition of *Gems & Jewelry Appraising: Techniques of Professional Practice* promises to become the new *"standard"* for gem and jewelry appraisers worldwide.

Antoinette Matlins, P.G.
Author of *Jewelry & Gems: The Buying Guide,*
*Engagement & Wedding Rings, Gem Identification Made
Easy,* and *The Pearl Book*

v

PREFACE TO THE SECOND EDITION

Since first publication of this work in 1988, industry politics, fashion trends, cultural changes, and world economics have created dramatic changes in the jewelry appraisal field. Over the past ten years there has been a great amount of pushing, shoving, and posturing by jewelry appraisal groups trying to establish special territories and marketing niche. Now, at least for the moment, groups and individuals seem to be working together for the good of the appraisal industry, the appraiser, and the jewelry consumer.

Today is an era in which the profile of both jewelry appraiser and jewelry consumer has changed. Over the last decade consumers have been inundated with information about jewelry prices, markets, designs, and differences. However, while the consumer is getting smarter about buying and owning jewelry, they have also grown more discriminating about receiving *value* for their money. When we entered this century people were flocking to buy jewelry made by machine. We leave it valuing fine jewelry items made by hand at a higher price.

Appraisers must face market reality. In order to stay—and grow—in business, continuing studies in valuation science are mandatory. Around the world qualified professional jewelry appraisers are in demand to address vital and complex questions about the *market value* of gems and jewelry for insurance, taxation, inheritance, and resale. In the next century the appraiser's world will grow even more complicated with *new complex technology*. On the international scale, all jewelry appraisers should understand and be able to deal with changing *world* markets. What do we see as the *future* of jewelry appraisers? Although value science education is the *key* to professional development, individuals will also need *courage, tenacity,* and *vision* to be successful jewelry appraisers in 2000 and beyond.

Anna M. Miller, G.G., M.G.A., R.M.V.
1999

PREFACE TO THE FIRST EDITION

Only a few years ago, if you needed an appraisal of gems and jewelry for any reason, you asked your local jeweler, who hastily scribbled a one-line handwritten note. He or she usually performed the appraisal for free, and did so with reluctance, accommodating you only because as a customer you held the promise of a future sale. The price your jeweler may have assigned to the jewelry was granted without the least regard for market research, legalities, or ethics. In most instances, the estimate was no more than a properly completed sales receipt.

Gemologists were usually pushed into the role of appraiser by their jeweler employers, who were eager to gain an advantage over their competitors by advertising an experienced, well-educated staff. Assured by their bosses and gemological instructors that gemological training constituted a knowledge of appraisal, gemologists took on this role and muddled through the subsequent difficulties. No one ever asked jewelers or gemologists if they knew (or cared) about the differences between value and price.

The first hint that a professional jewelry appraiser might be a distinct entity from a jeweler and separate from a gemologist occurred in the 1970s, during which gems and jewelry gained widespread popularity as investments. Consumers, newly conscious of the effect of grading standards for diamonds and gemstones on their price, began to demand precise reports with exact figures of "value." While gemologists could identify and grade, and jewelers could keystone merchandise to come up with a price, few were qualified to go into court to substantiate their "value" judgments or explain, logically, how it was estimated on a particular item. To make matters worse, no universal appraisal standards for jewelry appraisers were known or used industry-wide.

The revolution in the personal property appraisals field (of which jewelry is a part) is a little more than a decade old. There now exist uniform standards and procedures for personal property appraisers, classes in valuation techniques, and degree programs in the valuation sciences.

Professional jewelry appraisers are on the edge of a new vocation. Banks, insurance companies, and governmental agencies have all helped bring about the changes and contribute to the birth of the profession; they have realized that they can demand and get high standards of performance and integrity from jewelry appraisers, as they can from appraisers of real property.

This book is a guide to becoming a professional jewelry appraiser, not a textbook on gemology or value theory. Valuation theory is a complex study best obtained in structured classes. Similarly, you should already have gemological expertise if you plan to become an appraiser. This book, while recognizing that jewelry appraising as a learned profession is in its infancy, attempts to enlighten both the new and practicing appraiser in current valuation techniques, research methods, markets, liabilities, and legalities.

The prices and values stated in *Gems & Jewelry Appraising* are actual prices compiled from quotes by wholesale and retail gems and jewelry dealers, antique jewelry dealers, manufacturer's price lists, and New York spot commodity prices—precious metals and sales realized from auctions. Since the supply and demand of gems and jewelry vary greatly, sharp differences in price are likely to occur from one geographical location to another, based on regional tastes and local economy. The prices stated in the text are therefore to be viewed as guides rather than exact values.

Anna M. Miller, G.G., 1988

ACKNOWLEDGMENTS FOR THE SECOND EDITION

Colleagues worldwide have contributed ideas and information for the second edition of this book. A special thanks to friends and associates in Great Britain: Philip Stocker, John Benjamin, Jack Ogden, and John S. Harris; Donna Hawrelko and Linda DeVine in Canada; Sang-Ki Kim and the 100-plus Korean Master Valuers; Judy Grieder Jacobs, Dominick Mok, Anne Paul, and Carol C. Chiu in Hong Kong; Tay Thye Sun, Patrick Lee, Ginny Granger, Aw Toke Ghee, Neelan Amarasuriya, many members of the Singapore Gemologists Society, and Vijayalakshmi Hashim, a colleague in Bangkok. Thanks also to my colleagues Fred Ward, Michele Zabel, Michael Goldstein, Anne Reichel, Katrina Ricketts, Anne Blumer, Martin Fuller, Lois Berger, Lorin Atkinson, Amber Shigematsu, Anthony Clark, Gary Dulac, William R. Mann, K. K. Malhotra, Don Kay, and Robert Weisblut. To Dr. Ouida Felker, Dr. Gary Schneider, Dr. Don Hoover, Dr. Curtis Conley, John Caro, Carl Schmeider, Richard W. Hughes, Don Kay, and Eva Anuniewicz, my grateful thanks to you all for sharing knowledge, data, and scholarship to advance and expand the field of valuation science. A special tribute of thanks and recognition to William D. Hoefer, who provided information and advice for much of the updated text.

ACKNOWLEDGMENTS FOR THE FIRST EDITION

I owe a debt of gratitude to many people who have helped me with this book. Special thanks to Joanna Angel for editorial assistance. Acknowledgments go to people who specifically contributed information and suggestions to the manuscript: David S. Atlas, Pamela J. Abramson, Dona M. Dirlam, Fabio Graminga, Lynette Proler, Richard F. Digby, Carol P. Elkins, Edward Tripp, Marcia Hucker, Kay and Anthony Valente, Judith Osmer, Dianna Chatham, Dr. Richard Rickert, Shelly Kuehn, Lary Kuehn, Therese Kienstra, Kim Hurlbert, Gail B. Levine, Myra L. Waller, Erin Randall, Emyl Jenkins, Gerhard Becker, Denise DeLuca, Joy McGeorge, Silva Salakian, Tannis Bilkoski, Alfred Brown, Howard Rubin, Patricia Soucy, Berangere Hannedouche, and Ellen Epstein.

Many thanks to the members of the Association of Women Gemologists who enthusiastically participated in several years' research on appraisers and methods of valuation. Thanks to contributors of ideas and suggestions from individual members of the Gemological Institute of America, the American Society of Appraisers, the National Association of Jewelry Appraisers, the American Gem Society, the Accredited Gemologists Association, the Appraisers Association of America, and the International Society of Appraisers.

Special thanks to Dr. Charles D. Peavy, ASA; Joseph W. Tenhagen, ASA; Fred L. Iusi, ASA; and ASA Director of Education Arthur Wilson for providing useful critiques of the manuscript.

I express my appreciation to Elizabeth Hutchinson for the artwork and to Alfred Lee for providing some illustrations. To John Miller for countless hours spent reading the manuscript, thank you.

Finally, thanks to friend and mentor Sara Levy, who was there at the start.

CHAPTER 1

THE APPRAISER

"The whole subject of appraisal of property: it's not an art and it's not a science; in my opinion, it's a mystery."
—Tax Court Judge Carlisle B. Roberts
Astoria, Oregon, June 1974

Appraising is a profession that started booming a few years after Judge Roberts pronounced it "a mystery."

The practitioners are a far cry from the old-time traders and miners—those romantic figures of the Gold Rush years. The glamour men and women of the industry today are the gems and jewelry appraisers, who understand gemstone treatments and can determine the country of origin and fair market value of precious gemstones and metals.

For many years, jewelry appraising hardly commanded prestige. "It was more like another hat the retail jeweler put on when absolutely necessary," remembers a New York jeweler. "Most people thought there were a few good ones and the rest were sleazy."

The status and number of jewelry appraisers changed dramatically during the late 1970s, the period of investment gemstones, tax-shelter donations, and barter deals. The demand for independent jewelry appraisers to handle the burgeoning investment market as well as the need to establish ethical standards for appraising were met by a plethora of new appraisal organizations, while creative leadership and guides encouraging those already involved with personal-property valuations spewed forth from established appraisal societies.

Amid the turmoil, the new codes of ethics, the sanctions, and the certifications, something exciting happened. To this profession in transit, a separate and elite progeny was born: professional gems and jewelry appraisers. These men and women were wise enough to obtain state-of-the-art gemological and valuation training and aware enough to comprehend that the public's and industry's outcry for reform would probably result in government licensing and a new set of appraisal legislation.

Who Is a Professional Gems and Jewelry Appraiser?

Today's *Professional Jewelry Appraiser* has tools, market experience, and special appraisal education to perform what has become one of the industry's most exciting and challenging jobs. Indeed, there are many "experts" in jewelry appraising as comfortable in court in the role of "Expert Witness" as they are in a gemological laboratory. We need not worry about these appraisers, because they are the ones who attend and support continuing education in the gemological and appraisal fields. Jeopardizing appraisers who have worked hard to become professional are the gemologists and jewelers appraising merchandise *without any* formal appraisal education.

At the present time anyone can call oneself a professional appraiser. However, self-anointing does not confer expertise. The key is *education*. A gemologist or jeweler who has undergone gemological training, holds a degree or special education in valuation science, and has buying and selling experience either on a wholesale or retail level has the basic prerequisites of an appraiser. Those with a tested, certified ability to value, identify, and grade gems and precious metals, circa-date jewelry, determine manufacturing methods, and research, write, and support valuations set forth in a report have the fundamental skills required to gain a marketable reputation as professional appraiser.

Clientele who may be served by this specialized knowledge include diverse groups: jewelry retailers, wholesalers, collectors, the general public, investors, insurance agents, insurance claims adjusters, bank trust officers, attorneys, state and federal agencies—including the U.S. Customs and the Internal Revenue Services—auction houses, certified public accountants, museum curators, pawnshops, and so on. The possibilities are endless.

The evolution of the jeweler or gemologist into an independent, skilled appraisal specialist worthy of public trust is a welcome step in a trade with a history of misplaced ethics and misguided integrity. In refusing to be swayed from a strong code of ethics, or sense of moral obligation, appraisers will maintain their positions of trust and could act as catalysts to upgrade the credibility of the entire jewelry industry.

A Brief History of Appraising

It has been said that jewelry answers a deep human need for self-beautification. From the earliest known jewelry items, which consist of three fish vertebrae necklaces dating from the late Paleolithic era (25000 to 18000 B.C.), men and women have loved wearing jewelry. Every culture has a history of prizing necklaces, rings, bracelets, and other tokens. Most, if not all, have also treasured earrings. The collection, use, and love of jewelry have been motivated by emotions ranging from blind superstition to monetary security and social status.

The first great jewelry and gemstone collectors were royalty and the church. They were in lock step with the first valuation specialists—the tax collectors or assessors.

Like appraisers today, the tax collectors of old needed some knowledge of values. Interestingly, texts were available for their use from as early as the fourth century A.D. In an Indian text, the *Artha-Sastra,* developed between the fourth and six centuries A.D., a body of rules and standards regulating taxes and other charges were applied to diamonds and precious stones. The text, which has been translated as *The Estimation and Valuation of Precious Stones,* reveals an extensive knowledge of the subject that was used for over one thousand years before evolving into a genuine technical manual known as the *Ratna-Sastra.* This latter text, used by assessors, officials, merchants, and others, has a detailed list of factors to be considered in assessing the value of individual gemstones.

Mostly, however, the search for information about valuation methods throughout antiquity turns up only inventory lists, although the lists themselves can be highly informative and certainly entertaining. One example is the 1750 Treasure Inventory of the Hapsburg-Lorraine family of the House of Austria. It mentions a large holding of jewels, as well as works of art and such heirlooms of religious significance as the Agate Bowl, once believed to be the Holy Grail. To a jeweler and appraiser this inventory is exciting; it can still be viewed, along with much of the listed treasure, in the Kunsthistorische Museum in Vienna.

In 1874, H. M. Westropp wrote *A Manual of Precious Stones and Antique Gems,* in which he lists the items of the Townshend Collection, housed in the South Kensington Museum, London, and the British Museum's Blacas and Devonshire Gems, but does not give their values. He offers one interesting tidbit about value, however, in a quote from a September 25, 1874, issue of the London *Times:*

A valuable addition has just been made to the collection of gems in the British Museum, through the acquirement by purchase of a splendid specimen of the Zircon. It cost upwards of 700 £, and is no larger than a common garden pea. It is one of the finest known. It flashes and glows with a red luster that seems to denote the actual presence of fire and flame.

Westropp added that he was in a position to state on the best authority that the zircon weighed about three carats.

An early appraisal report can be found in the work of the *Ratnapariska* of Buddhabhatta, written in Sanskrit and now kept in the Bibliothèque Nationale, Paris. This fifth-century manuscript states: "A diamond weighing 20 tandula is worth 200,000 rupakas."

Earlier still, the value of a gemstone can be found in Book 37 of Pliny the Elder's *Historia Naturalis,* written in the second century A.D. He quotes Theophrastus (c. 372–c. 287 B.C.) in giving a price for an anthrax (probably a ruby): "A small ring stone used to sell for forty aurei" (about $205.00). Pliny does not state the price per carat of the gem but he does mention the value factors of gems, which seem to be the same as those still held today: beauty, rarity, and demand. In Pliny's time crystal was valuable for goblets, and aventurine's price increased with the "greater number of stars upon the stone." This sounds a lot like gemstone appraising today, where visual phenomena command a higher valuation.

Some precious jewelry, however, is difficult to place any value upon. Major-General H. D. W. Sitwell, Keeper of the Jewel House of the Tower of London, has declared it impossible and fallacious to affix any monetary figure to the royal regalia:

"It is impossible," he writes, "because the Regalia really represent three values: (a) as precious stones, gold and plate, the value of which might be estimated by a jeweler; (b) as museum pieces, the value of which might be doubtfully assessed by an expert valuer; (c) their traditional value as the Regalia of Great Britain and the British Commonwealth and

Empire, the most important value of all" (Sitwell, 1953, viii).

The majority of today's jewelry appraisers, of course, are not faced with the task of appraising crowns and coronets. Most see a lot of cluster rings, straight line bracelets, wedding sets, and pearl strands. They are delighted, however, when an especially elegant item from antiquity or elaborately jeweled object of unknown provenance turns up for valuation. It is this kind of variety that the appraisers enjoy most: the surfacing of a special treasure in an otherwise ordinary collection.

Qualifications and Equipment

Much has been written about who is qualified to appraise gems and jewelry. Does being a gemologist make you a qualified jewelry appraiser? No, but gemological training does provide one of the subskills necessary to appraise competently. Does being a jeweler, buying and selling goods every day, make a qualified appraiser? No, but it provides one of the tools of appraising: a necessary knowledge of the marketplace.

The fact is, many jewelers and gemologists who do appraisals are ignorant about what an appraisal really is: a statement of the value of an article in its common and most appropriate market, not its *price* in any one store in particular. Jewelers set prices; appraisers analyze prices in relevant markets to define value.

Just what is an appraisal? In the handbook "The Appraisal of Personal Property," the American Society of Appraisers gives this definition: "An appraisal prepared by a professional appraiser identifies clearly the appraisal question (objective) for the appraisal, the intended use (function) of the appraisal, and the type of value (purpose) being estimated." *Black's Law Dictionary* defines an appraisal as "a valuation or an estimation of value of property by disinterested persons of suitable qualifications."

Key words are "suitable qualifications." To determine value requires training and education in long-established appraisal principles, procedures, value theory, standards, and research methods. Further, a broad knowledge of good communications is paramount to report writing. Clearly the appraising of gems and jewelry is outside the scope of gemology and requires much more of the gemologist/appraiser than simply the knowledge of gemstone identification and grading. Similarly, the jeweler who appraises needs to know more than just the product he or she is selling. Although formal education in gemology and practical trade experience lay the groundwork, formal appraisal training is necessary to complete the framework for a professional gems and jewelry appraiser.

Several jewelry trade, gemological, and appraisal groups have considered the qualifications a professional appraiser must have and list the following basic requirements:

1. Formal education in gemology
2. Training in principles of valuation
3. Training in evaluating various manufacturing methods
4. Experience in buying and selling
5. Knowledge of various levels of value and how they affect the market from source to consumer
6. Knowledge of current wholesale and retail prices of gemstones, jewelry, and watches
7. Knowledge of actual sales prices with access to verifiable data
8. A complete gemological laboratory, which includes the following:
   - Binocular microscope with dark field illumination
   - Refractometer
   - Polariscope
   - Spectroscope
   - Dichroscope with calcite element
   - Ultraviolet lights, SW/LW
   - Leveridge or Presidium gauge
   - Table gauges
   - Diamond tester
   - Metal testing kit
   - Fiber-optic illuminator
   - Diamond color grading light
   - Master grading set of diamond stones, graded by the GIA; five stones minimum with weights of at least a quarter carat each
   - Photographic equipment that will photograph on a 1:1 ratio
   - Specific gravity liquids
   - Gold weight scale (dwt. scale or gram scale)
   - Diamond balance scale or carat weight scale
   - Colored gemstones grading system
   - Tweezers
   - Color filters
   - Chelsea filter

It should be clear that appraising is a discipline separate from gemology, with a recognized education and certification program for the appraiser to follow. As with any professional certification, however, mastery of principles and methods and allegiance to a code of ethics are only the start. Education must remain on a continuing basis for the appraiser to keep up with developing techniques, legal matters, and to hone professional skills to a fine point.

Gemological and Appraisal Organizations and Designations

In the early 1980s, only a handful of gemological and appraisal associations offered designations of members. With the recent proliferation of appraisal societies, however, the industry has found itself submerged in an alphabet soup of acronyms. It would be in the best interest of all concerned if each association and society required stringent testing and/or education of its members, but some do not, the only entry requirement being a fee. The following list should clarify the confusion about the abbreviations G, GG, FGA, DGG, and so on. Of course, only you can determine which association best suits your needs, but it is clear that your peers and the public will perceive your gemological expertise and professional standing in the field by the string of initials after your name.

Gemological Associations and Titles

Gemological Institute of America (GIA): Founded by Robert M. Shipley, a retail jeweler and one of America's first trained gemologists, in 1931. Shipley responded to requests for education and gemological information by his associates with a series of lectures that soon turned into the first home study gemological courses in the United States. Growth was swift and in the 1930s and 1940s the GIA established a laboratory for testing gems and grading diamonds. Improvements were made on existing instruments and new tools for gem testing were developed. Since becoming a nonprofit institution in 1942, the GIA has become a recognized worldwide leader in gem and jewelry studies and training.

Gemologist (G): This designation is given by the Gemological Institute of America, whose new headquarters are located in Carlsbad, California, to individuals who successfully complete courses in gem identification, diamonds, colored stones, and colored-stone grading, and who pass a written examination. This course is usually accomplished by home study.

Graduate Gemologist (GG): The designation is awarded to students who have met all gemologist requirements and attended additional classes in diamond appraising and gem identification. Conducted by GIA instructors, the classes are usually one week long each, and are offered in cities throughout the United States during the year.

In a class by itself is the *Graduate Gemologist in Residence* diploma. For many, this is the premier accomplishment. The course covers all subjects taught at the gemologist and graduate-gemologist levels, but the students are taught in residence at the GIA facility in Santa Monica, or at the institute's New York campus. The residency program lasts about seven months. Other courses can be added—such as retail jewelry training, pearls, appraisals, and jewelry design—that can extend the total training time to a little over a year.

Fellow of the Gemmological Association (FGA): This title is awarded to the successful candidate for the gemological diploma of the Gemmological Association of Great Britain, the United Kingdom's equivalent of the GIA. The program is a correspondence course backed by coaching and guidance from the GAGB. The course involves two years of study and is divided into two parts, preliminary and diploma. This diploma is recognized worldwide as having a high professional and scientific standing.

Fellow of the Gemmological Association of Australia (FGAA): A course of study closely equivalent to that of the Gemmological Association of Great Britain, leading to a diploma for the designation FGAA.

Gemmologist, Accredited Gemmologist (CIG): These titles are given by the Canadian Institute of Gemmology, a registered trade school in Vancouver, Canada. The gemmologist certificate is awarded to students who have successfully completed the introductory course in gemmology or an equivalent study, as well as the courses on diamond grading and advanced gemmology. The accredited gemmologist diploma requires the gemmologist certificate (or equivalent) and completion of courses in colored-stone grading and practical gemmology. A recertification after five years and annual maintenance fee are imposed.

German Gemological Society (DGG): The Deutsche Gemmologische Gesellschaft, or German Gemological Society, awards its members a diploma equivalent to the GIA's graduate gemologist diploma. Applicants must successfully complete a gemological study program in Idar-Oberstein, Germany, and pass an all-day written, oral, and practical examination. The program of study is similar to that given by the GIA.

Appraisal Organizations and Titles

The American Society of Appraisers (ASA): This group, founded in 1936, is open to individuals engaged in the appraisal or valuation profession or in related activities. The society has approximately five thousand members worldwide, with fewer than one hundred and fifty of these falling within the gems and jewelry discipline. The ASA has an affiliate level as well as three grades of membership: candidate, member, and senior member. The affiliate level is for those who wish to be associated with the ASA but do not desire to advance within the organization. Membership is on an individual basis, and is not offered to business firms. Persons applying for the entry-level candidate grade of membership are required to take and pass an ethics examination during their first year in the ASA. Those seeking to join the ASA at the member level or to be promoted to member must pass an eight-hour written examination testing the applicant's knowledge, expertise, and competence within his or her discipline; submit two sample appraisal reports; have two years of full-time appraisal experience; and possess a degree in evaluation sciences, engineering, accounting, law, or business administration from a qualified school, or the equivalent of such education, as approved by the ASA's Board of Examiners. Senior members must meet all of the above requirements and have a minimum of five years of full-time appraisal experience. Only senior members may use the designation ASA after their names. In addition, senior members must recertify every five years. Fellowships (FASA) may be bestowed upon senior members by the ASA Board of Governors, in recognition of outstanding services to the appraisal profession or to the society. Fellows are entitled to use the designation FASA.

Master Gemologist Appraiser (MGA): This program was developed by the Accredited Gemologists Association in 1983, and became part of the American Society of Appraisers in 1987.

International Society of Appraisers (ISA): Founded in 1979, there are three levels of membership: associate, member, and CAPP (certified appraiser of personal property), a certified grade. Associate is an entry-level membership that can be obtained by paying an entry fee. To be designated a member of ISA, one must attend three core courses and complete their examinations. The courses cover legal, ethical, and theoretical aspects of appraising, and are basic to all disciplines of personal property appraising. Earning the CAPP designation requires the successful completion of the core courses and exams as well as specialized appraisal education in the candidate's discipline. Home study, professional development activities, and specialty reports are also requirements.

Appraisers Association of America (AAA): This group began testing and certifying its members late in 1986. Based in New York, the group meets monthly and conducts seminars and special conferences.

The National Association of Jewelry Appraisers (NGJA, NJA): The NAJA grants an accreditation to members who meet requirements of documented education and appraisal experience. Designations granted are national jewelry appraiser (NJA), national gem and jewelry appraiser (NGJA), the senior member designation, and Certified Master Appraiser (CMA).

Educational and Vocational Programs for Appraisers

In addition to the programs offered by the various gemological and appraisal organizations, several United States colleges and universities offer baccalaureate and master's degrees in the valuation sciences, including Regis College, Denver, Colorado, and Lindenwood College, St. Charles, Missouri. Serious personal-property appraisers will find a degree in the valuation sciences to be an asset to their careers, and should give it earnest consideration.

Lindenwood College at St. Charles, Missouri, offers an appraisal degree program unique because of its format. A four-year program with annual two-week intensive course of study on campus at Lindenwood can enable a candidate to earn a bachelor's or master's degree in valuation science. Each two-week program is structured to provide the nine required credit hours for one trimester's work and meets the standards of the North Central States Accreditation Association. When the student leaves the course and returns home, he or she is then required to complete course requirements of research and writing. The program enables applicants to earn a bachelor's or master's degree in valuation sciences by combining existing college credits from an approved institution with the hours earned at Lindenwood. With appropriate transfer and other credits, students can normally earn a degree within four years. The thirty-six credit hours earned in the four trimesters are used to meet the requirements and complete the one hundred and twenty semester hours necessary for graduation for undergraduates; graduate students need thirty-six semester hours of credit for a master's degree.

The Master Valuer Program, the first correspondence course for gems and jewelry appraisers, began operations in 1993. The program consists of a 30-lesson correspondence course and a week-long hands-on practical jewelry appraising workshop. The program focuses on jewelry appraisal methodology, value theory, report writing, ethics, legalities, research via the internet, and communication skills needed by jewelry appraisers. The program was designed for an international audience and since its inception has been given in Hong Kong, Beijing, Seoul, Bangkok, Singapore, Johannesburg, Vancouver, Toronto, London, and dozens of cities in the United States. The program is currently being taught in residence by the Korean Institute of Gemmology, the Registered Valuers of the National Association of Goldsmiths, U.K., and at the University of South Florida in Tampa. The Canadian Jewellers Association accepts graduates of the Master Valuer Program as having fulfilled the educational requirements to obtain their Accredited Appraiser designation.

The American Society of Appraisers has a career development program consisting of four three-and-one-half-day courses. The courses explore the concepts of value theory and its application to the specific discipline, such as business valuation, fine arts, gems and jewelry, and machinery and equipment. The course of study for the disciplines of personal property and gems and jewelry are designed to expand comprehension of basic value theory as well as the report-writing and research skills necessary for professional appraisers.

A series of classes in the basics of appraising is also offered by the International Society of Appraisers (ISA), in conjunction with Indiana University's School of Continuing Studies. The classes are offered in different cities throughout the year and the curriculum includes instruction in professional ethics, business practice, methodology, and the legal aspects of appraising. Those willing to fulfill some additional requirements can earn the certified appraiser of personal property (CAPP) title.

National Certification of Appraisers

Although at this time appraisers may undertake formal training and education in the valuation sciences simply to increase their knowledge and gain greater professional status, it is inevitable that appraisers will soon have to undergo national testing and certification. Legislation on testing and certification is expected to be passed by the end of this decade.

In the House of Representatives, the Commerce, Consumer, and Monetary Affairs Subcommittee on Government Operations, chaired by Representative Doug Barnard, Jr. (D., GA), opened hearings in Washington late in 1985 concerning the impact of faulty and fraudulent appraisals on both real estate loans granted by federally insured financial institutions and on related real estate activities.

Congress became concerned. The testimony presented at the hearings painted a picture of a totally unregulated profession, with only 10 to 20 percent of all persons who do appraisals holding any form of membership in a national testing and certifying appraisal society. Moreover, the only kind of licensing that now exists is aimed at real estate appraisers and is based on an examination of basic real estate knowledge, not technical appraisal knowledge. Even this regulation has not been adopted by all states.

The vast majority of appraisers in this country—both real-property and personal-property appraisers—are not currently accountable under any licensing laws, standards of professional practice, codes, or professional ethics, nor have they been examined as to their knowledge of appraising. National certification may make it possible that any individuals found guilty of unethical and/or fraudulent appraisals could, upon proof of incompetence or unethical practice, be prevented from engaging in all future appraising.

At the request of the Congressional committee, representatives from nine appraisal groups got together and drafted the Uniform Standards of Professional Appraisal Practice. The nine organizations represented were the American Institute of Real Estate Appraisers; the American Society of Appraisers; the International Right of Way Association; the National Association of Independent Fee Appraisers; the Society of Real Estate Appraisers; the National Society of Real Estate Appraisers; the American Society of Farm Managers and Rural Appraisers; the International Association of Assessing Officers; and the Appraisal Institute of Canada.

The nine organizations formed an umbrella group called the *Appraisal Foundation,* which formed a standards and certification board. The outcome (in 1989) was revision and adoption of an expanded version of The Uniform Standards of Professional Appraisal Practice (USPAP). Over the last decade, the initiatory sponsors of The Appraisal Foundation have changed and merged, but the majority remain real property appraisers. *Appraisal Sponsors* as of July 1997 were: American Association of Certified Appraisers, American Society of Appraisers, American Society of Farm Managers & Rural Appraisers, Appraisal Institute, International Association of Assessing Officers, International Right of Way Association, National Association of Independent Fee Appraisers, and National Association of Master Appraisers. *Affiliate Sponsors* are American Bankers Association, Farm Credit Council, Mortgage Insurance Companies of America, and National Association of Realtors. There is now one *International Sponsor,* Appraisal Institute of Canada. The gemological and personal property appraisal organizations that are not sponsors of the Foundation generally adopt their standards anyway, and ask members to conform to them.

Uniform Standards Are the Rules Under Which Professional Appraisers Will Work

Today, *all* federal financial regulatory agencies that oversee federally related real estate transactions require compliance with USPAP as the *minimum* standards. And public and private agencies have, or will soon, adopt USPAP, usually along with supplemental standards that must also be followed by anyone working in those agencies. State appraisal registration boards have incorporated the standards into their regulatory laws, and violation of the standards can result in suspension or revocation of an appraiser's license or certification. Although USPAP applies to *all appraisal disciplines,* to date only *real estate appraisers and consultants* have been impacted by licensing and enforcement by state agencies. This means USPAP standards are *voluntarily* adhered to by gems and jewelry appraisers unless one is a member of an appraisal association that mandates the standards to its members, such as ASA. However, while USPAP standards have been incorporated into the rules of *all major* appraisal organizations, enforcement is the jurisdiction of peer review committees. To ensure compliance with USPAP standards, members and candidates of appraisal organizations such as ASA who wish to be recertified and/or designated must show evidence of having successfully completed a specifically organized course on USPAP. While not teaching a specific course on USPAP, the International Society of Appraisers does incorporate and teach USPAP standards in their Core appraisal courses.

The Introductory pages of the USPAP student manual pose the question, "What is the purpose and intent of USPAP?" with the answer, *"Standards have established the minimum basis for the development of and the reporting of an appraisal. The standards are intended to aid users of appraisal services as well as set minimum requirements for appraisal practitioners."* The Uniform Standards of Professional Appraisal Practice have already resulted in significant positive changes to the appraisal profession, and the majority of tested and certified personal property appraisal practitioners are in favor of such standards. Most professional appraisers realize that until government licensing of personal property appraisers becomes a reality, strict and impartial national codes may be the only way to keep the incompetent out of the industry.

Currently, a Personal Property Appraiser Qualification Criteria Task Force, made up of personal property appraisers with diverse backgrounds, is writing *minimum* qualification criteria for appraisers of tangible personal property. The goal is for the criteria to provide assistance to users of personal property appraisal services in selection of a personal property appraiser. However, the qualification criteria will be voluntarily met by appraisers and, indeed, the Task Force does not foresee any governmental body utilizing the guidelines as part of a regulatory program.

Standards That Apply to Personal Property Appraisers

Of the 10 USPAP standards, Standards 7 and 8 specifically apply to personal property appraisers. The guidelines admonish personal property appraisers to be aware of, understand, and correctly employ recognized methods and techniques necessary to produce credible appraisals. Standard 7 covers recognized methods and techniques and the manner in which they must be used to produce an accurate appraisal. It warns against doing appraisals in a careless or negli-

gent manner, and against leaving out significant information that could affect a conclusion of value. It also covers proper identification, purpose, function, valuation date, research, and market conditions at the time of research. Standard 8 advises appraisers to communicate analysis, opinion, and conclusion in a manner that is not misleading.

The independent professional appraiser not mandated by society membership to conform to USPAP will, nevertheless, be wise to adopt the standards immediately and conform to them in his or her appraisal practice. One of the questions attorneys have been asking of appraisers in court is "Are there any national standards for appraisals?" The practitioner who can recite the USPAP standards and explain them will be more acceptable and professional.

The Importance of Belonging to Associations

Since 1930 the Gemological Institute of America has graduated over ten thousand gemologists. It cannot be doubted that a large percentage of those people have combined work in the jewelry business with appraising as a means of making a living. And in a February 1993 article in *SmartMoney* magazine, a *Wall Street Journal* publication, a Graduate Diploma in Gemology from the Gemological Institute of America was declared one of the "Five Best Degrees for Your Money." Regardless of how they have used their gemological education, they have felt the need to assemble together from time to time to swap information with their peers and reassess their goals. History tells us that individuals with similar interests have always tended to congregate in one particular section of a city or town. This was true of the communities of jewelers and artisans in ancient Alexandria, Rome, and Smyrna. The early artisans recognized that by joining together to form a society or guild they could exert pressure upon the state and church, and thereby influence the politics and the economics of the country indirectly.

In a similar sense, this still holds true today. Many gemologists, jewelers, and appraisers belong to an association or society of their peers in order to gain the "protection" of the assembly and reap the benefits of the association's good reputation. Concurrently, gemological and appraisal associations, like the Marines, are always looking for "a few good men" and women to swell their membership. If fan mail is any barometer, certified jewelry appraisers are as good as gold—and just as eagerly sought.

In the early 1980s, the American Society of Appraisers received over ten thousand requests for appraisal help. In reply, the ASA sent names of its members. This is the first benefit of belonging to an association:

you establish credibility as an appraiser and profit from advertising provided by the association.

Belonging to an association of your peers can also give you greater potential media exposure. Local radio and television talk-show hosts are generally eager to find gemologists and appraisers to interview because the subject of gems is romantic, and determining value of an object mystifying and interesting. Hosts seek out articulate speakers by contacting gemological and appraisal associations, since they often perceive professionals belonging to such organizations as having greater status than those who operate alone and unaffiliated. In addition, newcomers to town are more likely to search the Yellow Pages for an association that they know from previous contact. Your listing under the association's umbrella advertisement may often turn out to be a substantial source of clientele.

Participation in local and national meetings helps you develop close bonds with other appraisers in your field, and this networking experience can be the most important tangible in your career. Before joining any group however, make sure that the organization will operate with your best interests in mind as a member of the team. Attend a meeting or two and meet the people with whom you will be sharing the title of member. Ask your friends and associates what they know about the organization and its members. Are they respected as professionals in the community because of their superior knowledge and ethics, or is the organization just a social club? You can find out a lot about an association with a simple question to a few of its members: What does this association do for you? Your decision to join should be based on careful attention to the answers you receive.

Ideally, an association should offer continually updated information in your special field, and should provide contacts to further your vocational goals.

The most vital reason, however, for belonging to an association is a legal one. If your career as a jewelry appraiser lasts long enough, you will almost certainly be called upon to serve as an expert witness at one time or another. When you do appear in court, your credentials will be carefully scrutinized; being a tested and certified member of a national association of appraisers can go a long way toward making you a credible witness. (See chapter 7 for further discussion of expert witnesses.)

On the other hand, some courts may accept any association as worthwhile and fail to distinguish among those indigenous to the field and those that are totally irrelevant.

A highly respected personal-property appraiser, Dr. Charles D. Peavy of Houston, testified in a trial and was quizzed about his credentials as expert witness.

Peavy explained that he was a senior member of the American Society of Appraisers and had been examined, tested, and certified by ASA in his discipline of personal property. The opposing witness, when asked about her credentials, stated that she was a Smithsonian Associate. The judge agreed with the opposing witness that the Smithsonian was a fine institution, and commented that he had never heard of the ASA.

Dr. Peavy was later able to explain to the court that being a Smithsonian Associate simply means that the member receives *Smithsonian* magazine and has discount buying privileges and a few other perquisites at the Washington facility. When opposing counsel tried to defend the SA title, Dr. Peavy observed, "I have just been elected to the National Geographic Society, but that doesn't make me a geographer."

Conflict of Interest

Because many appraisers are also jewelers, antiques dealers, auctioneers, consultants, and pawnshop owners, the question of whether a dealer can stop dealing during an appraisal is often raised. Can the obvious conflict of interest be kept under control? It is a much debated issue. Jewelers who appraise maintain that because they are active in the marketplace, they know what an item will sell for; thus, they reason, they are better qualified to know the true value of a gem or jewelry item than is an appraiser who is not a dealer. The number of professional gems and jewelry appraisers who handle only appraisals is growing, but until the demand for appraisers without vested interests is met, jewelers and appraisers may continue to coexist in the same business, if not the same body. The problem of conflict of interests has been addressed by the ASA in this way:

> . . . it is unethical and unprofessional for an appraiser to accept an assignment to appraise a property in which he has an interest or a contemplated future interest.
>
> However, if a prospective client, after full disclosure by the appraiser of his present or contemplated future interest in the subject property, still desires to have that appraiser do the work, the latter may properly accept the engagement, provided he discloses the nature and extent of his interest in his appraisal report (American Society of Appraisers, 1968).

By making a simple declaration, jewelers who buy, sell, and appraise can prevent possible misunderstandings.

Opening an Appraisal Service

Every year people try to escape from ordinary jobs and dreary vocations. It has been estimated that as many as twenty-five million Americans change jobs annually. Those who are in the jewelry business can easily believe these statistics, for it often seems that every other person they meet was once in the business, is in the business, or wants to be in the jewelry business. Gemstones and jewelry, with their aura of glitter, money, and excitement, draw many into the industry. However, it takes motivation and staying power to succeed.

The U.S. Census Bureau tells us that 60 percent of all new businesses fail, dissolve, or reorganize within the first two years of operation. Most failures can be traced to mismanagement; one-third fail from undercapitalization. A budding businessperson needs a clear concept of the business, clients, and goals. A sound plan of action is essential. Plan to do a lot of research before you make a commitment, and be sure to consider the following points.

How will you raise capital and how much money will you need to establish the new business? The first rule for opening your own business is to have enough cash on hand to cover all overhead expenses and forego drawing a personal salary for at least six months, and preferably for one year.

A major problem for many women, however, is raising the money for a new enterprise. Most banks are not interested in loaning venture capital money, although they do look favorably upon wage earners. When you consider how to raise money, it would seem wise to hold onto your present job while in the process of applying for a personal loan to be used for a new business.

The amount of money you will need for start-up will certainly be dictated by your personal lifestyle, ambition, and a careful analysis of projected business income and overhead. However, an operation can be launched on a shoestring for as little as five to seven thousand dollars if you already own gemological instruments or have access to them, as one woman gemologist in Tucson discovered. Bent on success, she borrowed money from a friend after her loan applications were turned down by banks, and opened a one-room 750-square-foot office in a strip shopping center. She furnished it with antiques from her own home and prepared appraisals off a desktop that doubled as a sales counter. It took a few years of devoted application to drumming up business and clientele, but her imagination and talent paid off. When she eventually expanded her business, she tripled her office space

and opened a completely equipped gem laboratory, diamond selling room, and retail sales area.

If you do not have sufficient capital, or are unable to obtain financing, you may consider a partnership. By combining money and talent, two partners can often accomplish what one cannot do alone. Be aware, however, that there are pitfalls involved in partnerships. A high degree of mutual trust is required for both parties.

There are two forms of partnerships that seem workable: the silent partnership, in which the silent partner puts up half the money in return for half of the profit but does not participate in the day-to-day business operations, and the limited partnership. Like the silent partner, the limited partner shares in the profits of the business and does not have a voice in management. However, the limited partner is liable only for the amount of his or her monetary contribution to the business. A limited partnership is often created for the express purpose of obtaining additional business funds.

Whichever you decide upon, be sure to have an attorney prepare a written agreement drawing up the terms of the partnership. The agreement will spell out exactly who has what authority and set the limits of individual expenditures. The agreement will also stipulate how the partnership may be dissolved, for reasons of disagreement or death.

If you are planning to be an independent appraiser working for a jewelry store or individual jeweler, the partnership will probably take the form of a handshake or gentlemen's agreement, with both parties filling the needs of the other. Some jewelry vendors who lease space in large department stores, including department store chains, hire independent appraisers to appraise in the store on a full-time or piecemeal basis.

A common and quick way to open a business is to rent an office in a building housing similar jewelry operations, usually wholesalers and jewelry repair shops. These people can be a good source of appraisal income and you may also get walk-in customers who have other jewelry business in the building. There are also cooperative offices in most large cities in which your contract for office space also pays for a group receptionist and telephone answering services.

After you have selected a site, check the location and the apparent prosperity of the neighboring businesses. Is the office or store in a stable, changing, or deteriorating part of town? Who are your neighbors? Do the surrounding businesses sell a product compatible with yours? How is the customer traffic? Is parking adequate or public transportation accessible? Will there be much competition from other jewelers, discounters, or department stores? Inquire about municipal codes that might affect your business, including any permits necessary or building codes regulating the remodeling or restoring of sites (especially historic buildings), and do the basic research needed to build a profile of customer demographics.

If yours is a low-budget operation, try not to spend money on fancy decorating, at least not initially. You can profit nicely with a few hundred feet of space divided into two rooms with a partition or clever furniture arrangement. The idea is to create a private area that you can use as a laboratory. Since many clients will not want to let their jewelry out of their sight, have extra chairs in the lab so that customers can watch as you conduct the examination. The front office should be furnished with a desk, computer, telephone, and comfortable chairs. A computer is no longer optional for a new business. And you will need fireproof filing cabinets to safeguard your records and a UL-approved high-security safe to store customer property if you plan to hold anything overnight.

Decorating can be accomplished with a bit of creative effort and imagination. Offices need not all be furnished from an office furniture store. An Indian- or Oriental-style rug, bookcases or armoires, and a few green plants can create a serene yet professional ambiance. Of course, you should hang your diplomas and certificates on the walls; be sure they are handsomely framed.

Painting and carpentry will not be a problem if you decide to locate in an office building. If you opt to move to a shopping center, find out whether you will be required by the terms of the lease to provide your own wall and floor coverings, do your own carpentry, and supply your own heating, cooling, and lighting systems. These are expenses you can do without when you are just going into business. If nothing but a shopping-center location will do, try to find a previously occupied space that needs little or no alteration. In most cities, you will have to pay a deposit for electrical service. Some office complexes include this in the rent.

Office buildings generally list each business in their directory, which is usually located in the lobby. Freestanding buildings and shopping centers, on the other hand, sometimes stipulate that individual business signs must conform to specific sizes, types of lettering, and materials. Most banks and office buildings will not permit freestanding signs.

Your professional letterhead and other basic appraisal documents need to be considered early in the process of opening an office. Quality printing takes time but is essential—your professionalism will be reflected in your stationery and appraisal forms.

You should contract for an advertisement in the Yellow Pages as soon as your lease is signed, since it will usually be several months before the advertisement appears in the next issue of the publication. It is unethical, however, to advertise a title or group affiliation in such a way as to imply that you have been tested by the organization for your appraisal expertise *if* the title does not involve certification for such proficiency, or if you have not been granted full rights to the title by the association.

You should have an attorney review any lease before you sign it. Many people, especially those in smaller communities, hesitate to hire professional consultants to assist them when they open a business. The main reason is cost—a good lawyer or accountant can charge a hundred dollars an hour or more. However, saving money by scrimping on consultants' fees can be costly in the long run. Many leases require you to join merchants' associations, adhere to specific opening and closing hours, or pay a variety of hidden extra fees. Similarly, it is worthwhile to hire a bookkeeper or accountant to set up your initial bookkeeping system. If you operate—or plan to operate—your business with the help of a computer, look into one of the fine jewelry software accounting programs. Even though initially time is needed to learn to operate the system, it may ultimately save time and money.

Find out if you need a resale number and obtain one if necessary. Most states require you to have a resale number even if you intend only to appraise and do not collect state sales tax for appraisals. A sales tax deposit must be paid to the State Tax Board when you obtain a resale number. It is based on store rent, projected sales, and so on. You will probably also need to apply for a business license; most cities mandate these.

If you do not already have Errors & Omissions insurance, you will need to obtain it. An E&O policy covers any claims for damages arising from negligence, errors, or omissions resulting from professional services rendered, or that should have been rendered. It also covers the cost of defense against suits alleging damages for the above reasons, even if the suit proves false, groundless, or fraudulent. A solid policy will cover claims made anywhere in the world. It does not cover bankruptcy; libel or slander; any dishonest, fraudulent, malicious, or criminal acts or omissions by the appraiser; punitive damages; bodily injury; or property damage. However, it does provide a security blanket for appraisers, in recognition that the technical problems involved in appraising gems and jewelry are such that there is always the danger of errors from which loss may result.

E&O insurance is expensive and can be difficult to obtain, especially for appraisers who cannot demonstrate a good track record. See whether your state jeweler's association offers group insurance rates (if you are a member) or, if you are an independent appraiser, try to obtain coverage through one of the appraisal organizations to which you belong.

Jewelers Mutual Insurance Company expanded its jewelry appraisal liability program for jewelers and jewelry appraisers in 1997. They offer jewelry appraisal liability coverage that can be added to a Jewelers Mutual's policy, Craftsman policy, or Combination Policy Program. To qualify for appraisal coverage, jewelers and jewelry appraisers must meet specific criteria such as appraisal education and jewelry appraising experience.

Becoming a Portable Appraiser

Many appraisers opt to be "portable"—that is, to maintain an office base in their home, but conduct appraisals at the client's home, office, or other location. There are many aspects to being a portable appraiser that do not apply to appraisers in fixed locations. The most obvious difference is that portable appraisers have no office or overhead costs. The second advantage is freedom of movement. In addition, portable appraisers do not have to fill out take-in forms or worry about clients accusing them of switching stones or damaging valuables, since they do not keep any jewelry overnight.

Of course, there are also disadvantages to working out of your home: Heavy loads of equipment must be carried to each appraisal, lighting and working conditions are often less than ideal, you may frequently have to put up with misbehaving children and/or pets, and the public will have access to you twenty-four hours a day unless you have a separate business telephone or answering machine. Also, you must gather, write, and interpret all information about the jewelry during the examination, for if you forget to check an item or option on an item, you may have to make another trip back to see the jewelry, thus losing time and money. Moreover, some people perceive portable appraisers as less professional than their storefront counterparts, although this attitude is changing. Many professionals—including real estate brokers, accountants, architects, and consulting engineers—work out of their homes. The United States economy is becoming more service oriented, and as a portable appraiser your services will be in demand.

All the equipment necessary to handle almost any appraisal can be carried in a small suitcase. The Gem Instruments Corporation sells the MaxiLab, and Gemological Products manufactures the Portalab (figs. 1-1, 1-2). Both are complete, self-contained gem testing laboratories that can be carried and used anywhere. With options, prices range around seven thousand dollars.

In addition to a portable lab, you will also need to

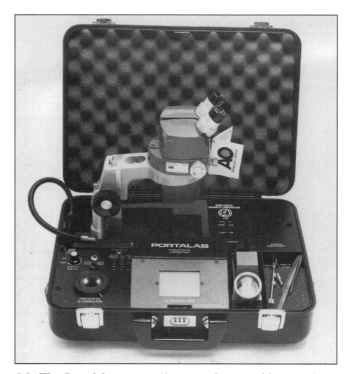

1-1. The Portalab, a convenient way for portable appraisers to carry a gemological laboratory into the field. *(Photograph courtesy of Gemological Products Corporation)*

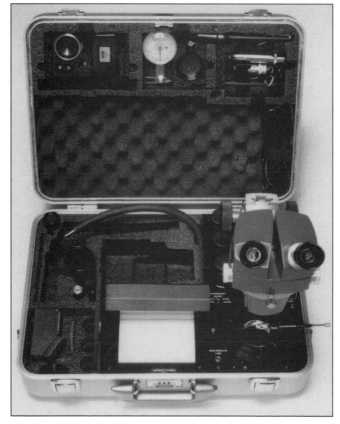

1-2. The MaxiLab, another portable gemological laboratory. *(Photograph courtesy of Gem Instruments Corporation)*

Table 1-1. The Costs Involved in Getting Started

1.	GIA TraveLab with GemoLite Super 60 Zoom Optics	$6,695.00	24. Ultra Fine Melee Tweezer	13.95
2.	Presidium Dial Gauge	225.00	25. 2X Adaptor Lens for Microscope	262.00
3.	Ricoh Digital Camera	600.00	26. GEM Cloth	3.75
4.	Mettler Jewelers Scale	1,795.00	27. Wire Stoneholder	65.00
5.	Fiberlite 250 intense light source	695.00	28. Parcel papers	8.95
6.	GIA DiamondMaster with warning buzzer	199.00	29. Loose stone boxes	40.00
7.	Gold Tester: G-XL-24 PRO	595.00	30. GIA Property Charts A & B	15.00
8.	Darkfield Loupe	215.00	31. Diamond labels for appraisal reports	5.95
9.	GEM Duplex II Refractometer	395.00	32. Dues to professional organizations:	
10.	Gem Instruments Illuminator Polariscope	225.00	*American Society of Appraisers*	425.00
11.	Replacement Interference Figure Sphere	6.50	*Appraisers Association of America*	300.00
12.	Polarizing Filter Sets	240.00	*Accredited Gemologists Association*	125.00
13.	File-A-Gem deluxe diamond wallet	65.00	*GIA Alumni Association*	120.00
14.	DG-X Diffraction Grating Spectroscope 110V	2,984.00	33. Subscriptions to price guides:	
15.	GEM SW/LW Ultraviolet Lamp	244.00	*The Guide*	180.00
16.	UV Viewing Cabinet	125.00	*Auction Market Resource*	195.00
17.	GEM Calcite Dichroscope	91.50	*Diamond Value Index*	100.00
18.	Chelsea Color Filter	49.00	34. *Gems and Gemology* subscription	59.95
19.	Diamond Master Stones: GIA GEM trade laboratory certificates (5)	4,500.00	35. *Jewelers-Circular Keystone* subscription	33.95
20.	PearlMaster Comparison Set	725.00	36. *Lapidary Journal* subscription	28.00
21.	Pearl gauge with carrying case	60.00	37. Gemology and Appraisal reference, text books	500.00
22.	OHAUS Scout portable gram scale	200.00	38. Stationery, forms, report covers, brochures, business cards	850.00
23.	GIA GemSet (Colored Stone Grading)	625.00	39. Desk, 3 chairs, 2 lamps, rug, gem pictures for walls, green plants, 2 bookcases	2,000.00

outfit another case with a movable office—a catalog or book salesperson's case is ideal. The case should contain photographic equipment and film, a pennyweight or gram-weight scale, a tape measure, a pocket calculator, a millimeter gauge, a carrying case of diamond masters, a diamond-weight scale, worksheets, and any other hand tools you believe will be necessary.

Table 1-1 shows a breakdown of the typical costs involved in starting a new business. It includes an itemized list of the equipment that one gemologist, who opened a new business in Kansas in 1997, needed to conduct appraisals both in his office and in the field. He already had a computer and hand tools. It cost him over twenty-six thousand dollars to start his new business, not including rent, deposits, or licenses.

Building a Clientele

Whether your business will be large or small, you will need to budget money for advertising. You should advertise directly to the public if you are an independent businessperson, and advertise in trade journals or through direct mailings if you are working with or for a jeweler. Advertising can take several forms and can be an elaborate or a simple do-it-yourself project, as your budget permits.

Advertising agencies and public relations firms exist throughout the United States and can help you launch a business, improve your public image, or build a high public profile. Some will set up an account for you and charge you according to the time spent on your project; others charge a percentage of the money you spend on advertising; still others do both. However, it is likely that no agency will want your business if the billing will run to only a few hundred dollars. They simply will not want to expend the energy on such a small return. You can do it by word processor or computer on your own and get good results by being creative, alert to opportunities, and persistent in making your own media and business contacts.

Whether you are opening up your own business or forming a partnership, you should announce the new business in the local newspaper first. You may also consider advertising in the local legal newspaper (most metropolitan cities have one), in club or religious newsletters, in trade publications, and in direct mailings to attorneys and insurance companies, whose names can be found in the Yellow Pages directory. Your local weekly or daily community newspapers are likely to be a good bet, as they tend to be receptive to running announcements and press releases. If you take out an advertisement in the paper, you can reasonably request a feature story on your business, too. Bear in mind that during the summer, many local papers are without the copy they usually devote to schools and sports, and may be looking for space-filling material. It is most important, however, to remember that many weekly papers are understaffed and also that they prepare their newspapers many days in advance of printing. To maximize your chances for publication, submit a press release that needs as little rewriting as possible, and send it in early. Follow the standard format for press releases:

1. Type the release, double-spaced, on standard 8½″ × 11″ paper.
2. Begin typing a third of the page down from the top.
3. Place the date in the upper right corner.
4. Place your identification—name, business address, and telephone number—in the upper left corner, so that the editor can contact you for further information if necessary.
5. In the first paragraph, explain the who, what, when, where, why, and how of your story; fit this within the first sentence if you can.
6. Be concise. If you have a second page (try not to), identify the story in the upper left corner and write "continued" at the bottom of the first page.
7. Indicate the end of the release by typing "30," ###, or "end" at the bottom of the page.

In addition, you should read the newspaper to which you intend to send the release for several days or weeks to determine on which page or section your release would be considered news. Business page? So-ciety page? Financial page? Call the newspaper to find out the name of the person who handles this page or section, and mail your press release to their attention. A sample press release announcing the opening of a new business is shown in figure 1-3. If the release does not get published, don't be disappointed. Try again.

Shortly after you open your doors to the public, you will be besieged by an army of salespeople badgering you to advertise in everything from civic newsletters to coupon mailings. Be prepared—have a plan of action already mapped out for your dollars and stick to it. Do not let anyone sign you up for services you do not need. Instead, focus on establishing your own personal mailing list of clients—it will become your most valuable resource for advertising gain. Begin your list of clients by keeping your customers' names, addresses, and telephone numbers in a card file. Keep it current and add the names and addresses of people who call you on the telephone to inquire about prices for appraisals. These calls should be followed up with a letter and brochure from your office. A sample follow-up letter is shown in figure 1-4. This list of clients will be used for all kinds of mailings from your office, from those suggesting updates on appraisals to those offering a diamond brokerage service. Learn to work your list; these customers already know you, so take advantage of this edge.

If you work out of your home, get a post office box to use as your mailing address. Advertise that all appraisal work is by appointment only. Use the card file

1-3. Sample press release announcing the opening of a new appraisal business.

Announcement

The grand opening of XYZ Gems and Jewelry Appraisers has been announced for this weekend in the ABC Building, 123 Main Street. An open house will be held from 9:00 A.M. through 3:00 P.M., Saturday and Sunday, November 1 and 2. A tour and explanation of the laboratory services will be offered.

Matthew Williams and Chris Williams, owners of the firm, are Graduate Gemologists of the Gemological Institute of America, and bring a combined total of twelve years of gems and jewelry appraising to the new business. The new facility uses state-of-the-art laboratory instruments and advanced technology for the examination and evaluation of diamonds, gemstones, precious metals, and jewelry items.

Each stone, loose or set, is checked to determine if it is genuine, synthetic, or imitation. It is examined for clarity, cut, and color, as well as size and carat weight. All jewelry is evaluated for its metal content, the quality of workmanship and design, and the period of its style. Color photographs of the jewelry accompany the Certified Appraisal Documents that XYZ Gems and Jewelry Appraisers render for insurance and estate purposes.

"We do not buy or sell," Matthew Williams said, "but we know fair market values and appreciation potentials, and we are familiar with replacement costs. Because of our portable equipment," he continued, "we can offer appraisals to our clients either in our office or at a site of their choosing."

Williams discussed the modest fees that they impose for appraisal work and emphasized that the charges are based on time, not on a percentage of the appraised value.

After this weekend, XYZ appraisers will be open from 9:00 A.M. to 5:00 P.M. Monday through Friday, and on weekends by appointment only. Call 555-1234 for additional information.

1-4. Sample follow-up letter to send to potential clients who have telephoned to inquire about appraisal prices.

Dear _____ :

As you have requested, I am sending you a brochure and business card to explain our gems and jewelry appraisal service more fully. I have also enclosed a list of my qualifications as an appraiser.

If, after reading this brochure, you have any questions regarding the professional appraisal of jewelry, please contact me at the number listed below.

XYZ Appraisers has portable gemological equipment as well as a fully equipped office, so appraisals can be conducted at your convenience at the site of your choice. You are welcome to watch the appraisal being conducted and to ask any questions pertinent to the appraisal.

Our work is by appointment, and we are available six days a week.

Thank you for your interest in XYZ Appraisers.

Sincerely,

---

mailing list for your personal clients; if you do work for a jeweler, establish a separate card file for those clients.

You need not limit your direct mail campaigns to customers you already have on file. Consider sending client solicitation letters to attorneys, bank trust officers, and insurance agents. Offer your services and let them know exactly why they would need expert jewelry appraisals—for probate, estate liquidations, community property settlements, and so on. Sample solicitation letters are shown in figures 1-5 and 1-6.

Networking is a very old method of getting business. It involves associating yourself with your peers and working the group with determination and diligence to get clientele. Get involved in committee work, attend meetings faithfully, and make yourself known to one and all. Send your card and brochure to each personal property appraiser in any appraisers' organization to which you belong—including jewelry and gemological associations.

Send a "Dear Colleague" letter to the jewelers in your area and let them know that you are available to perform their appraisals independently. If you are able to work in their store, advise them accordingly; if so, the jeweler can book appointments for you and then let you know when to come in and service the accounts. An offer of cooperative advertising announcing your visits may be of interest to the jeweler and help generate some appraising business.

Prepare a personal biography—a list of your qualifications as an appraiser—and have it printed, and use it as a handout to all potential customers; that is, anyone who shows an interest in getting an appraisal. Most consumers are not aware that qualified appraisers must undergo special training, and assume that all jewelers are appraisers.

Approach the professional groups of insurance agents in your community and offer to speak to them on the subject of proper appraisals for insur-

1-5. Sample client solicitation letter to send to attorneys, bank trust officers, and insurance agents.

Re: Personal Property Appraisals

Dear _____ :

We would like to offer our services to your clients who require appraisals of their gems and jewelry.

ABC Appraisers, a fully certified gems and jewelry appraisal organization, will conduct examinations of personal property for appraisals in homes, offices, or banks. This ensures client privacy and that no property leaves its place of safekeeping. Color photographs of the complete inventory are included with each appraisal report.

ABC Appraisers offers jewelry appraisals for probate, insurance, community property settlements, and estate purposes.

Appraisals are by appointment and fees are based upon hourly rates. A brochure that explains our services in greater detail is enclosed. For additional information or business references, please call 555-1234.

Cordially,

1-6. Sample client solicitation letter to send to insurance agents.

Dear _____ :

   In these unsettled times, more and more people are converting their cash to jewelry and gemstones. As this trend continues, there is greater demand for personal property insurance and, as part of that coverage, it becomes imperative to procure the best possible appraisals. Associated Gemologists is an independent appraisal firm that can fill this need.

   Authenticity, quality, design, and value are the four most important criteria that our expert staff is dedicated to explaining to the prospective client. Associated Gemologists offers personalized services, such as consultations, appraisals, certifications, identifications, lectures, and buying services with direct contacts to mines and gemstone vendors world-wide. We also maintain a well-equipped modern laboratory.

   Associated Gemologists wants to work with your company by offering our specialized services to you and your clients for their protection as well as for your own. Remember, an incorrect identification by an unqualified person could cause needless grief and expense.

   Please feel free to contact us if you have any questions about our services.

Cordially,

---

ance purposes. One appraiser has had good luck with giving presentations to agency managers and explaining how his fully certified and proper appraisals can be of benefit to them. Offer your services as speaker to any group that will hear you—this can be a very valuable source of clientele. When you are invited to speak, discuss jewelry and appraising, not yourself. The fact that you are addressing the group will establish you as an expert in the field. To find groups that may welcome you as a speaker, investigate whether your community offers public information shows.

In addition, look into opportunities for teaching either gemology clinics or adult education classes at the local museum, community college, or high school. People who attend these classes may later become your clients.

If writing is not difficult for you, think about writing a gems and jewelry column for your local newspaper. Like speaking on radio and television, this advertises your expertise in the field and establishes you as an individual to be trusted. In addition, examine the possibility of writing a quarterly newsletter to be sent to your clientele. The newsletter can be a chatty one-page mailing discussing new gemstones on the market, jewelry fashion tips, the history and lore of gemstones and jewelry, pricing variables, and any number of informative articles to titillate your clients while keeping your name in front of them. If you sell gems and jewelry along with appraising, the newsletter could be the perfect medium to combine client contact with information and low-profile advertising.

Maintaining Your Clientele

To serve and maintain your clientele, realize the impact your image has on your customer and make your customer rely on you for dependable service. According to one consumer focus group, some consumers who were tested on what they expected to receive and actually did receive in the way of service stated that a major gap exists between services expected and those actually rendered. According to the survey, reliability was by far the most important service quality to clients. Clients also complain about poor communication. They need to know that you understand the kinds of appraisals they need and that you listen and respond to their requests. How do you compare with your competitors? Do you give your clients what they actually need? Moreover, your clients are placing their trust in your ability to do market research and provide them with correct evaluations for insurance or estate purposes. Too many appraisers fail on this one issue.

Ethics play a large part when you advise clients on purchases, set fees, and give objective appraisals. Some jewelers/appraisers purposely undervalue the quality of the clients' valuables so they can tout their own "fine quality" items in the interest of future sales. This is not appraising. This is an unethical practice that should be beneath the dignity of all professional appraisers. Ethics do not come with the graduate gemologist diploma and are not automatically conveyed with appraisal association membership. However, your clients expect and deserve your most competent and ethical service—your peers deserve it, too.

1-7. Sample appraisal update notice. To personalize the mailing, write the client's name in by hand and sign each card.

Dear ————————————— :

    With your best interest in mind, we advise that you obtain an updated appraisal on the jewelry we have examined and evaluated for you, as well as on any items you may have acquired since.

    While you may be aware of the changing values of gems and diamonds, gold and other precious metals, we at XYZ Appraisals have computer access to prices in the key world marketplaces. It is likely that the monetary worth of your possessions has increased since your last appraisal.

    Please call for an appointment at your earliest convenience.

Sincerely,

Handling Appraisal Updates

For clients who need updated appraisals on their jewelry items, this service should be handled in the same way that a dentist lets you know it is time for a check-up—send out notices.

Most insurance companies recommend an update every three years and a yearly new appraisal for very expensive items. Send cards to your clients reminding them of the changeability of the precious gems and metals markets, and advise them not to be without adequate protection of their valuables. The form shown in figure 1-7 can be used on a reminder card.

Establishing a Professional Image

There are no statistics available to show how many appraisers of gems and jewelry there are in the United States, but the number must be substantial. The GIA has recorded that over sixty thousand jewelers have taken educational courses in gemology, retailing, and merchandising, so the odds are great that a high percentage of these jewelers are also appraisers.

Education is, of course, the first requirement to establishing a professional image. On a personal level, an appraiser builds image with proper dress, grooming, body language, communication skills, attitude, and the correct use of the English language. It has been said time and again that your vocabulary and the way in which you express yourself play a big part in how you are received by the client. The more articulate you are, the more credible you are perceived to be.

Some key points to remember include:

- Maintain a professional demeanor.
- Stay calm under criticism.
- Do not joke about the serious—the value of gems and jewelry is a serious subject to your clients.

- Maintain a friendly relationship with your competitors.

Roberta Ely, a personal property appraiser based in San Diego, teaches a course on the professional image. Ely points out that one's personal appearance is important. She admonishes appraisers in her classes to be well groomed, to carry neat briefcases, and to have a clean car if they visit clients in their homes. Ely warns it is not unusual for a client to peek out of the window to get a look at the appraiser and the car he or she is driving. "Clients pick up on subtle little things like body language. If you have vitality, grace, and a sense of authority, it will show and make an impression on the client." Ely adds, "You want them to remember you and your terrific work, not sloppy dress or bad manners."

Portable appraisers should keep their appointments as close to schedule as possible. No one likes to be kept waiting. If you are going to be delayed, call your client. If the appointment was made a week ago or longer, call to reconfirm before you start out. Do not book your appointments too closely together, as you never know what may delay you. Many clients, once they make an appointment for you to appraise one or two items of jewelry, end up bringing out several more pieces "because you are already here."

Most clients are eager to talk with the appraiser, be of help, ask questions, and watch what is going on. A few are nervous about getting in the appraiser's way. It is important to establish friendly client relations right away. First, establish the function of the appraisal (insurance, estate), then tell your clients what you are going to be doing (examining, taking inventory) and how you are going to do it (all the details of gemological instrumentation). Let them have a look at their jewelry or gems through your loupe. Most clients really appreciate the gesture. Ask for their assistance in providing any information that they may have about the provenance of the articles to aid in your valuation research.

There will come a moment when you will require quiet in which to do your work and most clients will respect this. Occasionally, there will be the nonstop conversationalist who makes your work difficult. If clients keep talking when you need to concentrate, ask them to write down all the information they can provide on an item or two—that will usually keep clients busy. If that ploy does not work to give you uninterrupted silence, however, you may have to remind them that you are working by the hour (if you are) and can finish faster without conversation. Of course, if you are charging the client by the item, you can always tell them that you have to hurry along because you have another appraisal job to attend. At the conclusion of your examination, pack away your tools, fold your worksheet, reiterate your payment policy, and tell your clients when they can expect a finished report. Later, if you find you cannot deliver the report by the finished date, notify your clients immediately.

Before leaving any on-site appraisal, be sure to check for overlooked items you may need to appraise. Is the client, for instance, wearing an expensive-looking wristwatch or earrings that should be appraised? Be alert and you may be able to expand the report validly.

Have all the contracts signed and obtain a retainer fee before you go. Do not quote any prices or values of items you have just examined, not even ballpark prices! You do not know what the client may do with the information and the market may have changed since you last checked it.

Attitude, it seems, has a lot to do with being a professional. In an article entitled "Professionalism and the International Society of Appraisers," C. Van Northrup writes: "Professionalism is a social process in which the individual must think and act as a professional in order to be recognized [as such] by the public" (Northrup, 1986, 10).

Protecting Your Reputation

Your reputation as a competent, fair, and trustworthy appraiser is your most valuable intangible. Guard and protect your reputation in several ways. First, refuse to do "freebies." Free appraisals are demeaning, and those who ask for free appraisals do not see you as a professional with years of education and experience. Off-the-cuff appraisals are worth exactly what someone pays for them—nothing—and they deprive you of the opportunity to extend your best professional appraisal of what may prove to be an important jewelry item. Second, dissociate yourself from gemologists and appraisers who handle questionable appraisals and jew-

elry deals. You know who they are. The trade journals spell out their sins of omission or commission and the appraisal association ethics committees work single-mindedly to oust them from membership. Third, check your valuations carefully and reread the report several times before you sign your name at the bottom. Remember that any appraisal could be questioned in court and be certain you are correct. Are you positive you can substantiate the statements you made in the document? Make no verbal appraisals—they can be as binding as written ones and turn out to be legal headaches. Fourth, read the Federal Trade Commission's guides for the jewelry industry to be aware of the legal definitions of such terms as "flawless." A careless use of terms could turn your client into a litigator with you as the respondent. Remember disclosure laws.

Setting Fees

Money is a sensitive area. Plenty of people in business for themselves do not realize that they should be drawing a salary and earning on their investment in the business. In other words, the business needs to make a profit beyond salaries and overhead. If you have never worked for yourself before or charged for personal services rendered, you may be shy about asking for money. Develop a tough hide from the start, ask for your money without apology, and get it up front. Most appraisers working with or for a jeweler will have worked out a base salary and/or commissions. If you have not, finding out how others handle the situation may help you decide which arrangement would be best for your circumstances.

Only a short time ago, the standard way to charge for appraisals was to request a percentage of the total value of the items, usually 1 to 1.5 percent. If you were appraising very expensive jewelry, you could add up a tidy sum for your fee in a short while. Many appraisers and jewelers were not beyond edging up the valuations by hundreds or thousands of dollars to make their fees fatter. This temptation to disregard ethics was not lost on gemological and appraisal associations, jewelry trade groups, or the IRS, all of which have issued policy statements over the years condemning this practice. They view the percentage fee as too much of a temptation to inflate an appraisal figure and hold that it is unethical. Most suggest that appraisers charge by the hour, the day, or per piece. A survey of one hundred gems and jewelry appraisers conducted by the Association of Women Gemologists reveals that most charge by the hour, asking from thirty-five to one hundred and fifty dollars. A large percentage of respondents charged by the item, from twenty dollars to seventy-five dollars depending upon the complexity of the piece. Per-item charges were always coupled with a minimum fee of approximately forty-five dollars for the first item.

An experienced appraiser may charge from two hundred and fifty dollars per half-day (with a minimum of one hundred and fifty dollars) to a thousand dollars for a full day's work. If you are portable, this includes your portal-to-portal time charge. Some appraisers combine several methods of charging: per diem when working for attorneys, banks, and courts; per item when working for the general public. Appraisers in California are able to charge a much higher per-item rate than are their counterparts in the Texas, Oklahoma, Louisiana, and Arkansas area. Prices in New York and Texas are similar, with a medium per-item charge of fifty dollars, but even in Texas the rates vary across the state: south Texas appraisers are frequently able to charge and get more per item than their colleagues can in north Texas. It greatly depends upon the economic conditions of your region of the country, the demand, and the competition.

Some laboratories and appraisers have found success in using a sliding table of prices that vary according to the size of the gemstone and number of stones, or time and complexity required for an appraisal (table 1-2). Some think that the most equitable way to charge for an appraisal is with an hourly rate designed to cover all the services the appraiser has to perform, including time spent on telephone calls and any extra insurance coverage that may be needed. The fee should also include any extra expenses incurred, such as the cost of obtaining an outside expert opinion or analysis from a gem laboratory.

On the other hand, some appraisers declare that to

Table 1-2. Sliding Scale of Appraisal Fees

Item	Price (in dollars)	Update Fee (in dollars)
All metal items	10.00	5.00
Single/multistone items, total weight up to .25 ct.	30.00	15.00
Single/multistone items, total weight .26 to 1.05 ct.	55.00	20.00
Additional carat or portion above 1.05 ct.	10.00	5.00
Watch, without diamonds	30.00	15.00
Watch, with diamonds	55.00	20.00
Beads (not pearls)	30.00	15.00
Pearls (cultured/imitation)	40.00	20.00
Gem identification	10.00	10.00
Coins	20.00	10.00
Photographs only	10.00	10.00
Gemprints	25.00	25.00

Note: Minimum fee for first item only, $55.00.

receive the same compensation for appraising a twenty-dollar item as for a twenty-thousand-dollar item is tantamount to insult. They argue that their years of experience as appraisers and the thousands of dollars they have spent in education and equipment entitle them to greater reward. Some appraisers charge a percentage of the value of the items they appraise while pointing out that the major auction houses commonly use the percentage-figure basis for fee structuring.

The entire issue of fees in the United States may ultimately be legislated. In Pennsylvania, Senator Stewart J. Greenleaf sponsored and passed a bill regulating jewelry appraisers' fees known as the *Jewelry Appraisal Act (Purdon's Pennsylvania Statute Annotated Title 73, CHP 29, Section 1983–1984)*. This statute requires jewelers who do appraisals in the state of Pennsylvania to charge a flat rate, and prohibits them from charging a fee based on a percentage of the value of the appraised jewelry item. Violators of the bill face a fine of one hundred dollars for the first offense and two hundred dollars for the second or any subsequent offense. So far this law targets jewelry appraisers only.

The fee structures of portable appraisers can get complex: one arrangement is used for the public when the appraiser is working independently; another method for appraisals done at a jewelry store, in which the appraiser is wholesaling his or her services to the jeweler. The number of ways in which portable appraisers handle billing is limited only to the number of creative individuals working in this field. Some popular fee formulas found during a research of the question include the appraiser who is paid a base salary and works for the jeweler full-time, but may solicit and keep all revenues from appraisals, or the appraiser who conducts appraisals in the jewelry store on an appointment basis. In the latter case, the appointments are made in advance by the jeweler, but the appraiser values the jewelry, sets the fee, and collects the money from the customer. The jeweler *may* receive a set percentage of the appraisal fee (anywhere from 10 to 30 percent). Another variation is for the fee (set higher to accommodate the jeweler's percentage) to be collected by the jeweler, who in turn gives the appraiser his or her share. The perfect system for the appraiser is, of course, to bill the customer directly, keep all fees, and simply use the jeweler's space as a place to conduct business. Some appraisers and jewelers adopt this arrangement and consider it equitable, as it affords the jeweler greater opportunities to sell—first when the customer brings the jewelry in to be examined, and second when the customer returns to pick up the appraisal report.

Another plus for jewelers who have independent appraisers work in their stores is the repair work that appraisals can generate. The responsible appraiser will point out to the client during the initial examination any repairs that should be made before the appraisal is undertaken. Such problems as broken or cracked shanks on rings, broken spring rings, prongs that need retipping or replacing, and/or stones that are loose should be reported and actually shown to the customer.

Jeweler/Independent Appraiser Relationships

This kind of arrangement requires total trust between appraiser and jeweler, and a strong bond of friendship. However, if the appraiser sells gemstones or jewelry on the side, there will be a gray area that may be difficult to overcome no matter how much the two trust each other. If the jeweler ever suspects that the appraiser is soliciting customers for sales along with appraisals, the entire fabric of trust will be shredded. A strong belief in fair play is necessary on both sides if this work arrangement is to be successful and mutually rewarding.

Appraisers, on the other hand, should be wary of any jeweler who wants expertise but is not willing to pay for it. You may be asked to "just look" at diamonds, colored stones, and other jewelry items while you are in the store between appointments. A certain amount of free information may reasonably be expected, but do not give away all of your expertise.

In addition, you could also be asked to value merchandise sold by a jeweler whose markups are greater than the area-established norms. If so, you may wish to plead conflict of interest and decline the evaluation. The conflict of interest arises from the implication that the jeweler wants to justify his or her markups with a validation from a professional appraiser, and the independent appraiser can lose the jeweler's patronage by pointing out that these mark-ups are excessive. It is a difficult position for the moral appraiser and calls for careful consideration of the available options.

Liability

Independent appraisers who work for jewelers can prepare their appraisal documents either on their own forms or on the store's forms. Regardless of whose forms you use, however, you are liable for the statements you make once you sign the document. Furthermore, even though you are an independent agent not affiliated with the jeweler's store in any way beyond appraising, the jeweler will also be liable to individuals damaged by you. If the setup gives the impression of partnership, it is legally considered a *partnership by estoppel*. In most cases, jewelers have no idea that they have undertaken such responsibility.

Independent appraisers should consider laminating their appraisal reports to preclude any tampering with the report numbers. Sadly, some retail merchants have been known to ask and pay for appraisals of store merchandise and then change either the valuation or the photograph on the report. If you suspect any merchant of this kind of offense, terminate your relationship with him or her.

The professional appraiser takes on a mantle of responsibilities and liabilities with each completed appraisal document. Although most appraisers understand their general responsibilities to the public and to the profession, they may be unaware of the legal mechanisms now existing that hold appraisers accountable for error and fraud. Some of the most notable areas of potential liability include the following:

Identification and authentication negligence. In a celebrated IRS challenge case in New York that resulted in back-tax penalties for the taxpayer, the taxpayer sought and received damages from the appraiser who provided the original report. Not only was the property overvalued, it was found to be misidentified and misdated.

Insurance losses. Insurance fraud of scheduled personal property based upon the valuation established in an appraisal has become prevalent in the past few years. Some insurance companies are now asking for verification of the appraiser's credentials plus a second-opinion appraisal. In some cases of suspected fraud, appraisers have been asked to give sworn statements of value.

Stolen property. The National Stolen Property Act amplifies the trade sanction agreement that was recently expanded and reinforced to protect the culturally important property of foreign countries. The sharply outlined liabilities state that anyone violating the provisions of the Act by buying, selling, storing, exhibiting, and appraising material protected under the treaty shall be liable to prosecution.

Donated property appraisals. Section 6659(c)(1) of the IRS Tax Code states that civil penalties can be assessed on the appraiser who is found guilty of gross valuation overstatement.

Questions Most Often Asked by Gemologists about Appraising

Five years of surveys of gemologists reveal that the following questions are most often on the minds of those who are considering getting into the field of appraising.

Q. What kind of equipment do I need to be an appraiser?
A. Among the essential tools are a binocular microscope, a refractometer, a polariscope, a Leveridge mi-

cromillimeter gauge, and ultraviolet lights. One of the great advantages to having a portable laboratory such as a MaxiLab or Portalab is that almost all of the instruments necessary for appraising are available in one container. Some appraisers who have fixed-lab locations buy regular laboratory instruments for their workstations; some buy and use only portable laboratories; some do both and have duplicate equipment. A host of hand tools are also necessary and desirable. For a list of other necessary appraisal instruments, see *Becoming a Portable Appraiser* in chapter 1.

Q. I have just finished the gem identification and colored-stone analysis portions of the GIA program. I plan to be an appraiser of diamonds and colored stones when I become a graduate gemologist. What kind of equipment or instruments should I buy right now?

A. You need to purchase a master set of diamond grading stones immediately. You should have at least five diamond master stones that have been color graded by the GIA laboratory. The diamonds should be at least a quarter-carat each, and larger if possible. The grading of colored stones is becoming more scientific, and you may wish to use one of the colored-stone grading systems on the market. A list of these and their manufacturers is given in *Colored Gemstones* in chapter 3.

A spectroscope is useful for distinguishing naturally colored green jadeite from treated jadeite, color-treated diamonds from natural colored diamonds, and some hues of natural corundum from synthetic versions. For a list of other essential tools, see *Becoming a Portable Appraiser* in chapter 1.

Q. How much should I charge for an appraisal?

A. There are several different ways of setting fees and most are dictated by individual circumstances of experience, overhead expenses, on-site or office appraisals, etc. Some charge a minimum fee for the first item (perhaps forty-five to sixty-five dollars), with another set fee for each additional item. Some appraisers charge by the hour, and some by the half-day or full day with an additional minimum. Fees are more fully discussed in *Setting Fees* in chapter 1.

Q. How do you evaluate gold teeth in an estate appraisal?

A. Treat it like scrap gold. It is usually around 16K.

Q. What do you say to a client who insists that a stone cannot be synthetic—that grandfather would never have bought grandmother a synthetic ring?

A. Tell the client that synthetic stones have been on the market since 1885, and that the original jeweler was probably unaware that this stone was synthetic.

Q. What steps can I take to maximize my personal security and increase the safety of my home or office?

A. If you are office-bound or hold jewelry overnight, you will need a secure safe, a well-written take-in form (see chapter 2), and possibly a buzzer system for the door as well as an alarm system for the store or office. You will also need Jeweler's Block Insurance to cover you in the event of a robbery or burglary.

Of course, if you conduct appraisals while the client waits and do not hold client jewelry overnight, security will be nearly a moot point.

For your bodily safety, vigilance is the best defense. Be alert going to and from your car when traveling to any appraisal appointment. If you travel out of town frequently, you should carry a mobile telephone.

Q. Where can I go to update the pricing of colored gemstones and jewelry yearly besides the regular market shows?

A. The Tucson Gem and Mineral Show is held every February. Make it a point to go—your competitors do.

Q. I am considering a career move. Is jewelry appraising a good choice? I have the background.

A. Selling gems and jewelry and doing jewelry appraisals can be good careers if you have the education and certain personality traits. Ask yourself if you are well organized, if you enjoy interacting with the public, whether you consider yourself someone with integrity, and whether you are motivated to be a self-starter.

Independent appraisers must be pleasantly aggressive and knowledgeable about market conditions. If you believe you meet the requirements, you can establish your business and maintain it as long as you care to work.

It is a *great* second career for women!

CHAPTER 2

APPRAISAL PROCEDURES AND THE NATURE OF VALUE

Establishing and substantiating the value of an item are what appraising is all about. There are several steps that occur between the initial examination of the client's property and the final estimate of the property, and the wise appraiser does not skip any of these. The six steps involved in the appraisal process, which are detailed in table 2-1, are as follows:

1. Establish the scope of the appraisal.
2. Plan the appraisal.
3. Collect and analyze data.
4. Apply a valuation approach.
5. Set limitations and contingency conditions.
6. Supply the final estimate of value.

Table 2-1 may also be used as a physical work plan.

In this chapter, the different types of appraisals are discussed, as are the primary valuation approaches and the recommended limiting and contingency conditions to be added to the final appraisal document. Chapter 3 provides a step-by-step guide to the other steps involved—the methods of jewelry analysis, evaluation, and documentation, including a breakdown of the identification and take-in stage, sources of data, and economic and item data analysis.

Establishing the scope of the appraisal. During the initial examination and inventory of the client's property, the appraiser asks why the client needs or wants the appraisal, in order to determine the purpose (type of value) and function (intended use) of the appraisal. In discussing the objectives of the appraisal, the appraiser has a responsibility to clarify the kind of value that is appropriate and to explain this to the client clearly.

It is important to establish both the purpose and function of the appraisal to ensure that the appraiser will provide the client with the correct appraisal document. For example, the client may say that the purpose of the appraisal is to determine the retail replacement of an item. This purpose, retail replacement, can serve any number of functions—insurance, comparison, hypothetical, damage, or barter—that may require the appraiser to submit particular information. Similarly, an appraisal to set the fair market value of an item could be used for such different estate functions as divorce settlement, probate, donation, or casualty loss. The term *estate* describes any preowned jewelry; secondhand, antique, or period as well as other items sold for fair market value. Be certain to qualify the purpose and function of an estate appraisal when this designation is used.

It is the appraiser's role to represent the interests of the client objectively during the appraisal and to perform three primary tasks: identification, quality analysis, and valuation. Researching the appropriate market for estimated costs is the appraiser's responsibility. It is important that the appraiser explain why the market and particular value or cost estimate have been deemed appropriate, in order to avoid misunderstanding and to prevent unwitting or deliberate misapplication.

In Henry A. Babcock's book *Appraisal Principles and Procedures*—a standard reference work for real and personal property appraisers—significant points are discussed about the *value* of property and how *value* tends to fluctuate due to economic factors. Babcock states that as a result of value fluctuations, an appraisal must state the *valuation date* as a date when the *value* figure is applicable. "Otherwise," he contends, "the figure is meaningless and therefore useless." Babcock defines *valuation date* as *the date when the appraised value was obtained.* And, he cautions, the *valuation date* is not to be confused with the *report date,* which means the date the report was finished (typed and ready for the client). Dates are especially sensitive in fair market value ap-

Table 2-1. The Appraisal Process

ESTABLISH THE SCOPE OF THE APPRAISAL

Identify and take inventory of client property Establish fee with client	Determine purpose of appraisal (type of value)	Note date of examination of the property	Establish function of appraisal (intended use)

PLAN THE APPRAISAL

Determine Data Needed:	List Sources of Data:	Other Sources of Expertise:	Schedule the Appraisal:
Current prices on precious stones and metals Hallmarks, maker's marks Trademarks research	Dealers Wholesalers Manufacturers Other	Laboratory analysis Other appraisers	Initial exam Research Preparation Delivery date

COLLECT AND ANALYZE DATA

Location:	Economic:	Item by Item:
Residence Office Bank Other	Market analysis Market trends Supply and demand Special circumstances Highest and best use	Identification Description Weights and measurements Photographs

APPLY A VALUATION APPROACH

Cost:	Market Data:	Income:*
Cost evaluation of intrinsic value, labor, mark-ups	Comparison of existing comparable items	Used in market value appraisals of income-producing property

SET LIMITATIONS AND CONTINGENCY CONDITIONS ON APPRAISAL DOCUMENT

VALUE CONCLUSION

*Rarely used by appraisers of gems and jewelry.

praisals for probate and estate tax, when an alternate valuation date may be used.

Planning the appraisal. The next step is determining what research data will be needed (such as price lists, books, and catalogs) and where this information may be found. If the article to be appraised is beyond the scope of the appraiser's expertise, it may be necessary to confer with other experts or to get authentication and identification from a laboratory, particularly if a gemstone's country of origin or gem treatment is an issue.

The amount of time needed for research and preparation should be calculated and the client should be advised of the estimated delivery date of the appraisal document.

Collecting and analyzing data. Making general notes on the location and atmosphere in which the initial examination and inventory take place is important. If the appraiser works under less-than-ideal conditions, this should be noted on the appraisal report as a limiting and contingent condition. It is difficult to work properly in a crowded bank safety-deposit room with limited lighting, or in an antagonistic atmosphere, such as in the residence of a couple undergoing a hostile divorce.

The appraisal report should also list the special economic, political, and social factors that influence the market: economic factors such as inflation, recession, and changes in tax laws; political events in countries where gemstones are mined that affect the supply of gemstones; and social and cultural trends and fads that sway property values.

Applying a valuation approach. Before proceeding to an explanation of the cost and market-data comparison approaches to valuation, let us consider the nature of value—what it is and how it can be established. In the gems and the jewelry discipline, value is determined by the appraiser's research and analysis of numerous substantiated sales of comparable items. This analysis establishes a *mode*, which is the most frequently occurring price found for an item during the appraiser's research. A statistical definition of *mode* is the number that occurs most frequently in a series of numbers. If seven out of ten jewelry stores carry a similar style of diamond ring priced at one thousand dollars, while three jewelry stores price the same style of ring at twenty-five hundred dollars, the mode of the ring is one thousand dollars. Realistically, a mode needs an absolute minimum of three numbers. If no frequency exists within those three numbers, the number of transactions has to be increased until a frequency develops.

Price is frequently confused with value. Price is set by a merchant according to his or her market or economic needs at the time of sale. The price of an item, however, may be more or less than its value. For example, if you offer a friend a ruby brooch for a certain figure, the friend may reject the figure but make you a counteroffer that you accept. The price of the brooch will have been established without regard to its value.

To determine the value of the particular items being appraised, gems and jewelry appraisers commonly rely on two processes, the market-data comparison approach and the cost approach, as the most viable means of valuation.

The *market-data comparison approach* involves researching the appropriate and most common markets for sales data of comparable jewelry or gemstones. It is used to establish an item's retail replacement value or to determine its fair market value for tax purposes. The considerations in the market-data approach include the number of sales, the period of time covered, the rate of turnover, the motivation of buyers or sellers, and the degree of comparability. Comparable items are those of an equivalent uniqueness, rarity, quality, condition, period of design, origin, designer or craftsman, quality of design execution, appropriate market, and purpose. The *cost approach* provides an estimate of how much an item would cost to replace in the current market if it were reproduced identically, and is commonly used when no comparable item exists. The cost of each jewelry component is analyzed separately: for a ring, the appraiser would analyze the metal, method of manufacture, metal fineness, heads, assembly labor, cost of the gemstone(s), and setting fees. This approach is used to estimate retail replacement value but is never used in determining fair market value for IRS purposes. Most appraisers like to use both methods and correlate the findings for a final estimate of value if a comparison item exists.

Another approach to valuation exists, the *income approach*. Although jewelry appraisers rarely use it, appraisers should at least be familiar with the approach. The income approach is typically used in appraisals of income-producing properties. It can also be used to estimate investment value—the subjective value of a property to a particular investor. For instance, if a jeweler is in the business of leasing fine jewelry and wants an appraisal of the items, the income approach would be used in order to analyze the property's capacity to generate monetary benefits as an indication of its present value.

Limiting and contingency conditions. Any conditions that are unique to your evaluation should be listed on the appraisal report. This subject is discussed more fully later in this chapter.

Final estimate of value. The final step in the process is the dollar figure estimated by the appraiser following due diligence in research of all information pertinent to the appraised property. Supporting data used in this estimate should be itemized, or at least acknowledged, on a reference page attached to the report.

The Purpose of the Appraisal

Retail Replacement (Insurance)

A retail replacement appraisal is required by an insurance company before it will schedule jewelry on an individual policy beyond a certain dollar amount. In insurance parlance, *scheduled property* is a list of personal valuables and the appraised value of each property item for which the insurance company will pay in the event of loss or damage. The appraisal is the record that will be consulted by the insurance firm to set the premium and determine the amount of insurance, depending on the terms of the insurance policy. Common examples of scheduled property include fine art, jewelry, furs, audiovisual equipment, stamp and coin collections, silverware, goldware, and plated items. Typical examples of unscheduled personal property include furniture, drapes, appliances, and other general furnishings of a residence.

The insurance appraisal must provide your client with sufficient information to ensure replacement with an item of equal quality and kind. Usually, the appraiser must supply for each item the *current market price* (mode), which is generally construed to mean the most frequent value of a like item found in the most appropriate market, but not any one store in particular, selling like merchandise within the geographical area.

The appraiser must be aware that more than one *replacement* cost exists and should consider the client's best interests before selecting the appropriate concept. The appraisal document should clearly indicate the option chosen:

1. *Replacement Value (New)* refers to the cost of replacement in the retail market of property as good as, but no better than, the item being replaced. The item should be identical to that being replaced, therefore this is useful for mass-produced jewelry. However, the term is useful *only* when a new identical item can be obtained.
2. *Comparable Replacement Value (New)* refers to replacement of an item with a comparable of like kind, quality, and condition. This is the appropriate option to

use in an insurance replacement appraisal for antique jewelry. It should be carefully noted on the report that the replacement is for a *comparable* item and not an exact duplicate.

3. *Comparable Replacement Value (Secondary Market).* This value is used when items are no longer in production, and a newly made item is not desirable or available. The secondary market is often a "used" market such as antique store, resale, jewelry broker, or pawnshop. The value is for an item of like kind, quality, and condition. It should be noted on the appraisal report that the value is for a similar item and not a reproduction, not an exact duplicate, and *not* new.

4. *Reproduction Value* is the current price of constructing an exact duplicate or replica jewelry item, using the same construction standards, materials, and design. This is normally used when replacing part of a set that has been lost or stolen, or when an unusual custom item has been lost or stolen. When one item in a pair or set is lost, the reproduction cost is often more than one-half of the value of the complete set or pair. Consideration must be given to the difficulty and cost of hand fabrication to match the existing piece. Insurance policy "Pair and Set" clauses should be carefully read.

State insurance codes vary widely from state to state. Some insurance companies will replace a lost or stolen item in like kind, some with the piece's monetary value, and some will deduct a discount from the monetary value. In Michigan, for instance, insurance replacement is defined as cash value less depreciation. Find out the insurance laws and limits in your state—your client will almost never know these facts and will appreciate your willingness to provide information, straight answers on values, and the necessary analysis of markets. For some very valuable items, the client and insurance agent may wish to negotiate value. This will be expressed as the price the insurance company is willing to accept as a risk and for which the customer accepts the premium. Although there is no easy formula for determining insurance value, it depends on proper appraising research.

Appraisers have long complained that insurance companies do not use the full description of the article, using instead a kind of insurance-company shorthand for the final schedule document. The truth is, insurance companies do not need to. They have a brief description of the article on the schedule and they have a copy of your full description on your report, which is filed with the client's other insurance paperwork. If you remain uneasy about your client's chances of getting back an item that is like in kind because your client's insurance schedule shows a shorthand version of your re-

port, you are within your rights to demand that the complete appraisal report appear on the schedule. The most important points to include are the quality grades. Many companies use a computer printout form that does not have enough space to hold your full description. In the event of a loss, the insurance company may not even pay the appraised value. The typical supplement contains a clause that reads "unless otherwise stated in this policy, the value of the property insured is not agreed upon but shall be ascertained at the time of loss or damage." Moreover, most insurance companies will not pay cash for lost or stolen jewelry. They will replace it, based on the appraiser's description, from their own wholesale sources, usually at 30 to 80 percent of the appraised value of the replacement price. For this reason, accurate and detailed descriptions and grading are absolutely essential. These descriptions not only determine the client's coverage, but assure him or her of receiving like-kind items if the need arises.

The declared price of valuation is the price upon which the premium is set, and reflects the retail costs that would be incurred to replace or reproduce any gems in like quality and jewelry mountings in like manufacture and degree of craftsmanship. This monetary figure is just a mathematical sum by which one's premium can be calculated. Therefore, the most important part of an insurance appraisal is the accurate descriptions of the appraised items because insurance companies insure the jewelry items, not their value. This may be a difficult point to convey to your client.

When researching the retail replacement values of custom-made jewelry items, or fine designer jewelry for insurance, it is necessary to determine if the client wants replacement by the same firm (for example, Tiffany's), or if they will be satisfied with an equal but not identical replacement from another company. For example: when writing insurance replacement on an item that came from Tiffany's and bears that company's trademark, the only appropriate value is replacement *from Tiffany's.* Trademarked Tiffany's jewelry can only be *replaced* with trademarked Tiffany's jewelry (copyright considerations) and the appraisal should state *"Retail Replacement Value Tiffany's (New)."* This applies equally to *all* designer and well-known manufacturer trademarked jewelry (Bulgari, Van Clef, Winstons, etc.). The other scenario in writing insurance appraisal for a designer piece of jewelry is if the client will settle for an identical replacement of *equal value,* but *not* from the original source. In the event the client will accept replacement of *equal value,* full explanation of the client's replacement request should be made on the appraisal report. While it is highly unlikely that a client with a fine designer piece of jewelry will opt for replacement from other than the original source, they should be given the opportunity to make a personal decision.

Jewelers often ask whether they can use the price they would replace an item for in their store as the appraised price of an item for insurance purposes. The answer is no. An appraisal is based on an analysis of numerous prices in the marketplace to determine the most often occurring price at which the item can be bought—this analysis cannot be based solely on one store's price. One store's price is a replacement cost estimate. Therefore, unless the jeweler has made direct market research, it would be wiser to offer the customer a "Statement of Replacement Cost" instead of an appraisal. This statement of replacement cost is generally written on the jeweler's letterhead and it is not called an appraisal anywhere on the form.

In 1996, the Jewelers Vigilance Committee set forth insurance documentation guidelines intended as an alternative standard for jewelry retailers *without* appraisal training. The guidelines provide a way for a merchant to document retail replacement cost of his *own merchandise* in *his* store for his clients' use in obtaining insurance. The JVC guidelines are voluntary and at the time of this writing have not been made mandatory by any jewelers' group. The guidelines limit the jeweler to using his cost based on his own sales records for both items he has sold, and items he will document that were sold by another jeweler. The insurance documentation is *not* an appraisal, but a statement ("Replacement Cost Estimate" has been suggested) of one store's actual selling price for an item. The guidelines require each report to disclose that the cost estimate represents only one store's actual selling price, which is presumed to prevent any misunderstandings. While the authors of the JVC guidelines admit the public will probably identify a "replacement cost estimate" as an appraisal regardless of what it is named, they believe the solution for public understanding is a written explanation and recommend the following be used on each document:

> Unless otherwise stated, the subject property was sold by (NAME) Jewelers and the replacement cost stated is the actual price paid. In any case, the replacement cost estimate is the most common actual sales price of the same, identical, or fully comparable property if sold by (NAME) Jewelers at this time.

If the report is prepared according to the JVC guidelines, it is clearly "price" that is being reported rather than "value." The JVC guidelines also state that a jeweler must have experience and knowledge to accurately identify and evaluate the quality of any item documented. Also, a knowledge of gemology, manufacturing techniques, and other factors (presumably economic)

affecting an item's replacement cost estimate is recommended for those preparing insurance documentation.

How do the JVC guidelines address the issue of jewelers providing insurance documentation for items they *do not* sell? "It would not be logical or appropriate to limit the JVC guidelines to items actually sold by the retailer," said Larry Phillips, G.G., a member of the JVC Task Force in a June 1996 letter to Jewelers' Circular-Keystone magazine. "If a retailer claims to have prepared his replacement cost estimate in conformance with the guidelines, the consumer and the insurer should be able to rely on the honesty of the report. If a retailer is knowledgeable enough to document his own merchandise, then he can logically document any item for which he has sales records and a regular, current line of supply. In other words, the key issue is not whether you sold the item, it is whether you can recognize it for what it is and whether you can replace it though your own usual source of supply."

Jewelers who have sold items at special discounted prices because of their own wise buys may ethically appraise the item at a higher price, provided the value is based on current market research and actually reflects the mode of the article in its appropriate market. In your zeal to protect your client, beware of overvaluation, which could be grounds for negligence on your part. Substantial overvaluation for an object that runs counter to the market may result in cancellation of the client's policy and litigation for the appraiser.

If a client has submitted a claim and rejects the insurance company's replacement offer, the cash payment can be limited to "the amount for which the insured could reasonably be expected to replace the article." A national insurance underwriters company has been quoted as saying that insurers are "likely to understand this amount to be their own replacement cost" (*Changing Times*, 1985, 64). They explain that since lost or damaged articles can be replaced at discounted prices, the insured can "reasonably be expected to replace" the jewelry for that price.

To avoid the cash-or-replacement option, your client can purchase an "agreed value" policy. This type of policy guarantees to pay claims in cash in accordance with the scheduled values.

A schedule will cost about ten to forty dollars for every added thousand dollars of jewelry coverage. Silverware and art objects are also subject to dollar limitations; you need to advise your client on protection of these items.

Counsel your client to ask the agent the following questions before you write an appraisal. The insurance agent's answers will help you and the client reach a greater understanding of the conditions affecting any claim subsequent to your valuation:

1. How are claims paid, in cash or replacement jewelry?
2. Would the client have a say in the selection of a replacement article?
3. What happens if an article is not replaceable?
4. Does the insurance cover all risks, including mysterious disappearance, and all geographic areas?
5. What are the exceptions and exclusions?
6. Is the client covered if negligence is involved in a loss?
7. Are there deductibles?
8. Is depreciation ever imposed? Which items are subject to depreciation and how is it computed?
9. What is the pair and set clause? Will the insurance provide an additional amount to cover the cost of matching a missing item in a set if the fact that there is a set or pair has not been previously stated?
10. What type of proof is needed to justify a claim?
11. Does the insurer require the appraiser to have special qualifications?

The last question in the preceding list may evoke some interesting answers. While some of the larger national companies are starting to make progress in requesting qualified appraisers, many set no standards for jewelry appraisers. Interviews with agents of twenty insurance agencies revealed that most companies do not require the jewelry appraiser to have appraisal knowledge or, for that matter, gemological knowledge. That explains why so many are willing to accept a handwritten receipt of sale as an "appraisal." The blame falls squarely on insurance underwriters who have failed to establish criteria for qualified appraiser practitioners.

At least one major insurance company has introduced printed materials, lessons, and videos to underwriters and adjusters spelling out *what appraisals are, how they are used,* and *what exactly should be in them.* Workbook notes declare, "Good appraisals may help assure us that the item we are insuring is what it is supposed to be," then go on to explain, "Knowing one item from another can help us distinguish the limit of liability that should be applied to them [jewelry items]." The following statement, written specifically to underwriters, shows the company is interested in clear descriptions and accurate statements of value: "Knowing what we are insuring is important in judging whether the appraised value appears accurate. A second appraisal is called for when the appraised value is more than *twice* the recent purchase price, and the appraiser does not indicate the reason for the discrepancy (such as distress sale, bargain purchase at auction, legitimate 'going out of business' sale, bankruptcy liquidation sale, etc.). An appraised value of $75,000 for an item recently purchased at a jewelry store for $30,000 would be an example." Most

insurance companies prefer the appraiser to be a gemologist and/or trained appraiser. They ask the underwriters to use a list of organizations with high standards for training appraisers and gemologists to see if the appraiser fulfills the major qualifications. Many insurance company underwriters and agents also use appraisal quick-check reference cards listing the critical elements that should be present on appraisals.

Writing an Accurate Appraisal

To be valuable to client as well as insurance company, an accurate and complete appraisal contains the following:

1. An overall description of the item.
2. Specific description information on all gems and precious metals.
3. Any elements of special consideration to the estimated value (for instance, proven provenance).

The general description of an item should depict a picture of the item and include:

1. The type of jewelry item involved, i.e., earrings, ring, necklace, bracelet, brooch, suite, etc.
2. Identification of gemstones or precious metals involved.
3. Measurements and overall weight of the item.
4. Quality grade and condition.
5. Type and weight of precious metals used in the mountings, settings, clasps, etc.
6. Type, number, measurements, estimated weights, and quality grades of gemstones.
7. Trademarks, hallmarks, or maker's marks on the mounting.
8. Description of the specific grading and testing procedures used.

Insurance appraisals should also include specifics on identifying, describing, and valuing *each element* in a jewelry item. For example, an appraisal of a diamond and pearl bracelet should include grading of both *diamonds and pearls* as well as quality grading of the precious metal. If the item being appraised for insurance purposes is antique, special appraisal considerations are mixed. Appraisers should document the value as: the *value the piece is likely to bring at auction,* the *cost to have the item duplicated today,* or the *cost to remake.* The most consistently accurate value is "the value the piece is likely to bring at auction." Whether the item is *irreplaceable* or a modern reproduction, all information should appear on the appraisal report.

The Home Shopping Network (HSN) is steadily gaining market share of jewelry purchases. And, if the prognosticators are correct, jewelry purchases over the Internet is the wave of the future. What market is researched to estimate value on jewelry purchased via television? The *most appropriate* market for a replacement figure is Home Shopping Network. At least one seller is known to mark the jewelry they sell with their initials, somewhat of an indication to the appraiser that the piece *can* be replaced by the seller. A note of caution, however: wording on the appraisal document should make a clear distinction between "cost" and "value." Write "Estimated Replacement Cost (HSN) $XX"— avoid using the word "value." If the client has bought jewelry from a television seller and the jewelry is not trademarked, research comparable merchandise sold at the level of the market, i.e., high retail, low retail, discount jeweler, appropriate to the jewelry being appraised. Write a complete explanation of the market(s) researched, and your analysis of the prices in the appraisal report. Internet jewelry sales require diligent research.

Fair Market Value: Estate

Fair market value is used for estate evaluation purposes, and is an assessment based on what a willing buyer and seller would agree to without a forced sale. Appraisal criteria for estates have been legislated to include specific information and data, but do not include the factors that an insurance replacement appraisal does, and so this is usually a lower value. The following is the U.S. Department of Treasury definition of fair market value:

> The fair market value is the price at which the property would change hands between a willing buyer and a willing seller, neither being under any compulsion to buy or to sell and both having reasonable knowledge of relevant facts. The fair market value of a particular item of property includible in the decedent's gross estate is not to be determined by a forced sale price. Nor is the fair market value of an item of property to be determined by the sale price of the item in a market other than that in which such item is most commonly sold to the public, taking into account the location of the item wherever appropriate. Thus, in the case of an item of property includible in the decedent's gross estate, which is generally obtained by the public in the retail market, the fair market value of such an item of property is the price at which the item or a comparable item would be sold at retail [Treasury Regulation 20.2031-1 (b)].

The definition of "retail" used in the context of fair market value is not the definition generally accepted in the jewelry business. As the IRS uses it, retail means any market where goods change hands and where the buyer is the ultimate consumer or end purchaser of the goods. There are numerous retail markets. Estate sales, second-hand stores, antique stores, flea markets—even auctions—can be considered retail if the buyer is the ultimate consumer and is not purchasing goods as a dealer or for wholesale.

The key words in this definition of fair market value are "most common market." It is the appraiser's responsibility to research and be able to document on the appraisal report the most common market, as well as to explain why this market level was chosen. The appraiser does not create markets but researches them, and his or her primary research is based on documented prices, not opinions or sales offerings.

For example, if a jewelry item being appraised for estate settlement is a fine Art Deco brooch in excellent condition, the most common market for the brooch would probably be an auction. By diligent research of the auction market, the appraiser could doubtless build a valid and defensible report. Similarly, the most appropriate market for an out-of-style man's wristwatch with a worn and engraved case would be a scrap dealer.

The scrap dealer is both *ultimate* consumer and *most common market* because he or she is the final purchaser of the item in *its current form*. The ultimate consumer of a worn, damaged wristwatch beyond repair is not the same consumer of the same watch in running condition. The analysis of "ultimate consumer" must be carefully considered. If the appraiser is researching fair market value of a parcel of loose, faceted, small aquamarine gemstones, who is the ultimate consumer for these gemstones? Logically, a jewelry manufacturer would utilize gems such as these in his or her production line. Therefore, the price paid by the *manufacturing jeweler* for the parcel of aquamarines in *their present condition* could be considered fair market value. If the scenario changed to a single aquamarine gemstone instead of a parcel, the likely ultimate consumer for the gem *as is* would be the *retail jeweler*. The fair market value would be based on what the retail jeweler pays for the stone when buying from the wholesaler. Although it can be confusing, the mental anxiety of defining fair market value on an item can be kept to a minimum by identifying what a piece will sell for in its *present state* and *most common market*.

The definition of fair market value is analyzed below. Every phase of this definition has been tested by the courts more than once.

Price at Which Property Would Change Hands. What is being defined is the hypothetical sale price. It is obvious that an actual sale of the property would be the best indicator of the value, but if no sale is available, a hypothetical sale is used. All factors that are taken into consideration in hypothecating a sale are set out in the definition of fair market value. In general, a hypothetical sale is considered a sale for cash; any additional increase or decrease in the value that might result from special financing is not considered. For example, if money were borrowed to buy the property, the interest paid on the borrowed money is not considered part of the property's value.

Between a Willing Buyer and a Willing Seller. Exactly who are the willing buyer and seller? If the buyer does not want to buy and the seller does not want to sell, either no sale takes place, or the sale that does take place (such as a forced liquidation sale) would not be representative of fair market value.

Both Having Reasonable Knowledge of all Relevant Facts as of the Valuation Date. The appraiser works under the assumption that both buyer and seller have a reasonable knowledge of the facts concerning the items being appraised—for example, that both know that the diamond is nearly flawless or that the carving is by Fabergé. If this is not the case, the sale is not determinative of value. The appraiser cannot be careless in this regard and must make sure that the appraisal document details the relevant facts on the valuation date. What the IRS calls the "valuation date," also known as the effective date of appraisal, identifies the market conditions that existed at the time appropriate for the function; in case of an estate settlement, it may be the date of death. In most cases, the executor will tell the appraiser what date to use, since the date of death is one date in an optional timeframe that can be chosen.

Marketplace. Marketplace is defined as the area in which the particular item is most commonly sold to the public. "Most commonly sold" and "public" are the key words in this definition. The courts have defined "public" as the greatest number of ultimate consumers of an item in its present form or condition buying for a purpose other than for resale. Types of markets include retail (to the ultimate consumer), wholesale, auction, collector, dealer to dealer, cutter, hobby, museum, scrap, and miscellaneous, depending on the jewelry.

The concept of marketplace also includes consideration of the location of the market. For example, if a wealthy person dies leaving a notable collection of jewelry, but her home is in a distant, remote part of the country, the cost of transporting the jewelry to a more accessible market for resale may be taken into account in the FMV appraisal. Conversely, there could be a reduction of appraised value if the collection is sold as is, where is.

It is useful to bear in mind that fair market value is a legal term, whereas market value is an economic concept. Fair market value often has special considerations for its determination, based on local legislation and rulings. In addition, the particular time requirements for disposition of the items may depend on supply and demand, and should be considered carefully. Fair market value applies when time *is not* of the essence, and the length of time needed for disposition of an item may vary from thirty to ninety days to over a year.

Appraisal Functions

Estate Settlement and Tax Liability Appraisal

Appraising in the area of estate settlement and tax liability calls for specialized knowledge, experience, and willingness to go the extra mile in researching values. Errors in tax appraising for probate may result in penalties to the client and fines to the appraiser. For example, the U.S. Treasury Department can bar any appraisers who are found deficient in valuing property for charitable donations from providing future appraisals for tax purposes.

Estate settlement appraisals are based on the fair market value of the items as of the decedent's date of death, or at the alternate valuation date. Probate is the process of testing or verifying the execution of a will. If one does not have a will, then the decedent is said to have died intestate. State statutes provide and prescribe the devolution of estates of persons who die without a will. An appraisal is necessary to determine the estate's tax liability. Although the decedent's date of death is the most often used valuation date for probate appraisals, the personal representative (executor/executrix, administrator/administratrix) of the estate has a several month time period in which to dispose of the property. To achieve the greatest tax advantages for the estate, the executor/executrix may require the appraiser to use an alternate valuation date. When undertaking an appraisal of this type, discuss which date you are to use as the *valuation date* with the attorney or executor/executrix handling the estate. An appraisal made in the course of administering an estate for tax liability must reflect cash received from the items of the estate, based on actual liquidation figures. Should the estate wish to keep possession of the items, fair market value is applied to the items at the appropriate secondary or primary retail market. An example is jewelry made by the decedent, a well-known artist. Gallery transaction prices where his work was sold would be considered the primary market used to estimate value.

If an appraiser is requested to provide a marketable cash value in the appropriate marketplace, the appraisal should be labeled "marketable cash value," not estate or inheritance value. The IRS position is that if the lowest cash value is desired, the items should be sold for cash and the cash receipts declared. If keeping the items in the estate is desired, then the items should be appraised for fair market value at the secondary retail level in the appropriate market.

The sentimental value of an item to the owner does not affect its fair market value. To sanction this false belief results in misvaluation in estate appraisals.

Since estate tax liability laws may vary from state to state, candid discussions with the attorney handling the probate are urged. All federal estate taxes must be prepared in compliance with the Internal Revenue Code. See Publication #448, Federal Estate and Gift Taxes, September 1984, for guidelines to federal estate tax regulations. Federal tax rulings—regulations governing inheritance tax appraisals—and revenue procedures are subject to change, so it is wise for appraisers to obtain a copy of the latest publication of regulations from the local IRS office before beginning an estate valuation.

Penalties for charitable donation appraisals may be applied to tax returns found to be 66⅔ percent or less of the "correct value." The penalty may not apply, however, if the undervaluation of an asset for gift purposes results in less than one thousand dollars of tax underpayment. If the client is a private individual and not a corporation, the taxpayer may be subject to an additional tax of up to 30 percent of the underpayment and the appraiser may be subject to a one thousand dollar fine per offense.

The courts have long upheld the concept that an item has one and the same fair market value regardless of whether it is being appraised for a donation claim or estate tax liability. They have consistently supported the definition of fair market value discussed in the preceding section.

Use caution before assigning "no value" to any items you may encounter in the jewelry estate. "No value" can apply only to gemstones so tiny, broken, or abraded that they virtually cannot be recovered by repolishing or recutting. If you do assign "no value," be certain to make a full explanation in your appraisal. Most estates have a cache of worn and broken gold and silver mountings that can generally be assigned scrap value, or the melt price.

Collateral Appraisal

Jewelry that is tendered in place of cash for payment purposes is a form of collateral and, accordingly, the loaner may require an appraisal. Bank loan officers frequently ask for this type of appraisal when they want to determine the cash value that they can reasonably expect to receive, in the event the loan is forfeited, upon liquidation of the jewelry or gemstones. Collateral appraisals provide the fair market value of the items; however, banks need to know their options for quick disposition of the property, so you may wish to include a liquidation value as well. Your appraisal report should cover a full range of disposal options for the bank.

Divorce Settlement/Dissolution of Marriage

In the United States, there are nine states with community property laws—Texas, Arizona, California, Idaho, Louisiana, Nevada, New Mexico, and Washington. Mississippi, Virginia, and West Virginia have changed in the past decade from title regulation states (a term no longer used) to equitable distribution of property states. Wisconsin became a community property state when it adopted a version of the uniform marital property act; the new statute was accepted January 1, 1986. This statute does not, however, apply to property division on divorce, but community property division while in a marriage, or upon death. All remaining states in the United States have dual property classification.

Community property states are those in which the property of the divorcing couple is divided according to its value. There is equitable distribution (one can get more than the other) or equal distribution (each one gets one half). In *equitable distribution* states a judge usually awards each party a certain percentage of the total value of the combined holdings; the percentages vary according to the circumstances of the marriage. No-fault divorce statutes in many states grant courts the power to distribute equitably upon divorce all property legally and beneficially acquired during marriage by husband and wife, or either of them, whether legal title lies in their joint or individual names. In the states with Dual Property Classification statutes, property is divided on the basis of either total marital properties, or marital/separate properties. Bill Hoefer, G.G., F.G.A., discusses all divorce property classifications on his website, "Appraiser Under Oath."

Divorce statutes are constantly in flux. Changes may occur in your state's laws that may require explanation by an attorney. Although in most divorce appraisals you will be directed to estimate fair market value for the jewelry, you cannot assume that *fair market value* is used in *all* community property states. For instance, California does not use fair market value, but relies on the evidence code or civil code as a default—one is fair market value, one is not.

There is hardly a divorce appraisal in which the subject of what belongs to whom and why will *not* arise. You are expected to know that the term *marital property* is used in states with community property and equitable distribution regulations. New York's definition is typical: marital property refers to all property acquired by either or both spouses during the marriage and before the signing of a separation agreement or the commencement of a divorce, regardless of the name in which the property is held. It applies to anything that the client acquires during the marriage, except for *separate property*, which is defined as property acquired before the marriage or acquired by inheritance or gift from someone other than the spouse; personal injury awards; property acquired in exchange for separate property, not including any appreciation that is due partly to the other spouse's contributions; and any property that the parties designate in a prenuptial agreement as separate property.

Community property is another term for marital property and defines the entire estate. California's definition is typical: all personal property, wherever located, that is acquired during the marriage by either spouse while living in California is community property.

The reason all of the foregoing is important to you as the appraiser will become apparent once you have accepted the job of appraising a client's jewelry for division of common property, gone to their home, and discovered that you must evaluate seven hundred items of jewelry, half of which must be individually removed from a variety of jewelry boxes. If other personal property is involved, such as hardstone carvings, silver flatware, or silver holloware, you must act in your client's best interest and resolutely question each article's ownership.

Ask your client's attorney to give you clear direction on how he or she wishes you to distinguish between separate and community property at the time of the inventory of articles and on the appraisal report. Frequently, the attorney will direct you to appraise everything. He or she may be planning to categorize the items with the client after your report is finished. This is a good arrangement; you can then be sure that you have included all jewelry items of the estate in your report.

Handling divorce settlements requires a certain perspective. When you accept this type of work, you will often witness a drama of revenge, malice, and despair—needless to say, sensitive appraisers may suffer from this stress. Remember that although it is natural to have empathy for your client, it is your duty and responsibility as a professional appraiser to decline the role of advocate and remain impartial.

Divorce valuation is not for appraisers who cannot work quickly, efficiently, and obtain all the necessary information in one examination. The spouse demanding the appraisal usually has only one chance for outside experts to enter the home, so you must be prepared to assemble all the information you need in one visit.

Only a small percentage of the appraisals the average valuer is called upon to perform are for divorce, as the jewelry estate must be substantial enough for this service to become necessary. One judge estimates 10 percent or less of the divorcing population has jewelry estates large enough to justify the employment of an appraiser. In our materialistic, upwardly mobile society, this percentage may rise dramatically in the years to come.

Liquidation Appraisal

Liquidation appraisal value is value determined when the client decides to convert jewelry items into immediate cash. The sale can be held under forced or limiting conditions and with time constraints, such as under court order or bankruptcy. Liquidation is the lowest measurable market, and results in the lowest net return to the client.

Since liquidation appraisals need research to determine what the client might expect to receive in a quick cash sale, the appraiser must obtain bid prices from several dealers who are in the business of buying and selling items similar to those being appraised. Executors and individuals seeking to liquidate usually have no idea what the items are worth; the appraiser is employed to identify, examine, inventory, and give a bottom-line figure (or estimate range) for which the items can be sold.

One market to research is the auction market. This represents the net sales price an item would probably realize at auction, minus fees and commissions. If the client has consigned goods to auction, he or she must also pay other charges: approximately 1 percent of the reserve price (the lowest for which the item can be sold) to insure the jewelry while it is in the hands of the auction house and two hundred and fifty dollars for color photographs or one hundred dollars for black-and-white photographs of the item, to be used in the auction catalog. Most auction representatives concur that the reserve price can be figured at about 80 percent of the lowest presale catalog estimated price. This is handy information for the appraiser, who can then figure the lowest possible price an individual would take for an item.

The appraiser should not become too complacent about using auction prices, however, because if the item has been auctioned at a small regional sale, there is usually no minimum reserve and the seller has no control over the outcome of the sale. Even at major auctions, anything can happen. The state of the economy or international problems can reduce the number of prospective bidders in a room. Conversely, bidding wars can spur the price of an item to unrealistic highs. An appraiser attempting to pinpoint auction values needs to proceed cautiously and do as much research as possible on events surrounding the sale of comparable items. Attending many auctions personally is the best way to gain an understanding of this market.

If the client wants to consign goods to a jewelry or gemstone retail outlet and wants to know what to expect in the way of value, the answer is that the client can usually expect to get 10 to 20 percent more than the current wholesale value of the items.

Comparison Appraisal

A client may bring in a jewelry or gemstone item to verify its identity and/or quality as claimed by the seller. Some jeweler/appraisers will refuse to do such appraisals because they fear repercussions from their customers and colleagues if they provide appraisals that are too high or too low. Independent jewelry appraisers are without a vested interest in such cases and do not have this problem; they can render an ethical and professional appraisal based on careful research of the market in the valuer's locale without fearing any reprisals. Comparison appraisals *usually* reflect the jewelry at their most common *retail* replacement price; however, this type of appraisal can also reflect comparisons in auction, wholesale, or broker markets. This is an appraisal more complicated than it first appears. Sometimes clients are seeking to find if they have purchased an item at the lowest price, but often they want to double check a *verbal guarantee* given them by a sales clerk's allegation: "This will appraise for twice what you are paying in retail replacement value." The first step is to establish the market level where the item was purchased: Retail? Wholesale? Auction? Liquidation? When the market level where the jewelry was purchased is identified, *that* is the appropriate market to research and make sales comparisons for a realistic estimate of retail replacement value.

Estimate to Replace

An estimate to replace is used to establish the value of a previously undocumented item that has been lost or stolen. It is a hypothetical appraisal that is based on information supplied by the client, such as any photographs and the client's description of the item. Use the following disclaimer on your report: "This estimate to replace has been determined solely from the customer's information about the item. The appraiser did not personally inspect the subject jewelry."

Your report will be seen as more credible by insurance companies if you explain how you determined the stated values. State the procedures you followed and itemize, by date and name or title, the catalogs, wholesalers, and any other markets you have used for this estimate. If you are a jeweler, be sure to note in your report that the valuation you have supplied is an estimate of what you would charge to replace the item in your store, not an appraisal of market replacement.

Damage Report

A damage report expresses the difference in value that has resulted from breakage and estimates the cost of the removal, recutting, and resetting of the stone, as well as the value of the recut stone (loss of weight). In general, diamonds cost around one hundred to one hundred and twenty-five dollars per carat to recut. Consult with a gem cutter if you are not able to determine the exact weight loss involved in recutting. You must get a release of liability from your client if recutting the stone will be conducted through your facilities, as most gem cutters will not accept liability for recutting stones.

A damage report should contain the following:

1. Purpose of the appraisal.
2. Value of the item prior to the incident.
3. Current value as a damaged item.
4. Weight loss of a diamond or colored stone that is expected to result from the recutting.
5. Charge for repair to the item.
6. Value of the item once repaired or recut (if gemstone).

The insurance company has the option to replace a damaged item with one like in kind; repair or otherwise restore the item to its condition immediately prior to the damage; provide a cash settlement covering the amount for which the property could reasonably be replaced with identical property; or simply provide the applicable amount of insurance. Generally, insurance companies opt for whichever of the above methods will cost them the least. A settlement that satisfies the client depends largely upon the individual insurance company adjuster and the local laws.

An important point for the appraiser to remember is that if a damage report relates only to the cost of repair of the damage to a stone, the report should state that the cost to restore the jewelry to new condition is *not* included. To restore the jewelry to new condition when only the stone is warranted is called a *betterment*. If *betterment* occurs, the insurance company can deduct or try to recover money differences already paid in the claim.

Casualty Loss

In a casualty appraisal, the appraiser tries to determine the fair market value of a lost, stolen, or destroyed jewelry item that has not been previously documented. The Internal Revenue Service allows an income tax deduction of some portion of the value of lost, stolen, or destroyed articles with a proper casualty loss appraisal. The allowable deduction for damaged items is the difference in fair market value before and after the damage to the item. For stolen or lost articles, the allowable is fair market value of the article before the incident.

There are IRS parameters of which you need to be aware, so it would be wise to check with the local district director before completing the appraisal, since regulations and interpretations change frequently. However, to establish value, the appraiser will use the original cost of the subject item or, if the original cost is unknown, the fair market value of the item at the date of its acquisition.

Donation Appraisal

Few *donation* jewelry appraisals are being made in the late 1990s. Museums and other nonprofit institutions requesting them are having a difficult time finding qualified appraisers willing to undertake such assignments and accept the liabilities that accompany this type of appraisal. Spokespersons in the government and appraisal societies have made valuers thoroughly aware of the risk of fines, job restrictions, and professional sanctions, for cavalierly undertaking *donation* appraisals. This fearful attitude may be attributed to some stringent laws that went into effect in 1985, known as the Deficit Reduction Tax Act. The Act was aimed at some unethical appraisers who were conducting charitable donation appraisals with a "sky is the limit" attitude. For the most part, the appraisals were pushed by gem sellers who would set up the donation and provide inflated appraisals of the items being sold. In some cases, the reports were furnished to gem sellers by unscrupulous appraisers, who took a higher than usual fee to provide the inflated values. Appraisals with items highly overvalued brought the entire appraisal industry under the scrutiny of the IRS, and the 1984 Tax Act was the result. It is a lengthy and complicated bill that not only increased penalties on taxpayers for donation overvaluations, but regulated the appraiser as to the kinds of appraisals acceptable, and imposed fines and/or barred unscrupulous appraisers from providing future tax-related appraisals.

A donation appraisal, as for a gift to a museum, university, or other nonprofit institution, is based on fair market value. One should use the most common market for the articles, and accommodate the "willing buyer, willing seller" concept. The most common market will be the market having the greatest number of transactions, between willing buyers and willing sellers, of comparable merchandise.

Among other points, the bill has provisions for donations of an aggregate value of goods exceeding five hundred dollars but not five thousand dollars, and for donations of goods valued over five thousand dollars. The bill states that the valuation must be made by a qualified appraiser not earlier than sixty days prior to the date of donation. It must be prepared, signed, and dated by a qualified appraiser.

A separate qualified appraisal is required for each item of property that is not included in a group of similar items of property. Only one qualified appraisal is required for each group of similar items of property, but a donor may obtain separate qualified appraisals for each item of property.

The following information must be included in a qualified appraisal:

1. A description of the property in sufficient detail to enable a person who is not generally familiar with the type of property to ascertain that the appraised property is also the contributed property. A photograph of the property must be included as well.
2. The physical condition of tangible property must be described.
3. The date (or expected date) of contribution.
4. The terms of any agreement or understanding entered into or expected to be entered into by or on behalf of the donor relating to the use, sale, or other disposition of the property contributed.
5. The name, address, and taxpayer identification number (Social Security Number) of the appraiser.
6. The qualifications of the appraiser, including his or her background, experience, education, and membership in professional appraisal associations. (One note: the IRS does not believe that special education or membership in a professional organization gives the appraiser uncontested approval.)
7. A statement that the appraisal was prepared for income tax purposes.
8. The date or dates on which the property was valued.
9. The method of valuation used to determine the property's fair market value.
10. The manner and date of acquisition of property by the donor or, if the property was created, produced, or manufactured by or for the donor, a statement to that effect and the date the property was substantially completed.
11. The specific basis for the valuation, if any, such as comparable sales.
12. The fee arrangement between the donor and appraiser.

Along with the appraisal report, you must complete and give to the client IRS Form 8283 for deductions of noncash charitable contributions. You must also complete section B, the Appraisal Summary part of the form, when the donated property exceeds five thousand dollars. You must also sign the form and certify that you are an independent appraiser, and that your fee is not based on a percentage of the property's value, since the IRS no longer accepts appraisals provided by appraisers who charge fees in this manner. Your signature makes you liable for civil penalties under section 6701(a) of the tax code.

To police the appraiser's work further, the IRS has Form 8282, which requires the donee to submit a statement to the IRS if the donated property is sold, exchanged, or traded within a two-year time period. This form is intended to check possible collusion between the donor and donee. However, it is possible that once the item is traded again, it may drop in value from your original appraised price. To protect yourself in the event that the IRS later asks you for information about your previous appraisal, keep records of substantiation so that you can prove that the market has since fallen. One example is the 1979–1980 peak market for "D" flawless diamonds retailing for sixty-four thousand dollars per carat! The diamond market plunged to twelve thousand dollars per carat (D-flawless, wholesale) in 1985, then fluttered up and down over the next ten years before settling around fourteen thousand dollars per carat (wholesale) at the end of 1997. Lesson learned: Subscribe to price guides and *save them!*

Can you use auction market prices when researching fair market value for a donation appraisal? Yes, if you can prove it is the most appropriate and common market. In 1986, Joseph W. Tenhagen, current president of the Diamond Dealers Club of Florida, was employed by the IRS to find the fair market value of a 48.20-carat natural alexandrite stone at the time of donation, December 1979. Tenhagen met the government's criteria for FMV by using the market data approach of comparable gemstones. The auction and retail markets proved to be the most appropriate and common markets. The differences and similarities of comparable items were analyzed and correlated. Analysis included date of sale, size, amount of color change, clarity, cutting, and country of origin. The data reflected information obtained from eleven actual sales, two museum specimens, three stones that were offered (but did not sell) at auction, and sales information from three gemstone dealers with like stones for sale. Tenhagen established value and built a defensible document on the basic appraisal principle: research. His report can be found in the appendix. It is a good example of due diligence in using auction-recorded prices to establish fair market value for a donation appraisal.

From 1982 to 1987, approximately three hundred cases of tax deductions for gem donations, claiming many millions of dollars, were reviewed by IRS personnel. In each case, the U.S. Tax Court defined the ultimate consumer, or end user, as the person buying the property, for a purpose other than resale, in its present condition in the most common market. The tax court repeatedly held that if a recent transaction of the gems was in question, the price paid in the transaction was the best evidence of value, providing that no evidence existed that the price was extraordinary to the market. However, in several 1987 court decisions, the taxpayers were allowed to deduct *less* than they paid for the gem(s). The courts are no longer relying solely on the cost of the gems as the figure a taxpayer can use for a donation.

Table 2-2 lists ten representative cases decided from 1985 to 1987. Six were decided at the taxpayer's purchase price, not at the appraised value supplied by the taxpayer. In *Anselmo v. Commissioner,* the IRS offered to settle out of court at the taxpayer's purchase price plus an added 12 percent inflation sum; the other settlements ranged from slightly above the taxpayer's purchase price to below actual purchase price.

The IRS now asserts that only qualified appraisers may do tax-related appraisals. They define qualified appraisers as those who represent themselves to the public as appraisers of the type of property being valued, and who cannot be considered "excluded appraisers." *Excluded appraisers* include the donor, the donee, any party to the transaction in which the donor acquired the property (unless the property is donated within twelve months of the date of acquisition and the appraised value does not exceed the acquisition price), anyone employed by any of the named persons, and any person whose relationship to those involved in the donation would cause a reasonable person to question the independence of the appraiser.

You must declare on the appraisal that you meet the listed requirements, understand that a false or fraudulent overstatement of value of the property may subject you to a penalty for aiding and abetting an understatement of tax liability, and know that it may cause this and future tax appraisals that you perform to be disregarded. You must also question your client about the original cost of the item and provide extensive documentation. A thorough and detailed cover letter must accompany the appraisal, and must include the market information that was the basis of the evaluation for each item as well as references and comparable sales data. This reflects the effort of the IRS to prevent a person from buying in the wholesale market and selling or donating as a retailer. Before you begin any type of donation appraisal, consult IRS publication 561, "Determining the Value of Donated Property" (revised November 1986) and also see publication 526, "Charitable Contributions."

Fear of Signing IRS Form 8283

To sign or not to sign this form has become a concern to many jewelry appraisers. Many, conscious of the substantial amount of paperwork involved in doing ap-

Table 2-2. 1985–1987 Court Decisions on Gemstone Donation Tax Shelters

Case and Trial Location	Taxpayer Donation and Cost	Tax Appraisal	IRS Stat Notice	IRS Appraisal	Published Court Date and Decision	
Anselmo v. Commissioner Washington, D.C.	numerous parcels, 15,000	80,680	16,800	1) 7,900 2) 8,100	4/16/85	16,800
Robert C. Chiu v. Commissioner Washington, D.C.	tax year 1 (78) 2 @ 10,412	51,095	10,750	1) 5,919 2) 12,000	4/15/85	10,750
	tax year 2 (79) 13 @ 22,039	119,464	26,555	1) 44,571 2) 25,887	4/15/85	26,555
	tax year 3 (80) 28 @ 20,000	92,790	20,000	2) 20,974	4/15/85	20,000
Pliney A. Price v. Commissioner Washington, D.C.	parcel tourmaline 3,093	15,910	3,093		4/15/85	3,093
	parcel sapphire 3,786	15,910	3,786	2,125	4/15/85	3,786
Ali A. Talabi v. Commissioner & *Chait Palantekin v. Commissioner* Washington, D.C.	tax year 1 (78) kunzite 21,943	46,812	21,943	18,408	4/15/85	21,943
	tax year 2 (79) blue topaz 5,677	26,698	5,677	2,212	4/15/85	5,677
Chris B. Theodotou v. Commissioner Washington, D.C.	kunzite 2,641	15,849	2,641	2,377	4/15/85	2,641
	opal 380	2,280	380	577	4/15/85	380
	blue topaz 18,944	186,852	18,944	16,941	4/15/85	18,944
J & H Lampe v. Commissioner Dallas, Texas	9 @ 4,500	1) 22,023 2) 10,415	4,500	3,150	5/16/85	4,500
Dale B. Dubin v. Commissioner Washington, D.C.	topaz crystal 750	1,200,000	750	750	9/11/86	750
	jade desk set 55,000	225,000	55,000	55,000	9/11/86	55,000
Clark R. Hecker v. Commissioner St. Louis, Mo.	8 tourmalines 5,100	24,164	3,400	(av. of 2) 4,337	6/16/87	4,337
	9 mineral specimens 5,100	19,500	3,400	5,540	6/16/87	5,540
Edwin J. Cunningham, Jr. v. Commissioner St. Louis, Mo.	sapphire pendant 4,000	22,450	5,000	1)2,972 2)3,744	6/16/87	3,744
	emerald/diamond pendant 5,000	26,985	3,335	1)5,200 2)4,982	6/16/87	5,091
	garnet pendant 3,000	16,205	2,000	1)2,100 2)4,480	6/16/87	3,290
Leo J. Malone, Jr. v. Commissioner St. Louis, Mo.	rubellite tourmaline mineral collection	tax year (80) 27,500	3,771	2,600 485 1)2,386 2)1,857	6/16/87	4,721 5,535
	yellowish/gr. tourmaline 5,657 pendant & ring 4,600	tax year (81) 21,028	3,066	1)2,608 2)2,000 1)3,712 2)2,750	6/16/87	

Note: Where appraisals were done by more than one appraiser, the numbers 1) and 2) are indicated. All figures are rounded to the nearest dollar.

praisals for donation purposes, simply refuse such work. More serious, however, is the fact that signing the form renders the appraiser accountable for *all* statements made on the form. As Emyl Jenkins, a personal property appraiser, points out, she is concerned that the IRS requires her to attest that all information given by the *donor* on the form is correct. She writes: "I now expect almost everyone to try to fudge just a little bit, especially when they're dealing with the IRS. I've concluded that IRS forms bring out the closet embezzler in most people" (Jenkins, 1986, 37).

Jenkins has raised a serious question. How can you protect yourself when asked to certify the truth of the donor's statement? One way is to hire an attorney to help you devise a statement to accompany each tax form you sign. The statement should, in part, declare that you cannot be held responsible for the donor's claim of when and how the item was acquired and the cost or adjusted basis for the gift.

Jenkins, who is a senior member of the American Society of Appraisers as well as an author and lecturer on personal property appraising, has developed the following statement, which she attaches to every completed Form 8283:

> Donation of personal property by (donor's name) to (donee) on (date gift given): An appraisal to comply with IRS requirements for gifts with a value over $5,000.
>
> Accompanying is a complete description of the property donated by (donor's name) and my qualifications as an appraiser to make this appraisal. The fee for this appraisal was based on an hourly charge for the time the appraiser spent researching and preparing the appraisal, plus direct costs in the preparation of the appraisal document including telephone and incidental expenses to confer with other experts. This appraisal has been made for income tax purposes to accompany IRS Form 8283 and it is intended to provide the information required in Part II 2 (a) and (c), and II 3. The appraiser is not responsible for the information provided in Part II 2 (b), (c), and (d) of that form. The fair market value has been established by the use, in part, of published auction prices. The appraiser does not certify or warrant the accuracy of published auction prices, but maintains that such publications represent an accepted definition of "market" for the type of property described in this appraisal. The appraiser has no interest in the property appraised and is an independent contractor and not an employee of either the donor or donee.

Other Functions of an Appraisal

A *qualitative report* gives information about an item but does not include a statement of value. This type of report is used merely to establish or confirm identity and to describe gemstones, precious metals, and other jewelry components. A client might, for example, want to know whether certain gemstones are natural or synthetic, whether a stone has recutting potential, or might want to determine the country of origin of a jewelry item.

A *customs appraisal* is a report prepared for a client who wishes to take jewelry abroad and avoid any problems upon reentry into the United States. On the document you confirm the existence of a particular item of jewelry in the possession of the client on a particular date (and time, if the client is leaving the country the same day). Note serial numbers, trademarks, maker's marks, and furnish a detailed description of the jewelry along with a photograph of the item, if possible.

Limiting and Contingency Conditions for Appraisal Documents

The list below includes recommended limiting and contingency conditions to be attached to your appraisal report document as needed. Your actual document should be developed with the assistance of an attorney. You may wish to include several additional considerations to the report to meet any special circumstances. These statements should be in 8-point type or a larger size, depending upon legal requirements in your state. Remember, however, that while you can limit your liability to disclose whatever prevented you from operating at a subscribed industry standard, you cannot disclaim it totally.

1. Mounted stones are examined and evaluated only to the extent that the mounting permits.
2. All weights and measurements are estimates, unless otherwise stated.
3. Ordinary wear common to this type of item is not noted.
4. If the item is antique or out of style, say that the valuation is for the replacement of an item of similar size, type, and quality, not for an exact duplication.
5. Identification of metals and methods of constructions are determined only to the extent that the design permits.
6. If the take-in date is not the date of the valuation of the jewelry, distinguish the two dates clearly on the report.
7. If the appraisal has been prepared away from your normal working environment, state the location and make note of any working conditions that may have limited the proper examination and evaluation of the items, such as lighting or space limitations, or time constraints.
8. Unless otherwise stated, all colored stones listed on this appraisal report have probably been subjected to a stable and possibly undetectable color en-

hancement process. Prevailing market values are based on these processes, which are universally practiced and accepted by the gems and jewelry trade.

9. No change in this appraisal report can be made by anyone other than the named appraiser; the appraiser will not be responsible for unauthorized changes.

10. Possession of this document does not confer the right of publication. This report may not be used by anyone other than the above-named client without written permission of the appraiser, and then may be used only in its entirety.

11. All value conclusions are valid only for the purpose stated.

12. It is understood and agreed that fees paid for this appraisal do not include the services of the appraiser for any other matter whatsoever. In particular, fees paid to date do not include any of the appraiser's time or services in connection with any statement, testimony, or other matters before an insurance company, its agents, employees, or any court or other body in connection with the property herein described.

13. It is understood and agreed that if the appraiser is required to testify or to make any such statements to any third party concerning the described property appraisal, applicant shall pay the appraiser for all time and services so rendered at appraiser's then-current rates for such services with half of the estimated fee paid in advance to appraiser before any testimony commences.

For fair market value appraisals, you might append the following contingencies.

1. The prices of subject items are estimates of their current fair market value in their present condition and within the existing local market. Primary research has been conducted in the following manner: (list marketplaces and prices analyzed to estimate value).

2. As used in this appraisal, "fair market value" is defined as the price at which such property would change hands between a willing buyer and a willing seller, neither being under compulsion to buy or sell and both having reasonable knowledge of relevant facts, in the most common market that is reasonable and appropriate for a purchaser who is the ultimate consumer of the property.

For Estimate To Replace appraisals, you may want to append the following limiting conditions: This appraisal sets value estimates at the current market value at which the appraised items may be purchased in a retail jewelry

store engaged in the business of selling comparable merchandise, and does not necessarily reflect the price of any one particular jewelry store. Jewelry appraisal and evaluation is subjective; therefore, estimates of value may vary from one appraiser to another and such variance does not necessarily constitute error on the part of the appraiser. This appraisal should not be used as a basis for purchase or sale of the items valued, and is only an estimate of the approximate replacement values of subject items at this time and in this locale.

Handling Insurance Replacements

You do not need to be a retail jeweler to expand your business by handling the replacement of gems and jewelry on insurance claims. By working as a broker, you will be in a good position to offer strong discounts to insurance companies and draw their business to you.

Insurance claims adjusters and agents need current information about replacement costs and the availability of jewelry they have on claim, so the first step is to contact them, tell them who you are, and explain how you can help them. Most will respond to you by contacting you for information at first. After working with you on several replacements, insurance representatives will probably begin sending you their clients for insurance appraisals.

While different insurance companies may have their own methods of handling claims, the basic procedures remain the same nationwide. The chain of events leading to your involvement with the jewelry replacements is as follows:

1. A client gets a retail replacement "floater," "rider," or "schedule" on his or her insurance policy for an item of jewelry.

2. The client's jewelry is later lost, stolen, or damaged, and the client files a claim. If the article is stolen, the client must file a report with the local police before notifying the insurance company.

3. The claim goes to the Claims Department of the insurance company, bypassing the underwriter, who is no longer involved.

4. If the Claims Department believes that the claim is legitimate, it will want to give the client a replacement item of jewelry rather than the item's cash value. The insurance company would rather replace than "cash out" the item even if the company would save money by "cashing out." The reasoning is that if the article is replaced, it will probably continue to be insured and the premium will be maintained.

5. The claims representative will want to replace the lost, damaged, or stolen article at a cost of at least 10

to 50 percent less than local sources. This is where you, the appraiser/insurance replacement specialist, come into the picture.

The claims representative, whom you have contacted earlier, calls and gives you details about the article to be replaced. You can use a quotation form such as the example shown in figure 2-1 to write down all the necessary information and work up your quote for replacement based on the description furnished by the agent. The agent will want a *written quotation,* the price for which you will deliver a comparable replacement article, according to the former insurance appraisal, to the client. You must quote the exact item by description; if it is a diamond, describe the four "C's" of color, cut, clarity, and carats.

After you have presented your quotation, you should get a letter from the insurance adjuster authorizing replacement. Make sure you have written authorization to replace before you start work. The cost of replacement (with the discount) is established between you and the insurance adjuster—do *not* discuss this with the customer. Ask the agent if there is a deductible and if local taxes are included or should be added.

If the item for replacement is a chipped or damaged diamond or colored gemstone, you must do a major damage report and review. If the damaged stone does not change dramatically in visual size after the recutting or repair, the client must accept the repair of the stone plus payment for the loss in value of the weight. The insurance company pays for cost of repair. If, however, damage to the stone is severe and the stone is estimated to become considerably smaller after recutting (insurance companies vary on the minimum acceptable size after recutting; consult with the agent), the company keeps the damaged stone and gives the client another of the same original size and quality. The insurance company then sells the smaller recut stone. If you are going to do quotations for diamond recutting, make sure you are proficient at this type of estimation, or consult with a diamond or colored-stone cutter. Protect yourself with the usual plots and photographs and explain to the client the risks of recutting the stone. A sample damage report form is shown in figure 2-2.

Authorization to Proceed

After the insurance claims representative receives your quotation and gives you the go-ahead to proceed with the replacement, you will either secure the item from your previously researched source or build a replacement (if you are a bench jeweler and able to perform this service), as you will have already stated. When the replacement item is ready, there may be yet another form for you to fill out completely and have the

claimant sign—the customer satisfaction and insurance payment authorization form (fig. 2-3). Not all states require this, but where it is used, its importance cannot be stressed too strongly—this form must be signed and returned to the insurance company before you can be paid for your services.

In Florida, for example, instead of a customer satisfaction form, the insurance company issues a two-party check with the names of the client and the insurance firm replacing the items. The cancelled check becomes an acknowledgment of satisfaction. If you are using a customer satisfaction form, have the claimant sign the form affirming that he or she is satisfied with the replacement jewelry. Next, fill in the percentage of discount extended to the insurance company below the retail replacement total. Include the amount due you at the bottom. If the client has paid you a deductible, as is the norm, subtract it from the total due. That bottom line is the amount the insurance company owes you for replacing the item. Sign the form and send the bill to the claims representative with whom you have been working.

Questions and Answers about Developing Insurance Replacement Business

Q. How can I get started?

A. Solicit claims representatives by mail, telephone, and by visiting in person. Invite insurance agents to your office or store and express your willingness to travel from your place of business to the claimant. If you wish to meet many claims adjusters in a short time, plan a seminar and invite agents to listen to you explain what you can do for them.

A Houston, Texas, gemologist/appraiser has compiled a training manual for claims representatives explaining common metals, diamond, and colored-stone terminology. She distributes the manuals to insurance agents and underwriters at seminars that she gives several times a year. Included in the booklet is a list of questions for agents to ask claimants about lost items, as well as a minimum requirements list of information needed for accurate jewelry appraisals. Appraisal methodology, and some "Meaningless Terminology" narration such as Pigeon-blood red and Blue White Diamond, helps get across the need for well written descriptions.

Q. What kind of mark-up margin should I allow?

A. The insurance replacement specialist's usual mark-up is about 20 percent above wholesale. If you really want to go after the business, go as low as you must over wholesale (but no lower than 5 percent) to get the job. Just make sure that you can deliver what you promise.

Q. Will the insurance company pay me to supply a quotation?

A. Yes. The average charge for a quotation is about thirty-five dollars, regardless of whether you do the replacement. But, as some will refuse to pay this fee if you contract for replacement of the jewelry, the matter of quotation fee must be settled between you and the adjuster when you are contacted to submit a written quote.

2-1. Sample written quotation for replacing an insured article.

COMPANY NAME
(Logo)

REPLACEMENT FORM

Date: _____

INSURANCE COMPANY: _____

ADDRESS: _____

CITY, STATE _____ ZIP _____ TELEPHONE _____

Adjuster's Name: _____

CLIENT: _____

ADDRESS: _____

CITY, STATE _____ ZIP _____ TELEPHONE _____

Policy # _____ Coverage _____

Claim # _____ Deductible _____

Article to Be Replaced: (Based upon descriptions furnished)   Preliminary Estimate:

_____

_____

_____

_____

_____

_____

_____

Estimated prices are current as of above date and subject to market fluctuations.

Quotation Authorized by: _____

2-2. Sample insurance damage report.

COMPANY NAME
(Logo)

DAMAGE REPORT

Prepared For: _____ Regarding: _____

_____ _____

_____ _____

_____ _____

Claim and Policy # _____

Type of Stone: _____

Original Shape: _____

Estimated Weight Before Damage: _____ carat

Present Weight: _____ carat (measured weight) (estimated weight)

Present Measurements: _____ x _____ x _____ x _____ mm

Description of Damage: _____

_____

_____

Recut Estimated By: _____   [PLOT]

Recut Time: _____

Recommended Recut Shape: _____

Estimated Recut Weight: _____

Weight Loss: _____

Estimated Recut Measurements: _____ x

_____ x _____ x _____ mm

Estimated Quality Before Damage: _____ clarity/color

Estimated Present Quality: _____

Estimated Quality After Repair: _____

Estimated Value Before Damage $_____ Estimated Present Value $_____

Estimated Recut Cost $_____ (retail)

Estimated Value After Repair: _____

Salvage Value $_____

Date _____ _____

Signature

2-3. Sample certificate of satisfaction form.

COMPANY NAME
(Logo)

Certificate of Satisfaction

Insurance Company: Insured: Policy No. _____

    Name_____   Name_____

    Address_____   Address_____

    City_____State_____Zip_____   City_____State_____Zip_____

    Attention:_____   Claim No._____Telephone_____

DESCRIPTION OF ITEM(S) TO BE REPLACED:

Items: Replacement Cost:

_____

_____

_____

_____

_____

_____

_____

_____

_____

    Sub Total_____

    Sales Tax_____

    Total_____

    _____

    _____

    _____

This is to certify that the above facts are true and that the repair or replacement has been made to my satisfaction and in full settlement of its obligation under my policy shown above for said loss, I authorize my insurer to pay:

This certificate of satisfaction has been executed on the   _____

_____day of_____19____.   Company

                                                         _____

                                                        Insured Signature

CHAPTER 3

CONDUCTING THE APPRAISAL

I counted the large balass rubies on the great throne, and there are about 108, all cabuchons, the least of which weighs 100 carats, but there are some which weigh apparently 200 or more. As for the emeralds, there are plenty of good colour, but they have many flaws; the largest may weigh 60 carats, and the least 30 carats. I counted about 116; thus there are more emeralds than rubies.

Tavernier, *Travels in India*, 1676

Imagine that you are a gemologist or jeweler who is facing an appraisal of jewelry for the first time. The items are spread out in front of you and your refractometer, microscope, and other necessary tools are close at hand. You are ready to begin, but not sure where to start. The take-in form shown in figure 3-1 will help you proceed smoothly. The steps involved in appraising are as follows.

Initial Examination and Take-In

Determine the purpose, type of value, and function (intended use) of the appraisal and find out how many items you will be appraising. Explain your fee structure and obtain the client's approval to proceed. Next, fill out the client's name and address and the date and time of day on the take-in form. Itemize each piece to be appraised and list the client's estimate of the jewelry's value. If you plan to hold the jewelry overnight, place each item in a separate take-in envelope or plastic bag, mark the appraisal take-in form number on the outside of the bag, and number the bags in sequential order after the initial exam is finished.

Note any damage to stones or mountings on the take-in form and point this out to the client. Discuss the condition of each piece and show the client, under the microscope, any damage and/or needed repairs. This is the appropriate time to discuss the overall quality of gemstones and indicate any particular aspects that may affect the value of the items you will appraise. If the client does not know how to look for damage on stones or mountings, show him/her how to use a loupe. You may make a friend and patron for life if you do so taking the time to explain exactly what the client is viewing. Diamonds and colored stones that may be positively identified by their inclusions, fractures, chips, breaks, or other internal or external features should be plotted on the take-in form as the customer watches. A copy of the form is given to the customer, who should be assured that he/she will have the opportunity to look at their gemstones upon return and can use the plot to be certain they are the same gemstones.

When you list the jewelry items on the take-in form, describe all stones generically. Never make a positive identification of metal or gemstones unless you have done the tests at that time. For example, write "one yellow metal ring containing one round faceted red stone and two near-colorless transparent stones. Shank stamped 14K."

Note any special instructions on the take-in form, such as "Do not clean ring; owner does not wish to lose patina."

Next, have your customer read, understand, and sign the take-in form, or, if you are a portable appraiser, the contract (fig. 3-2). Follow the same procedure a storefront jeweler would in advising the client about damaged items or repairs that should be made before the appraisal begins. Make a note of these on a worksheet (a sample worksheet is shown in figure 3-3). Give the client a copy of the take-in form and notify him or her to present this copy in order to retrieve the jewelry later. If the jewelry is left with you, put it in your safe as soon as the client leaves until you are ready to begin work on the actual appraisal.

Advise the client of the various identification and testing procedures that you could perform, explaining both the risks involved in conducting the tests and the additional charges you will impose for the procedures.

3-1. Sample appraisal take-in form.

COMPANY NAME
(Logo)

APPRAISAL TAKE-IN FORM

Name _____   Page _____ of _____.

Address _____   No. _____

City, State, Zip _____   Date Received _____

Telephone _____   Completion Date _____

Name on Appraisal _____   Appraisal Form (check one)

Address _____   Insurance _____ Estate _____

City, State, Zip _____   Other _____

Appraisal Type _____   Total Number of Items _____

                                              Estimated Fee _____

Item No.	Items	Customer's Declared Value

SERVICE AGREEMENT

"The description and value of the article(s) listed on this form are correct. By accepting said article(s) Customer agrees that neither the appraiser, its parent company, nor any of its employees or officers shall be responsible for the identification or condition of the jewelry or stones at the time of the receipt. I further agree that the responsibility for any damage or loss to said article(s) shall be limited to the actual cost to the appraiser and/or its parent company to repair or replace the article(s), and in no event shall said repair or replacement cost exceed Customer's evaluation as shown on this form. If Customer fails to list said value(s), the Customer agrees that the said value(s) of said article(s) do not exceed the sum of $100. I acknowledge that the above terms have been fully explained to me by the appraiser or a company employee whose name or initials appear on this form and that I agree to these terms and conditions."

Client's Signature _____

3-2. Portable appraisers should have their clients sign a formal authorization form such as this one before beginning the initial examination.

Authorization for Appraisal Service

In consideration of this Employment Agreement between_____

hereinafter referred to as the appraiser, and_____

hereinafter referred to as the employer, said parties_____
do hereby agree as follows:
The appraiser agrees to make a study of the property:_____

_____located at_____

_____

_____

PURPOSE OF THE APPRAISAL

_____

_____

_____

and to deliver (   ) copies of a_____report to the

employer on or before_____.

In return for said services and appraisal report, employer hereby agrees to compensate appraiser in the amount of $_____, payable as follows: $_____ upon the signing of this agreement and the balance of $_____ upon delivery of said report.

Should additional services of the appraiser be requested by the employer, his agent, his attorney, or the court, such as pre-trial conferences, court appearances, court preparation, etc., the employer agrees to compensate the appraiser at the rate of $_____ per hour provided such additional services are performed within one year after delivery of said report. In the event that such services shall be required more than one year after delivery of said report, the compensation shall be at the customary per diem rate charged by said appraiser as of that date.

The cost of preparing exhibits for court, photo enlargements, maps, etc., shall be borne by employer, and the appraiser shall, in addition to his compensation, be reimbursed by the employer for such costs advanced by the appraiser.

Payment for such additional services shall become due upon receipt of statement rendered by the appraiser.

It is further understood and agreed that if any portion of the above compensation or costs due to the appraiser becomes delinquent, the employer agrees to pay interest thereon at the rate of _____% per annum on said account from the due date until paid, and further agrees to pay all costs of collection thereof, including reasonable attorney's fees, court costs, etc.

In the event that employer desires to cancel this authorization, written notice thereof shall be delivered to the appraiser, and it is agreed that the appraiser shall receive compensation from the employer for all services rendered at the rate of $_____ per day for the time actually spent prior to receipt of written notice to stop work plus all costs advanced in connection with said appraisal prior to receipt of such written notice.

_____
I hereby accept these terms and conditions and order the appraisal to be made.

_____   _____
  Employer/Fiduciary   Date

Appraiser hereby acknowledges receipt of $_____ retainer.

_____   _____
  Appraiser   Date

3-3. Sample appraisal worksheet, for use with colored gemstone jewelry and other articles.

APPRAISAL WORKSHEET

Job # _____ Item # _____
Date _____ Date Due _____
Purpose: RR _____ FMV _____
Function _____

General Description

Jewelry Type (check) Woman's _____ Man's _____

Ring _____ Bracelet _____ Brooch _____ Chain _____

Charm _____ Earrings _____ Necklace _____

Pendent _____ Other _____

Word Description

Damage seen: _____

Measurements

Height _____ mm Width _____ mm Depth _____ mm

Length _____ mm (watches, necklaces, chains)

Rings: Widest point _____ mm Narrowest point _____ mm

Ring Size _____   Photo (y/n) _____   (ratio 1:1)

Stones

Information Source: Dia. form _____   Col. Stone Form _____   Melee form _____   None _____

Number of Stones	shape/cut	type	size	color	clarity	make	Total weight	Price (per ct.)	$ Total
							Total stone wt.	Total stone cost (wholesale)	

Metals

Metal Type: (check)

Gold _____   Silver _____   Plat. _____

Gd. Pl. _____   White _____

Yellow _____   Other _____

Tested (y/n) _____   Stamped (y/n) _____

Hallmark _____

Fineness _____

Construction

Manufacture Type (check)

Handmade _____   Cast _____

Die-Struck _____   Quality _____

Setting Type (check)

Prong _____   Gypsy _____   Bezel _____

Tube _____   Bead _____   Pavé _____

Channel _____   Illus. _____

Tension _____   Fishtail _____

Cluster Illus. _____   Basket _____

Other _____

Style (check)

Antique ___ Modern ___ Art Deco ___

Weight

_____ dwt (including stones)

_____ stones ct. wt. X .13

_____ net weight of metal

Cost of Metal

spot price $\dfrac{\_\_\_\_}{480}$ X $\dfrac{\_\_\_\_}{\text{(fineness)}}$ = $\dfrac{\$\_\_\_\_}{\text{(per dwt)}}$

$\dfrac{\$\_\_\_\_}{\text{(per dwt)}}$ X $\dfrac{\_\_\_\_}{\text{(metal wt.)}}$ = $\dfrac{\_\_\_\_}{\text{(total cost of metal)}}$

$\dfrac{\$\_\_\_\_}{\text{(cost of metal)}}$ X $\dfrac{\_\_\_\_}{\text{(labor \%)}}$ = $\dfrac{\_\_\_\_}{\text{(wholesale cost)}}$

Equipment Used:
- ❑ microscope
- ❑ refractometer
- ❑ polariscope
- ❑ dicroscope
- ❑ utility light
- ❑ S.G.
- ❑ spectroscope
- ❑ U.V.
- ❑ color filter
- ❑ leveridge gauge
- ❑ diamond master set
- ❑ photo equipment
- ❑ thermal probe
- ❑ GIA color grading chips
- ❑ gold tester
- ❑ carat scale
- ❑ pennyweight scale

Comparables (for market analysis)

Source

1

2

3

4

5

Finish Costs

Setting and labor _____

Stone Totals _____

Metal Totals _____

Wholesale Total $ _____

Retail Mark-up _____

Apposite Value $ _____

Reprinted with permission K. Louise Crowell, G.G.

Identifying Treated Stones

Approximately 90% of all colored stones sold in the average retail jewelry or department store are treated, with the techniques ranging from low/high temperature heating to irradiation, diffusion, staining/dyeing, coating, oiling, bleaching, luster enhancement, and impregnation, among other procedures. Appraisers should discuss with their clients the fact that most colored gemstones are heated to obtain better color, emeralds are routinely oiled, resin treatments are increasingly being used to enhance the clarity, and diamonds are treated with a special material to make inclusions less visible. Further, all the aforementioned gemstones need special care to keep them in good condition. Even if you are an appraiser only, and not the seller of the stones, it might be prudent to have the client sign a short statement at the bottom of the take-in form declaring they have been informed about the gemstone's treatment or enhancement and understand how to care for the stone. It should be explained to the client that some treatments are discoverable only through laboratory analysis, and depending upon the individual situation, you may wish to recommend a lab examination. Stipulate to the client that if they do *not* want you or a laboratory to perform extensive or additional testing, your report will reflect the assumption that one or more enhancement techniques may have been applied to the gemstone. If the colored stones are large, expensive, and one of the top three sellers—ruby, sapphire, and emerald—confirmation of treatment by independent laboratory testing is becoming necessary with the burgeoning problem of identification. The FTC guidelines "Guides for the Jewelry Industry, 16 CFR Part 23" have held that disclosure of gemstone treatments and synthetics be required since 1979. In May 1996, a revision to *"Guides for the Jewelry, Precious Metals and Pewter Industries,"* Part 23 of Title 16 of the Code of Federal Regulations (CFR)—16 CFR Part 23—put new emphasis on the disclosure and treatment information required at all levels of jewelry commerce. This includes wholesalers, manufacturers, retailers, catalog and catalog sales, mail order firms, television, advertisers, and of course, gemologists and appraisers. The following comments are found in a note to the *"Guides"*:

The main effect of including appraisers or those identifying and grading industry products among those covered by the Guides would be to ensure they would be guided by the same definitions and standards as those selling the products.

The Commission concluded it would be unfair or deceptive for appraisers to ascribe meanings to standard terms used in the jewelry industry that are different from the meanings attached to those terms by sellers of the products. Thus, appraisers and those identifying and grading industry products are advised to follow the admonitions of the "Guides". (SUP67)

There are new directives from the FTC on using the terms "enhancement" and "treatment." Sec. 23.22 states: "It is unfair or deceptive to fail to disclose that a gemstone has been treated in any manner that is not permanent or that creates special care requirements, and to fail to disclose that the treatment is not permanent, if such is the case. The following are examples of treatment that should be disclosed because they usually are not permanent or create special care requirements: coating, impregnation, irradiating, heating, use of nuclear bombardment, application of colored or colorless oil or epoxy-like resins, wax, plastic or glass, surface diffusion, or dyeing."

The FTC "Guides" continue: "Enhancement is the term used by the trade to describe the treatment of gemstones to improve their color or otherwise improve their appearance. However, the Commission has determined that a more accurate term is 'treatment' and has added this term, in lieu of 'enhancement,' to the list of attributes that should not be misrepresented." The "Guides" go on to declare that nonpermanent treatments of various types (not just treatments that affect color) or any treatment creating *special care requirements* of the gemstone should be disclosed. At this writing, there is a single disclosure issue that remains: the lasering of diamond inclusions. FTC "Guides" do *not* require disclosure of this treatment. Most appraisers, however, consider this important information, and feel that, ethically, lasering should be disclosed on the appraisal document. Revised FTC guides may require disclosure.

The Real Problem

Most appraisers are anxious to disclose gem treatments and, thus, protect themselves from a litigious situation. However, given the sophistication of treatments today, the real problem is knowing *when* there is something to disclose! Jewelry retailers and appraisers are asking: "If the retailer does not know his stones are treated and need to be disclosed, can he be held responsible if the stone he sold *as natural and/or untreated* turns out to be *synthetic and/or treated?*" And, what about the appraiser who fails to disclose a problem because he or she just doesn't see it? It is a problem with no clear solution, and retailers and appraisers alike lament: "We cannot disclose what we do not know." Today, a major problem is that stones originally heat treated and disclosed as such may have that data lost when moving through the supply chain. "This is especially true in corundums," according to one stone dealer, "because heating is such a standard process; they are often almost indistinguishable from untreated natural stones."

The case that set a legal precedent for disclosure issues occurred in 1994, when a St. Louis, Missouri, jewelry store owner was accused of selling fracture-filled diamonds without revealing it to his customers. The store eventually paid out over $600,000 in customer refunds and a $50,000 fine ordered by the court. And in 1997, nondisclosure of the existence of a fracture in a 3.65-carat Colombian emerald, and use of Opticon filler to conceal it, were the leading charges against the jeweler who sold it and the independent appraiser who valued it. A stunning judgment was brought against the jeweler and appraiser even though both had examined the emerald *independently* in *different* laboratories at the time of sale, *found no evidence* of *any type* of filler or severe fracture, and documented it. The problem is that in the last decade, the types of gemstone treatments and enhancements have grown so sophisticated, recognizing them is an immense challenge to the average appraiser, gemologist, and jeweler.

Appraisal Methodology

With the take-in form completed and all contracts and agreements signed, you are ready to begin the steps to valuation. Each step listed below is discussed in greater depth in the following text.

1. Clean the items if necessary and note on your worksheet any damage or special features that you failed to notice earlier.
2. Photograph the items to be appraised.
3. Identify and measure the gemstones. Note on the worksheet all tests made to identify the gems. Itemize the equipment you used.
4. Analyze the metal fineness of the mountings.
5. Weigh and measure mountings and analyze the method quality and style of their manufacture.
6. Note hallmarks and stampings. Determine circa date, if possible.
7. Research the market and evaluate items accordingly.
8. Type or use a word processor to transfer all information from your worksheet to the final appraisal document. Plot the inclusions of major stones. Include photographs and be sure to define the ratios at which they were shot. List the reference sources you used and sign the form.

9. File a duplicate copy of the appraisal in the client's folder.
10. Deliver, mail, or call the client to pick up the completed appraisal document.

Before you begin work on the inventory, pause to draw yourself together mentally and concentrate upon one item at a time. There is a tendency for appraisers to scan the job hastily and take in many impressions at once. Since you want to draw every possible ounce of information from each item, focus is important.

Excellent lighting conditions are required for working with diamonds and colored gems, because the degree of color observed by the appraiser is dictated by the light under which the stone is examined. Color researchers recommend using a light source that duplicates north daylight. The source is generally fluorescent light. Although fluorescent "daylight" fixtures do not exactly duplicate north light, they can produce a constant, uniform light. Two acceptable light sources are the fluorescent lamps Vita-Lite, made by Duro-Test Corporation, and Verilux, produced by the Verilux Corporation. The GE Chroma 50 lamp may also be used for color grading.

It is important to realize that all "daylight" fluorescent tubes are not identical and that they are subject to manufacturing fluctuations. Look for a fluorescent lamp with a high color-rendering index, about ninety. The index ranges from zero to one hundred, with one hundred equalling north daylight.

Since proper lighting may not be available in the client's home, office, or bank, some portable appraisers take their own light sources with them.

Photographing the Jewelry

Photograph the jewelry before you begin the detailed examination of the articles. Then, during your examination if you find pieces that need extra photographic attention (such as special elements of design or function) to adequately document the item, take more detailed pictures.

While there is time and expense involved in photographing items for appraisals, there is a variety of cameras that can be used. Keep in mind that the first objective of the appraisal is to establish the existence of an item, and the second is to give an account of design, size, and materials. Useful appraisal photographs can easily be obtained with an instant photo system such as Polaroid CU5, Polaroid 100EE, or Polaroid Image II. The Jewelry Pro II system, used with additional close up supplementary lens and supporting stands, is small enough to be portable. When using the

1:1 ratio, the image area is large enough for a watch, or a group of five rings to be shown actual size.

For today's computer-literate appraiser, perhaps a more efficient method with greater scope is the use of a digital camera. Digital cameras have been getting a lot of attention from jewelry appraisers. When linked to a computer system and the appropriate printer, a digital camera can provide "filmless" picture taking. Digital cameras allow you to capture images with the press of a button, see them instantly on a built-in screen, transfer them to a computer, and arrange, group, or enlarge images directly on the appraisal document. Kansas independent jewelry appraiser Mary Desmarteau, G.G., speaks with enthusiasm about the Ricoh RDC-2 multimedia digital camera used in her laboratory (fig. 3-4). She believes this technology is a great advancement to professional jewelry appraisal presentation by adding clear, detailed, quality photographs to the appraisal documents.

John S. Harris, F.G.A., retail jeweler, photography expert, and appraiser in Great Britain agrees that the digital photographic system is efficient but has this to say: "This system [digital] presents great advantages, but the quality of the printer in particular, and the paper used, will dictate *quality* of image. The cost of equipment and image production is high. Although printing can be done on plain typing paper, a special gloss paper produced for the system is better, but more expensive. However, color and resolution are good and results are impressive for presentation with valuation documents."

Harris, who lectures frequently on the subject of jewelry photography, suggests that the best remedy for

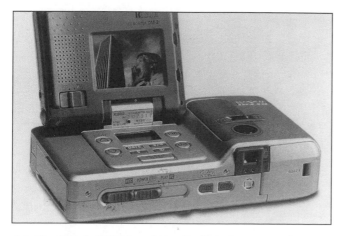

3-4. The Ricoh RDC-2 multimedia digital camera allows the appraiser to go beyond the current shooting/developing film process by making and transporting photos directly into the appraisal document. Further, high resolution images are captured in razor-sharp, color-accurate pictures. *(Photo courtesy Ricoh Corporation)*

most appraisers is to become adept with a standard 35mm single-lens reflex camera. The following, in Harris's words, is how to accommodate a 35mm camera for use in appraisal documents.

First Consideration. A secure area in which to work where the lighting and background set-up can remain. Often, the item to be photographed can be retained only for a limited time.

The Camera. Although any simple fixed-lens camera can be adapted to take close-up photographs, the problem of parallax sets in as you approach *really* close; that means the view through the view finder is not that of the lens. Therefore the 35mm single-lens reflex camera is more adaptable where the internal mirror system enables the operator to see *through the lens*. The advantage of being able to remove the lens and adapt extra attachments to aid magnification is important. Manual operation is preferable for close work rather than a fully automatic camera, because you will have more control over the various functions of the camera.

Close-Focus Photography. Whether a subject is large—such as a silver platter—or a group of *smaller* items that can be arranged within an area of about 8 x 10 inches (250 x 200 cm), a standard 50mm lens at a distance of 18 inches (450 cm) can be used and still maintain sharp focus with the resulting magnification about 0.13×. No great detail is achieved but a *record of the items is obtained.*

Close-Up Photograph. We consider a small silver dish, a bangle, or perhaps a brooch (fig. 3-5), which will provide an image on 35mm film about 0.33× magnification; that means the image size on film is about one third of the subject size. To do this you will need to use extra extension on the 50mm lens and get closer to the subject. You can use a lens called a Macro Converter Lens, fitted between the standard 50mm lens and camera body. A 2× Macro Converter will double the focal length of the prime lens. A set of extension tubes can also be used but the working distance between lens and subject will be reduced. Using either of the above set-ups will enable you to achieve magnification up to 1×, which as actual size on a 35mm format will give a good detailed image of a cluster ring. By using extension tubes magnification can rise to 3.25×, at which point details of *maker's marks, damage to mountings,* and *surface* and *internal marks* in gemstones can be recorded (fig. 3-6). The Macro Lens, made especially for close up photography (figs. 3-7 and 3-8), is a highly recommended tool because *working distance, light loss,* and *spherical aberration* have been taken into account in the production of its optics. When using an extension, Macro Lens, and standard 50mm lens, it is important to consider film speed in relation to the loss of light at the high magnifications. The choice is between a fine

3-5. Close-up photography. A 19th-century swallow brooch of 15 karat gold with silver top. This piece was being appraised and the missing diamond was to be replaced. At take-in the client was shown the previous poor repair work on a wing of the front swallow, along with the smoked diamonds (caused by careless repair work), before continuing the assignment. By pointing out these existing conditions to the client, any later claim that the appraiser was somehow responsible for the damage is avoided. (Kodachrome 200, Pentax 35mm, 50mm f/1.7, 2× macro, 2 sec. Exposure at f/11). *(Photo by John S. Harris)*

3-6. Detail of the swallow brooch at 2× magnification shows extent of poor repair with lumps of solder and some burned diamonds. The solder and damage reduce the value of an otherwise highly collectible item. *(Photo by John S. Harris)*

grain slow speed film such as Kodachrome 64, which requires a greater exposure, or using a shorter exposure on a faster film like Kodachrome 200 with fine details lost because of the larger grain film.

Films and Filters. Black-and-white film is often sufficient and particularly suitable for silverware, metal statuettes, and simple gold or silver jewelry. A panchromatic film with speed rating ISO25 to ISO50 will have a fine grain structure that will yield a sharp image detail in hand-engraved ornaments of gold and silver. At this speed, good lighting and a vibration-free support are essential because of the longer exposure times required. For most appraisal work, color film will render a quality image for stone set jewelry, enameled work, or stone carved figurines. If color tones must be accurate, use the appropriate lighting for film whether it is sensitive to daylight or artificial light. In the event of using film in the wrong type of light, remember to use a compensation filter to balance the color.

Support and Lighting. Good support for the camera is essential. In close-up photography the high magnifications required will demand slow shutter speeds, rather than a wider aperture, to capture sufficient light and still maintain a good depth of field. As a result of this, camera shake due to vibration is a possibility. Various tripods or macro stands are on the market. The use of a cable shutter release with a time delay mechanism

can also help to allow vibrations to settle before final exposure. Apart from *providing* sufficient light, it is also important to *control* it by diffusing glare from gemstone facets, or using a narrow beam at a low angle to enhance the contours of a cameo. The color temperature of the light used must be compatible with the film. For example, if the lighting is artificial, such as photoflood bulbs, and a daylight type film is used, then a pale blue filter No. 80B will correct color balance; otherwise the diamonds will look yellow in the photograph. If you have a diamond-grading light with a temperature of

3-7. Lapis lazuli brooch with three 7.9mm cabochons in a silver gilt mount. This item was purchased by a jeweler in a mixed lot of items with the intention of reusing the stones. The small indentions on the catch and stem are maker's marks. (Pentax camera, 2× macro converter, Ektachrome 400, 1 sec. F/16). *(Photo by John S. Harris)*

3-8. Further research on the lapis brooch revealed the marks as silver import marks used by the Austro-Hungarian Empire between 1872 and 1902. The letter "G" appears in the top left corner, which represents the town of Graz in Austria. What appeared to be an insignificant brooch became a very collectible item. (Kodachrome 64, 8 sec. F/22). *(Photo by John S. Harris)*

about 5,500°K, you are close to average daylight. However, as with all fluorescent light sources, it produces an overall greenish cast with daylight type films. It is necessary to use a FL-D filter (pale salmon pink color) to eliminate this effect. If using an electronic flash for close focus work from 3 ft. to 1 ft., use a ring flash to envelop the subject and avoid harsh shadows. Experiments with lighting techniques may prompt you to photograph the fluorescent patterns produced by some multi-stone set diamond jewelry. This type of photograph can provide the unique *fingerprint* type evidence crucial in proving identification of a recovered piece of property. The light source should be ultraviolet LW, and carried out in a darkroom. An aperture of f/5.6 should be sufficient with speeds anywhere between 15 seconds and several minutes depending upon the amount of fluorescence. The film should be sensitive, such as Ektachrome 400. Take a matching photograph in normal lighting for comparison.

Photomicrography. This is not only for those with complicated laboratory equipment, but is well within the scope of the average appraiser. Almost any camera will do. After the visual image is brought into focus in your microscope, a simple fixed-lens camera can be placed on top of the vertical tube of a monocular microscope, with its lens just above the eyepiece. Aperture plays no part in controlling depth of field, so it is set wide open with focus at infinity. Estimate your exposure and release the shutter. Trial and error is a great tutor. The 35mm SLR camera is much more adaptable and, if using one, remove the camera lens and remove the

eyepiece from the microscope. The camera back only is fitted to the microscope tube (monocular, or to one binocular or binocular photo tube) by means of a suitable microscope adapter. The image is now seen in the camera viewfinder and, as the microscope objective lens has now replaced the camera lens, it can be brought into focus using the microscope in the normal way. The image should fill the full frame of the 35mm film. Since an artificial tungsten light is generally used in photomicrography, the best choice for film is a tungsten type such as Ektachrome 160. There is no need for a color correction filter. However, if the photo shoot is being made in *daylight,* use an orange filter No. 85B. If a daylight film such as Ektachrome 400 is used, correct with a blue filter No. 80A; otherwise an orange tint is produced. Color balance is of less importance in photographing gemstone inclusions unless research work is being undertaken. As the higher magnifications from 10× to 40× will produce images at a low light level, the slower shutter speeds will tend to encourage vibrations, so a rigid set-up is important. If the subject is in an immersion liquid, the slightest vibration will be recorded as a blurred image if viewed from above the surface of the liquid. With a horizontal immersion microscope, this is avoided by viewing through the side of the immersion cell. Where vibration is inevitable, it is better to work in the dark— open the shutter and use the light on and off for the required exposure time.

Arranging the Subjects

Depending upon how many items of jewelry you have to appraise, include one to six items per photograph. The number of items in a picture depends on the type of appraisal and size of the individual items. For instance, if you were appraising one hundred items for a divorcing couple, you would not need or want one hundred individual photos of the jewelry, but could photograph the items by category, grouping together rings, pendants, and so on. For a probate appraisal in which several heirs will eventually divide the estate, it might be more convenient for the heirs to have individual photos of the jewelry. Use a gray background for best contrast.

For an insurance appraisal, you can cluster items in a photo. The most effective way to do this is to use a ring box grooved for individual items. If you have three items in two rows, number them from top to bottom, left to right, to provide an easy crossmatch with the written report.

For insurance or divorce appraisals, this cluster technique will save you film while affording you a complete and accurate photo record of the jewelry. If there are only one or two jewelry items to appraise, it is neater and more professional to photograph them separately.

Cleaning the Jewelry

The jewelry will probably need to be cleaned. Most items will be covered with a film of skin oil and cosmetics that must be removed before you can make a thorough inspection of the gemstones.

Cleaning jewelry in a client's home or in a bank will require some creativity on your part. Cleaning tools you will need to carry routinely include a small bottle of any commercial jewelry-cleaning product such as Gem Kleener, a child's toothbrush, and a small bottle of Grease Relief or a similar grease-removing product.

You may also want to buy a compressed-air product called Dust-off, used to clean camera lenses, slides, and delicate instruments. It can also be used to clean jewelry as long as the jewelry is not caked with grime.

As a responsible gemologist, you already know that many gemstones require special handling when they are cleaned. Diamonds can be cleaned in a steam or ultrasonic cleaner, but colored gemstones should *never* be put in an ultrasonic unit, and some species can also be damaged in a steam cleaner. Most colored gemstones have inclusions that can force internal cracks to the surface if the gems are subject to vibration. Emeralds, which are almost always oiled, will leach the oil if cleaned in an ultrasonic or steam cleaner and may emerge from the unit dull, grayish, and with every fissure in the stone announcing its presence. Emeralds can be re-oiled if they are immersed in a vial of warmed cedarwood oil and the oil is kept warm for several hours or more; place the vial on top of a steam cleaner to keep the oil heated. To clean emeralds, use lukewarm water, baking soda, and a soft brush; do not rinse in alcohol.

Other stones that should not be cleaned in an ultrasonic or steam unit include jade, lapis lazuli, amber, ivory, pearls, coral, and turquoise. Dyed lapis lazuli will leach its color, turquoise will turn green, and the others will suffer various misfortunes. Similarly, Indian corundum star stones should be kept away from steam and ultrasonic cleaners, as they are heavily oiled and, like emerald, will come out of the unit with every crack showing and color drained.

Avoid sudden changes in solution temperatures even when cleaning colored gemstones by hand. Tanzanite, aquamarine, peridot, and kunzite can all be damaged by exposure to sudden temperature variations.

Pearls. Be cautious when cleaning strings of pearls and beads. They may have weak strands ready to break with the slightest pull. If this appears likely, advise the customer to have the pearls restrung before you begin the appraisal, or obtain a release from liability for this hazard. Clean the pearls with a soft cloth, soft brush, and a paste of baking soda and water. Extra cleaning care should be given around the bead hole, as this is where most cosmetics will tend to accumulate and bead holes must be clean so you can investigate the thickness of the nacre. Strands of pearls and beads need to be supported with both hands after they have been cleaned and then left on a table to dry. Advise the client that the pearls must be left to dry for at least twenty-four hours to allow enough time for the string inside the bead holes to dry. Never clean pearls in ammonia; it will dissolve the nacre.

Diamonds. Dip ring in a solution of water, detergent, and ammonia, brush with a soft brush, rinse in alcohol, and dry. Or, if you want to clean diamonds the way the professionals do, boil a small amount of mild soap flakes and a little ammonia in two cups of water. Put the diamond ring in a wire tea strainer and swish it in the hot suds for a few moments. Let the ring cool and then dip it in alcohol to cut the soap scum. Place it on a paper towel to dry. Do not boil the diamond if the jewelry contains any colored stones.

Mother-of-Pearl. Wash in a solution of a small amount of powdered whiting and cold water. Do not use hot water or soap. (Whiting is a very fine preparation of chalk that can be bought at paint stores.)

Ivory and bone. Ivory includes elephant, walrus, sperm whale, hippo, and narwhal ivory. Wipe clean with a soft, clean, damp cloth. If necessary, wash in warm water and use a soft brush. *Do not soak, bleach, or store in very dry conditions.* Organic materials are easily damaged by heat, chemicals, or dry conditions. Store away from strong light in even temperature and humidity. *Old ivory is easily warped* when exposed to heat and dampness. If the condition of the object makes the use of water infeasible, try dry-cleaning with whiting.

Glued-in Stones. Stones that are obviously glued into place should not be cleaned unless you have supplies available to reglue them. Do not clean foilbacked stones of any kind, including cabochons and faceted stones. These are frequently found in costume as well as antique jewelry.

Lockets. These should be handled with care, especially antique hair lockets. Hair lockets are made of plaited, woven, and curled hair, and should never be cleaned! Not only would you damage the hair, but antique items must not be cleaned or the patina on the metal will be destroyed.

Enameled Jewelry. Enameled pieces should be handled carefully, as they may contain soft enamel, which can easily be washed out. Examine the piece first to see whether it has any soft enamel—the soft enamel will appear dull under magnification. Hard enamels are usually safe enough to clean by hand, but you should avoid the ultrasonic cleaner at all costs.

Charms. Some charms may contain paper prayers, booklets, or folded paper money. Check contents carefully before you start cleaning.

Watches. Unless you are an experienced watchmaker, do *not* attempt to clean a watch. To clean a watch successfully requires removing the movement and leather or fabric bands. Also, many watches are not waterproof; it is better to appraise them in as-is condition and save yourself a possible lawsuit for negligence.

Advise Your Client

Playing sports and wearing jewelry do not go together very well, even though a popular piece of jewelry is called a *tennis bracelet!* Bumps, knocks, and abrasions can damage any piece of jewelry including diamonds, but especially amber, emerald, kunzite, tanzanite, zircon, topaz, and peridot. Chlorine and other chemicals and pollutants in water can cause severe damage to pearls, coral, turquoise, gold, and silver. Clients with home pools, or those who swim regularly, should be advised that chlorine can dissolve enough gold to loosen and destroy prongs holding gems in the settings. Chlorine can also tarnish silver, and cause gold to turn black or green.

Identifying, Measuring, and Weighing Gemstones

Examining gemstones, calculating their weight, and grading gems for color and clarity is what gemology is all about and the point at which real jewelry appraising begins. In most appraisals, gemstones, whether diamonds or colored stones, are the greater portion of the value of the item, although there are exceptions to this rule.

All gemologists, no matter how experienced, will sometimes come across a gemstone that they cannot positively identify. This situation calls for a consultation with another gemologist or gemological laboratory. If you are not sure of a gem's identity, don't guess. Advise your client of the identity problem and defer the appraisal until you can resolve the matter. In some cases, mountings may restrict positive identification and removing the gem from the mounting may be all that is necessary to solve the problem. Be sure to get a waiver of liability from your client in writing before you proceed.

Diamonds

Measure diamonds with a Leveridge gauge and write down the specific data. Make a special diamond appraisal worksheet to use for all major diamonds so that you do not forget to include any important tests. See the sample form shown in figure 3-9.

On the diamond appraisal worksheet, note the shape of the stone; the color, graded against master diamond-grading stones; the clarity, graded under magnification; a plot of the inclusions for all diamonds of one carat or more; and the quality of the cut. Also note any unusual inclusions and other reasons you had to assign the grade you did to the stone. Finally, note any damage to the stone, both on your worksheet (under "Miscellaneous") and on the worksheet plot.

There are several grading systems in use today to describe diamond color, clarity, and other characteristics such as finish, proportion, and so on. The GIA system is the most widely used in the United States, but is not the only system. Figures 3-10 and 3-11 show comparison grading systems employed worldwide. To ensure that your appraisal will have gradings recognizable to any concerned party, use terms that have been carefully defined and widely published. If, however, you find it more convenient to use other grading plans, comparison bars should be included on your report to the more popular and universally understood terms.

Cutting Styles

Standard cutting styles are illustrated in the appendix. Several styles have been designed recently that contain more facets than the brilliant cut. The purpose of these more complicated cuts is to achieve a greater degree of brilliance in the finished gemstone. Some of the fancy cuts are the *jubilee cut* (80 facets), the *king cut* (86 facets), the *magna cut* (102 facets), the *royal cut* (154 facets), the *radiant cut* (70 facets), the *quadrillion* (70 facets), and the *barion cut* (62 facets). The *Trillion* is a patented triangular brilliant cut diamond, with 50 facets—41 including the table and culet, plus nine girdle facets.

Famous diamond cutter Gabi Tolkowsky, whose uncle's mathematically derived "Tolkowsky cut" formed the basis for the modern round stone, released the "triple brilliant" cut in 1996. The cut, which has been named *"The Gabrielle"* in his honor, features 105 facets. Tolkowsky got the idea for the new cut while working on the Centenary Diamond, the 278-

3-9. Sample diamond appraisal worksheet.

Name _____   Job # _____

Address _____   Date _____

City/State/Zip_____   Date Due _____

Shape and Cut_____   Loose _____   Mounted _____

Weight _____   Estimated _____   Measured _____

Diameter or Dimensions _____   Depth _____   Table Measurement _____
                    length and width

Depth Percentage_____

Table Diameter Percentage_____

Girdle Thickness _____

Finish
Girdle Surface _____

Symmetry _____

Culet _____

Polish_____

Cut Grade _____

Clarity Grade _____

Color Grade _____   Proportion Grade _____   Finish Grade _____

Fluorescence _____   COMMENTS:

Base Price per Carat _____

Base Price per Stone _____

Est. Replacement Cost (retail) _____

Engraved Diamond # _____

List Instruments Used:

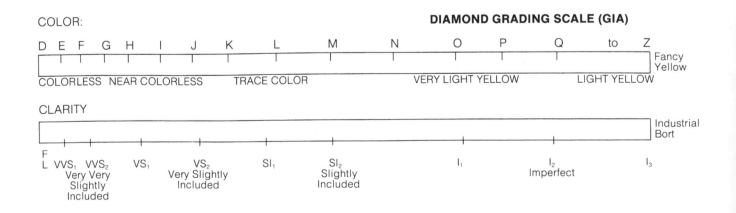

3-10. Color grading standards for diamonds.

Left margin labels (bracketing the rows): *Mounted stones appear colorless* (D–J); *Small mounted stones appear colorless* (D–K).

GIA [USA]	Hong Kong	AGS [USA]	Scandinavia 0.50ct & over	Russia	France	Great Britain	Switzerland
D	100	0	RIVER	RAREST WHITE	BLANC EXCEPTIONNEL	FINEST WHITE	RIVER
E	99.5						
F	99	1	TOP WESSELTON	FINEST WHITE	EXTRA BLANC	FINE WHITE	TOP WESSELTON
F	98.5						
F	98						
G	97.5						
G	97	2					WESSELTON
H	96.5						
H	96	3	WESSELTON	WHITE	BLANC	WHITE	TOP CRYSTAL
I	95.5						
I	95	4	TOP CRYSTAL	FINEST CRYSTAL	BLANC NUANCÉ	COMMERCIAL WHITE	CRYSTAL
J	94.5						
J	94	5	CRYSTAL	COMMERCIAL WHITE	LÉGÈREMENT TEINTÉ	TOP SILVER CAPE	
K	93.5						
K	93						
L	92.5	6	TOP CAPE	FINEST CAPE	TEINTÉ	SILVER CAPE	TOP CAPE
L	92						
M	91	7	CAPE	CAPE		LIGHT CAPE	CAPE
M	90						
N	89						
O	88	8		COMMERCIAL CAPE		CAPE	
P	87		LIGHT YELLOW				
P	86						

carat stone with 247 facets that is considered his crowning achievement.

Old European- and Old Mine-Cut Diamonds

Many clients will ask your advice about having their old diamonds recut. They will want to know how they can release the presumably finer stone that is now "trapped" within the existing stone, and whether the recut stone is likely to be of fine quality. In general, the only old-cut diamonds you should consider advising your client to recut should fall into a better color grade than KLM and should have a very high clarity grade. This may rule out most of the old-cut stones you may see, which are likely to be Dutch White (KLM colors).

3-11. Clarity grading standards for diamonds.

GIA [USA]	Scandinavia	Exchanges	Russia	Alternate W. Europe
FL	FL	PURE	10X CLEAN	IF
IF	IF	PURE	10X CLEAN	IF
VVS1	VVSI1	PURE	10X CLEANISH	VVSI
VVS2	VVSI2	VVS	10X CLEANISH	VVSI
VS1	VSI1	VVS	10X VERY SLIGHT	VSI
VS2	VSI2	SI	10X VERY SLIGHT	VSI
SI1	SI1	SI	10X SLIGHT; EYE CLEAN	SI
SI2	SI2	PIQUE	10X SLIGHT; EYE CLEAN	SI
I1	PIQUE 1	PIQUE	VERY SLIGHT TO EYE	PIQUE 1
I2	PIQUE 2	PIQUE	SLIGHT TO EYE	PIQUE 2
I3	PIQUE 3	PIQUE	MARKED TO EYE	PIQUE 3

Normally, a stone is not recut with weight retention in mind. However, old mine-cut diamonds tend to lose about 35 percent of their existing weight when recut because of their square lines, and old European-cut diamonds tend to lose about 15 percent. This is not a hard-and-fast percentage, however; some "old miners" have been known to lose as much as 60 percent of their original weight without any great improvement in appearance, whereas some old European-cut stones have been improved in appearance with only a slight reworking and 10 percent loss of weight (figures 3-12, 3-13, and 3-14).

If you have any difficulty in assessing old cuts, try to get instruction from a cutter. An experienced cutter can give you more information in a brief session than you might obtain from an entire day spent digging information out of reference books.

Some old mine-cut diamonds are almost like rough diamonds in terms of shape. You can learn to assess their probable quality when recut by checking the stones for strain under a polariscope. The majority of old diamonds are not recut and have found a market niche with designers and consumers, who seek out the old-cut stones.

Some companies deal routinely or exclusively with old-cut stones, and are excellent sources of information on both recutting and pricing. One well-known firm is D. Atlas & Company, 732 Sansom Street, Philadelphia. David Atlas cites overestimation of color grade as the mistake most frequently made in estimating the potential quality of stones to be recut. He explains that the leakage of light through the large culets reduces color concentration and can make the color grade seem higher. Also, he warns: "Platinum prongs can make JK colors look like HI colors, and it's easy to be three color grades too high." He recommends that

3-14. Fine quality old mine-cut diamonds in a woman's ring. *(From the Lynette Proler Antique Jeweller's Collection)*

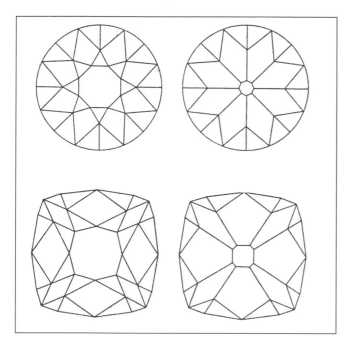

3-12. *Top row:* Old European-cut diamonds. *Bottom row:* Old mine-cut diamonds.

extreme care be taken in evaluating old miners in antique Georgian jewelry with sealed backs, noting that "the stones look large but are usually thin. Bruted (frosted) girdles instead of polished ones will cause

3-13. Citrine quartz and diamond presentation brooch has cushion-cut citrine in the center surrounded by approximately seventy-two old European-cut and several rose-cut diamonds. *(Photograph © 1986 Sotheby's, Inc.)*

the stone in the jewelry to look whiter than it really is." Atlas also explains that an old-cut diamond with an R or S grade color should be treated in the opposite way from the norm, and should be turned into a fancy cut to improve it to the fullest extent.

Atlas has a "Rule of Ten" test that he believes will help gemologist appraisers calculate the probable weight lost in recutting. First, make a list of all "repairs" that must be made to the stone. For old mine-cut diamonds, award ten points for *each* necessary repair: girdle, pavilion refaced, crown refaced, pavilion depth, crown depth, and shape surgery. For old European-cut diamonds, award ten points each for repairs made to the girdle, crown, table, culet, and pavilion (lower girdle facets). If you can add up as much as 50 points for an old mine-cut diamond, cutting weight loss will probably be about 60 percent. For old European-cut diamonds, you may lose 30 percent or more weight in recutting, with the average weight loss at 10 to 20 percent.

With a growing demand for old-cut stones over the last few years, New York diamond dealer Michael Goldstein has found a niche in the specialized marketing of old European- and old mine-cut diamonds. Goldstein is also an excellent source for replacement of difficult-to-find rose-cut and table-cut diamonds. He maintains a buy/sell pricing chart for old-cut diamonds, free upon request, that is an invaluable reference for appraisers. Contact Goldstein at 580 Fifth Avenue, Suite 903, New York, New York 10036.

Colored Gemstones

First, identify the material. Is it synthetic or natural? Is it color enhanced? (See table 3-1.) Are there any unusual treatments, such as glass-filled inclusions? Make a note of these, and incorporate the following steps in your regular examination routine.

1. Color. Evaluate the stone in terms of *hue* (the basic color), *intensity* (the strength of the color), *tone* (how dark or light the color is on a scale of black to white), and *color distribution,* if irregular (such as the zoning in sapphires).
2. Clarity.
3. Cut. Evaluate in terms of shape and quality.
4. Take the size of the stone in millimeter measurements and carats.
5. Note whether the stone is transparent, translucent, or opaque.
6. Note any nicks, cracks, damage, or unusual properties of the stone.
7. Plot the inclusions of important stones.
8. List the instruments used in the examination.

Color and Clarity

For decades the jewelry industry has been wrestling with the problem of how to describe color for colored gemstones and fancy color diamonds. Why is this so important? Because color is the name of the game in evaluating *colored* gemstones. Moreover, the intensity of color is the *number one* factor affecting the price, and can account for as much as 85% of the value of the stone. Furthermore, the perception of color changes under different lighting conditions. Examine the color of a stone under normal daylight, fluorescent, and incandescent light to understand the extent of color alteration that occurs when the light source is changed. Fluorescent light intensifies the color of blue sapphires; incandescent does the same for rubies. Because grading color is so subjective, the appraiser should clearly note on the appraisal report the type of illumination used to examine the gemstones.

Currently, there is no international color-grading system accepted by all gemologists, appraisers, or the jewelry industry at large. Of several color communications systems on the market, the two most widely used today are Gemological Institute of America's *GemSet,* and Howard Rubin's *GemDialogue.* Both systems agree on the essential components of color: hue, saturation (intensity), and tone. Both operate on a matching process, but each system uses a different medium for sample color presentation.

GemDialogue (fig. 3-15), which has been adopted by the American Gem Trade Association as its official color communication system and is recommended by many appraisal professionals, is a highly portable method that gives over 60,000 colors to match against. It does so with the use of 21 transparent color charts,

each of which shows 10 different saturation levels for each color from strong to weak. The charts are in color sequence and a small spreadsheet tells you how to mix the charts to get all the "in between" colors, which are needed to complete the color circle. The charts are all pure colors and give you a color scale against which to match your stone. If any black or brown is visible in the stone, a black and a brown transparent "color mask" (also in 10 different saturation levels) are included. When you choose the color and saturation level you may then use the mask to simulate the amount of color hidden by black or brown. GemDialogue allows you to describe a pure color in two dimensions, by hue and saturation level, and add the third dimension (black or brown) only if seen in the stone.

The system comes with a grading manual that explains how to get a final grade for a gemstone after starting with an initial color grade. The worksheet, included in the instruction manual, lets you fill in all the necessary grading factors and add or subtract, to or from the initial grade, based on each factor. To get the initial color grade of 15 gem species included has a table showing on which color charts the stone is found, and offers initial grades on a 10-1 rating. When you achieve the final grade you may use the prices found in the "Guide," a gemstone pricing handbook. According to Howard Rubin, developer of the system, "Much of the color-grading sequence is actually what goes through a dealer's mind when looking at a gemstone."

Distressed by the lack of communication between color-grading systems, Howard Rubin and Gail Brett Levine have put together a book that cross-references the majority of the other color systems with GemDialogue. The work is called *GemDialogue Color Toolbox* and covers nearly 2,100 physical comparisons of color

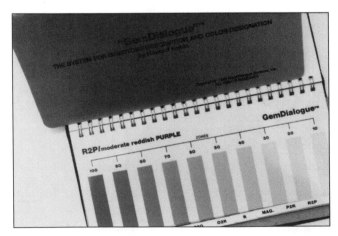

3-15. The GemDialogue gemstone description and color-matching system, devised by Howard Rubin.

done under Durotest Vitalite fluorescent bulbs rated at 5,300 kelvin temperature. Systems cross-reference Munsell®, The World of Color®, Colorscan®, and GIA GemSet®. Users of the "Toolbox" are able to easily convert GemDialogue terminology to that of the other systems, or their terminology to that of GemDialogue. Most importantly, appraisers using different systems are now able to communicate more effectively between systems for more standardized color grading.

GIA's GemSet is a handy, portable, color-grading communication tool. GemSet (fig. 3-16) is a system that makes color comparisons with the use of small plastic color tabs molded to resemble actual gemstones in the shape of faceted round brilliant-cut stones. Each of the 324 color master stones is identified in GIA colored-stone-grading nomenclature. This color system provides a color reference that, according to appraisers who use the system, remains consistent with repeated use, and establishes a basis for value. GIA's GemSet communicates color by referring to the three essential elements of color: hue—the basic color sensation; tone (value)—the lightness or darkness; and saturation (chrome)—the purity or dullness. The system allows the user to select a gem's color from among 31 hues, seven tone levels and six saturation steps. The results are conveyed in abbreviations imprinted on 324 three-dimensional color comparators (fig. 3-17).

From colored stones to diamonds, cut affects almost every element that makes a stone beautiful and desirable. It is logical, therefore, that the *quality* of cutting on a gemstone has considerable impact upon its value. A well-cut stone has good shape and proportions. The symmetry of a clearly defined outline shape relates directly to how pleasing it is in the eye of the beholder. Cutting affects a stone's brilliance, the flashes of light that are returned to the eye. Most faceting styles can be classified as brilliant, step, or mixed cuts. Round brilliant cuts have facets that radiate from the table or culet to the girdle. Step cuts have concentric facets. These styles can be adapted to almost any shape. The light that enters into a poorly cut gemstone leaks out the pavilion instead of reflecting from the pavilion facets and back from the crown. While it is true that better-cut gems command a higher price, the majority of *colored gemstones* on the market today are poorly cut. Joseph Tenhagen says most colored gemstones have a 70–80 percent pavilion depth, which is considerable, and poorly cut stones usually have a "window." "In this category," Tenhagen says, "are stones cut so shallow that there is little or no life in the center of the stone and they exhibit a window; you can see through the stone as you can through a pane of windowglass."

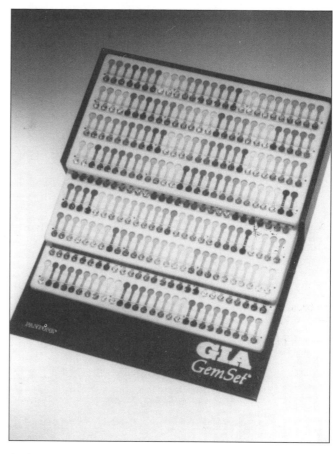

3-16. The Gemological Institute of America's GemSet color-matching system. *(Photo courtesy of GIA GEM Instruments and Bookstore.)*

3-17. The Gemological Institute of America calls this a color-matching comparator. Each of 324 colors are identified in GIA colored-stone-grading nomenclature: The first letter represents hue; the first number indicates color tone; the second number is the saturation. This comparator reads: 0 5/5, meaning a medium, strong orange.

Table 3-1. Common Gemstone Treatments and Detection Tests

Gemstone	Treatment	Test	Reaction/Result *
Aquamarine	Heat	None	Not applicable
Chalcedony	Dye	Spectrum/spectroscope Chelsea filter	Shows broad absorption bands Blue and green dyed material shows pinkish filter reaction
Corundum: Sapphire	Heat Surface diffusion Cavity filling	Ultraviolet fluorescence Immersion in methylene iodide Magnification	Chalky green fluorescence Shows blotchy color zoning and evidence of a thin color layer Surface-reaching cavities, pits, and voids are filled with plastic, glass, etc. Distinguishable with magnification
Ruby	Heat Cavity filling	Ultraviolet fluorescence Magnification Magnification	Not distinguishable with limited testing May see glassy fractures or changes in the structure of the inclusions Glass infilling may result as a byproduct of heat treatment
Diamond	Fracture-filled Laser drilled	Magnification Magnification	Flash-effect colors
Emerald	Oiling Dye Filling surface cavities or fractures with synthetic polymer, resin	Ultraviolet fluorescence Magnification Ultraviolet LW	Oil may fluoresce yellow Dye may be seen in fissures Whitish/blue and sometimes orangy yellow colors
Ivory	Dye	Magnification	Color (dyed to improve color)
Jadeite: Green	Dye Dye	Chemically bleached and polymer impregnated often dyed & impregnated Spectroscope	ID with infrared spectroscopy May show 4370 A.U. line: 6300–6700 broad band proves presence of dye
Lavender	Dye	Magnification	Dye concentration in cracks
Lapis lazuli	Dye Wax	Acetone Magnification/hot point	Discoloration of swab Sweating effect of wax with hot point held to stone
Opal	Plastic Smoke	Hot needle/hot point Magnification	Extreme softness of material; acrid plastic odor Unnatural color confined to surface
Pearl	Dye	Diluted solution of nitric acid	Discoloration of swab
Quartz	Dye Heat	Magnification None	Unnatural color, chatoyant band Undetectable
Topaz	Irradiation	Fade test *may* work	Treatment is often unstable and gem stone is subject to fading
Turquoise	Paraffin or plastic	Hot point/hot needle	Acrid plastic odor if treated with plastic; if wax treated, will show sweating effect when hot needle is held 1mm from stone
Zircon	Heat	None	Not applicable
Zoisite (Tanzanite)	Heat	None	Color probably does not occur in nature; when the naturally brown zoisite is heated, it turns blue

* Reaction or result will be present if gemstone has been treated.

Stones that are lumpy or cut with unbalanced outlines and outrageous pavilion bulge also fall in the lower-cost category and appropriate discounts should be factored into the valuation. Additionally, Tenhagen points out how poor cutting can cause dark areas in a stone, which affects the apparent color: shallow angles lighten, deeper angles darken a color.

It is easy to understand that changing the apparent color of a colored gemstone or diamond affects its per carat price, in some cases doubling or tripling the per carat price. More difficult to understand is with the good cutting technology available today, why all gemstones are not well cut. The answer is a simple one and grounded in economics. Most cutters try to obtain as much yield as possible from the rough, which often means skipping fine cutting. Also, the species of gemstone being cut helps determine the cutter's approach to the stone because the material often dictates *how* it will be cut. Cutting liberties that are *not excessive* in colored stones have slight effect on a stone's value if the stone is a particularly rare or fine stone. Therefore, while fine and expensive materials may be graded with more leniency, poor cutting in the abundant and inexpensive colored stones, such as quartz, cannot be tolerated.

One exception is the fantasy-cut stone, which has its own set of standards. For fantasy-cuts, cutting is *everything*. These stones are judged on their proportions, balance, use of light, and superiority of cutting craftsmanship.

Cut of a Diamond

When evaluating diamond cuts, Tenhagen insists "Cut" is the last and most misunderstood diamond parameter. "It is well known to diamond cutters and dealers that with all other factors being equal, a poorly proportioned diamond may sell for as much as 50% less than a well-proportioned diamond. The interrelationship of the table percentage, crown height, girdle thickness, and pavilion depth constitute a diamond's proportions." As diamond cutters vary proportions, the diamond's price per carat varies. Tenhagen offers crucial information to the appraiser: "The greater the variance in cutting proportions from 'excellent,' the more dramatic the price reduction to the knowledgeable buyer. Knowing the cutting proportions of a diamond leads an appraiser or diamond buyer to a realistic diamond price. Within the diamond world more time is spent negotiating price because of proportions than on *any other* aspect of diamond buying!"

Tenhagen is the author and publisher of *The Diamond Value Index,* a subscription publication interpreting the various proportions of diamonds into market prices for similarly proportioned diamonds. For infor-

mation and subscription prices write Joseph W. Tenhagen, Diamond Value Index, 36 NE 1st Street, Suite 419, Miami, Florida 33132.

Analyzing Metal Fineness

Testing kits for analyzing metal fineness are available from major jewelry supply houses. Each consists of a wooden box with five plastic bottles of prepared balanced acids and a black basalt block for testing. The liquid is used on a clean surface of the block and is not mixed with other liquids or water. The bottles dispense the acid one drop at a time; each bottle should be kept tightly closed when not in use to prevent spillage or evaporation.

To test a metal, first ensure that the surface of the mounting is dry and clean. Make a long streak of metal on the black testing-stone surface. Press hard into the surface of the mounting under test to ensure that any plated covering is penetrated and the underlying base metal is smeared on the testing stone. Next, apply a small drop of the appropriate liquid onto the streak and study the reaction very carefully. The liquids are marked 18, 14, 10, S, and P. After finishing the test, clean the waste from the surface of the testing stone. When the stone is dry, it is ready for reuse.

Testing Gold, Silver, and Platinum

Gold. Start by applying a drop of the liquid marked 18. If the gold is 18K or higher, the streak will remain for at least five seconds. Count off the time. If the test streak disappears immediately, the gold jewelry is of a lower karat fineness and you should restreak the stone and apply the 14 liquid. The 14 liquid requires ten seconds to react. If the streak disappears in fewer than ten seconds, the gold is not 14K and you should repeat the test with 10 liquid. The 10 liquid also requires ten seconds to react.

Silver. If the liquid S turns the trace on the test block a milky white, the jewelry in question is sterling silver. If the trace remains intact, disappears, or turns green, this indicates some other metal.

Platinum. It takes one minute for the liquid marked P to affect the trace on the test stone. If the streak is still in place at the end of one minute, you can consider it platinum. The streak will turn gray if the item is gold. On silverplated or base metals, the streak will disappear.

Some appraisers and jewelers still like using a kit containing gold test needles, a testing stone, and acids for testing metals. This system requires practice for good results. In this test kit you have three one-ounce ground-glass-stoppered bottles in a wooden box. These are not portable and the acid can be easily spilled. The bottles should be kept upright since the acid is dangerous, corrosive, and toxic. If the contents are accidentally spilled on your fingers or hands, the area should be flushed immediately with plenty of cold water. In the kit, pure nitric acid is used for testing 10K gold or less. Aqua regia—a combination of one part nitric and three parts hydrochloric acids, in which gold is soluble—is used to determine fineness from 18K up. Gold from 14K to 18K should be tested with a mixture of one part hydrochloric acid, forty-nine parts nitric, and twelve-and-one-half parts distilled water.

The test needles are a keychain-like arrangement of metal "fingers" tipped with gold from 4K to 20K. Testing begins when you take the keychain of needles and make a streak on the testing stone of 18K, 14K, and 10K. Below these streaks, add a streak from the item of jewelry you are testing. With a drop of liquid on the glass dropper, draw the liquid across the streaks in a straight line and compare the fade time of the 18K and 14K with the fade time of your jewelry streak. If both your jewelry streak and one of the gold needle streaks do not disappear, the karat content of the jewelry in question is the same as the test streak it matches.

The kit does not include test needles for platinum or silver but a platinum streak tested with nitric acid will exhibit slow fading (a few seconds), and a platinum streak tested with hydrochloric acid will exhibit extinction with a brownish surface float. A silver streak tested with nitric acid will have slow to quick extinction; tested with hydrochloric acid, the silver will show extinction with a white powdery float.

The appraiser should know that some 14K gold alloys will first give a greenish reaction similar to brass and then a normal 14K gold reaction. It should never be assumed that the quality marks found on an item of jewelry are correct, especially on items of foreign manufacture. Some foreign manufacturers start with 18K gold, but owing to the contamination of solder or another base metal, the final quality can drop as low as 8K. Also, there have been instances of manufacturers stamping any metal as 14K or 18K without regard to gold content. If it is impossible to reach different parts of the mounting or finding (as in layered construction) but the *majority* of the mounting checks out as stamped, then it is acceptable to write on your report: "The portion of the mounting that cannot be assayed because of its construction appears to be (whatever quality the rest of the item has been assayed to be)."

Use caution in appraising class rings, as they sometimes have double metals. A 10K gold overlay on a base metal is not uncommon. Plating may cause you some problems with correct assaying unless you take care to obtain a rub that bites beyond the plating. Similarly, rhodium plating on white gold or silver may react just as platinum or high-karat gold would, and rings stamped 14 without the K usually have inner protective bands of 14K gold, but the remainder of the ring may be another metal. Assay wedding bands without quality marks carefully. These may test 14K but may actually consist of a gold overlay on copper or stainless steel.

The heft of a jewelry item will provide another clue to its metal content. Some chains and bracelets of foreign manufacture may be marked as 14K or 18K, but prove in the final analysis to be gold-plated silver. These will have a certain heaviness or lack of heaviness that will alert you that the stamping may be false. Sometimes an item's clasp may be genuine gold but the band or chain will be plated. Conversely, you will find 14K chains and bracelets with gold-filled or -plated clasps. In these cases, the original clasps usually have been replaced. In general, do not make any assumptions based on face value. Test each item.

Gold teeth are often encountered in estate appraisals. They are usually about 16–19K fineness.

Gold Content and Stamping

The Federal Trade Commission has ruled that the terms *gold* and *solid gold* can be used only to refer to *fine gold;* that is, gold of 24-karat quality. Technically, only gold with no additives can be called pure. However, such gold—labeled "24K"—is too soft to be used in jewelry, so various metals are used with the gold, such as silver, copper, nickel, palladium, or zinc. Once the metals are mixed it is called an alloy. To be called karat gold in the U.S., a piece must be at least 10K, or 41.67%, gold. Almost all gold used in jewelry is an alloy and requires a karat designation (i.e., 14K) be used before advertising "gold." A piece of gold jewelry must assay (test) close to the quality mark. The National Gold and Silver Stamping Act states the fineness of gold in a piece of jewelry cannot be more than three one-thousandths (.003) *less* than the fineness indicated by the karatage mark. Pieces of jewelry using solder or additions of gold alloys of less fineness cannot be below their mark by more than seven one-thousandth parts (.007). Most consumers buy gold jewelry that is either 14K (14 parts pure gold and 10 parts other metals) or 18K (18 parts pure gold and six parts other metals). For 10K, *the lowest fineness allowable for gold jewelry in the U.S.,* there are 10 parts pure gold and 14 parts other metals.

At the time this book was first printed in 1988, gold manufacturers were stamping their products as *plumb* to conform to federal law. By law, gold articles must be marked to reflect their karat content accurately. Gold stamped 14K is correctly stamped as *plumb gold*. This means the piece is *exactly* the fineness indicated, i.e., a *plumb-gold ring* stamped 14K *will not be less than 14K* gold.

Articles manufactured after 1961 required the karat quality mark be accompanied by a registered trademark mark, or name of the person or concern who applied the gold marking. However, you may occasionally see a piece of karat gold jewelry without markings or quality stampings. The absence of a stamp—i.e., 14K or 18K—is *legal* because the government does not require manufacturers to stamp the amount of gold in a piece of jewelry. However, if a manufacturer *does* use a gold mark, federal law requires it to be accurate and accompanied by a maker's mark, the company's initials, or registered trademark. The quality marks in most European and Asian jewelry is expressed in metric terms. The proportion of gold to other metals is measured in parts per 1,000. For instance, 24K = 999, 18K = 750, 14K = 585, 10K = 416, 8K = 250. See table 3-2 for a breakdown of the gold content of karat alloys.

Gold Filled, Gold Overlay, and Rolled Gold Plate typically have a layer of 10K or better quality gold mechanically bonded to all significant surfaces. These are subject to the same three one-thousandths part tolerance. The ten percent tolerance allowed under the old *Voluntary Product Standards* is no longer recognized. To use the term *gold filled*, the object must contain a surface plating applied mechanically. This plating cannot be covered with nickel washed with gold, as the FTC says it would be misleading, *unless* there is *disclosure* about the primary gold coating covered with a base metal that is gold washed.

Gold Electroplate requires a minimum of 7/1,000,000th of an inch fine gold, with a coating not less than 10K. Any less than that is considered *gold flash* or *gold wash*. There has been an important change in the term *Gold electroplate*. While *gold plate* was restricted to jewelry mechanically bonded, *gold plate* may now be used to describe jewelry that is electroplated gold, providing it contains a minimum of 1 micron thickness (or 40 millionths) of an inch of 23 karat gold. Gold electroplate can now be abbreviated as GEP.

Vermeil has a new standard. *Vermeil* is the term given to gold with a minimum fineness of 10 karats mechanically bonded or electroplated over *sterling silver*. The thickness of the gold must be at least 120 millionths of an inch. FTC guides say: "If a nickel barrier is used, that must be disclosed," i.e., "the sterling silver is covered with a base metal that is gold plated."

Liquid Gold. This is a solution of chemicals, including 12 percent gold used as a surface decoration, that is literally painted on, then fired to 1004 degrees Fahrenheit.

The following list provides the gold qualities commonly used in jewelry produced in these countries:

- Austria: 14K, 18K
- Belgium: 18K
- Denmark: 8K, 14K, 18K
- France: 18K, 22K
- Germany: 8K, 14K, 18K
- Greece: 14K, 18K, 22K
- Italy: 18K
- The Netherlands: 8K, 14K, 18K
- Norway: 14K, 18K
- Portugal: 19K
- Spain: 18K
- Switzerland: 9K, 14K, 18K
- United Kingdom: 9K, 14K, 18K, 22K
- United States: 10K, 14K, 18K
- Hong Kong: 14K, 18K, 24K
- Japan: 8K, 14K, 18K, 22K
- South Africa: 9K, 10K, 14K, 18K, 22K

The Platinum Group

Six metals form the platinum group: platinum, palladium, iridium, rhodium, ruthenium, and osmium. They are always found together in their natural state and have certain characteristics in common. All but osmium have been used in jewelry. Palladium, next to platinum, is the most extensively used and is brilliant white in color. It is a precious metal in its own right

Table 3-2. Gold Content of Karat Alloys

Gold Percentage	Karat
100.00	24
95.83	23
91.67	22
87.50	21
83.33	20
79.17	19
75.00	18
70.83	17
66.67	16
62.50	15
58.33	14
54.17	13
50.00	12
45.83	11
41.67	10
37.50	9
33.33	8
29.17	7
25.00	6

and often described as the "twin sister" of platinum, which it closely resembles. Palladium, however, is much lighter in weight than platinum.

What are the new FTC guides for marking platinum jewelry? The guides state that jewelry with 950 parts or more per thousand of pure platinum can be correctly marked and described as "Platinum" without the use of any qualifying statements. As used in the guides, 850 to 950 parts per thousand can be marked in accordance with international standards "950Plat" or " 950 Pt.," "900 Plat" or "900 Pt.," "850 Plat" or "850 Pt." The revised guides permit the use of two- or four-letter abbreviations for platinum. Additionally, alloyed articles containing 500 parts per thousand of pure platinum and at least 950 parts per thousand *platinum group* metals should be marked with the parts per thousand of pure platinum, followed by the parts per thousand of each *platinum group* metal. For example, "600 Plat. 350 Irid." ("platinum and iridium") or "600 Pt. 350 Ir." Both dominant metal names *must* be used together on the stamping, such as platinum iridium or platinum ruthenium. Both iridium and ruthenium are used to harden platinum. Rhodium, seldom used to harden platinum alloys, is used with ruthenium to harden palladium alloys. Rhodium is also used to plate silver and white gold to prevent tarnish. Osmium alloys are used for compass bearings. *Less than 500 parts per thousand* pure platinum *cannot* be marked with the word *platinum* or any abbreviation.

Copies of the Jewelry Guides are available from the FTC's website at http://www.ftc.gov and also from the FTC's Public Reference Branch, Room 130, 6th Street and Pennsylvania Avenue NW, Washington, DC 20580.

Silver Content and Stamping

Sterling silver is defined as an alloy of at least 925/1000 parts silver, the other parts being such base metals as copper, nickel, tin, and antimony. Sterling has also been called *solid silver,* but it actually contains 75/1000 parts of metal other than silver. The term "sterling" does not signify the weight or gauge of the article, as a sterling silver item, such as a bracelet, can be very light or thin.

Silverplated. A silverplated item is made of base metal with silver electroplating. The thickness of silver on electroplated items may be only about 1/100,000 of an inch. If an article has an alloy containing not less than 900/1000 parts fine silver, it is called *coin* or *coin silver.*

Nickel Silver or German Silver. Items marked with either of these terms are alloys containing *no* silver. When used as a base for silverplated ware, it usually consists of 65 percent copper, 5 to 25 percent nickel, and 10 to 30 percent zinc.

Colored Gold

We all know that gold comes in two colors—yellow and white. Sometimes we see various shades of yellow gold, from dark to light and even rose. More and more designers and manufacturers are turning to an amazing rainbow of colored golds for attention, shock value, and to offer something new. If you are curious or have had questions from your clients about the alloys involved in the party-colored golds, see table 3-3.

Peter Gainsbury, design and technology director at the Goldsmiths' Company in London, says that some of the colored golds are not what they seem. He asserts: "Black gold is a contradiction in terms, blue gold is a myth, and purple gold is not a metal." Gainsbury has made studies that prove black gold to be only a film of black copper or nickel oxide on an alloy surface, or a surface coated and colored in the same way a plating solution would coat and color.

The British Assay Office will not permit the use of the term "blue gold." Blue gold, Gainsbury claims, is nothing new—the term can be found in old textbooks as 18K gold iron alloy. He says that the blueness may be the result of the development of iron oxide film on the surface of the alloy, as is the case for "black gold." Blue watch dials, we are told, are produced either by coating the gold surface with a transparent blue lacquer, nickelplating the gold dial and chemically coloring the nickel, or implanting cobalt atoms into a gold alloy surface to produce a blue color.

Purple gold exists, Gainsbury points out, but it is not a metal. It is obtained by melting together a mixture of 75 percent gold and 25 percent aluminum, but the result—instead of being an alloy—is a chemical compound of gold and aluminum that has few of the essential properties of a metal.

Weighing, Measuring, and Noting the Manufacturer

The weight of the item is a convenient way to evaluate gold and silver jewelry. It helps you distinguish between thin- and heavy-gauge metal jewelry, and whether the item is hollow or solid metal.

If you need to determine only the weight of the mounting of an item containing gemstones, use this formula:

1. Note the total weight of the item in grams.
2. Calculate, from measurements, the total gemstone weight in carats.
3. Convert carat weight into grams with the formula: carat weight × 0.2 = grams.

Table 3-3. Content Breakdown of Colored Gold Alloys

Color/Karat	Alloy Content
Bright yellow, 22K	91.67% 24K gold; 5% fine silver; 2% copper; 1.33% zinc
Bright yellow, 18K	75% 24K gold; 9.5% fine silver; 15.5% copper
Medium green, 18K	75% 24K gold; 5% fine silver; 20% copper
Very deep green, 18K	75% 24K gold; 15% fine silver; 4% cadmium; 6% copper
Deep rose, 18K	75% 24K gold; 25% copper
Pink, 18K	75% 24K gold; 5% fine silver; 20% copper
Bright red,* 18K	75% 24K gold; 25% aluminum
Bright purple, 20K	83.3% 24K gold; 16.7% aluminum
Blue, 18K	75% 24K gold; 25% iron
Gray, 18K	75% 24K gold; 8% copper; 17% iron
Black, 14K	58.3% 24K gold; 41.7% iron
Brown, 18K	75% 24K gold; 18.75% palladium; 6.25% fine silver
Orange, 14K	58.33% 24K gold; 6% fine silver; 35.67% copper

*Tends to be brittle.

4. Deduct this gemstone gram weight from total gram weight of the item.

Another formula for computing the net weight in pennyweights of metal in mounted goods: net weight = gross weight minus carat weight × .13. If the identity of the stone is unknown, use an estimated specific gravity of 3.00.

Weigh chains separately from any pendants that hang upon them. The labor required to produce chains reflects a much smaller percentage of its total price. Charms that are soldered on bracelets and cannot be removed can be weighed by resting the charm(s), one at a time, on a gram scale while you hold the bracelet in your hand and support your arm on a counter or desk. You should list the value of each charm on an insurance replacement appraisal. Make sure that the client has a complete list by design and style in case replacement is needed. The total weight of the charm bracelet can be determined by subtracting the total weight of charms from the total weight of the bracelet and charms.

When taking measurements, list the overall size of the item in millimeters or inches. Use a small tape measure and include the clasp when you take the total measurement of a necklace. A millimeter gauge should be used to establish the widths and depths of chains, bracelets, watch bands, rings, brooches, earrings, and so on. If you are working with a strand of pearls or beads, note the length of the strand and count the number of beads or pearls. Use a millimeter gauge or a pearl gauge to obtain the size of beads or pearls and note the figure on your worksheet.

Construction Analysis

Examine each item of jewelry to determine the type of construction. Is it handmade, cast, or die struck? A combination? Knowing the construction is important because the cost of handmade jewelry is higher than that of similar pieces cast from wax patterns or die struck. Chains that are mass produced by machine cost much less than those that are hand assembled and finished.

Cast jewelry usually shows pits and rough areas in the small recesses on the underside of jewelry, where polishing is difficult. Open pit marks, cavities, and stressed areas reveal that an item was hastily cast. Pinpoint holes indicate porosity, another sign of careless casting undertaken without consideration for detail. In cast jewelry, you will also find small cast settings; intricate work will not look quite finished.

Handmade jewelry items will often show a different color solder in the joints; even well-constructed items often reveal small areas of solder. Although handmade jewelry will normally have a higher value than other construction, if the piece has been poorly made and finished it may be less valuable than an item cast and finished with care. "Handmade" does not necessarily mean "quality." If an item looks as good on the inside as it does on the outside, you probably have a hand-constructed piece or a die-struck item finished by hand. Handmade and handfinished jewelry may show deeper and uneven cuts, overlapping or incomplete cut ends that do not join other parts of a design, layout lines on the back sides, or tool marks. Other signs of poor workmanship include file marks that should have been polished out and obvious, pitted solder joints.

Note the condition of filigree jewelry in particular. There is a big price difference between hand-cut and cast filigree jewelry. Learn to detect the differences and, if possible, enlist the aid of a bench jeweler to help you.

Die-struck jewelry is formed by pressing metal into dies and is usually mass produced. Stamping is a two-step process. The item is first stamped into the metal and then the shape is cut out. Much inexpensive gold jewelry, especially pendants and earrings, is made by these methods. Die-struck and stamped items are characterized by a bright finish in the small recesses. Die-struck items are frequently heavier than are their cast counterparts because of the denser metal used in the manufacturing process.

During an examination, look for prong breakage, prong shear, and stress corrosion in the jewelry. If prong damage is found, it is prudent to advise the client—point out the damage, using magnification if necessary. The causes for prong breakage points to two problem areas: (1) exposure of jewelry products to household chemicals such as cleansers; cleaning products containing chlorine, florine, or bromine; or swimming pool chlorine products, and (2) jeweler's error including poor craftsmanship and improper stone setting techniques. *Stress corrosion* is seen more often in nickel-based *white gold alloys* and is due to the nickel, which tends to concentrate along the grain boundaries. The problem in stress corrosion is generally the metallurgical nature of nickel-based white gold and *not* the quality of construction.

Flashing, the slightly raised or overlapped metal that exists on the back side of punched-out jewelry, is a typical clue to machine-finished work. Often you will find the pressed-in look of the design showing on the back side of the jewelry. It is also important to note the finish of the jewelry on the appraisal report. See the appendix for a glossary of finishing terms.

Evaluating Chain Construction

Pay particular attention to chains when you are evaluating the construction of items in an appraisal. They are quite popular and abound in most jewelry collections. See figures 3-18 through 3-22 for illustrations of twenty-seven popular kinds of chains.

Run the chain through your hands. How does it feel? Are there rough edges? You can cut your finger on a badly finished chain, for which the manufacturer sacrificed labor to achieve a certain price. A rough-edged chain was most likely mass produced and sold for a low retail cost.

Check the chain for flexibility. Many cheap chains are stiff. Does the chain kink up when handled or worn? Watch the complexion of the diamond cutting to see whether there are *chatter marks,* the small grooves or jumpy ridges that indicate the machine did not run smoothly over the gold, and show that the manufacturer used shortcuts. Check the corners of hexagonal chains to see whether they are beveled. This simple technique makes the chain smoother to the touch and whispers "better quality" to the appraiser. On rope chains, there should not be a gap between the two lengths wrapped around each other; if there is a gap, it will cause the chain to hang badly on the neck. Examine the ends of chains to see how they

3-18. *Top to bottom:* Rope chain; Boston chain; double herringbone chain with beveled edge; zipper chain; king chain; double-link chain.

were made; machine-made chain is cut off a long spool. Is each chain end capped to give it a clean look, or are the ends simply pressed together? Finally, look at the clasp. Is it a spring ring of good quality and the right weight for the chain?

Nomenclature for Jewelry Findings, Mountings, and Chains

It cannot be stressed too often that correct description is essential to proper documentation. If you do not know how to describe the various parts of a jewelry piece, how can you convey to your client or to a third party what the items look like? Furthermore, are you describing the piece with the same terminology your peers use?

Findings are the small metal components used by jewelers to make or repair various articles. Mass produced by machine, findings include bolt rings, gallery strips, settings for stones, brooch catch plates, and links for cufflinks. When made by hand, these are sometimes called *fittings*. In describing mountings, be sure to include the following information:

1. Whether the item is for a man or woman
2. Type of article

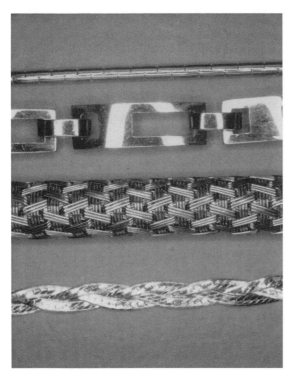

3-19. *Top to bottom:* Round c chain; buckle chain; basketweave chain; braided and beveled herringbone chain.

3-21. *Top to bottom:* Cable chain; spun rope chain; Frenchlink chain; round disc chain.

3-20. *Top to bottom:* Foxtail chain; flat curb-link chain; c-link chain; round mesh chain; ultra-link chain.

3-22. *Top to bottom:* Mirror chain; nugget chain; box chain; serpentine chain; cobra chain; wheat chain; stirrup chain; infinity chain.

3. Metal, metal fineness, and metal color
4. Method of manufacture and manufacturer's marks
5. Style or motif
6. Metal finish
7. Metal weight

Rings manufactured by more than one process, such as die-struck and hand-assembled rings, should be described in terms of their composition, manufacturing method, and assembly. For items containing a number of gemstones, report the number, cuts, types, measurements, weights, and analyses of all stones. Common findings, mountings, and chains are illustrated in figures 3-23 through 3-26.

Trademarks and Hallmarks

Trademarks identify a particular manufacturer. A trademark can be a monogram (two or more letters alphabetized according to the first letter on the left), designs without letters, company names, or numbers. Trademarks have been used for hundreds of years and in the beginning consisted of pictures, designs, or trade symbols to help the illiterate identify the source of a commodity. When the early guilds of Europe were established and the reliability of an artisan's product was of prime importance, the trademark came into use as a method for guilds to trace the makers of certain items, to ensure that proper standards were being met. This use of trademarks still holds today; quality is associated with a manufacturer's trademark. The National Gold and Silver Stamping Act requires manufacturers of jewelry and precious metals to stamp their trademarks next to the quality marks of their goods. Trademarks must be registered in the United States Patent and Trademark Office.

For the appraiser, trademarks and stamped marks offer one of the few ways to establish the provenance of any particular jewelry item. A good reference source for trademarks is the Jewelers' Circular-

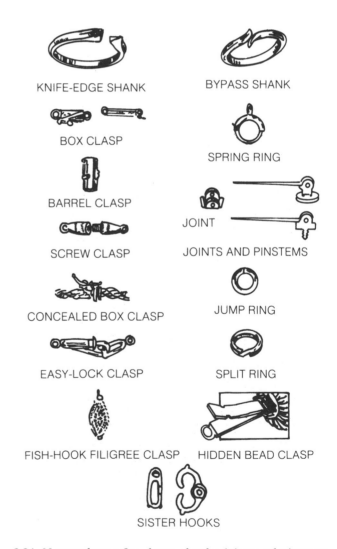

3-23. Nomenclature for ring heads, mountings, settings.

3-24. Nomenclature for clasps, shanks, joints and pinstems, hooks, and ring closures.

3-25. Nomenclature for settings, ear wires, and heads.

3-26. Mounting styles.

Keystone *Brand Name and Trademark Guide,* which lists over eleven thousand names and symbols used by nearly five thousand makers of jewelry. The *Canadian Jeweller Trade Mark Index,* a comprehensive directory of Canadian jewelry trademarks as well as brand names of other precious-metal products from around the world, is equally impressive. This index of trademarks currently registered with the Canadian government includes jewelry and silverware marks and the brand names of watches, clocks, giftware, and accessories. The directory is updated annually.

Hallmarks

The systematic marking of gold articles began in 1300 in England, when a law was introduced to protect the public against the fraudulent use of adulterated gold and silver by dishonest smiths. Originally, all wares were marked in London and at first only one mark, a leopard's head, was punched into gold and silver. Later, other marks indicating quality, place, date,

and maker came into use. Today, almost all countries use some form of hallmarking on gold articles.

Standards used by other countries and marked on *gold* items include the following (not a comprehensive list):

- Argentina: .750, .500
- Australia: 9, 12, 14, 18, 22
- Austria: 986/1000, 900/1000, 750/1000, 585/1000
- Belgium: 500/1000
- Bulgaria: 920/1000, 840/1000, 750/1000, 583/1000, 500/1000, 330/1000

- Canada: 9, 12, 14, 18
- Czech Republic: 9, 14, 18
- Egypt: 12, 14, 15, 18, 21, 23
- Finland: 969/1000, 750/1000, 585/1000
- France: 18, 20, 22
- Hungary: 14, 18, 22
- Ireland: 9, 14, 18, 20, 22
- Israel: 9, 14, 18, 21
- Italy: 750/1000, 585/1000, 500/1000, 333/1000
- Japan: 375/1000 to 1000/1000
- Malta: 9, 12, 15, 18, 22
- Netherlands: 585/1000, 750/1000, 833/1000
- Norway: 14K, 18K
- Poland: 375/1000, 500/1000, 583/1000, 750/1000, 960/1000
- Portugal: 800/1000 (minimum legal standard) Watches may be .583 or .750
- Romania: 375/1000 to 958/1000
- Russia: 583/1000, 750/1000, 958/1000
- Sweden: 18K, 20K, 23K
- Switzerland: 14K, 18K
- Tunisia: 583/1000, 750/1000, 840/1000, 875/1000
- Turkey: 12K to 22K
- Yugoslavia: 583/1000, 750/1000, 840/1000, 950/1000

Also see table 3-4 for a list of some gold hallmarks used in England and Ireland. For in-depth information about gold and silver markings and hallmarks as well as complete dates, town lists, and maker's marks, consult Tardy's *Poincons d'Or et de Platine* and Tardy's *International Hallmarks on Silver*. Both are listed in the bibliography.

In Great Britain, sterling silver is indicated by a lion passant. Britannia silver is 958.4/1000 parts fine silver and the rest base metal. The quality mark for this alloy is the Lady Britannia, seated with a shield and spear.

French silver that is marked with a crab is 800/1000 parts fine silver. Marked with the head of Minerva in an octagonal shield, the silver is 950/1000 parts fine silver.

Irish sterling silver is marked with a crowned harp or with the Hibernia, the seated figure of a woman with a small harp in her hand and a spray of palm leaves. In Scotland, sterling silver is indicated either by a thistle or a thistle with a lion rampant.

In Russia, silver marked 84 and 88 is of a quality below sterling; silver marked 91 indicates a quality slightly above sterling.

Conducting Market Research

Jewelry items that are stamped with the name of the manufacturer and the production number of the arti-cle, as is often the case, will present few problems to the appraiser in obtaining a retail replacement cost. By contacting the manufacturer and giving the details of the item and the production number, the appraiser is usually able to obtain the manufacturer's wholesale price. By applying the retail mark-up that is most commonly used by the average fine jewelry store in his or her geographical locale, the appraiser can then determine the retail replacement price.

If, on the other hand, you do not know the manufacturer, the firm is out of business, or comparables are unavailable, one of the most expedient ways to price the item at retail replacement is to use the cost approach—what some appraisers called the "bricks-and-mortar" breakdown of an item. Take the intrinsic parts (the weight of metal and gemstones), multiply their respective weights (per karat and per carat) by the current wholesale costs, add any other factors, such as setting and/or labor charges, and then add a retail mark-up. You will end up with the average cost of a new reproduction.

To find the value of a ring that weighs 5 dwt. and is stamped 14K, multiply the current price of gold (say, $400) by .585 (14K) and divide by 20 dwt. (there are 20 pennyweights per troy ounce of gold). This formula will give you the price per pennyweight of gold on any particular day if you use the most current price of gold. The pennyweight price is then multiplied by the weight of the ring to obtain the intrinsic value of the gold ring.

The intrinsic value figure is multiplied by 1.8, the average manufacturer's mark-up. (Mark-up can be as high as 2.5 for some items—see the *Other Considerations* section below.) The price you have will be the approximate wholesale selling price for most cast rings and for some die-struck rings. The formula is as follows:

Current gold price × gold fineness ÷ 20 (dwts. per gold oz.) × weight of item × 1.8 (mfg. mark-up) = wholesale cost to average jeweler.

To determine the wholesale cost of sterling silver in jewelry items, use the above formula, substituting the current price of silver and using .925 for metal fineness. For fine silver, use .999 for metal fineness.

For platinum, use the above formula, substituting the current price of platinum and using .950 for metal fineness. After multiplying by the 1.8 percent manufacturer's mark-up, add an additional 20 to 30 percent to the total sum to reflect the fact that platinum is labor intensive and requires additional heating and more preparation.

Table 3-4. Gold Hallmarks of Ireland and Great Britain

Irish Hallmarks	Quality	Date of Usage
Crowned harp	22K	1784–1975
916	22K	1975–present
Plume of feathers	20K	1784–1975
English Hallmarks		
Crown over 22	22K	1844–1975
Crown over 18	18K	1798–1975
15.625*	15K	1854–1932
12.5*	12K	1854–1932
9.375*	9K	1854–1932
750*	18K	1973–present
Uncrowned king's head	18K	1808–1815

*These will be found with a lowercase *e* in a square shield followed by a leopard's head in a circle.

Other Considerations

Different manufacturers' mark-up percentages will be used in the previous formula, depending on the amount of work required to produce the item and the value of the gold or other metal. To determine manufacturer's mark-up for an article that is very intricate or a one-of-a-kind cast, multiply the intrinsic gold or other metal content by 2 or 2.25 to account for the time required and the wax model making. For very heavy gold items, multiply the intrinsic gold content by at least 2.5 to determine mark-up.

For two- or three-color gold, multiply the intrinsic value of the gold by approximately 2.2 to determine mark-up; use a slightly higher factor for die-struck jewelry. For designer jewelry it is best to contact the manufacturer of the item if possible.

Setting and Labor Costs

You need to be familiar with setting and labor costs to make accurate calculations when you use the cost approach to valuation. Visit a jewelry repair company in your area and ask for a copy of their price list. If there is no jewelry repair company in your immediate area, use the following compilation of average prices charged at keystone in the Atlanta area at the time of writing. See table 3-5 to obtain a quick computation of plumb gold at current gold prices.

Average Setting Prices

The following average retail setting prices are based upon a 2.5× mark-up on findings and stones. Labor is approximately triple key. David S. Geller of Jewelry Artisan, 510 Sutters Point Drive NE, Atlanta, Georgia 30328, publishes a book from which the following examples were taken. Geller's *Repair and Design Price Book* would be a helpful addition to any appraiser's library. Is knowing the price of jewelry design and repair important? Yes, because if the Cost Approach is being used to estimate value (calculating the value of the item by the individual components) the appraiser must have knowledge of the current prices jeweler's charge for all bench work. The following prices are retail as quoted to the customer.

Four Prong Low Base Head

Diamonds and colored stones. *Price is retail* and includes the head, soldering it into place, and setting the stone.

- Up to 10 points — 20.50
- 11 to 15 points — 25.50
- 16 to 49 points — 32.50
- 50 to 74 points — 49.50
- 75 pts to 1.00 carat — 65.00
- 1.01 cts to 1.50 cts — 95.00
- 1.51 cts to 2.50 cts. — 115.00

Four Prong Yg/Wg Basket Head: Round, Oval, Emerald, Heart, Pear Shapes

- 4 × 3mm — 35.00
- 5 × 4mm — 38.00
- 6 × 4mm — 42.00
- 7 × 5mm — 49.00
- 8 × 6mm — 55.00
- 9 × 7mm — 88.00
- 10 × 8mm — 94.00
- 11 × 9mm — 100.00
- 12 × 10mm — 110.00
- 16 × 12mm — 165.00
- 20 × 15mm to 22 × 16mm — 195.00

Four Prong Tiffany Heads, 14K Wg/Yg: Round, Square, Princess, Emerald Cut

- Up to 25 points — 59.00
- 26 to 60 points — 65.00
- 61 to 75 points — 79.00
- 76 pts to 1.0 carats — 95.00
- 1.01 to 2.0 carats — 132.00

Prong and tip repair (10K and 14K)

- First Tip — 14.00
- Each additional Tip — 9.00

Tips: 18K yellow and white

- First Tip — 17.00
- Each Additional Tip — 11.00

Platinum
- First Tip   26.00
- Each Additional Tip   20.00

Removing & Resetting Stones
- Prong set, low base, all shapes, up to ½ ct   15.00
- Prong set, Tiffany & larger, colored stones   40.00
- Bezel set stones, up to 7 × 5   35.00
- Bezel set stones, 8 × 6 and larger   55.00
- Channel set stones, up to ½ carat   28.00
- Channel set stones, over ½ carat   45.00

Prongs
10K and 14K yellow, white, and pink prongs:
- First prong   18.00
- Each additional prong   13.50

18K yellow and white prongs:
- First prong   22.50
- Each additional prong   16.50

Platinum prongs:
- First prong   39.00
- Each additional prong   25.00

Baguettes
Tapered and straight baguettes. Price includes head, soldering into place, and setting:
- 1.5mm to 3mm long   25.00
- 3.5mm to 5mm long   28.50
- 5.5mm to 6mm long   38.50

Miscellaneous
Handmade 14K bezels for cameos
- 18 × 13mm oval   155.00
- 25 × 18mm oval   190.00
- 30 × 22mm oval   215.00
- 40 × 30mm oval   285.00
- 50 × 40mm oval   300.00

Lobster Claw Catch, 14K Yellow Gold   22.75

Barrel Clasps, 14K
- 2mm   35.00
- 3mm   39.00
- 4mm   48.00

Pearl Clasps, Filigree, 14K Yellow Gold
- 11 × 5½mm, small size   19.00
- 12 × 5mm, medium size   27.00
- 13 × 5mm, large size   29.00

Figure "8" Safety Devices, 14K YG   23.00

Bezel Setting Round Stones
(Labor only—does not include furnishing the bezel)
- Up to 12 points   16.50
- 13 to 25 points   18.00
- 26 to 50 points   21.00
- 51 to 74 points   25.00
- 75 pts to 1.00 carat   50.00

Bead Setting Round Stones (Pavé)
- Up to 15 points   14.00
- 16 to 50 points   18.50
- 51 to 75 points   26.00
- 76 pts to 1.50 cts   50.00
- 1.51 to 3 cts   70.00

Channel Setting Round Stones
- Up to 15 points   18.00
- 16 to 50 points   25.00
- 51 to 75 points   30.00
- 76 pts to 1.50 cts   55.00
- 1.51 to 3 cts.   70.00

Research Sources
Where will you research the jewelry you are valuing? Have you a clear idea of where to look and whom to call for information? Keep records of all the research you do on items, and list on your appraisal worksheet the people and companies you contact and the information gathered.

Market data research sources include:

- Retail stores carrying like merchandise
- Wholesale jewelers who sell like merchandise
- Auction houses
- Jewelry trade shows
- Gem and mineral shows—an excellent but often overlooked source of information
- Manufacturers
- Casting houses and findings companies
- Jewelry designers (individuals)
- Books and trade magazines or periodicals
- Price guides directed at specific markets, such as diamonds, colored stones, pearls
- Your own records
- Computer networks (Internet) with access to historical records and/or current prices of gemstones and precious metals
- Museum catalogs and special exhibits

Using Price Guides
Almost every jewelry appraiser will use or at least consult a price guide at some point. A price guide can be a book on antique jewelry, an auction house catalog with the hammer sale prices of the articles auctioned,

Table 3-5. Cost of Plumb Gold Content by Pennyweight

$ per troy oz. of gold	$ value per dwt. (rounded off to nearest 5¢)						$ per troy oz. of gold	$ value per dwt. (rounded off to nearest 5¢)					
	9½K	10K	12½K	14K	17½K	18K		9½K	10K	12½K	14K	17½K	18K
300	5.95	6.25	8.45	8.75	11.00	11.30	510	10.10	10.65	14.35	14.90	18.65	19.15
310	6.15	6.45	8.70	9.05	11.30	11.60	520	10.30	10.85	14.60	15.15	19.00	19.50
320	6.35	6.70	8.95	9.35	11.70	12.00	530	10.50	11.10	14.90	15.45	19.35	19.90
330	6.55	6.90	9.25	9.65	12.05	12.40	540	10.70	11.30	15.20	15.75	19.70	20.30
340	6.70	7.10	9.55	9.90	12.40	12.75	550	10.90	11.50	15.45	16.00	20.10	20.65
350	6.90	7.30	9.80	10.20	12.80	13.10	560	11.10	11.70	15.70	16.30	20.45	21.05
360	7.10	7.50	10.10	10.50	13.15	13.50	570	11.30	11.90	16.00	16.60	20.80	21.40
370	7.30	7.75	10.40	10.80	13.50	13.90	580	11.50	12.10	16.30	16.90	21.20	21.80
380	7.50	7.95	10.70	11.10	13.90	14.30	590	11.70	12.30	16.60	17.20	21.60	22.20
390	7.70	8.15	10.95	11.35	14.25	14.65	600	11.90	12.50	16.90	17.50	22.00	22.60
400	7.90	8.35	11.20	11.65	14.60	15.00	620	12.30	13.00	17.40	18.10	22.60	23.20
410	8.10	8.55	11.50	11.95	14.95	15.40	640	12.70	13.40	17.90	18.70	23.40	24.00
420	8.30	8.80	11.80	12.15	15.35	15.80	660	13.10	13.80	18.50	19.30	24.10	24.80
430	8.50	9.00	12.05	12.50	15.70	16.15	680	13.40	14.20	19.10	19.80	24.80	25.50
440	8.70	9.20	12.35	12.80	16.10	16.50	700	13.80	14.60	19.60	20.40	25.60	26.20
450	8.90	9.40	12.65	13.10	16.45	16.90	720	14.20	15.00	20.20	21.00	26.30	27.00
460	9.10	9.60	12.95	13.40	16.80	17.30	740	14.60	15.50	20.80	21.60	27.00	27.80
470	9.30	9.80	13.20	13.70	17.15	17.65	760	15.05	15.90	21.40	22.20	27.80	28.60
480	9.50	10.00	13.50	14.00	17.55	18.00	780	15.45	16.30	21.95	22.80	28.50	29.30
490	9.70	10.25	13.75	14.30	17.90	18.40	800	15.85	16.70	22.50	23.40	29.20	30.00
500	9.90	10.45	14.05	14.60	18.25	18.80							

Reprinted with permission of Jewelers' Circular-Keystone.

wholesale price lists of jewelry manufacturers, or the price lists of specific items, such as diamonds and colored stones that are privately sold by subscription.

Price guides have one thing in common. The prices stated can and do fluctuate and should be used only as guides, and not as gospels, of price. Industry price guides are not valid primary sources of market value. Primary research is information based on established, substantiated prices (the mode of prices most frequently occurring in the marketplace), not on opinion or prediction. Gemstone price guides are largely hypothetical, based on one individual's opinions or calculations of future prices. Moreover, price guides generally give the dealer's asking price, not the actual selling price. To be accurate, ethical, and legal, the appraiser must use verifiable sales data.

The Guide is a diamonds and colored-stone price guide with an army of "pricing advisors" taking notes on diamonds, colored stones, and pearls from wholesalers (foreign and domestic) and at gem and jewelry shows all over the country. Since there is so much diverse pricing input, it is logical to assume that *The Guide* reflects wholesale market prices a lot more accurately than prices compiled by a single individual.

However, the single most important issue that has troubled appraisers relying on any price guide is "What is the *legality* of using the prices offered to determine value?" While the use of a price guide is not a substitute for using due diligence in arriving at an opinion, the American legal system will accept use of data from price guides as *hearsay* evidence. The following citation from the Federal Evidence Code Rule 803 now seems to allow the appraiser to use a publication such as *The Guide* with impunity:

Hearsay Exceptions

(17) Market Reports, Commercial Publications—Market quotations, tabulations, lists, directories, or other published compilations, generally used and relied upon by the public or by persons in particular occupations.

Federal Evidence Code Rule 803

Federal Code 122F.2d 143:

Testimony and respect of the market value of personal property is admissible when based upon recognized current catalogs or price lists.

The appraiser is still charged with using a reliable method to arrive at his/her opinion because the expert's opinion is still the issue. The appraiser should understand the law as it applies to his/her state, because there is variance among states. Price guides have a place in the appraiser's reference library when used as tools to establish, through comparison, a range of prices to which the appraiser adds specific data and can make a final value judgment based upon his/her own expertise and local markets.

All appraisers should keep records of the prices of gemstones and jewelry they appraise, as well as the dates and sources of these prices. No other tool is as handy or dependable as your own records, which are also valid as a body of substantiated information that you can use to verify your appraisal document in court. The idea is not new—appraisers and jewelers have been making notes about sales and levels of pricing at gem shows and jewelry markets for years. If you find that it is too time consuming to take notes at gem shows, consider using a microtape recorder. You can murmur unobtrusively into a recorder jewelry descriptions, sales transactions and prices, and your impressions of the various styles and designs. Transcribe the information into your notebook when you return to your office.

If you are establishing a range of prices from auction catalogs, be cognizant of the many variables that can affect the final sale price. Damage or needed repairs are not always disclosed, and provenance is rarely guaranteed. Furthermore, auction catalog photos cannot be relied upon to give a true idea of a gem or jewelry piece, as photos are shot from only one side and angle. Of course, if you are able to inspect the auction articles personally, the piece can be used as a point of reference if you can be sure that the hammer price reflects value in the market and is not unduly high or low because of the auction time, place, location, attendance, and so on. Remember that using a similar item in an auction catalog does not in itself provide enough description or information about quality and condition to be used as the sole comparable piece for the item you are appraising.

If you are using auction prices to help establish fair market value, remember that FMV data must come from sales of comparable items to the ultimate consumer—the end user of the property. Many auctions are attended by dealers who are presumably buying for resale. If a dealer is the purchaser, an item's hammer price may not be used to establish fair market value. Auction prices are useful, however, for items most commonly sold to the public. These include antiques, period pieces, and designer jewelry. For donation appraisals and fair market values used for estate purposes, the hammer price alone—not including buyer's or seller's commission—is used.

The following price guides are available by subscription:

1. *Auction Market Resource,* P.O. Box 7683, Rego Park, New York 11374. Publisher Gail Brett Levine gives auction price information for antique to modern jewelry.
2. *The Guide* published by Gemworld International, Inc., 650 Dundee Road, Suite 465, Northbrook, Illinois 60062-2758. Publisher Richard B. Drucker, G.G., offers a comprehensive pricing guide used by many jewelry appraisers.
3. *Rapaport Diamond Report,* 15 West 47th Street, New York, New York 10036. First diamond guide in the industry.
4. *Diamond Value Index,* published by Joseph W. Tenhagen, 36 NE 1st Street #419, Miami, Florida 33132. Analysis of diamonds based upon specific cutting parameters, with selling prices.

Which Retail Mark-Ups Should Be Used?

Average mark-ups work in principle but not always in practice, where retail selling prices are often discounted in competitive markets. Furthermore, mark-ups fluctuate depending on general business conditions and the economy.

Most jewelers say that they use few formulas to determine their mark-ups, but vary mark-up according to the individual article. Today, retail jewelry markups are shrinking. Some jewelers cite these reasons for mark-up variables: higher or lower demand for a particular item, keen competition, jewelry that simply looks better and can support a higher mark-up, jewelry that has been bought at a lower rate and can be marked up high—even a gut feeling about how an article may sell. Cash flow problems can also cause a jeweler to alter the mark-up commonly used. Alarmed that retail jewelers' markups were deteriorating, *Jewelers Circular Keystone* magazine confirmed the shrinking mark-ups in a 1995 industry markup survey. The JCK article pinpointed a more competitive market as one reason for the changing mark-ups. It has been shown, however, that jewelers generally stick to the mark-up that they have established. Once the appraiser knows how jewelers in their local area mark-up merchandise, he/she can establish a mode based on those prices and build a ratio chart that can be quite accurate. It should be noted however, that the *actual selling price* of an item should not be confused with the *suggested retail price*. Jewelers often tag a piece of jewelry with a high selling price, but discount it under pressure of a binding retail sale. Therefore, in many retail jewelry stores the *selling price* on a jewelry tag may not be the *actual sales price*, unless the jeweler commonly make sales at that higher price.

A list of average diamond and colored-stone mark-ups used across the United States is provided in table 3-6, and how to use mark-ups in table 3-7. Table 3-6 was compiled by *The Guide* based on their own in-house research and a 1995 JCK Retail Panel members' survey.

Why Are Some Mark-Ups Higher?

Once a *wholesale* value for an appraised item has been determined, the appraiser generally applies an appropriate mark-up to arrive at an acceptable retail value. This is the standard way to use the Cost Approach, right? The approach is correct, but what the appraiser must keep in mind is that not all jewelers pay the same *wholesale* price for an item. With geographic variation in wholesale prices, the appraiser will find variance in retail prices—usually for the identical article. An independent appraiser impulsively using *wholesale* prices found in a price guide and then marking them up according to his/her regional mode, might complain that the price guide numbers are above retail in his/her locale. Not all jewelers get the benefit of identical wholesale prices for merchandise; buying power and credit buying are two reasons for the disparity.

Table 3-6. Breakdown of Percentage Mark-Ups. The JCK retail median for this category was based on $200 cost and a 2.25 mark-up. *The Guide* adjusted its tables to reflect a $250 cost. Tables courtesy of *The Guide*.

DIAMONDS

$ Cost	Mark-Up × Cost			Retail Median $	JCK '95 Retail Median $
	Mode	Average	Median		
100	2.0	2.26	2.2	220	225
250	2.0	2.19	2.0	500	563*
500	2.0	2.10	2.0	1,000	1,125
1,000	2.0	1.94	2.0	2,000	2,250
1,500	2.0	1.85	1.85	2,775	2,750
3,000	1.5	1.66	1.6	4,800	5,250
5,000	1.5	1.54	1.5	7,500	8,750
7,500	1.5	1.50	1.46	10,950	10,625
10,000	1.5	1.45	1.4	14,000	13,500
15,000	1.5	1.39	1.33	19,950	–
20,000	1.25	1.35	1.3	26,000	–
25,000	1.2	1.33	1.28	32,000	–

COLORED STONES

$ Cost	Mark-Up × Cost			Retail Median $
	Mode	Average	Median	
100	2.0	2.46	2.4	240
250	2.0	2.34	2.4	500
500	2.0	2.25	2.2	1,100
1,000	2.0	2.10	2.0	2,000
1,500	2.0	2.00	2.0	3,000
3,000	2.0	1.80	1.8	5,400
5,000	1.5	1.65	1.65	8,250
7,500	1.5	1.58	1.53	11,475
10,000	1.5	1.53	1.5	15,000
15,000	1.5	1.45	1.4	21,000
20,000	1.25	1.42	1.35	27,000
25,000	1.2	1.39	1.32	33,000

The Principle of Qualitative Ranking

The Principle of Qualitative Ranking is one of the most important, but often misunderstood, of the principles of valuation. Jewelry appraisers *especially* need to put this principle into use in order to justify their estimated values on an appraisal assignment. Why? Because, to report price on an object, you only have to *know* the price. But to report quality and value, you must *understand* both *quality* and *value*. Using a Qualitative Ranking system implies that you *do* understand.

Defining Value and Quality. "Value" as defined in the American Society of Appraisers *Appraisal of Personal*

Table 3-7. Retail Jewelry Mark-Ups

Important Pricing Considerations

Do you know the correct formula used to "mark-up" a piece of jewelry for an estimate of value?

If you are simply multiplying a *mark-up percentage* (such as 150%, 200%) against the wholesale cost—or, if in using the Cost Approach this is the last element factored in before the value estimate—*you may be missing a step and underpricing.*

Example:

If you are doing this:

Wholesale cost of jewelry item:	$1000
Mark-up you want to use:	× 200% (2.00)

You end up with this:

Your Estimated Appraised Value:	$2,000

You have left out a step and gotten a valuation figure that may be too low!

Some of the confusion exists in the terms "mark-up" and "keystone." If you want to *keystone* a jewelry item you double the wholesale cost and the resulting figure would be the estimate of value. However, If you want to *mark-up* the jewelry (for example 200%), you must also *calculate in the wholesale cost of the item.* You do this by adding the wholesale cost to the mark-up percentage you are using.

The Formula is:

Wholesale Cost × Mark-Up % + Wholesale Cost
= Estimated Value

Example:

Wholesale cost	$1,000	
Mark-up percentage	200%	= 2.00
		(decimal conversion)
Plus wholesale cost	$1,000	

◆

Or, $1,000 × 2.00 + $1,000 = $3,000
(giving you 200% mark-up)

This chart will help you calculate the desired mark-up:

If you want this mark-up:	Use this decimal that includes the percentage for wholesale cost
50%	1.50
75%	1.75
100%	2.00 (*Keystone*)
125%	2.25
150%	2.50
175%	2.75
200%	3.00 (*Triple Keystone*)
225%	3.25
250%	3.50
275%	3.75
300%	4.00

Property handbook: "Value is a social agreement; it is the consensus among people interested in a property of what is a reasonable price for that property."

To find "value" (a numerical figure), appraisers research and establish a market "mode" for the subject property.

"Quality," according to *Webster's Third International Dictionary,* is a term defined as: "A degree of excellence or fineness; a degree of conformity to a standard—as in a product or craftsmanship; a measure of inherent or intrinsic excellence of character or type."

Another *Webster's* definition defines "quality control" (which applies to jewelry and the qualitative ranking principle) as "a critical study of design, materials, processes, equipment, and workmanship."

Therefore, when appraisers use the principle of Qualitative Ranking to categorize jewelry and estimate value, they are applying a method that classifies and organizes various quality levels of manufactured jewelry from Poor to Best. The Qualitative Ranking principle states that a sound opinion of the quality of a piece of jewelry can be derived from a comparison of the characteristics and features with the corresponding features of *another similar item with a known standard for such comparison.* In simple terms, gemstones as well as jewelry can be grouped in Poor, Good, Better, and Best categories (also relates to value) by using a comparative process with like items.

As practical as this process is, however, there is a basic flaw. In order to be able to accurately and justifiably classify a gem or piece of jewelry as Poor or Best, one must have actually *seen* examples from the poorest to the best of an item. This applies to natural as well as synthetic gemstones, *all methods of manufactured jewelry,* designer jewelry, and antique jewelry. *Broad* experience in the jewelry field is needed before employing a Qualitative Ranking system, and a strong argument can be made that appraisers using the system are more exact if they are gemologists, have market experience in retail sales, are familiar with jewelry manufacturing processes, and understand jewelry repair and alterations.

It is particularly negligent to assign quality ranking to jadeite, rubies, and designer jewelry without research, hands-on examination, and personal knowledge of all quality levels of the property from Poor to Best. In regard to designer jewelry, this means the appraiser should have comprehensive understanding of the jewelry made by various artists and be familiar with their complete production.

Quality Ranking Antique Jewelry

Can we apply the same standards of quality ranking to *antique jewelry* that we use for contemporary jewelry? No. Because antique jewelry (defined as 100 years old or more) cannot be judged by modern standards. The craftsmanship and gemstone cutting on antique jewelry must be judged by the prevalent standards of its time. What was considered to be the "best" craftsmanship in the past may not be the "best" in today's vocabulary because of new technology, techniques, and tools. Also, in antique jewelry, the entire piece including the provenance (if any) must be considered and not just the craftsmanship or materials. Quality grading and appraising antique jewelry requires special expertise, market research, and an explicit chart for comparison and ranking.

Can We Judge Design?

Is design a part of the quality ranking system? Yes and no. *Design* and *design judgment* must be addressed as separate topics. Good design involves some standard elements. In the simplest terms design is the orderly arrangement of lines and shapes in such a way that the result is pleasing to view. There are two kinds of design: pure design and representation, and one or the other always dominates.

What Elements Are Considered?

Here are *some* elements to be considered when assessing jewelry on a ranking scale:

1. How is the piece manufactured: Cast? Die-Struck? Handmade? Other?
2. What is the quality of the manufacturing? Porosity present? Unfinished backs? Finished prongs? Are prongs thin, or correct proportion to the stones?
3. If the item is a ring, is the shank worn, too thin, or strong without structural problems?
4. Is the piece well finished, with polishing on the undersides, between filigree and in grooves? Tumble polished or finished by hand?
5. Has attention been paid to the details of the mounting: Is the piece even? Lines straight? Angles equal? Piece balanced?
6. Have there been any repairs? If so, how well done are they?
7. If repairs have been made, was the correct solder used? If lead solder was used, how extensively was it used? Does solder have pits or flow out of a seam?
8. Have repairs substantially altered the item?
9. Is the article durable for normal wear or has the designer cut corners in the manufacturing process to obtain a selling price? What corners were cut?

10. Does the item have a stamp for metal fineness? Manufacturers mark?
11. Are gemstones well set? Are channel settings straight and level?
12. What is the present condition of the piece? Pristine? Normal wear? Major wear? (Does the piece exhibit major scuffing? Scratches? Finish worn off?)
13. Clasps: Are clasps the correct size for the article? Are they in good working condition?
14. Weight: Is the item of a "wearable" weight and size currently used in the retail jewelry market? If not, why not?

Using the Chart

The Qualitative Ranking Chart (table 3-8) should be used with the understanding that the chart is a "guide" and not the definitive industry standard, because one does not exist. Further, it must be used with logic. For example, there are many articles of foreign manufactured jewelry that appraisers are called upon to value. It must be clearly understood that country of origin does not automatically determine the quality rank of the jewelry. Also, the quality of jewelry is not affected by the name of a designer, karat stamp, or a trademark. However, there are legal considerations requiring trademarks to be placed with karat stamped items, and other legal requirements to be met in regard to metal fineness. And, while the name of a designer may have a positive effect on the market value of an item (especially in ranks 8–10), the name of the designer does not dictate the quality of the product.

Note Grading Limitations on Worksheet and Appraisal Report

Quality grading judgments are most often made with mounted gemstones. Mountings tend to mask some important jewelry construction elements that can only be seen before the gems are set. Since subtle quality variations can cause a difference in the final estimated value of an item (for example, damage under prongs) state on the appraisal document that examinations including identifications, estimated weights from measurements, and quality gradings were done with *gemstones in the mountings*. The valuer should make notations on the worksheet about the research conducted, current market data collected (including mode of markups), and the names of those consulted for value information. State if taxes are included in the final valuation. Retain a copy of the appraisal in the client's file along with original worksheet. This is vital information in the event of any future court action.

Table 3-8. Quality Ranking Jewelry

The following definitions are currently used in *The Master Valuer Program* course work as benchmarks of quality that might be found in various market levels. Levels of "quality" are not standardized in the jewelry industry. A quality ranking system is necessary in order to class jewelry commonly found in various markets. Where a category does not completely fit the appraised item, a "split-rank" system can be used with comments on each individual component included in the appraisal report, i.e., manufacture, design, craftsmanship, polish, finish, wearability, quality marks, trademarks, and sometimes the designer.

> Scale of 1–10 with 10 as Best:(Best—10) (Better—9) (Very Good—8) (Good—7) (Fair—6) (Déclassé—5–1)

Best ranks 10 on a scale of 1–10 with 10 being virtually perfect in all respects.

Item may be handmade or machine made. Totally polished on all surfaces. Craftsmanship, design, proportions, and artistry all in the master class. Perfect setting of stones. Free of any faults.

Better ranks 9.

Item may have been made by any method. Produced with attention to design, proportions, and artistry. Carefully mounted stones. Angles of prongs graduated or uniform, symmetry of all elements. Total polish on all surfaces. No signs of seams o solder. Master class workmanship. Nearly a fault-free item.

Very Good ranks 8.

High quality craftsmanship, possibly of the master class. Good design, proportion, and artistry. Good polish on *nearly* all surfaces. Well-set stones. This is the highest level for cast items that show any porosity or other visible material defects. Any porosity must be invisible during wear and most porosity should be properly filled. There cannot be a great deal of porosity at this level, filled or hidden. The item should be well polished on top but may have partial finishing of the underside. Setting of stones should be secure and stones level with one another. *Slight* variance in channel setting lines, prong tips, or finish is acceptable. Bearings for stone settings should support the undersides of the stones. This is likely a product of a journeyman class or well-trained jeweler, but *not* at the master level of craftsmanship, design, proportion, or artistry.

Good ranks 7.

May also be called *Production Quality*. Most typical of production lines, moderately mass-produced items. This rank covers some items from television sales shows, although much would be ranked lower and only occasionally any higher. Tumbling for some of the finish process may round off some design elements. Settings may be cast in place. Galleries and undersides may be only partly finished. Porosity may be visible. Some porosity may show signs of filling with solder. Setting needs to be secure and stones need to look even to the wearer or untrained observer. Bearing surfaces and prong tips should generally be properly made, but may show some degree of irregularity and flashes of an unfinished nature. Much antique reproduction jewelry and museum reproductions fall into this category.

Fair ranks 6.

May be termed *Commercial Quality*. Mass-produced items, arts and crafts items, semi-professionally made silver jewelry. Made by reasonably competent craftsmen. Much 9K and 10K jewelry is made at this rank although karat content does not dictate quality ranking alone. Many plated items are made at this level. Sometimes inexpensive cabochon gemstones are seen set in this level of jewelry, but cabochons can be set in any level of jewelry. Polishing is not well done. Structural integrity of the item may have been compromised due to faulty design, workmanship, or the desire to keep the item inexpensive.

Déclassé rankings 5–1

Déclassé/5: This ranking indicates handmade or machine-made jewelry that may have individually satisfactory elements of design, craftsmanship, proportions, or artistry, but the overall effect is of an item that *is not well made*. Stones are not well set.

Déclassé/4: No attempt has been made to secure stone settings, level stones, or use proper gauge prong tips. Setting deficiencies show in careless channel lines or other craftsman procedures. Structural problems may exist that will lead to premature bending, damage, stone loss, or premature wear.

Déclassé/3: Some of this category of jewelry is made in foreign countries and does not conform in any manner to U.S. manufacturing standards. In this category we find *very* poorly machine-crafted and handmade jewelry. This category includes *extremely* thin metal jewelry (gold-foil type) not intended for daily wear, and novelty jewelry made for sale by amateurs at flea markets and jewelry fairs.

Déclassé/2–1: Jewelry that falls into this category is so worn as to be useless. Broken and unrepairable items that *may have functional, economic,* or *technological obsolescence.*

Computer Network Communications

The future is here. Today and into a technologically advanced 21st-century jewelry appraisers are going to be using the Internet and World Wide Web for research. This means new terms to learn, new nomenclature to define, and new skills to attain. It is the cutting edge of jewelry marketing, buying, selling, and appraisal research. The computer and communications revolution has swept the jewelry industry with an estimated 90% of retail jewelers now using a personal computer for some aspect of their business. Further, over one-third have access to the Internet, and sign on regularly either from their store, at home, or elsewhere. The numbers of jewelers and jewelry suppliers with their own web sites continues to grow. Leading the industry's move into cyberspace is Polygon Network, Inc., a provider of on-line services to the jewelry industry since 1983.

Polygon was developed by Jacques Voorhees (fig. 3-27) twenty years ago in New York City as a joint venture with Xerox to provide diamond investors with a trading network. However, when the diamond-investing market declined in the 1980s, Voorhees re-created Polygon into an information and trading service for jewelers. Polygon is today known as "The Internet Specialist For The Jewelry Industry™" and offers a number of services that have become vital business tools for many jewelers and appraisers. Some of the most important of these are:

Polygon Trading Network, an on-line trading and discussion resource, accessible either via Internet or directly by modem. Features include a large database of diamond inventory from dozens of diamonds dealers around the United States and overseas on a 24-hours-a-day basis. This database, called CertNet, is a great resource for appraisers as it records approximately $100 million of loose diamonds, updated daily, with prices shown on each listing and the name of the company offering it. An invaluable resource, CertNet makes it is possible to specify virtually any size, shape, or quality of diamond and see an up-to-the-minute wholesale listing of stones that fit the parameters, with their prices. This type of accurate, current market data, supported by actual competitive listings gives the appraiser justification for the estimate of value.

CertNet represents a fraction of the activity on the Trading Network. Most buying and selling actually occurs on the "trading channels," which are open bulletin-board style format, offering and requesting various types of merchandise. The Trading Network also includes discussion and conversation channels so members can "talk shop" 24 hours a day. One of the

3-27. Jacques Voorhees started Polygon twenty years ago. It is now the largest computer information and trading service for jewelers. *(Photo courtesy Polygon/Matt Lit.)*

discussion channels is "Appraisal Discussion," in which all aspects of appraising are discussed—and sometimes hotly debated.

What distinguishes Polygon's trading and discussion resources from other bulletin board services is the fact that the quantity and quality of the participation is so high. Over 4,000 broadcast messages per day go out over Polygon's trading and discussion channels. Participants include many industry leaders, editors of trade journals like JCK and *National Jeweler,* heads of industry associations, retail jewelers, appraisers, and wholesalers.

Website Programs. In addition to the Trading Network, Polygon is also the largest provider of websites to the jewelry industry. At the time of this writing Polygon is operating over 20,000 websites for retail jewelers, manufacturers, and others in the trade. Polygon has gone international with set-up of Polygon/South Africa and Polygon/Australia. Those involved in the jewelry industry in any capacity, including appraisers, will find Polygon the most comprehensive network in delivering market information. The Polygon network is easily accessed via their website, http://www.polygon.net, or for more information write Polygon Network, Inc., P.O. Box 4806, Dillon, Colorado 80435. The latest website for jewelry is www.gemkey.com.

About the Internet

The Internet was started by the U.S. Department of Defense in the 1960s. Later, colleges and science agencies were linked through this network. The Internet was made available to the general public in 1984 and since that time millions of computer users have connected to other computers around the world. First, in order to get "online" an Internet Service Provider (ISP) is needed. This service usually provides software and help hooking up to the Internet. Commercial service providers such as America OnLine, Prodigy, Microsoft, or Compuserve all provide access to the Internet for a monthly fee. Getting on the Internet is the first step to accessing the World Wide Web (www), which stores information within the Internet. WWW has thousands of informational sites, many with links connecting the site to other sites. Users can "click on a link" without having to type in an address. Linking from site to site is called "surfing." The Internet and World Wide Web have become essential research sources for jewelry appraisers. There is a caveat, however: There is an abundance of information available on the Internet with no regulations; therefore, the appraiser must carefully consider the accuracy of all statements.

Choosing Computer Software for Jewelry Appraising

There are several software programs developed specifically for jewelers, gemologists, and appraisers. The most helpful programs will be databased. A database is a collection of data efficiently arranged for quick search and retrieval. Windows-format databased software is available, letting the individual create and modify custom programs. This kind of software is called relational database or database management system. Following is a brief review of several databased software programs with the name and address of the developer. This is not a comprehensive list, but a brief survey of several popular programs. New programs come to the market regularly, so shop around.

Adamas Advantage Software

This software is designed to help gemologists and appraisers identify and analyze gemstones. The program also has color graphic capabilities that represent gemstone proportions, plot inclusions, and a color system that supports a universal color language, Commission Internationale D'Eclairage. *Adamas Advantage* features a vast database of gemstone properties, terms, colors, specific gravity, refractive index, heft, pleochroism, fluorescence, fracture, and luster. Covering more than 500 gem and mineral materials from amber to zoisite, *Adamas* also covers some of the more obscure minerals like jeremjevite in its database.

In the *appraisal* package, plotting, dimensions, and reporting of a diamond is simplified by entering a stone's data into the program. Then, based upon table size and crown height, a gemstone is automatically drawn to correct proportions in up to three dimensions. This is a good addition to the appraisal document.

The system may also be used to generate a diamond or colored-stone *quality analysis report, gemstone identification report,* or upgrade gem knowledge by testing via the *Gem I.D. Quiz Kit.* Another feature is the program's ability to illustrate light loss in diamonds by turning out a high-resolution plot showing ray tracing. Developer of the program is Martin D. Haske, G.G., Adamas Gemological Laboratory, 77 Pond Avenue, Suite C-609, Brookline, Massachusetts 02146.

CARAT™ Professional Appraisal Software

This is an advanced computer program designed to facilitate jewelers/appraisers in preparation of jewelry appraisals. CARAT™ is a sophisticated, easy-to-use program helping appraisers produce accurate appraisal documents via computer. The multisections of CARAT™ include detailed information on: diamonds, colored gemstones, pearls, precious metals, a customizing chart for certificates, a chart of instruments used in the appraisal, and *GIA Cut Class Grades* for round brilliant diamonds. An Appraisal Database maintains a complete record of the appraiser's work, as well as a comprehensive list of clients and their appraisals. CARAT™ prepares and prints multipage appraisal certificates, including an optional cover letter, disclaimer page, and explanations. A photo of the jewelry piece and diagram of the stone can be included and printed in color. The user can choose whether to use Gemological Institute of America or American Gemological Society grading codes and can customize the format of the appraisal certificate with a letterhead and logo. A feature of special interest to independent appraisers working for several jewelers, CARAT™ allows the appraiser to customize appraisals for up to twenty different companies. Included in the CARAT™ software package are *Price/Value* windows for diamonds, pearls, precious metals, and colored stones. As good as CARAT™ is, however, the developers insist that it should be viewed "only as a tool that assists in the formal appraisal process. Professional knowledge, training, expertise and experience should never be compromised." CARAT™ is available from Joseph Dvash, G.G., at Brilliant Software, Inc., 171 North Plank Road, Newburgh, New York 12550.

Gemology Tools (Windows Version)

This is a program that everyone likes and anyone can learn to use with ease. Designed and originally programmed by William R. Wise, G.G., *Gemology Tools* offers a stress-free way of generating important sales or appraisal information via computer: Diamond weight estimations, colored-stone weight estimations, diamond cut grading, Akoya pearl strand grading, analysis of round diamond proportions, calculation of crown angles, quick reference for gemstones, quick reference weight charts, even a place to schedule appointments. Some very important information for appraisers using the program are the "Crown Angle" and "Pavilion Angle" calculators. With the better cutting of diamonds and colored-stones receiving so much demand and attention from the industry, this tool comes in especially handy for the appraiser who either cannot make a crown angle call, or wants to confirm the estimate. *Gemology Tools* is available from Bill Wise, Wise Jewelry Applications, 61-8 Koala Court, Waldorf, Maryland 20603.

The Jewelry Judge

This is an attractive, affordable jewelry appraisal system that promises to save time for jewelers/gemologists/appraisers, and make appraisals into a profitable part of the jewelry business. There is little doubt that this program can deliver on its promises. The system is a complete appraisal-writing package that even those with little computer experience can manage. "The Jewelry Judge," says developer Steven A. Knight, G.G., "is designed so that *anyone* can work with it instantly." The program becomes a worksheet, price list, and calculator in a computer. An easy-to-follow menu system guides appraisers to pertinent appraisal facts necessary for accurate descriptions. A bonus for users of the system is on-screen plotting, a *GM Cut Class Grade* calculation section, and calculation of weights on *fancy cut diamonds*. One of the most helpful and unusual features of *The Jewelry Judge* is the built-in pricing of virtually all colored stones, opals, pearls, jade, diamonds, gold, silver, and platinum. Knight claims over one million prices on twenty shapes of diamonds, and over one hundred colored stone prices that are interactive with *The Guide* and *Rapaport*. The program permits separate detailing of diamonds and colored stones, all with GIA grading formats. One unique feature of this program allows customer information to be compiled in a mailing list and printed by ZIP code and other demographic categories. This is a *complete* appraisal package. For more information contact: The Jewelry Judge, Steven A. Knight, G.G., 252 James Street South, Suite 201, Hamilton, Ontario, Canada, L8N 3B5.

Helpful CD-ROM

A CD-ROM featuring great jewelry research is available to the appraiser. *Metal Arts Source Book 11*, covering more than 380 American, Canadian, Australian, and European artists along with over 1,400 pictures showing their works, is a must-have for the appraiser. You can zoom in to see more detail (up to 800%) or zoom down for a thumbnail size view. There is excellent information on platinum, precious metal clay, reactive metals, multiple casting, marketing retail presentations, and public relations.

Included in the disk is a Gallery Directory with over 500 names, addresses and contacts, a supplier directory with over 150 suppliers along with a description of services, and a school directory listing over 650 schools that teach jewelry making, both here and abroad. The disk is available from Bob Mitchell, Bob Mitchell Productions, 5009 Londonderry Drive, Tampa, Florida 33647.

Quantum Leap Software Solutions

Thom Underwood, G.G., founded the company in 1987 with its cornerstone product, Professional Appraisal Software. Originally called *Quantum Leap Appraisal Software,* the product was popular because it allowed appraisers to computerize the appraisal document and encouraged professional-looking reports. The original software was a DOS product, but moved to Windows in 1994. The features of the current product include: (1) ability to import graphics or pictures of appraised items; (2) variety of template designs for various types of appraising; (3) system functions in grams or pennyweights; (4) Cost or Market Approach can be selected for use; (5) appraiser's own words or choice of words on the document; (6) uses *The Guide* pricing with an update on diskette every month. For detailed information about *Quantum Leap,* Thom Underwood can be reached at his website http://www.qlss.com or by mail at Quantum leap, 3309 Juanita Street, San Diego, California 92105.

CHAPTER 4

RESEARCH AND ANALYSIS: HOW TO ESTIMATE VALUE

A competent appraiser is also a good investigator, searching through libraries and other information sources to document an item's worth. Charts, tables, formulas, and guide books are all part of the appraiser's arsenal of research and analysis. However, an appraiser must beware of falling into the complacent use of only one reference source or value table. No single book, chart, table, or reference is comprehensive enough to cover all market variables.

Old-Cut Diamonds: What Are They, and Where Did They Come From?

The earliest table-cut diamonds can be attributed to the 14th century because there is evidence of a diamond polishers guild in Nuremberg in 1373. In 1412, there is precise evidence for the existence of both table-cut and lozenge-cut diamonds. The rose-cut, first produced in 1520, is a flat base design unfaceted, with a dome-shaped top covered with 12 to 36 triangular facets grouped symmetrically around the girdle. Rose-cuts have also been called *Mazarins* because Cardinal Mazarin (1602–1661) was attracted to this shape and encouraged its production. However, he is wrongly credited with having invented the design.

At the end of the 17th century, Vincenzio Peruzi of Venice invented the brilliant-cut design with 58 facets: 33 above the girdle in the crown, and 25 in the pavilion. This form of brilliant-cut had a nearly square girdle outline with a high crown, small table, deep pavilion, and large open culet. The Peruzi cut is what was later to become known as the old mine-cut. The *GM Dictionary of Gems and Gemology, Sixth Edition* by Robert M. Shipley points out that the term brilliant-cut is misapplied: "[This term] incorrectly applied to a modern style of brilliant cut that also has a much higher crown and table than the modern brilliant cut, but whose girdle outline is circular or approximately circular, a style of cutting that is more properly called *old European-cut.*" The old European-cut diamond is found in early jewelry up to about 1930. Most old European-cut diamonds are light to medium yellowish color. This diamond color appeared after the South African diamond rush of 1870. In those early years of diamond mining, yellowish South African diamonds were famous, just as "champagne" diamonds today are famous for their Australian origins. Appraisers often encounter a modern modification of the old European-cut known as a *transition cut*. This diamond cut has a small table, closed culet, and short lower girdle facets. Around 1900, mechanical bruting and sawing was introduced and the *standard brilliant* was given a more circular outline and new height proportions.

Pricing Old-Cut Diamonds

Few old European-cut or old mine-cut diamonds are actually recut in the commercial marketplace, but they are invariably evaluated as if they will be. In the past the Gemological Institute of America instructed students to evaluate the older-cut diamonds by estimating recut weight to ideal proportions, even though there may have been no real intention to recut the stone. Today's gem appraisers evaluate old cuts in their *present* condition because they understand that a viable, trackable market exists for the old stones, although estimated replacement prices can be a problem. In the last decade several diamond wholesalers have begun to service the old-cut diamond market and develop their own specialty diamond niche. However, while one appraiser may see old-cut stones frequently, and another

Table 4-1. Old European-Cut Diamond Price Guide.

	.01–.03	.04–.07	.08–.14	.15–.17	.18–.22	.23–.29	.30–.36	.37–.43
D–F vvs–vs	575	580	650	730	875	1185	1600	1875
SI	475	475	550	615	675	750	1250	1375
I1	400	400	415	450	475	525	800	900
G–I vvs–vs	525	540	575	625	750	1000–1200	1500	1100
SI	450	475	510	575	625	675	1100	1300
I1	375	375	395	425	450	500	625	800
J–L vvs–vs	420	440	510	550	650	725	950	1100
SI	350	375	450	475	525	600	750	875
I1	275	295	345	380	395	450	550	600

	.44–.49	.50–.59	.60–.69	.70–.84	.85–.89	.90–.95	.96–.99	1.00–1.49
D–F vvs–vs	1950	2250	2600	2900	3100	3400–4000	3600–4400	4400–6000
SI	1550	1750	1850	2200–2500	2500	2750	3000	3300–3700
I1	1150	1250	1400	1550	1650	1900	2000	2200
G–I vvs–vs	1700	2000	2300	2500	2750	2750–3500	2800–3600	3000–4000
SI	1300	1475	1675	1975	2250	2475	2700	3000–3500
I1	900	1000	1075	1375	1500	1700	1800	2000–2800
J–L vvs–vs	1175	1275	1375	1650	1900	1700–2700	1750–2950	2300–3500
SI	950	1150	1200	1400	1600	1800	1950	2200–2600
I1	660	720	780	950	1150	1250	1400	1500–1800

Chart courtesy of Michael Goldstein, Michael Goldstein, Ltd.

rarely, both will have to diligently research the current regional and national markets to collect reliable pricing information.

A price reference chart shown in table 4-1 was compiled by wholesale diamond dealer Michael Goldstein of Goldstein Ltd. for his use in buying and selling old-cut diamonds, including rose- and table-cut stones. The chart shows a matrix of current base-price information for various sizes, colors, and clarity grades of old European-cut diamonds. The numbers represent his *wholesale* selling prices. For liquidation value discount 75% of the price. "The prices," says Goldstein, "represent prices for well-cut and well-proportioned old European-cut with circular outline. They provide a *guideline* for wholesale base prices."

When supplying retail replacement appraisals for insurance purposes on jewelry articles with old mine-cut and old European-cut diamonds, give two figures on your report. Give the cost of the old-cut stones replaced with comparable old-cut stones and give the price of a replacement diamond of modern cut with the same color and clarity grades of your old-cut diamonds. State these figures separately on the appraisal and indicate clearly that you are providing dual values for complete protection of the client, in case of loss or damage of the gemstones.

Be certain that you know the difference between an old European-cut and an old mine-cut diamond and can explain the distinctions to your client.

Phenomenal Gems

Some jewelry articles and gemstones have their own inherent set of value factors, including such phenomenal gemstones as star, change-of-color, and cat's-eye stones. All appraisers would like to possess an easy formula to apply to these items for valuation, but unfortunately no such formula exists. Many special articles must be judged on the merits created by their uniqueness and supply and demand in the consumer market.

When giving value to phenomenal stones, the following questions must be answered.

Cat's-Eye Stones

1. What is the sharpness of the eye?
2. How well is the eye centered?
3. Is the opening and closing of the eye distinct?
4. Does the stone exhibit a "milk and honey" effect?
5. What is the pavilion bulge factor?
6. Is the stone opaque? Translucent?
7. Are there any internal cracks or gas inclusions that could endanger the stone?
8. Are there external blemishes?

Star Stones

1. Is the star centered?
2. How many rays are there? Are they straight or wavy?
3. How sharp is the star?
4. How much weight is below the bezel?
5. Does the stone have belly bulge?
6. What is the bottom of the stone like? Is it chipped or cracked?
7. How good is the contrast between the star and the background?

Change-of-Color Stones
(Alexandrite, Sapphire, Garnet)

1. What colors show under various lighting sources?
2. Is the stone cabochon-cut or faceted?
3. How much weight is below the girdle?
4. Is the stone transparent, translucent, or opaque?
5. If you shine a penlight through the stone, does it reveal any internal cracks or gas inclusions that may endanger the stone?
6. What is the clarity?
7. Are there external blemishes, scratches, or abrasions?
8. What is the degree of color change?
9. How good is the contrast of change?

All cabochon-cut stones should be examined under a single overhead light beam, such as a penlight, and moved from side to side under the light for good observation of the star or cat's eye.

Fantasy-Cut Gemstones

The German term used to describe a fantasy-cut gemstone is *freischleiferi,* or free cutting. Two German master cutters of this highly acclaimed avant-garde style are Bernd Munsteiner and Erhart Jung. Figures 4-1 and 4-2 illustrate examples of their work. Fantasy-cut stones are unique, nearly three-dimensional in effect; each stone refracts and reflects light at a different angle. Jung and Munsteiner angle and place grooved cuts, curves, and straight planes to achieve total reflection of light. The fewest possible facets are used to obtain the effect. All are one-of-a-kind pieces and impossible to automate, although the Japanese are copying the cuts. One key to recognizing gems from the wheels of the master German cutters to the Japanese knock-offs is the ability of the Germans to achieve an incredibly high quality of polish. Attention to detail requires twenty-five to thirty hours of labor per stone. Munsteiner's studio alone is able to turn out only a thousand to fifteen hundred gemstones per year. Since

4-1. Green fantasy-cut 14.22 carat tourmaline by Bernd Munsteiner. *(Photograph by Lary Kuehn)*

4-2. Pair of fantasy-cut citrines, 12.61 carats each, by Erhard Jung. *(Photograph by Lary Kuehn)*

the stones are not cut in standard sizes, jewelry mountings must be custom designed to fit the stone's size and aesthetics.

Bernd Munsteiner is the most famous gem cutter in the capital of gemstone cutting, Idar-Oberstein, Germany. He has been called a "cutter's cutter," and is admired because he is a master of traditional cutting techniques as well as a breaker of tradition with his freestyle cutting. "Jewelry should develop to fit the times," he has been quoted as saying. Since 1985, Munsteiner has signed his gemstones with three triangles or the letters BM, either on the girdle of the stone or on one of the facets near the girdle. His signature alone will guarantee that his gemstones will command a higher market price in years to come. For the moment, however, appraisers are as interested in the weight estimation of a set fantasy-cut stone as in authenticating the cutter. What does one do about a formula to estimate weight? A survey of dealers who sell the stones and designers who use the cut in their work failed to turn up any standard formula that would give an accurate estimate of weight.

Gem dealer Lary Kuehn of Dallas is a wholesaler of gems cut by both Jung and Munsteiner. When the formula problem was presented to him, he supposed the best method would be to use the standard formula that would best apply to the stone if it were cut in the normal manner—that is, if it were a rectangle, emerald, oval, or so on. Then, approximately 20 percent should be deducted from that estimated weight. Kuehn cautioned that this "formula" is only a supposition, however: "As far as I know, no formula has been published for fantasy-cut gemstone weight estimation."

Once you can get an estimate of the weight, how do you price these stones? "By keeping in mind the uniqueness of this cutting and the fact that they are all hand cut," Kuehn suggests.

Fantasy-cut gems must be individually valued against work by the same cutter and cannot be compared to the work of other artists or to material of similar color or similar species. Using a per carat basis to calculate this highly specialized form of gemstone art is impossible and will lead to undervalued goods.

A tourmaline of good commercial green color and of about 10 carats in weight normally would sell for three hundred to five hundred dollars per carat wholesale. In comparison, if the same stone, same color, same weight, and same clarity grade were Munsteinercut, it would sell for around five hundred and fifty to seven hundred and seventy-five dollars per carat wholesale.

Ivory

Ivory has been sought after, cut, polished, sold, bartered, and coveted since the earliest times. Ivory jewelry will surely cross your desk from time to time, and your first thought will be: Is it fake or real? Great imitations have existed for decades.

The characteristic crosshatching (sometimes called crossgraining) effect of elephant tusk ivory makes it the easiest ivory to identify. Crosshatching may be difficult to locate on small items, requiring determined examination. Both mammoth and mastodon ivory tusks can still be found in part (figs. 4-3 and 4-4). These ancestors of the modern elephant had ivory tusks varying in color from creamy white to rich dark brown, or sometimes steely gray. Mammoth and mastodon tusks also have a crosshatch line, but much of the ivory found is useless owing to cracking and calcification that have occurred over the years. However, many new jewelry crafters like using this material be-

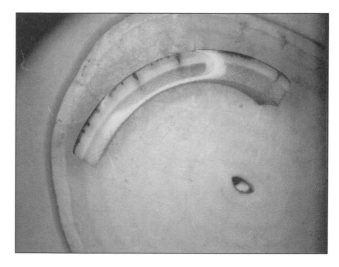

4-3. Small section of mastodon ivory, showing crosshatching and resting on another section of elephant ivory tusk.

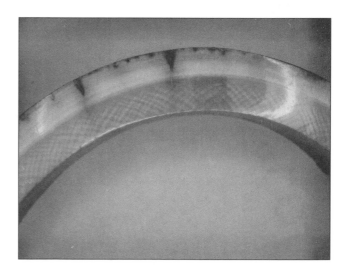

4-4. Close-up view of ivory crosshatching.

cause it is pliable and easily worked. Tusks that have been buried next to phosphate of iron are normally bluish or greenish; this ivory is known as *odontolite*. You may also encounter ivory from other animals such as walrus, whale, boar, shark, bear, elk, camel, beaver, and hippopotamus. Vegetable ivory—not a true ivory but from the ivory palm *Phytelephas macrocarpae*, which produces tagua nuts—handles, cuts, works, and ages in the same manner as animal ivory. Tagua-nut ivory was an especially popular medium for buttons, thimbles, needle cases, bracelets, pendants, belts, and scarf pins in the late 1800s. Factories producing vegetable ivory buttons were established in England and France about 1862 and two years later in Massachusetts. You may find many estate items carved from vegetable ivory.

Shirl Schabilion, gemstone dealer and collector of vegetable ivory, says that tagua-nut ivory can be identified by its distinctive wavy, circular grain, which resembles moire taffeta or watermark silk. Once you see this pattern, you will find it easy to identify vegetable ivory, which is the only ivory that shows this unusual, recognizable pattern.

Animal ivory in mint condition has a mellow, warm, translucent appearance, almost as if it had been soaked in oil. Very little suggestion of grain is seen. Asiatic ivory is a denser white than African ivory, is coarser in texture, and yellows easily. Ivory from Africa is characterized by its translucency and the fact that it bleaches whiter with age.

Inform your client who has ivory that heat is the chief enemy of this material. If your client wants to know how to clean it, recommend the method of swishing in a mild soap-flakes solution and quickly patting it dry.

The factors that govern value in ivory are color, translucency, polish, workmanship, and condition.

Jet

The heyday of the jet jewelry industry was in the 1870s, when two hundred to three hundred miners of jet were employed in the area around Whitby, England. Mining began there in about 1840 and ceased in 1920. Unless antique jewelry appraising is your specialty, you will probably not encounter much jet jewelry.

Jet is a variety of brown coal known as *lignite*. Because of its somber color, the material was used to make mourning jewelry and was popular in the Victorian era. It can be confused with such imitations as vulcanite, bog oak, Bakelite, and black glass, which is also called *French jet*. The conclusive test is a hot needle, which in jet produces a smell of burning coal. A hot needle used on Bakelite will result in a smell of phenol, or carbolic acid; vulcanite tested with a hot needle has the unmistakable smell of burning rubber. Bog oak is a fossilized wood and shows a woody structure; since it is easily identified by sight, testing is not necessary. French jet is also not difficult to identify, since glass is cold to the touch, and both heavier and harder than jet. It cannot be scratched with a pin and a hot needle produces no effect.

The factors that govern value in jet jewelry are as follows:

- The purity of the black color
- The degree of freedom from inclusions of other minerals, especially pyrite and sulphur
- Absence of cracks

- High polish (a dull polish diminishes the value)
- The degree of the jet's density, compactness, and hardness—the more dense, compact, and hard, the more valuable

Jet has been used to produce a variety of jewelry items, including necklaces, bracelets, crosses, pendants, and hair ornaments. Carvings, picture frames, cane heads, and related articles were also made of jet.

Examples of retail prices for assorted jet items are as follows:

- Cross pendant, 4¼″ × ¾,″ circa 1860: $250
- Cross, 2½″ × 4″: $250
- Necklace with carved beads, 12mm, 18″ long: $400
- Necklace, carved 12mm beads, 23″ long: $475
- Necklace, round graduated beads, 27″ long: $300
- Necklace, faceted beads, 19″ long: $400
- Necklace, oval carved beads, 18″ long: $400
- Earrings with 2″ × ¾″ jet dangles, circa 1860: $225
- Earrings with jet dangles having pin shell cameo centers, 2¼″ × 1″: $425
- Locket/pendant, 2″ × 1¾,″ circa 1870: $250
- Bracelet, 8″ long with carved chain links: $275

Coral

Coral has been a popular jewelry medium since antiquity. Its widespread use as a material of personal adornment has been duly noted by such peripatetic adventurers as Marco Polo and Jean-Baptiste Tavernier. Thirteenth-century explorer Marco Polo noted the use of coral for fashioning idols in Asian temples and the popularity of coral has hardly waned through subsequent centuries.

Much coral comes to Japan and Taiwan for processing from the Midway Island area, and some Mediterranean coral is also imported to Taiwan for processing. Mediterranean coral has long been held by experts to be the finest. Modern travelers to Italy will surely bring back jewelry from the coral-cutting center at Torre del Greco near Naples for you to appraise, and you will see this coral in shades from white to deepest red.

Coral is seldom confused with any other material except plastic, and is usually found in either cabochon-cut stones or beads. There are several different shapes of beads indigenous to Italian coral: round; tubular (small cylinder shapes); *spezzati* (small, rough nuggets); *cupolini* (small pieces of straight branch coral); basic nuggets; *fabrica* (large, chunky nuggets); and *frangia* (long, straight, curved pieces of branch coral). These shapes are illustrated in figure 4-5. Fig-

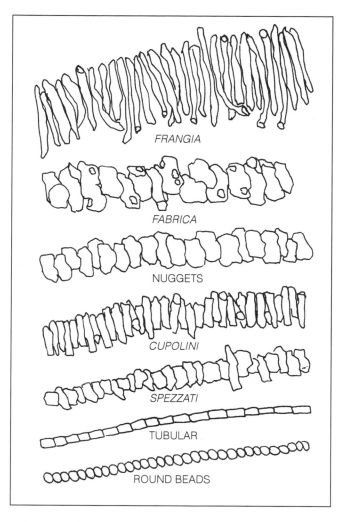

4-5. Assorted shapes of Mediterranean red coral beads.

FRANGIA

FABRICA

NUGGETS

CUPOLINI

SPEZZATI

TUBULAR

ROUND BEADS

4-6. These Italian coral carvings range in color from angel skin to deep oxblood, and vary from ½ inch to 2½ inches in size. *(Photograph courtesy of Timeless Gem Designs)*

ures 4-6 and 4-7 also show products of the Italian coral carver's art.

Color is the main value factor of coral. Oxblood red coral is the most expensive, followed by salmon, angel skin, white, and black coral. Most experts also consider intensity and uniformity of color to be major factors. Cleanliness is another value factor. The material must be compact and free of spots, cracks, inclusions, or holes of any kind. The cleaning of any organic substance such as coral, shell, or mother-of-pearl should be undertaken gently and carefully. Do not use solvent of any kind, as it will attack the material. Instead, use a weak detergent-and-water mixture to remove grime, followed by a careful rinsing.

Coral is often dyed to color enhance it. To detect the presence of dye, use a drop of nail polish remover on a cotton swab and test the underside of the coral. If color comes off on the swab, the coral has been dyed.

4-7. Mediterranean red coral worked by Italian carvers. The carving is 50mm wide and weighs 94 grams. *(Photograph courtesy of Timeless Gem Designs)*

To test for genuine coral, place one drop of a bland acid such as vinegar on the coral carefully. If the coral is genuine, the acid will cause the coral to effervesce.

It should be noted that there are over 300 varieties of coral, and many color variations. *Red* ranges from *orange-red* to *oxblood*. *Pink* ranges from *angel-skin* to *pale pink*. *White* ranges from *white* to a *"touch of pink."* There is a natural gold color coral found in the deep waters off the Hawaiian island of Oahu, first harvested in 1973. A Philippine coral *treated* to a golden color was introduced into the market a few years later. They are seldom seen in the marketplace today.

Coral polish should be excellent. Some traders may mask poor coral by using wax to produce a shine, so be alert. Strands of coral beads should be uniform in bead size, unless the necklace is of graduated beads, and the material should have no holes or blemishes. Bead holes should be drilled directly through the middle of the beads so that they lie on the neck properly. Round bead necklaces are the most expensive of the coral necklace shapes, and vary in price according to color and grade. The wholesale price of some round-bead coral necklaces is as follows:

Red Coral
- 4mm beads, 16″ strand: $60–90
- 6mm beads, 16″ strand: $160–250
- 8mm beads, 16″ strand: $350

Pink Coral
- 4mm beads, 16″ strand: $40–60
- 6mm beads, 16″ strand: $65–90
- 8mm beads, 16″ strand: $125–250

White Coral
- 4mm beads, 16″ strand: $20
- 6mm beads, 16″ strand: $35
- 8mm beads, 16″ strand: $50

Salmon Coral
- 4mm beads, 20″ triple (twisted) strand: $180

Amber

Amber is the condensed sunshine of a pine forest. Some say it is a fragment of eternity, for it is fossilized tree resin thirty to sixty million years old. Amber's warm golden color has been popular since the Stone Age and it has always been an excellent material for beads. Although you will probably see only amber beads to appraise, contemporary jewelry designers are now putting amber to use in rings, bracelets, pendants, and earrings. The material is soft but durable. Caution your customer to handle amber with care and not to wear it in the swimming pool (where chlorine will be present) or put it in an ultrasonic cleaner. To clean amber, wash it with mild soap and water and polish it dry with a soft cloth. Sometimes the luster of amber can be restored by polishing it with a soft cloth saturated in olive oil, then rubbing with a soft cloth to remove the excess oil. Under no circumstances should solvent ever be used to clean amber—solvent can dissolve the soft material. Avoid excessive heat and hot water in cleaning amber.

Amber is very light in weight and always warm to the touch. Colors range from bright "banana" yellow to deep rose.

Amber ranges in clarity from opaque to transparent and is found with or without inclusions. A product known as reconstructed or pressed amber (sometimes called *amberoid*) is made by melting small pieces of amber and compressing them into blocks by hydraulic pressure, usually with the addition of linseed oil. The blocks are then stained in various colors and shaped. Pressed amber turns white when it is old and is less valuable than natural amber.

Antique amber is prized by collectors who enjoy the aged reddish or brownish colors. However, appraisers should be aware that some specimens may not be what they seem and may have been artificially aged by immersion in salt water for several weeks.

Warnings about amber treatments and substitutes were being given as early as the sixth century A.D. Much of the amber jewelry from the late nineteenth and early twentieth centuries is really Bakelite, celluloid, or casein, all synthetic resins. Testing is essential.

The hot needle test is commonly used to distinguish genuine amber from its many plastic imitators. Celluloid beads will emit an odor of camphor, and celluloid may even adhere to the needle point. Bakelite and other plastics will give off an acrid odor when touched with a hot point while genuine amber gives off a "piney" odor. A touch of the hot point to casein will produce the odor of burned milk. In *Amber, Golden Gem of the Ages,* Patty Rice provides a useful clue in distinguishing imitation from genuine beads—examining the bead hole. Since amber is softer than most plastics, Rice says, the constant rubbing of the string in old bead necklaces will eventually erode the amber near the bead hole, and edges will chip as the beads rub together. She claims that even beads made of Bakelite that have been strung for sixty or seventy years or more will still have clean, smooth bead holes.

Genuine Baltic amber is of premium value because of its increasing scarcity. Baltic amber ranges in color from white to near black; most is yellow, gold, or light brown, with clarity varying from transparent to opaque

4-8. Baltic amber from the collection of Reynolds McNear, San Rafael, California. The large amber nugget in the center has an entombed cockroach. *(Photograph courtesy of Reynolds McNear)*

(fig. 4-8). The material takes a higher polish than other amber and is considered to be the finest in the world.

Amber from the Dominican Republic is also of very high quality. This is the amber area where fine and rare fossils are found. For many years, the primary worldwide source of amber was the Baltic region. Today, however, most of the amber in the U.S. comes from the Dominican Republic. Amber is also found in Mexico, Canada, Siberia, and Lebanon.

Amber Imitators

There are many fake pieces of amber in the market. Fakes generally fall into two categories: plastics colored to look like amber, and natural plant resins partially fossilized. Many plastics have insects inserted into the plastic while it is still in a liquid state, but since plastic is heavier than amber it can be separated by using a specific gravity (SG) test. Partially fossilized fakes are called copal. These are sometimes melted with heat on a stove and then have inclusions inserted into them. Since most insects used in fakes are large, the SG test will not differentiate between amber and copal. However, a solvent test is effective. Put several drops of 95% ethanol alcohol or acetone on a small surface of the item and leave for 20 seconds or until the solvent has nearly evaporated. If the surface is sticky when touched with a finger, the piece is copal and not amber. Copal is softer than amber and melts more easily. It does not take a high gloss polish.

Ambroid: Pressed or Reconstituted Amber

Small quality pieces of natural amber can be fused together under pressure in a vacuum. The semi-solid resin is extruded into cylinders of pressed or reconstituted amber. Beads can be made directly in a mold and many of the faceted amber necklaces seen today are produced in this manner. Reconstituted amber is stronger than natural because minute fractures or flaws inherent in the material have been eliminated. Although slightly heavier, the refractive index is the same as natural amber. Modern techniques have enabled processors to induce the "sun spangle" inclusions that formerly were a sign of natural amber. Sun spangles, also called fish scales, spores, etc., are enclosed air bubbles that have been forced by heat and pressure into iridescent discs. So far, the Dominican Republic amber has not been subjected to this process.

Inclusions in amber are a matter of personal preference. Some amber dealers believe that organic inclusions, such as leaves or insects, add value to the amber, especially if the inclusion is exactly centered in the material. If the appraiser has such material to value, using individual comparables priced in the current wholesale market is the only logical approach. Value factors for amber include color—fine golden and translucent reds are the most valuable—size, transparency, intensity of color, and flawlessness, or conversely, exceptional inclusions.

Reynolds and McNear, two amber dealers based in San Rafael, California, list the following wholesale prices in their catalog:

- Clear flat beads, graduated, 32″ long with gold plated clasp: $225.00
- Baroque polished beads, graduated, 24″ with 14K clasp: $97.50
- Flat beads, various colors and sizes, 28–55″ long: $90–190
- Faceted graduated beads, 28–30″ long with 14K gold clasp: $275.00
- Hand-faceted beads, 24″ strand: $200–250 (prices vary according to quality)
- Graduated small free-form beads, 24″ with gold-filled clasp: $50.00
- Semi-polished varicolored beads, 28″ long: $100–140
- Round beads, hand shaped, 26″ long stand: $75–200 (price varies with bead size)
- Light color large round beads, 30–32″ long with 14K clasp: $200–250
- Baroque opaque beads, 24–28″: $60–75.00
- Baroque, graduated polished beads, 24″ with gold-filled clasp: $87.50
- Clear square beads, 25–26″ with gold-filled clasp: $60.00
- Long rectangular beads, opaque, 25″ with gold-filled clasp: $60.00

- Rough chips, graduated, 25–28″: $8–10.00
- Heart-shaped amber pendant: $10–14.00
- Teardrop and freeform amber pieces for pendant: $8–14.00
- Amber with insect inclusions: $10–80.00

Opal

Appraising opal has never been easier. Especially since Dr. Paul Downing put his book *Opal Identification & Value* on the market in 1992. Downing wrote the book to provide appraisers with necessary information to identify all the relevant characteristics of any particular opal, then use those characteristics to estimate value. The information is concise and easy to follow. Although previous attempts have been made to establish guidelines for determining opal prices, they have been unsuccessful because of the gem's infinite variation in color pattern. There is no governing body to set the prices for opal; prices are the result of what the international market is prepared to pay in order to obtain the gem, simply supply and demand. For appraisers, the question of value is what keeps them in business, and it is not an easy question to answer when the subject is opals. Because opal is such a distinctive gemstone, there is no *one-price-fits-all* system. There must be diligent research because of multi levels of market; the *retail* price paid at a gem and mineral show may be different from the *retail* price paid in a fine jewelry store. *Demand* is connected to the consumer who is influenced by fashion and market trends. And even though the client may be vocalizing "What is the value?" he or she is more likely to be asking "How much would an equivalent stone sell for?"

Pricing opals mounted or loose is a challenge to most appraisers. In the U.S. fine quality opal costs less than the top four gems (diamonds, emeralds, rubies, and sapphires) and is sold on a per piece or per carat basis. Because most consumers do not think of opal in the same emotionally charged way they think of diamonds or rubies, dealers importing opal into the U.S. usually stick to three types: small, calibrated, mostly white cabochons with little play-of-color, doublets, and triplets. In his book *Opals,* author Fred Ward, G.G., says: "The majority of U.S. opal buyers usually are not shopping at the high end of the market. They may not even be aware a high-end opal market exists. Almost all the best *black* opal goes to Japan and other Asian countries."

There are new finds of opal being made regularly. The latest mining claims are in British Columbia, the United States, and Ethiopia, one of the newest opal finds. The Ethiopian mine is accessible only by mule or foot, and opal is currently mined with hand tools. Telahun Yohannes, minerals engineer, is the president of Ethio-American Resource Development, the company that oversees the mine. Paul Downing has called the new find "fantastic," and Dr. Gary B. Schneider, a geologist/gemologist/appraiser has estimated $200–800 per carat for cabochon-cut stones with good fire, shape, weight, and finish.

There are a number of factors that influence opal values. According to Dr. Paul Downing, price is determined by analyzing the following:

1. *Type of Opal.* Solid, boulder, matrix, treated, dyed, man-man, assembled, simulated
2. *Base Color.* Color or tone of the base: black, gray, white, orange, etc.
3. *Clarity.* Is it transparent, translucent, semi-crystal, opaque?
4. *Brightness.* What is the amount of refracted light returning to the eye?
5. *Weight.* What is the carat weight of the stone? Stones under 1 carat are less per carat than those over 1 carat. Stones over 15 carats are less per carat than those under 15 carats. Addressing a group of appraisers recently, Downing said it was necessary to decide how much weight to give all the above elements. "While most opal experts agree with the list of factors, *none* agree completely on the degree to which each influences market value." He continued, "influence depends upon the market being assessed. For example, red multicolor is the most preferred in the U.S., while green/blue is the favorite in Japan."

Synthetic Opal

What about synthetic opal? Downing cautions appraisers that the Gilson opal and several synthetics look so good now many cannot distinguish between them and natural. "Especially," Downing says, "those stones under a carat size. You used to be able to make a distinction between synthetic opals and natural opals by the snakeskin characteristic of the synthetics—not anymore." According to Downing there is no simple instrument used by gemologists that will make the separation between synthetic and natural. Downing suggests sending stones that need positive identification to a lab with an infrared spectroscopy (FTIR). At the present time, GIA laboratory has an FTIR to distinguish between natural and synthetic opal.

Care of Opals

Clients who have opals will ask you whether they should soak the stones to keep them from cracking.

There are several theories regarding the storage of opals, including soaking them in water, mineral oil, or glycerin, but none has been proven effective and the techniques may even damage the stones. *Neither oiling nor storing in water prevents cracking or crazing.* The water in some localities contains harsh minerals that may react and discolor opal after several weeks, and opal kept in mineral oil or glycerin will develop a hard-to-remove film of grease. Avoid ultrasonic cleaners, steamers, bleach, and chemicals of all types. Clean opal gently with plain warm water (no soap) and dry carefully with a soft cloth.

When describing opal in the appraisal report, note the predominant color of the opal, the background color, other colors that are visible, and distribution as well as intensity of opal colors. In addition, use a penlight, shining the light through the stone from the back, to examine for cracks and flaws.

Jade

The name "jade" is a collective term used to describe two separate minerals: nephrite and jadeite. In the market both are called *jade.* Nephrite has the longest historical association, while jadeite offers the most popular emerald-green colors. To the Chinese jade is a gem more precious than gold or any other stone. The earliest jade for Chinese carvers came from a mine near Khotan, in eastern Turkestan. Dark green nephrite that occurs near Lake Baikal in Siberia is found not far from the original tribal lands of Genghis Khan. Nephrite is fibrous and usually a spinach-green color, often with flecks of black. *Black jade* is actually *chloromelanite,* rich in iron and if viewed with high intensity lighting will be seen to be dark green. Stone Age people used nephrite to carve tools and weapons because of its great strength and toughness. Valuing nephrite is as much an art as science. Instead of being sold by the carat like most gemstones, both nephrite and jadeite are sold by the piece. In their finer qualities, jadeite can be among the most expensive stones in the world. However, modern mined and worked nephrite is of low value, and the finest nephrite cabochons rarely exceed a few hundred dollars. There is no scarcity of nephrite, and this is reflected in the price. The most valuable nephrite jade is *white* in color with *good translucency.* Because of the disparity in prices between nephrite and jadeite, it is recommended appraisers identify the material on the appraisal document not simply as jade, but specify if it is nephrite or jadeite. Jadeite from Burma was introduced into China around the mid-18th century and quickly supplanted nephrite in demand. Although

4-9. Burma is the sole source of fine jadeite, but Hong Kong is the place most often thought of as the center of the jade market. Hong Kong has hundreds of jade workshops turning out a steady stream of jade objects from artistically made to tourist junk.

Burma is the sole source of fine jadeite, and Thailand its prime entry point into the market, Hong Kong is the place most often thought of as the center of the jade marketplace (fig. 4-9). The chief value element in jadeite is color. The best stones have what Edmond Chin, Director of Christie's Hong Kong jewelry department, calls a "thick gooey green." Fine jadeite has also been described as "viscous," with the color likened to Palmolive dishwashing liquid. As stones get lighter, the color becomes more glassy.

Appraising Jadeite: Color
The most valuable colors of *jadeite* are green, lavender, red, yellow, and white. For valuation purposes one pure color is best, but combinations such as green and lavender, red and green, or white with green are all desirable. In all cases except white, the degree of translucence increases the value, while a lack of translucence lowers value. Mr. Don Kay, jade expert at Mason-Kay Company in Denver, Colorado, lectures to many industry groups about jade. He makes this important point on the way that color affects jade value: "A piece of jadeite with good color and fair translucency is valuable. But, a *colorless* piece of jadeite with excellent *transparency* is worth far less."

Transparency
In the United States, material with fissures, i.e., cabochons, bangles, and beads of good commercial color, can command a reasonable price *despite* the fis-

sures. In contrast, in Asia commercial color jades with fissures are *rejection* materials. Jadeite ranges from transparent to opaque. The best and most expensive has a translucent body color that resembles honey. Although jadeite cannot be as transparent as the best quality emerald, the highest possible transparency is more highly valued. To achieve a top price color zoning must be minimal.

Texture

The texture of jade ranges from fine to coarse and can be examined with magnification. The best texture is smooth and uniform, free from cracks and inclusions. These features are best viewed holding the jade against a light, or placed over a small light—such as a penlight—and observed by transmitted light. Logic affirms that a fine textured piece of jade with a high luster and good polish will command a higher market price.

Size

There is no simple formula to relate size of jadeite to price. Fine cabochons are number one on the list of desirable jade pieces. Well-cut cabochons with a smooth uniform curvatures free from humps and dips, with fine color, can be very expensive. Carved jade is not as valuable as a smooth piece because of the trade practice that a piece of jade is carved to remove/hide flaws and carving is done for marketing purposes. Don Kay affirms this market practice: "Smooth, uncarved pieces are more valuable than worked pieces of the same size and quality." According to Kay, fewer beads and bangles of jadeite are being cut today because of the huge waste of material during cutting. "When cutting beads," Kay says, "you have approximately 50% waste." The value of a pair of fine jadeite bangle bracelets is worth more than twice the price of one bracelet. And, the more colors in a bangle bracelet, the higher the price. Today in Hong Kong, bracelets are being made in ½" widths, which is wider than those made in the past. Higher values are also given to bangle bracelets, jadeite drop earrings, chained items, and matched pairs and suites because of the waste of materials in cutting. Color-matched pieces of jewelry, such as matched pairs or multiple matched pieces, should be priced 35 percent or more higher, even though the shapes may not be identical. Pricing of jade has been made even more difficult with the introduction of "B" jade. "B" jade quietly came into the market in the 1980s, but quickly produced a major turmoil. The industry could not distinguish between the treated and dyed jades which were named "A," "B," and "C" jadeite.

Jade ABC's

"A" jadeite is jade that is not enhanced. This is jadeite in its natural color and completely untreated except for surface waxing.

"B" jadeite is a process that originated in Hong Kong and refers to jadeite that has been subjected to a two-step process of *bleaching* and *polymer impregnation*.

"C" means dyed jadeite that is usually combined with either "A" or "B" jade.

In the past few years bleached jadeite has caused problems for the jewelers and appraisers. How can the average appraiser distinguish between the "A" and "B" jade? Even though GIA has detailed some basic techniques for identifying "B" jade, some of the recommendations, such as use of specific gravity and examination under long-wave ultraviolet lights, *do not work*. Currently, the most conclusive identification between natural colored jadeite and bleached polymer-impregnated jadeite is made with a Fourier-Transform Infrared Spectroscopy (FTIR) (fig. 4-10).

The FTIR machinery is expensive, and thus far in the United States there are only two units being used in the jewelry trade. GIA has one, and jadeite specialists Mason-Kay the other. At this writing, Mason-Kay is the only jade supplier in the United States who can certify their products as natural color, unbleached, without polymer impregnation. Several labs in Hong

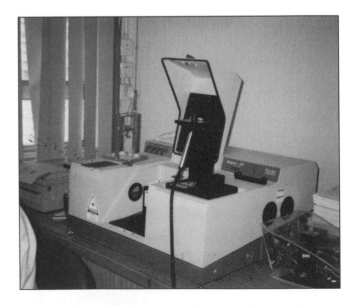

4-10. At this writing, the Fourier-Transform Infrared Spectroscope (FTIR) is the only sure method for detecting bleached and polymer-impregnated jadeite. In Hong Kong, the Hong Kong Jade & Stone Manufacturers Association has a respected laboratory for issuing certificates identifying "A" and "B" jadeite. GIA in California and Mason-Kay Company in Denver also have the FTIR.

Kong and the Far East Gemological Laboratory in Singapore have invested in the costly FTIR machine in order to issue certificates to the trade. The certificates are based upon conclusive results with the infrared spectroscope and a jade item.

What does the infrared spectroscope show? That absorption peaks around 3,000cm in the infrared region of the electromagnetic spectrum offer conclusive proof of polymer-impregnated "B" jade. Further, the mere presence of polymer in jadeite implies that the jadeite has been bleached before impregnation.

Gemstone scientists Tay Thye Sun, S. Paul, and Dr. C. M. Puah of Singapore have written a scholarly, detailed, comprehensive article about test results using a *Scanning Electron Microscope (SEM)* to distinguish natural jadeite from "B" bleached polymer-impregnated jadeite. The article appeared in the *Australian Gemmologist* magazine, Third Quarter, 1996 edition. Data from a battery of tests suggests that the Scanning Electron Microscope can be used to effectively distinguish bleached polymer-impregnated jadeite from natural colored jadeite. However, the SEM equipment is rare, difficult to use, and prohibitively expensive.

Identifying bleached and polymer-impregnated jadeite is a question that will not go away. Separating natural from bleached and impregnated jadeite—easily and conclusively—is destined to become the big buying and selling issue of the next decade (fig. 4-11). Don Kay, lecturing to gemologists/appraisers makes this comment: "The *majority* of jade pieces seen on the market today are "B" jades." Caveat appraiser!

4-11. In the Hong Kong Jade Market, most vendors display a sign like the one pictured that says: "Natural Genuine Burma Jade—No Chemical & Color Treatment." Regardless of the sign, the majority of the pieces in the jade market are "B" jade.

Appraising Jadeite

From an appraiser's point of view, the three most important elements in a jade stone are color, translucency, and uniformity of color. A fine color without translucency can bring a high price, but high translucency without body color has little value. To achieve a top price, "zoning" of color must be minimal. Jade is not sold by the carat, but by the piece. Jadeite is rarely cut in standard sizes and asymmetrical cabochons are common. Occasionally the appraiser will notice grooves under cabochons or on the flat backs behind carved jades. These grooves indicate that the piece had a previous, specialized use (for instance as a bead). Fine jade is site specific: jewelry quality jadeite jade comes from Burma and Guatemala. Nephrite, the more common form of jade, is mined in Alaska, Russia, Taiwan, Australia, and other sites.

How can the appraiser be sure what is seen is natural jadeite and not "B" jade? Some anecdotal results of direct observation are supplied by Don Kay, who reminds that scientific certainty only comes from infrared spectroscopy.

1. With magnification:
     Polymer flow can sometimes be seen
     Floating platelets
     Concentration of the impregnating substances can sometimes be seen in the fractures and cavities
2. A hot point tester used on a surface point will emit a distinctive odor if the piece is "B" jade.
3. Examine a strand of beads near the drill holes for evidence of polymer-impregnation, obvious near sharp edges.
4. When "B" jade is struck by a metal rod, or another piece of jade, the sound emitted is not as clear or high pitched as pure jade. This is most evident in one-piece bangle bracelets.

For the appraiser valuing jade, it is recommended that *extensive, diligent research* be employed. Market research is the key to writing an accurate appraisal document with a justifiable estimate of value. Don Kay has compiled the following charts (tables 4-2, 4-3, and 4-4) as *guideposts* to aid in valuation.

Wholesale prices for "A" jadeite items (natural color, completely untreated). Jadeite prices change regularly. The following prices are not definitive, but should be viewed as a starting point in research of this important market:

Fine Green 6 carved cabochons bracelet, 14K Chinese character separators: $985

Fine Green bangle bracelet, intense green with some lavender: $12,500

Table 4-2. Appraiser Quick Reference for Appraising Jadeite Cabochons

IF the stone is:	Add	No Effect	Subtract
Translucent	X		
Oval		X	
Round		X	
Marquise			X
Pear shaped			X
One-piece saddle	X		
Carved			X
Flat, rectangular			X
<2mm thick			X
>6mm thick	X		
<8×6mm			X

Table 4-3. Appraiser Quick Reference when Appraising Carvings

IF the carving is:	Add	No Effect	Subtract
High quality	X		
Good "use" of material	X		
<3mm thick			X
Visible internal fractures			X
Surface-breaking fractures			X
One consistent color	X		
Two or more mixed colors		X	
Two or more well-defined colors (depends on relative color strength)	X		
Carving subject matter		X	

Table 4-4. Appraiser Quick Reference to Appraising Bangles

IF the jade is:	Add	No Effect	Subtract
One piece, unhinged	X		
Two piece, hinged		X	
Three or more pieces			X
Carved			X
Translucent	X		
Visible internal fractures			X
Surface breaking fractures			X
One consistent color	X		
Two or more mixed colors		X	
Two or more well-defined colors (depends on the relative color strength)	X		
Not round cross-section		X	

Charts compiled by Don Kay, Mason-Kay, reprinted with permission

Fine Green carved wings and 14K yellow gold butterfly brooch: $1,600

Lavender jadeite earrings with cabs bezel set in 14K yellow gold: $600

Intense Lavender bangle bracelet: $1,375

Commercial Green Jade strand of beads, 8mm, 17" long, 14K clasp: $390

Commercial Green jade, small cabochon 8x6mm, set in 14K lady's ring: $330

Multicolor jadeite beads with 14K clasp; 6mm beads, 17" long: $175

Multicolor jadeite cabochon earrings & 14K yellow gold mountings: $160

Pearls

Many factors combine to stimulate consumer interest in pearls, primarily fashion. Pearls are either in fashion or in decline. The popularity of pearls has never been higher than it is today, with their classic beauty and new range of sizes and shapes on the market. This is an area of expertise where the appraiser will have many opportunities to invoke his or her special training in pearl evaluation.

When grading cultured pearls, the appraiser needs a standard by which comparisons can be made. Pearl-grading masters, developed by Gemworld International, Inc., and International Cultured Pearls of the Orient, Inc., are offered through Gemological Institute of America Gem Instruments. In grading round cultured pearls (Japanese akoya) there are several factors to consider: (1) Size, (2) Color, (3) Shape, (4) Luster, (5) Nacre, (6) Blemishes, and (7) Matching.

Size

The Japanese akoya cultured pearl is produced up to 10mm in size. There may be a ½mm tolerance in size for matching strands. Therefore an 8½mm strand will consist of pearls from 8 to 8½mm. The more exact the size match, the smaller the mm tolerance. Prices rise sharply for each 1mm change in size, especially over 7mm. The most popular size of cultured pearls in the United States are from 6½ to 8mm.

- Choker: 14"–16" long
- Princess: 17"–18" long
- Matinee: 20"–24" long
- Opera: 28"–30" long
- Bib: Necklace with more than three strands
- Rope (lariat, sautoir): 45" and longer

Pearl necklaces are either in graduated size, in which the smaller pearls are close to the clasp and the largest pearls are at the center, or in uniform size, in which all are equal in size. The unit of measure for pearls is *momme:* 18.75 carats (3.75 grams) = 1 *momme.*

Color

This is a matter of personal preference, but most of the world's pearl fanciers like a pearl with a slight rose cast. Color is regarded in two components: body color and overtone. There are four basic body colors: silver-white, cream, pink, and yellow. Overtones on cultured pearls can be rose or green and sometimes bluish or purplish. The overtones on pearls are like blush powder on a woman's face; they affect the surface color. Rose is the most common overtone. With the exception of black pearls, the more rose overtone color present, the higher the pearl value. The more green overtone present, the lower the value. There may also be combinations of overtone or no overtone at all. While many appraisers believe color is the number one value element (as it is in colored gemstones), luster and nacre thickness have a greater effect on price.

Pearls are graded for color on a white background. North daylight is the ideal grading light, but overhead fluorescent lighting will do. Never grade pearls under incandescent light. If there are golden pearls to appraise, notice that a top gold-color pearl looks a lot like 22K or 24K gold. Yellow pearls range in color from a "melted butter" look to the hue of a legal-size yellow tablet. Beware of pearls that have been dyed bright colors: inspect both cultured and freshwater pearls for signs of dye. Cream-colored, green, and yellow pearls are often dyed to look rose. Investigate the pearl drill hole and if the pearls have been dyed, the drill holes may appear unnaturally red. Similarly, the string may look slightly pink if the pearls have been dyed.

Shape

One of the most important elements in judging salt water cultured pearls is roundness. The rounder, the better. Any sign of elongation reduces the price of the pearl. Irregularly shaped pearls, often called baroques, are judged by different factors. There may be a variety of reasons for the irregular shape. The shape can be influenced by blemishes, irritants, trapped gas, filled cavities, hollow cavities, and more. Most baroques have tails that often chip when drilled. Chipping devalues the pearl.

Luster

The pearl should have luster, which makes it shine like a mirrored ball. To determine luster, the appraiser should look at the pearl by the light of an overhead fluorescent light.

On a pearl with high luster, the light will appear as a thin, curved line. On low-luster pearls, the light will look fuzzier and more diffused. Luster and nacre are related because pearls with a thick nacre can be finished to a higher luster. Luster is also dependent upon the transparency and conditions under which the pearls are cultivated. The colder the water, the slower the nacre grows with the result a finer-grained nacre, more transparent, and taking a higher polish with higher luster. When evaluating a strand of cultured pearls, note the age of the pearls and age-related effect on appearance. Luster and nacre are related because pearls with a thick nacre can be finished to a higher luster. However, older pearls oxidize over time and lose some luster. A strand with thick nacre and low luster probably had a much higher luster when it was new; therefore, to compensate in replacement, figure the cost of a new *equally thick nacre* pearl strand, and do not be misguided by the low luster.

Nacre

According to GIA, nacre thickness is the most difficult category to judge in cultured pearl grading and appraising. The standard method is to rotate the strand near a light source and observe to what extent a blinking effect occurs, and to look down the bead hole for a cross view of the nacre. An ideal nacre thickness is ½mm on each side. The mother-of-pearl bead is about 60 percent of the production. To see the nacre, use a jeweler's loupe and tilt the pearl so that the drill hole is angled at between 12 o'clock and 2 o'clock placement. The nacre deposit appears as light colored and somewhat transparent. The Japanese akoya take approximately two years of cultivation to have thick nacre accretion.

Blemishes (Cleanliness, Spotting)

Blemishes in cultured pearls, as with other gems, reduce value. When judging blemishes on cultured pearls use the unaided eye only. Rotate the pearls looking in all directions for cracks, spots, blotches, and what is called an "orange peel" effect.

Matching

This is an evaluation of how well individual pearls match in the entire strand. They may be well matched or mismatched. Cultured pearl manufacturers generally attempt to match pearls with the same size, color, shape, luster, nacre, and blemishes; however, the appraiser must observe carefully. Some companies make a practice of stringing good and poor pearls together in an effort to make the strand look finer than it is. Inspect each pearl, especially those on each end of the strand.

South Sea Pearls

Pearl imports rose 140 percent in the 1996–1997 period over past years, with no slackening demand in sight. The reason for the record imports and sales is due to South Sea pearls. The hottest thing in South Sea pearls today is the natural color Tahitian black. Moshe Kaufman, whose family L. Kaufman & Sons, New York, has been in the South Sea pearl business for over thirty years, offers this comment: "Tahitian black pearls are selling very well. Sizes over 13mm in better quality remain very strong and the price is stable. There is *always* a demand for very fine quality black South Sea pearls in big sizes. And, the question of color—natural or dyed—does not seem to be an issue." A few years ago, black pearls were suspect of being dyed. Kaufman says there are so many Tahitian natural black pearls on the market today that it costs more to dye a black pearl than it does to buy a black pearl. Is there a Tahitian white South Sea pearl? "Yes," says Kaufman, "but they are light grayish, and not like the silvery-white Australian pearls."

When valuing South Sea pearls, use the same criteria used to value Japanese cultured salt water pearls, but keep in mind that blemish-free South Sea pearls are very rare gems. A Tahitian necklace with 10×13mm pearls is in the wholesale range $15–25,000.

Once the pearls become baroque or off-shape, the price falls sharply. As to a valuation formula on South Sea pearls, Kaufman says: "You *cannot* take measurements of a pearl at the end and in the middle of a necklace to average them out for an estimate of value. If some pearls at the end of the strand are 11mm, with a 15mm center pearl, you cannot multiply by the average 33 pearls (in a strand) to figure the cost of the necklace. There is *no comparison* of the price between an 11mm pearl and the 15mm pearl of the same quality. For example, an 11mm pearl may be about $2,000, and the same quality in a 15mm $8–9,000." Valuing South Sea pearls is a research project for the appraiser, who needs plenty of documentation to back up his or her estimate of value.

Burma used to be the locale of the finest South Sea pearls, but today Australia, Indonesia, and the Philippines are quantity producers. Australia is producing very high quality white and golden color South Sea pearls; while the white and golden pearls out of Indonesia and the Philippines tend to have a lower dull luster, creamy color, and greenish overtones. Golden South Sea pearls are hot, according to Kaufman. But he warns appraisers, "If you don't have experience with them, don't attempt to put a price on them because you will never be accurate. There are a lot of shades of color. A necklace 11–13mm of fine golden pearls may wholesale $50–80,000. Yet that same neck-

4-12. Australian white South Sea pearl necklace from L. Kaufman & Sons, New York City. This fine necklace, 17″ long, has 14×17½mm well-matched pearls with a minimum of size difference. (*Photo courtesy L. Kaufman & Sons, Inc.*)

lace two shades off color, slightly brown or green will be less than half that price." The same holds true for prices between Australian white pearls and Tahitian white pearls. For example, an 11mm fine quality Australian pearl may be priced at $1,000 but a Tahitian white of equal quality may only be $700.

South Sea pearls grow to be quite large, generally from 12mm to 14mm. The 16mm–17mm South Sea pearls are so rare that it is almost impossible to have a necklace containing only pearls of this size. Graduated strands may have a 2–3mm difference in size from the center pearl to the ends of the strand. The typical South Sea pearl necklace is 18 inches long (fig. 4-12).

Natural Pearls

Natural pearls are rare and becoming more rare with each passing decade, given the pollution of the world's waters and other factors. To appreciate the rarity and exceptional value of fine natural pearls, consider that their equivalent in value is a strand of perfectly matched fine Burmese natural rubies. At the peak of their popularity between 1895 and 1930, a strand of natural pearls could cost as much as 1.5 million dollars. American natural pearls were as treasured as those from the Orient, and in the early 1920s, Tiffany's assembled two necklaces that sold for over a million dollars each, and a hundred that sold in the range of a hundred thousand dollars each. If you have natural pearls (verified as such by X-ray) and are trying to get some idea of current pricing, research the major auction house catalogs. Natural pearls appear with some frequency in their jewelry catalogs. In October 1983, Christie's sold a short choker of natural pearls, graduated in size from 10.2mm to 15.2mm at the center, for three hundred seventy-four thousand dollars. They had estimated the sale price to range from two hundred and twenty thousand to two hundred and forty thousand dollars. A pair of natural pearl button earrings sold at Sotheby's in 1985 for two thousand eight hundred and sixty dollars.

Although all natural pearls have, by industry tradition, been called *Oriental* pearls, the Federal Trade Commission has narrowed the definition and ruled that only natural pearls fished from the Persian Gulf can rightfully be called Oriental.

Freshwater Cultured Pearls

These can be divided into three categories: Biwa, Chinese, and American. The mantle tissue (irritant) of freshwater cultured pearls is 95 percent of the final product. How are they different from saltwater cultured pearls? Colors are light, medium, and dark orange, purple, lavender, violet, and multihued. Many freshwater pearls are iridescent and might be baroque, flat, or elongated instead of round. There are usually low-luster areas on portions of the pearls. Most are sold on the basis of weight alone. The majority are from Lake Biwa, Japan, and have fullness, sheen, and texture on all sides of the pearl. The average Chinese freshwater pearls are domed, have a flat bottom, and an irregular sheen and texture. This devalues them since it is impossible to conceal irregularities while wearing them. To evaluate the quality of the pearls, lay them on white tissue paper. The paper will provide sufficient contrast to define color and luster.

There are two American freshwater-pearl farms in Tennessee, and growers are making plans for farms in other states. Harvests have been limited, but growers remain enthusiastic about future yields.

Chinese Round Akoya Cultured Pearls

Chinese cultured round white pearls are in competition with the Japanese akoya cultured pearl. However, with the help of Japanese technicians, the Chinese are now in the cultured round pearl business while continuing to produce freshwater rice pearls, Keshi or seed pearls, and potato pearls. Although the akoya oyster is being used in China, there is a major difference between farming Japanese and Chinese akoya pearls: the water they grow in. Chinese round pearls do not have the luster of the Japanese pearls because growing in cold water is what gives them a fine sheen. Chinese waters are warm the majority of the time. Although Chinese pearls have a thick nacre and good color, luster in the Japanese pearls is better. Moshe Kaufman says that the most popular size strand of 6–6½mm Chinese round pearls sells for about $450–650 (wholesale) per strand. "Basically they are producing 4mm to 6.5mm and fine 6.5–7mm pearls in nice qualities. Exports *will* increase in the next few years and we will see many 4–5–6mm necklaces *mixed* with Chinese and Japanese pearls. When you combine the *best* of the Chinese round pearls with *medium-to-better* commercial quality Japanese, they are almost impossible to tell apart. Does it matter if a pearl is Chinese or a mixture? No, It does not matter. Although the Chinese pearls are less expensive than the Japanese, your eye cannot tell the difference in the top quality when all pearls are perfectly round, and currently there is no instrumentation to distinguish between them."

Chinese Freshwater Pearls

All is not well in Chinese fresh water pearl production. Lois H. Berger, G.G., Fuller & Associates, Washington, D.C., made an extensive survey of the pearl market at the Tucson Gem Show in February 1997 and had this to say about what she found: "I was surprised to see mountains of dull, chalk-like, poor quality pearls in all sizes being presented for sale. In conversations with the dealers, I was told that due to liberalization of imports and exports in China in 1994, there had been an increase in the number of pearl farms and trading companies. These companies operate for immediate profit and return on investment, harvesting their pearls after *six months* of cultivation." In 1995 a dumping of low quality pearls onto the market forced many pearl farmers into bankruptcy. According to one dealer, dumping was an attempt to sell poorer quality goods cheaply in order to generate revenues to reinvest in pearl farming.

Chinese freshwater pearls have natural colors, including orange, salmon, lavender, and mauve—many with overtones of bronze, peach, pink, and apricot. However, colors such as peach and lavender fade in sunlight. Chinese off-round freshwater pearls are available in white, light lavender, orange-pink, orange, peach, peacock, bronze-peacock, and silver. Berger says that only about 10–15% of white pearls are natural colored with the majority of off-white pearls bleached with peroxide. "The peroxide treatment creates a dull chalky white look and you can smell the peroxide," Berger said and added, "If a pearl has an unpopular color, it will be dyed or irradiated, yielding an unnatural color not found in nature."

During extensive research into the Chinese freshwater pearl market, Berger compiled several charts (tables 4-5 through 4-8) representing thousands of strands of the current Chinese production.

Prices quoted on the charts reflect wholesale cost of a single 16″ temporary strand with no knots. If a discount is noted, it should be deducted from the listed price. All prices are negotiable and quantity buying merits discounted prices. The method used for grading was Richard Drucker's Akoya Cultured Pearl Grading System (now GIA Gem PearlMaster) adapted for freshwater pearl comparison.

Table 4-5. Shape: Off-Round. Compiled by Lois H. Berger, G.G. Prices are in U.S. Dollars.

Size	Color	Shape	Luster	Blemishes	Matching	Price $	Comment
4.5–5mm	White	Off-round	High	Unblemished	Very good	10	25% off price
4.5–5mm	White	Off-round	High	Unblemished	Excellent	18	
5–5.5mm	White	Off-round	High	Unblemished	Excellent	5	
5–5.5mm	White	Off-round	High	Unblemished	Excellent	20	Beautiful
5–5.5mm	White	Off-round	High	Unblemished	Excellent	25	
5–5.5mm	White	Off-round	High	Unblemished	Excellent	35	
6mm	White	Off-round	Medium	Unblemished	Very good	40	25% off price
5mm	Lt. lavender	Off-round	Very high	Very sl. blem.	Very good	18	Excellent buy
5mm	Orange-pink	Off-round	Very high	Very sl. blem.	VV good	28	
5.5mm	Orange	Off-round	Very high	VV sl. blem.	VV good	40	Beautiful
6mm	Peach	Off-round	Very high	VV sl. blem.	VV good	38	
6mm	Lt. peach	Off-round	Very high	VV sl. blem.	Very good	60	
6mm	Peacock	Off-round	Very high	Very sl. blem.	Very good	65	
7 mm	Bronze-Peacock	Off-round	Very high	Very sl. blem.	Very good	85	
7–7.5mm	Peach	Off-round	High	Slightly blem.	Good	85	
7–8mm	Lt. mauve	Off-round	High	Slightly blem.	Good	125	Mauve variations
8mm	Silver	Off-round	High	Slightly blem.	Fair	25	
9–9.5mm	Peach	Off-round	Low-medium	Slightly blem.	Good	450	

Table 4-6. Shape: Rice. Compiled by Lois H. Berger, G.G. Prices are in U.S. Dollars.

Size	Color	Shape	Luster	Blemishes	Matching	Price $	Comment
3–3.5mm	White	Rice: long drilled	Low	Very blemished	Poor	0.25	Rice Crispies
3–3.5mm	White	Rice: long drilled	High	Unblemished	Very good	5.75	
3.5–4mm	White	Rice: long drilled	High	Slightly blem.	Very good	5.5	Sl. banding
4–4.5mm	White	Rice: long drilled	High	Very sl. blem.	Very good	4.5	
4.5–5mm	White	Rice: long drilled	Medium high	Blemished	Good	4	25% off
5–5.5mm	White	Rice: long drilled	High	Slightly blem.	Very good	5	
5–5.5mm	White	Rice: long drilled	High	Blemished	Good	3	
5.5–6mm	White	Rice: long drilled	Very high	Unblemished	Excellent	12.5	
5.5–6mm	White	Rice: long drilled	High	Blemished	Good	7.5	
6.5–7mm	White	Rice: long drilled	Medium	Slightly blem.	Good	14	25% off
7–8mm	White	Rice: long drilled	High	Very blemished	Good	28	
7–8.5mm	White	Rice: long drilled	High	Very sl. blem.	Excellent	80	
7–7–8mm	White	Rice: long drilled	High	Very sl. blem.	Excellent	120	
7–8.5mm	White	Rice: long drilled	High	Very sl. blem.	Very good	90	
8–9mm	White	Rice: long drilled	High	Slightly blem.	Very good	440	Sl. banding
8–10mm	White	Rice: long drilled	Low	Very blemished	Very poor	16	V heavy banding
8–11mm	White	Rice: long drilled	Low	Very blemished	Very poor	20	Heavy banding
8–11mm	White	Rice: long drilled	Medium	Very blemished	Poor	24	
8.5–9.5mm	White	Rice: long drilled	Low	Very blemished	Poor	20	V heavy banding
9.5–13mm	White	Rice: long drilled	Low medium	Very blemished	Poor	80	Heavy banding
9.5–15mm	White	Rice: long drilled	Medium	Slightly blem.	Poor	28	

Table 4-7. Shape: Potato. Compiled by Lois H. Berger, G.G. Prices are in U.S. Dollars.

Size	Color	Shape	Luster	Blemishes	Matching	Price $	Comment
3–3.5mm	White	Potato: side-drilled	High	Slightly blem.	Good	3.5	
3–3.5mm	White	Potato: side-drilled	Very high	Slightly blem.	Very good	7	30% off price
3–3.5mm	White	Potato: side-drilled	Very high	V sl. blem.	Excellent	15	AAA 30% off
4–4.5mm	White	Potato: side-drilled	Very high	Slightly blem.	Very good	15	30% off
4–5.5mm	White	Potato: side-drilled	High	Unblemished	Very good	3	
4.5–5mm	White	Potato: side-drilled	Medium high	Slightly blem.	Very good	13	A 30% off
5–5.5mm	White	Potato: side-drilled	Medium high	Unblemished	Very good	33	AA+ 30% off
5–5.5mm	White	Potato: side-drilled	Very low	Slightly blem.	Very good	15	
5–6mm	White	Potato: side-drilled	Medium high	Unblemished	Excellent	17	30% off
6mm	White	Potato: side-drilled	Medium	Unblemished	Excellent	16	
7–7.5mm	White	Potato: side-drilled	Very low	Blemished	Fair	40	B rating 30% off
7.5–8mm	White	Potato: side-drilled	Very low	Slightly blem.	Very good	80	AB 30% off
7.5–8mm	Off white	Potato: side-drilled	High	Slightly blem.	Fair	200	A 30% off
9–7mm	Off white	Potato: side-drilled	Medium high	VV blemished	Good	9	
9–7mm	Off white	Potato: side-drilled	Low medium	Blemished	Very good	12.75	
9–8mm	Off white	Potato: side-drilled	Medium high	VV blemished	Good	34	
9–10mm	Off white	Potato: side-drilled	Medium high	VV blemished	Very good	75	
10–8mm	Off white	Potato: side-drilled	Medium high	V blemished	Very good	32	Great buy
10–8.5mm	Off white	Potato: side-drilled	Low medium	VVV blemished	Good	30	25% off
11–10mm	Off white	Potato: side-drilled	Medium high	Blemished	Good	560	Bands, pits, bleach
11.5–12mm	Off white	Potato: side-drilled	High	VV blemished	Very good	85	Marked banding
12–10mm	Off white	Potato: side-drilled	Medium	VV blemished	Good	400	Marked banding

Table 4-8. Shape: Corn-Button. Compiled by Lois H. Berger, G.G. Prices are in U.S. Dollars.

Size	Color	Shape	Luster	Blemishes	Matching	Price $	Comment
3–5mm	Silver-black	Corn-button	Low medium	VV sl. blem.	Very good	2.5	
4–4.5mm	Peacock	Corn-button	High	VV sl. blem.	Excellent	8	
4–4.5mm	Lt. lavender	Corn-button	Very high	Unblemished	Excellent	8	AAA 30% off
4–4.5mm	Lt. lavender	Corn-button	Very high	Unblemished	Excellent	19	
4.5–6mm	Bronze	Corn-button	High	VV sl. blem.	Poor	12	
5–5.5mm	Silver	Corn-button	Very low	Very blemished	Poor	8	
6mm	Silver	Corn-button	High	Slightly blem.	Fair	30	
6mm	Lt. lavender	Corn-button	High	Unblemished	VV good	22	
7mm	Dark brown	Corn-button	Very high	Slightly blem.	Excellent	38	
7mm	Peacock	Corn-button	Very high	Very blemished	Very poor	14	
7.5–8mm	Lavender	Corn-button	Very high	Unblemished	Excellent	50	
7.5–8mm	Silver	Corn-button	High	Unblemished	Very good	55	
7.5–8mm	Lt. bronze	Corn-button	Very high	Slightly blem.	Poor	38	
7.5–8mm	Lt. lavender	Corn-button	Very high	Unblemished	Excellent	64	AA 30% off
7.5–8mm	Lavender	Corn-button	Very high	Unblemished	Excellent	70	AA 30% off
7.5–8mm	Silver	Corn-button	Very high	Unblemished	Very good	50	
8mm	Dark silver	Corn-button	High	Unblemished	Very good	58	
8mm	Bronze	Corn-button	Very high	Unblemished	Good	45	
8mm	Peach	Corn-button	Very high	Slightly blem.	Good	40	
8mm	Lt. peacock	Corn-button	High	Blemished	Fair	40	

Imitation Pearls

Imitation or simulated pearls have been around for centuries, long before the existence of cultured pearls. Plastic, glass, and shells are used to create these pearls, and a substance made of fish scales is often applied to the surface, giving the pearls a lustrous, nacrelike appearance. Majorica pearls are simulated pearls that are often mistaken for cultured pearls. Majorica strands range in price from twenty-five to seventy-five dollars in the better department stores. To tell the difference between these imposters and cultured pearls, rub the suspect pearl against the bottom edge of your upper teeth; cultured and natural pearls have a coarse, gritty feel, whereas simulated and imitation pearls are smooth.

Mabe

Mabe, or mobe, pearls are a form of blister pearl, grown on the shell of an oyster. The pearls are domelike and frequently measure up to one inch in diameter. They are usually used in earrings, rings, and other jewelry where a flat back is desired. Prices of mabes range from sixteen dollars for a 10mm pearl to about seventy-five dollars for one approximately 20mm; 14mm, a popular size, are about thirty dollars each.

Table 4-9 offers the appraiser a guide to the quality of saltwater cultured pearls. The chart should be used only as an indicator of quality and combined with the appraiser's research and firsthand knowledge of value characteristics.

Writing the Pearl Report

On your appraisal report, be certain to note the following value factors for strands of pearls:

1. Whether the strand is uniform or graduated.
2. Whether the strand is single, double, or triple (fig. 4-10).
3. The number of pearls and their size in millimeters.
4. All quality information on the pearls.
5. The overall length of the pearl strand or bracelet.
6. The metal fineness and style of the clasp, if any, and any gemstones and/or pearls set in it.
7. Note whether the drill holes in the pearls are centered. Off-centered drill holes convey sloppy and hurried workmanship and lower the value of the pearls. The best way to spot off-center drilling is to lay the strand out in front of you on a desk or counter and, holding each end of the strand, roll it toward you. Off-center drilling will make badly drilled pearls wobble and easy to spot.
8. Use the correct nomenclature for the shape. Pearls are reported in the following shapes: seed, three-quarters, half, rice, oval, drop, long drop, long stick, flat, twin, triangle, round, semi-round (or off-round), egg, semibaroque, baroque, button, twin, top, circle, and bridge.
9. If the pearls have been verified as natural by X-ray, note when and where the verification took place.

Answers to Questions Your Clients Will Ask about Pearls

Q. How long does it take a pearl to grow?
A. Pearls require from three to seven years, depending upon the size and quality desired and part of the world in which they are cultivated. Most cultured saltwater pearls on the market today are in the water only three years—sometimes less.
Q. Will wearing my pearls make them look better?
A. Regardless of what you have read or been told, pearls do not improve by being worn.
Q. What material should be used to string pearls?
A. For durability and beauty, pearls should be strung on silk cord, which should be knotted to protect from loss in case of strand breakage.
Q. How do I clean my pearls?
A. Do *not* use commercial jewelry cleaners, ultrasonic or steam cleaners. Remove any concentrations of dirt, makeup, or grease with a fingernail or a soft tissue. Soak the pearl strand for ten to fifteen minutes in a lukewarm, nondetergent solution such as Ivory or Woolite. With a complexion brush, scrub the knots and around the bead hole. Do not scrub too vigorously or the nacre could be damaged. Rinse pearls in clean, lukewarm water for at least ten minutes. After washing, it is vital to support the pearl strand with *both hands* when picking it up to keep it from stretching or breaking. Pat the strand with a paper towel or cloth to absorb water, arrange it in a circle with the clasp closed, and lay it on a towel to dry at room temperature. Drying time will take at least twenty-four hours; it takes this long for the string in the drill hole to dry completely.

Bead Necklaces

Beads are worn in all countries and are among the oldest items for bodily adornment. Beads have been used in religious ceremonies and to indicate status. Beads are always fashionable; the appraiser will see strands of the most precious and the most outrageous materials. Pearls are the fashion favorites of all time, but amber, lapis lazuli, turquoise, coral, and jade intrigue generation after generation with their mystical beauty.

Beaded necklaces are available in many materials

Table 4-9. Cultured Pearl Quality Determination

Quality	Cleanliness	Color	Cultivation*	Luster	Shape
Gem	Nearly 100% spotless	Rosé, white-pink, silver-pink, white-silver	Thick, even layers, silky smooth	Mirrorlike glow	Round in all
Fine	Very few spots	Cream rosé, rosé, white-pink, silver-pink, white-silver	Heavy, even layers	Bright, glassy look; bright surface sheen	Round in most
Top commercial	Few spots	Rosé, white-pink, silver-white, white-light green, pink, white	Medium to heavy even layers	Bright luster, bright surface	Round in most to very slight off-round
Better commercial	Few to some spots	White-pink, white to light green, pink, white	Medium layers	Average brightness	Round to slight off-round
Commercial	Spots	White to yellow	Thin, uneven layers	May have slight brightness	Round to slight off-round to semibaroque
Promotional	Spotty to very spotty	Chalky white to dark brown and yellow	Very thin, not evenly layered	Little if any; usually very dull	Round to baroque

*Nacre thickness.
Source: Cultured Pearl Association of America.

and shapes—spheres, ovals, cylinders; beads may be plain-surfaced or faceted. Frequently they are carved.

From an appraisal standpoint, the most inexpensive are smooth spherical beads, because they can be mass-produced and are sometimes finished by tumbling them in polishing barrels; many other shapes must be done by hand. Faceted beads are available from Germany, Japan, and India. The bead prices depend upon the accuracy of the faceting, with the best work being done in Germany. The most expensive beads are those made from the most expensive gemstones (rubies, sapphires, emeralds) and are partly or wholly carved and/or faceted.

Many necklaces of fine opal beads have come onto the market in the last few years. They are sold by the carat with prices ranging from an 18-inch strand of strong blue and green flash of 377 carats at twenty dollars per carat wholesale, to a 16-inch strand of top color and red flash beads, 3mm to 6mm at seventy-five dollars per carat (for 57 beads) wholesale. With some materials, such as opal, emerald, and ruby, it is difficult to find beads of the same color and flawlessness.

The larger beads of more costly material are more difficult to match and therefore more expensive.

Beads made from materials available in abundance, such as tigereye, quartz, lapis lazuli, and malachite, are more easily matched and are less expensive, because supply is sufficient to meet the demand.

Many types of chalcedonic quartz are dyed to imitate more costly gemstones, especially lapis lazuli and turquoise. The lapis imitations are sometimes called *Swiss lapis* or *Italian lapis*. Always check lapis beads for signs of dye. If you suspect the beads have been dyed, inform your client immediately and get permission before you test. A quick and simple test is performed with a cotton swab dipped in fingernail polish remover. If the swab shows blue coloring after dabbing at a bead hole, the material is dyed.

Problems deciding whether or not you have genuine lapis or its substitute sodalite can be resolved with the hydrochloric acid test. Carefully place one drop of the acid in an unobtrusive spot on the bead. Genuine lapis will immediately emit the odor of rotten eggs. Wipe this spot off quickly; if left too long, the acid will erode the finish of the lapis.

When judging the quality of the beads and bead necklaces and writing them up on the appraisal report, observe and list the following:

1. Type and quality of the material.
2. Workmanship. Are the beads round or faceted? If they are faceted, square, or octagonal, are the planes flat with uniform polish? If they are round, do they have any flat spots? Grade them as you would a cabochon for round beads and a faceted stone for faceted beads. List their measurements in millimeters.
3. Closeness of the match in the material that has patterns and color variations. Note if the strand is uniform or graduated in size.
4. Note the accuracy of the bead sizes in uniform strands and the accuracy of the smooth taper in graduated-size beads.
5. Quality of the drilling. Are all the holes drilled exactly through the center of the bead? Beads inaccurately drilled do not hang well; this is immediately noticeable when the necklace is worn. Drill holes that were not finished smoothly and correctly around the edges may also rub against the cord and cause the necklace to break.
6. Is the strand knotted?
7. If other materials are used with the beads (gold spacers, etc.), note type and fineness of metal.
8. Note the polish on the beads. Is it bright and even?
9. Finally, note the strand length and clasp.

Also record the number of beads on the strand and list any phenomena such as *adularescence,* the floating, billowing blue to white light the stone may exhibit when turned. The formula for computing bead weight according to formula expert Richard Homer:

$$\text{Diameter}^3 \times \frac{\text{S.G.}}{10} \times 2.618 = \text{Carat weight}$$

Rare and Collector Gems

The pricing of rare gemstones is little understood. Although the value of any gemstone is determined largely by its color, clarity, carat size, cut, and historical desirability, the basis for pricing rare stones has a twist—the degree of rarity dominates all other factors. Since a large and continuing market demand cannot be met, a systematic tracking of the market and market value is not possible. In this situation, every transaction is a one-of-a-kind deal.

The price of rare gemstones is determined by what the seller thinks the market will bear at the time of sale; the price is usually set by comparing known sales of similar material. If no such sales exist, and if there is not much similarity between the stone in question and the closest comparable recent sale, the price is set and subject to negotiation. As appraiser, you should make an effort to acquire data through reading, attending gem shows and sales, canvassing rare stone dealers, and even building your own collection of rare stones, even if the collection must be very small at first. Collectors and dealers of rare stones are a closely knit group of individuals; unless you can join the group of collectors, you may find it difficult to get price information upon which you can rely.

Availability as a criterion for value is very important. You may have customers with gemstones of such rarity that virtually no established price guidelines exist, because not enough of the particular stones are traded. Some stones are so rare that they are of interest only to collectors who may pay very high prices. These stones must be valued on an individual basis using the actual price paid by the customer as the best indication of market value; this, in effect, sets the price and the value.

Is Bigger Better?

Appraisers should be aware that a huge stone is not automatically more valuable if no commercial demand for it exists. In theory, as the size of the stone increases, so does the price per carat—all other factors being equal—but this is true only to a point. In other words: How big is too big?

If a stone is suitable only for museum display, and its main asset is sheer volume (which gives the stone its color), the appraiser must use the "highest and best use" approach to value. For gems and jewelry appraisers, the concept of "highest and best use" is the reasonable and most probable use that will support the highest present value of the item. This is further defined as the most physically possible use, legally permissible use, financially feasible use, and the most productive use. The appraisal report should include proof that no other use for the item can produce greater benefit, and must also contain a complete identification of the property. In all FMV cases, the appraiser must explain on the report how the current state of the market relates to the highest and best use, how the size and rarity of the material relates to value, and the general and current supply and demand. For example, the appraiser must be able to prove that an existing doorstop-sized gemstone is attractive and rare enough to find a home in a museum, and address the issue of whether a museum can be found that would accept it.

There is a danger of misusing the word "highest" to mean either the biggest in size or the highest in quality. There is a point at which gemstone size actually lowers the value. For example, a study by the American Gem Market System has shown on a correlated weight-and-price chart that aquamarines become less marketable and drop in price as they increase in size. At approximately the 10 carat size, a small percentage drops off the current price per carat; when the stone reaches the 60 carat size and larger, it is worth about half the current price per carat.

Two Are Better Than One

Would a pair of matched stones be priced higher than a single stone? Yes and no. A lot depends on the kind of material as well as the quality match of the stones and their size. This is a research and judgment call. Obviously, a pair of carnelian cabochon-cut stones in a pair of earrings would not command a higher price than normal because carnelians are common and not much in demand. A pair of chrysoberyl cat's-eye stones (matched in quality and size) would bring a premium. A price list of faceted rare gems is given in table 4-10.

Synthetic Gemstones

If your clients plead that their stones cannot be synthetic because they belonged to their grandmother, tell them that even the ancient Egyptians developed artificial gems, and that these played an exalted role in those days. In fact, lists of precious materials from that time show imitation lapis lazuli prized above gold and used to pay tribute to the Pharaohs. The thought that the stone was not natural was trivial compared to its beauty.

Who puts the value on synthetic gemstones and why do some manmade stones soar in price while others drop in value? The most stably priced synthetics are luxury synthetics: Ramaura rubies, Chatham Created emeralds, sapphires, and rubies, Kashan rubies, and Gilson opals. How will the appraiser value these? By recognizing that all synthetics are not created equal. Much of the value has to do with the manufacturing process. Melt-grown and pulled crystals are simple and fast methods used to create products quickly. Because technology and labor are less significant factors in developing these stones, they are very inexpensive, wholesaling from thirty cents to two dollars per cut carat. On the other hand, flux-fusion and hydrothermally grown stones require a slow growth process that imitates the natural growth and takes up to a year. In addition, vast amounts of electric power are needed to maintain their special growing environment and only expensive platinum crucibles can be used as growth chambers. Luxury synthetics are therefore costly due to high production cost and high risk.

The rational procedure for the appraiser seeking

Table 4-10. Price List of Rare Gems

Stone	Ct. Wt.	Shape	Clarity	Color	Origin	Per Carat
Andalusite	1.80	Oval	F	Reddish-Green	Brazil	$55
Benitoite	.55	Triangle	VS1+	Blue	USA	600
Boracite	.26	FF Step	S1	Lt. Blue-Green	Germany	400
Clinohumite	.38	Emerald	VS1	Golden Yellow	Russia	450
Crocoite	1.38	Sq. Emerald	VS1	Orange-Red	Tasmania	150
Cuprite	1.00	Round	F	Dark Red	?	85
Chrysocolla	.86	FF Oval	TL	Blue-Green	Arizona	40
Datolite	1.20	Barion Tri	VS1+	Colorless	USA	180
Dumortierite	.13	Oval	VS1	Blue-Green	Madagascar	700
Euclase	1.20	Oval	F	V. Lt. Blue	?	200
Hackmanite	.40	Keystone	VS1	Lt. Yellow/Pink	Canada	750
Hauynite	.12	Oval	VS1+	Blue	Germany	950
Lazulite	.39	Emerald	VS1	Blue	Brazil	400
Libyan Desert Glass	5.30	Pear	S1	Lt. Yellow	Libyan-Egypt border	30
Mimetite	.26	Sq. Emerald	VS1+	Lt. Yellow	Namibia	1,000
Phosphophyll	.57	Emerald	F	Blue-Green	Bolivia	850
Smithsonite	1.91	Round	F	Lt. Yellow	Namibia	100
Taaffeite	1.20	Triangle	VS1+	Blue/Mauve-Blue	Sri Lanka	450
Wulfenite	1.44	Emerald	VS1+	Colorless	Namibia	300
Yugawaralite	.77	Emerald	S1	Colorless	India	450
Zinkite	1.06	Oval	TL	Dark Red	USA	130

Courtesy of K. K. Malhotra, K&K International, Falls Church, Virginia value on synthetic gems is to use the cost approach, first identifying the synthetic generically (that is, flux-fusion, hydrothermal, and so on) and then grading the stone. All synthetics have quality grades. Master grading stones are available from the manufacturers of synthetic materials.

When estimating replacement value on synthetics, be certain to figure replacement in like kind, i.e., Chatham for Chatham, Ramaura for Ramaura. The luxury synthetics are more expensive than those made by earlier methods.

Table 4-11 provides a wholesale price list of stones from J. O. Crystal Company; tables 4-12 and 4-13 provide wholesale prices from Chatham Created Gems along with Chatham's Size and Weight Chart. This estimated weight chart is for *natural* and Chatham Created gemstones. Weights are approximate, allow plus or minus 10%. Table 4-14 is a chronological guide to the development of synthetic gemstones, including the various processes and manufacturers. Table 4-15 lists the common identifying characteristics of synthetic stones.

Table 4-12. Chatham Created Gems, Inc., Wholesale Price List. All prices quoted are per carat.

Emerald	Gem	Fine	A
.01–4.99 cts.	$180	$140	$80
5.00–10 cts.	$225	$175	$100
10.01 cts. & up	$315	$245	$140

Rubies	Gem	Fine	A
.01–4.99 cts.	$170	$120	$80
5.00–10 cts.	$215	$150	$100
10.01 cts. & up	$300	$210	$140

Chatham Created Alexandrite & Chatham Created Sapphire

Blue, pink and padparadscha. Available in one quality: Clean/Fine

Alexandrite & Sapphire

1–4.99 cts.	$120
5.00–10 cts.	$150
10.01 cts. & up	$210

Chatham Grading System (all stones are top color)

Gem:	Eye Clean
Fine:	Slightly included
A:	Less brilliance, more heavily included
B:	Heavily included (on request)

Price lists courtesy of Chatham Created Gems, Inc., San Francisco, California.

Table 4-11. Ramaura Cultured Gems: Cultured Ruby, Empress Cultured Emerald from J. O. Crystal Company. All prices are per carat wholesale prices.

RAMAURA CULTURED RUBY

Carat Weight	Gem+ (Flawless)	Gem (Eye Clean)	Fine (Sl. Included)	A (Mod. Included)
0.01–2.99 cts.	$200	$160	$120	$75
3.00–5.00 cts.	$300	$200	$150	$100

EMPRESS CULTURED EMERALD

Carat Weight	Gem+ (Flawless)	Gem (Eye Clean)	Fine (Sl. Included)	A (Mod. Included)
0.01–4.99 cts.	$200	$160	$130	$80
5.00–10.00 cts.	$300	$200	$160	$100

Nicholas Created Alexandrite–Gem Grade: Cut to yield 99% color change $100 per carat.

Table 4-13. Chatham's Size and Weight Chart.

For natural and Chatham Created gemstones. Weights are approximate/allow plus or minus 10%.

Round	diamond	emerald	ruby/sapphire	alexandrite
2.0	.03	.03	.04	.04
2.5	.06	.06	.08	.08
3.0	.10	.10	.15	.14
3.5	.16	.15	.22	.19
4.0	.22	.22	.34	.33
4.5	.33	.32	.45	.43
5.0	.45	.45	.66	.59
5.5	.59	.57	.83	.75
6.0	.77	.72	1.09	1.05
6.5	1.00	.95	1.36	1.23
7.0	1.25	1.10	1.64	1.63
7.5	1.55	1.40	2.12	2.00
8.0	1.85	1.75	2.50	2.35

Oval	diamond	emerald	ruby/sapphire	alexandrite
5×3	.25	.20	.29	.29
6×4	.52	.40	.59	.54
7×5	.93	.66	1.06	1.00
8×6	1.45	1.13	1.65	1.50
9×7	2.07	1.60	2.36	2.20
10×8	3.08	2.40	3.50	3.26
11×9	4.31	3.40	4.90	4.10
12×10	5.98	4.10	6.80	5.60

Trillion	diamond	emerald	ruby/sapphire	alexandrite
3×3	.11	.09	.12	.12
4×4	.27	.22	.32	.29
5×5	.52	.43	.65	.55
6×6	.91	.68	.95	.87
7×7	1.43	1.10	1.60	1.43
8×8	1.77	1.55	2.00	1.89
9×9	3.04	2.25	3.42	3.00

Marquise	diamond	emerald	ruby/sapphire	alexandrite
4×2	.10	.08	.12	.10
4.5×2.5	.13	.10	.15	.14
5×2.5	.18	.12	.20	.19
5×3	.21	.16	.24	.22
6×3	.25	.21	.29	.27
7×3.5	.35	.32	.45	.40
8×4	.73	.50	.75	.66
9×4.5	.90	.65	1.00	.95
10×5	1.00	.95	1.30	1.22
12×6	2.00	1.50	2.06	1.90

Octagon	diamond	emerald	ruby/sapphire	alexandrite
5×3	.25	.25	.35	.33
6×4	.50	.48	.70	.65
7×5	1.00	.87	1.30	1.20
8×6	1.76	1.35	2.00	1.86
9×7	2.70	2.16	3.10	2.86
10×8	3.90	3.00	4.40	4.18
11×9	5.50	4.00	6.18	6.00
12×10	7.40	5.10	8.30	7.90

Pear	diamond	emerald	ruby/sapphire	alexandrite
5×3	.22	.20	.25	.23
6×4	.46	.35	.53	.49
7×5	.76	.58	.87	.80
8×5	.90	.76	1.02	.95
9×6	1.42	1.05	1.62	1.45
10×7	2.14	1.59	2.43	2.27
11×9	3.72	3.00	4.18	3.95

Heart	diamond	emerald	ruby/sapphire	alexandrite
3×3	.11	.09	.15	.14
4×4	.27	.22	.32	.31
5×5	.52	.43	.65	.57
6×6	.91	.68	1.00	.90
7×7	1.43	1.10	1.60	1.52
8×8	1.77	1.55	2.00	2.05
9x9	3.04	2.25	3.42	3.10

Square	diamond	emerald	ruby/sapphire	alexandrite
2×2	.06	.04	.06	.07
3×3	.20	.12	.22	.21
4×4	.50	.28	.56	.45
5×5	.60	.50	.80	.75

Baguette	diamond	emerald	ruby/sapphire	alexandrite
4×2	.11	.10	.14	.12
5×3	.27	.20	.32	.28
6×4	.60	.47	.66	.63
7×5	1.05	.90	1.20	1.11

Table 4-14. Chronology of Synthetic Gemstones.

Date	Gemstone	Process	Manufacturer	Reference
BERYL				
EMERALD				
(1848)	Emerald	Flux	Ebelmen	N.80,128
1938	Emerald	Flux	Chatham	C.Pers.Com.,85; N.80,141
1960	Emerald	Hydrothermal	Lechleitner	N.80,149; G&G.81,98
1961	Emerald	Hydrothermal	Linde	S.81,297; JofG.65,427; N.80,150
1963	Emerald	Flux	Gilson	S.81,297; N.80,144
1964	Emerald	Hydrothermal	Linde	N.80,150
1964	Emerald	Hydrothermal	Zerfass	N.80,130
1979	Emerald	Hydrothermal	USSR	G&G.85,79
1979	Emerald	Flux	USSR	G&G.85,79
1980	Emerald	Flux	Lens Lens	JofG.80,73
1981	Emerald	Flux	Seiko	RJ.4/19/84,16
1981	Emerald	Hydrothermal	Regency/Linde	LJ.79,Cover
1981	Emerald	Overgrowth	Lechleitner	G&G.81,98
1985	Emerald	Hydrothermal	Biron	AG.82,344
1994	Emerald	Hydrothermal	Tairus	G&G.96,32
Other Beryl				
(1979)	Watermelon beryl	Vapor Phase	Adachi Shin/Japan	G&G.86,55
(1981)	Aquamarine, red beryl	Hydrothermal	Vacuum Ventures	N.90,50; G&G.81,57
1988	Aquamarine, red and other colors	Hydrothermal	Lebedev/USSR	G&G.88,252; G&G.90,206
1994	Red Beryl	Hydrothermal	Tairus	G&G.96,32
CHRYSOBERYL				
1970	Alexandrite	Flux	Kyocera/Inamori	N.80,246
1973	Alexandrite	Flux	Creative Crystals	N.80,246; E.79,145
1978	Alexandrite	Floating Zone	Bijoreve/Seiko	G&G.84,60
1979	Chrysoberyl (cat's-eye)	Floating Zone	NIRIM	JGSJ.80,3
1980	Alexandrite	Czochralski	Allied Chemical	N.90,50
1980	Alexandrite	Hydrothermal	Novosibirsk	JofG.88,232; ZTS.97,70
1983	Chrysoberyl (cat's-eye)	Floating Zone	Sumitomo	G&G.83,186; JofG.88,232
1987	Alexandrite (cat's-eye)	Floating Zone	Sumitomo and Seiko	N.90,50
1991	Alexandrite	Czochralski	J. O. Crystal Co.	G&G.91,53
CORAL				
1978	Coral—Simulant	Ceramic	Gilson	G&G.79,227; N.80,276
CORUNDUM				
1885	Ruby	Flame Fusion	Geneva	N.80,42
1891P	Ruby	Flux	Fremy & Verneuil	F.1891; N.80,39
1902	Ruby	Verneuil	Verneuil	N.80,27
1903	Ruby	Verneuil	Hoquiam	N.80,54
1907	Sapphire, blue	Verneuil	Bailovsky	N.80,66; N.97,486
1918	Ruby	Czochralski	Union Carbide	N.80,87; E.79,52
1942	Ruby	Verneuil	Linde	N.80,69
1947	Star corundrum	Verneuil	Linde	N.80,69; N.80,75
1958	Ruby	Flux	Chatham	N.80,83; C.Pers.Com.,85
1958	Ruby	Flux	Bell Tel. Labs	N.80,78; E.79,53
1964	Ruby	Vapor Phase	White	N.80,91; N.97,486
1965	Ruby	Czochralski	Linde	N.80,84; N.97,486
1969	Ruby	Flux	Brown/Kashan	E.79,51; JofG.85,469
1971	Sapphire, colorless	Czochralski	Tyco	N.80,87; E.79,55
1974	Sapphire, blue	Flux	Chatham	G&G.82,140; C.Pers.Com.,85

Table 4-14. (Continued)

Date	Gemstone	Process	Manufacturer	Reference
1980	Orange sapphire (padparadscha)	Flux	Chatham	G&G.82,140; C.Pers.Com.,85
1982	Ruby	Flux	Knischka	G&G.82,165
1983	Ruby	Flux	J. O. Crystal/Ramaura	G&G.83,130
1983	Ruby, sapphire	Floating Zone	Seiko	G&G.84,60
1983	Ruby and sapphire; ruby overgrowth	Flux	Lechleitner/Austria	N.90,53; JofG.85,557; G&G.85,35
1984	Star Ruby	Verneuil	Kyocera	T.Pers.Com.,85
1990	Pink sapphire	Czochralski	Union Carbide	G&G.92,66; G&G.95,188,214
1993	Ruby	Flux	Douros	G&G.94,72; G&G.95,295

DIAMOND

Date	Gemstone	Process	Manufacturer	Reference
1954	Diamond	High Pressure	General Electric	N.80,174
1964	Carbonado	High Pressure	General Electric	N.80,194; N.97,487
1970	Diamond: yellow, blue, colorless	High Pressure	General Electric	N.80,186; G&G.91,254
1985	Diamond: yellow	High Pressure	De Beers	G&G.87,187; N.90,58; G&G.93,38
1985	Diamond: yellow	High Pressure	Sumitomo	G&G.86,192; N.90,58
1990	Diamond	High Pressure	General Electric	G&G.93,191
1993	Diamond: pink, red, purple	High Pressure	Many producers	G&G.93,38,191; G&G.94,123; G&G.96,52,128
1993	Diamond: blue, yellow, colorless	High Pressure	Many producers	G&G.93,182,228; G&G.95,53; JofG.95,363

DIAMOND SIMULANTS

Date	Gemstone	Process	Manufacturer	Reference
1948	Rutile	Verneuil	National Lead/ Union Carbide	N.80,211
1955	Strontium Titanate	Verneuil	National Lead	N.80,214
1960	Garnet-YAG & GGG	Flux	Bell Tel. Labs	N.80,249
1968	Garnet-YAG	Czochralski	Bell Tel. Labs	N.80,223; N.80,345
1975	Garnet-GGG	Czochralski	Bell Tel. Labs	N.80,345
1976	Cubic Zirconia (CZ)	Skull Melting	Aleksandrov et al.	N.80,232
1976	CZ	Skull Melting	Ceres	G&G.81,9
1978	CZ: many colors	Skull Melting	Ceres	G&G.81,9; JofG.81,602
1982	CZ: blue, green (C-OX)	Skull Melting	Lebedev	N.90,50
1983	CZ: opaque white	Skull Melting	Ceres	G&G.91,240
1983	CZ: opaque pink, white, black	Skull Melting	USSR	G&G.91,240
1997	Moissanite	Sublimation in Vapor Phase		C3 G&G.96,52; N.97,488

FORSTERITE AND PERIDOT

Date	Gemstone	Process	Manufacturer	Reference
(1963)	Forsterite	Czochralski	Shankland & Hemmenway	G&G.94,102
(1971)	Forsterite	Czochralski	Finch & Clark	G&G.94,102
(1991)	Peridot	Floating Zone	Hanson	G&G.94,102
1992	Forsterite	Czochralski	Mitsui Mining	G&G.94,102

JADEITE

Date	Gemstone	Process	Manufacturer	Reference
(1953)	Jadeite	Medium Pressure Solidification	Norton	G&G.87,27; N.90,50
(1979)	Jadeite	Medium Pressure Solidification	General Electric	G&G.87,27; N.90,50

LAPIS LAZULI

Date	Gemstone	Process	Manufacturer	Reference
1976	Lapis Lazuli	Ceramic	Gilson	G&G.79,227; N.80,264

Table 4-14. (Continued)

Date	Gemstone	Process	Manufacturer	Reference
MALACHITE				
1982	Malachite	Hydrothermal	Balitskii et al.	G&G.87,152; N.90,50
OPAL				
1972	Opal, white	Chemical Deposition	Gilson	N.80,259; N.90,50
1974	Opal, black	Chemical Deposition	Gilson	N.80,259; N.90,50
(1975)	Fire Opal	Chemical Deposition	Gilson	N.90,50; JofG.84,43; G&G.85,110
1983	Opal	Chemical Deposition	Inamori	G&G.83,234
1985	Opal	Chemical Deposition	Kyocera	G&G.95,137,267
QUARTZ				
1851	Quartz	Hydrothermal	Senarmont	N.80,100
(1898)	Quartz	Hydrothermal	Spezia	N.80,100; JofG.84,240
(1898)	Quartz	Hydrothermal	Nacken	N.80,101
1940	Quartz	Hydrothermal	Bell Tel. Labs	N.80,102
1940	Quartz	Hydrothermal	Clevite	N.80,102
(1942)	Smoky Quartz	Hydrothermal	Bell Tel. Labs	N.80,114
1954	Quartz, colorless	Hydrothermal	USSR	G&G.94,279
(1958)	Citrine	Hydrothermal	USSR	N.90,50
(1959)	Amethyst	Hydrothermal	USSR	N.90,50
1974	Citrine	Hydrothermal & Irradiation	Many producers	N.80,116
1975	Amethyst	Hydrothermal & Irradiation	Many producers	N.80,117
(1980)	Amethyst/Citrine (Ametrine)	Hydrothermal & Irradiation	Bell Tel. Labs	G&G.81,37
(1985)	Rose Quartz	Hydrothermal	Hosaka et al.	N.90,50
SODALITE				
(1973)	Sodalite, colorless	Hydrothermal	Airtron	N.97,488
(1991)	Sodalite: blue, colorless	Hydrothermal	Liu/China	G&G.92,139
SPINEL, GAHNITE SPINEL				
(1848)	Spinel	Flux	Eberlman	N.80,210,247
(1907)	Spinel	Verneuil	Paris	N.80,210,247
1908	Spinel	Verneuil	Verneuil	N.80,210,247
(1960)	Spinel and Gahnite Spinel, various colors	Flux	White et al.	N.97,488; E.79,54
(1960)	Spinel and Gahnite Spinel, various colors	Flux	Bell Tel. Labs	N.97,488
1989	Spinel, red, blue	Flux	Lebedev	G&G.89,250; G&G.93,81
1993	Spinel	Flame Fusion	Germany	G&G.93,141
TURQUOISE				
1972	Turquoise	Ceramic	Gilson	G&G.81,62; G&G.87,55
ZOISITE				
1996	Tanzanite Simulants:			
	Glass	Fused	Many producers	G&G.96,270
	Synthetic Corundum	Flame Fusion	Many producers	G&G.96,270; ZTS.97,67
	Synthetic Spinel	Flux	Many producers	G&G.91,55; G&G.96,270
	YAG	Czochralski	Many producers	G&G.96,270; G&G.97; ZTS.97,67

Table 4-14. Continued

References (source and year, page number)

AG	*Australian Gemmologist*
C	Tom Chatham, personal communication, 1985
CI	*Chemistry and Industry*
E	Dennis Elwell, *Man-Made Gemstones,* 1979
F	Edmond Fremy, *Syntheses du Rubis,* 1891
G&G	*Gems & Gemology*
G&S	*Gold und Silber*
J	Gary Johnson, personal communication, 1985
JCG	*Journal of Crystal Growth*
JGSJ	*Journal of the Gemmological Society of Japan*
JofG	*Journal of Gemmology*
LJ	*Lapidary Journal*
N80	Nassau, K., 1980. *Gems Made by Man,* Chilton. Reprinted by Gemological Institute of America, Santa Monica
N90	Nassau, K., 1990. Synthetic gem materials in the 1980s. *Gems & Gemology,* Vol. 26, No. 1, pp. 50–63
N97	Nassau, K., 1997. The chronology of synthetic gemstones. *Journal of Gemmology,* Vol. 25, No. 7, pp. 483–490
Nature	*Nature*
NIRIM	National Institute of Research in Inorganic Materials
O	Judith Osmer, personal communication, 1985
RJ	*Retail Jeweller*
S	John Sinkankas, 1981. *Emerald & Other Beryls,* Chilton Press, Radnor, Pa.
T	Ken Takada, personal communication, 1985
ZTS	*Zeitschrift der Deutschen Gemmologischen Gesellschaft;* became *Gemmologie; Zeitschrift der Deutschen Gemmologischen Gesellschaft*

Dates

Date	appeared in quantity on the market [experimental work may be earlier]
(Date)	experimental work produced results
P	date reported in publication

Table compiled by Dona Dirlam, Cathy Jonathan, Elaine Ferrari-Santhon, and Ruth Patchick, GIA Research Librarians

Table 4-15. The ABCs of Synthetic Stone Detection*

Stone	Maker	Method	Common Identifying Characteristics
Alexandrite	Creative Crystals (Concord, Calif.)	Flux	Strong short-wave red fluorescence, platinum crystals; flux inclusions; color change: bluish-green to reddish-purple, sometimes dissimilar to natural stones
	Inamori (Kyocera, Japan)	Not disclosed	Very clean and therefore suspect; strong short-wave red fluorescence; color change: blue-green to purple, dissimilar to most natural stones
Amethyst	Russian; Japanese	Hydrothermal	Possible seed plate; "bread crumb" inclusions; possible liquid inclusions resembling fingerprints; all other properties the same as natural, thus making this material extremely difficult to detect. Note: the Russians also make synthetic citrine
Emerald	Chatham (San Francisco, Calif.), Gilson (Geneva, Switzerland)	Flux	Low refractive index; long-wave red fluorecence; flux fingerprints and other inclusions, wispy veils
	Regency	Hydrothermal	Low refractive index; long-wave red fluorescence; hydrothermal inclusions; seed plate; 2-phase "nail-head" inclusions perpendicular to seed plate
	Biron (Western Australia)	Hydrothermal	Refractive index closer to natural, no long-wave red fluorescence; hydrothermal inclusions; seed plate
	Lechleitner (Distributed through Idar Oberstein, Germany)	Hydrothermal	Synthetic emerald overgrown on faceted natural colorless beryl; crazing between natural and synthetic layers of the material; faint long-wave red fluorescence

Table 4-15. The ABCs of Synthetic Stone Detection*

Stone	Maker	Method	Common Identifying Characteristics
Garnet YAG (yttrium aluminum garnet)		Czochralski	Not true synthetic garnet since natural garnets are silicates; colorless variety used as diamond imitation; see-through effect; refractive index: 1.83
GGG (Gadolinium gallium garnet)			Used as a diamond imitation; high specific gravity (7.02); low hardness (7); see-through effect; refractive index: 1.97
Lapis lazuli	Gilson (Geneva, Switzerland)	Ceramics	Specific gravity is lower than natural stone; material is more porous than natural
Opal	Gilson (Geneva, Switzerland)	Precipitation	Not truly a synthetic; magnification reveals "chicken wire" or "lincoln log" structure absent in natural
Ruby		Flame fusion (Verneuil)	Curved striae; gas bubbles; strong red fluorescence
	Kashan (Austin, Tex.)	Flux	"Rain"; flux fingerprints; "Comet tail" inclusions; parallel growth layers that meet at an angle but do not intersect; fractures and healed fractures
	Chatham (San Francisco, Calif.)	Flux	Residual flux; platinum crystals; growth and color zoning; transparent, near colorless crystals, sometimes with rounded corners; strong short-wave red fluorescence
	Inamori (Kyocera, Japan)	Czochralski (suspected)	Phantom smoke wisps under oblique fiber optic lighting; very strong short-wave red fluorescence
	Ramaura (Redondo Beach, Calif.)	Flux	Residual unmelted flux, often appearing as sulphur-yellow globules; flux fingerprints ranging from flat to wispy; growth and color zoning
	Knischka (Steyr, Austria)	Flux	Dense, white cloud-like areas; irregular color zoning; distinct 2-phase inclusions; flux inclusions, including platinum crystals; spherical and elongated gas bubbles; some cut stones with original natural ruby seed may contain natural inclusions
Sapphire: Blue; fancy colors		Flame fusion (Verneuil)	Short-wave chalky blue fluorescence; Plato test with crossed polaroid filters reveals strain within stone; curved striae and gas bubbles (difficult to see in pink and orange stones)
"Alexandrite"		Flame fusion	This synthetic color-change corundum is commonly mistaken for alexandrite; strong short-wave red fluorescence; color change: bluish-purple to purple, totally dissimilar to natural alexandrite; curved striae; gas bubbles
Linde Star Sapphire	Union Carbide (Danbury, Conn.)	Flame fusion	"L" trademark on back of cabochon; curved striae; gas bubnification: needles that comprise star are not distinctly visible, as opposed to those in natural stones; short-wave chalky blue fluorescence
Pink, orange "padparadscha"	Inamori (Kyocera, Japan)	Czochralski (suspected)	Very strong short-wave red fluorescence: phantom smoke wisps under oblique fiber optic lighting
Pink Spinel	Kashan (Austin, Tex.)	Flux Flame fusion	See ruby, "Kashan" Not truly a synthetic; usually very distinctive fluorescence; cross-hatch anomalous double refraction in the polariscope; refractive index: 1.73 (higher than natural spinel); sometimes made into triplets using green cement to look like emeralds (these stones are easily identified with spectroscope)
Turquoise	Gilson (Geneva, Switzerland)	Ceramics	No iron line in spectroscope; "tapioca" effect under high magnification

*Reprinted courtesy *Modern Jeweler*

CHAPTER 5

JEWELRY FROM ANTIQUITY TO THE MODERN ERA

A piece of fine antique jewelry is not only an ornament; it is art. It tells a story and offers a glimpse into the lifestyles of people who lived a long time ago. For the appraiser to interpret the significance and place values on antique jewelry requires connoisseurship in the cultures, social customs, and fashions of the era.

Values seem to be constantly rising for items in this field due, in part, to high collector demand, which is generally greater than the supply. The public mania for buying antique and estate jewelry was vividly demonstrated in the April 1987 sale of the Duchess of Windsor's jewels by Sotheby's in Geneva, Switzerland. Bids came from twenty-three countries, and this was the biggest jewelry auction in history. The auction was originally estimated to bring in 7 million dollars and the final figure was 45 million, not including a 10 percent buyer's fee.

For the appraisers who are challenged by this area of jewelry, some basic requirements include an exhaustive knowledge of the materials used in antiquity to determine if their use was technically possible at the time proposed for a subject item, and of the preference during any given era for a particular kind of jewelry, design, motif, or gemstone.

Jewelry Antiquities

There is a fascinating category of jewelry so obscure and specialized that obtaining any value information is difficult to impossible. The class is called jewelry antiquities. Hand-wrought, sometimes wondrously detailed fragments of other civilizations, these ancient gems and jewelry treasures are most often seen in museums—protected in glass display cases from the light, elements, and the public. There is a small collector's market for jewelry antiquities, and various pieces are

auctioned with some regularity in New York and in Europe. Putting a value on these objects can be one of the most challenging and frustrating jobs ever undertaken by the appraiser.

To begin with, you cannot assume that all you must do is canvass museums and ask curators for price ranges. Most museums will not allow their staff members to quote values. Even during the "heirloom" or "discovery" days when the public brings items into the museum, the articles are only identified and dated, not valued. In fact, on a recent tour of the Asian Arts Museum in San Francisco, the appraisers in the group were warned by the leader of the tour not to embarrass themselves or the curator by asking the specific worth of any of the display items. Somebody did anyway, but the curator gracefully circled the question and stepped over to another exhibit.

To the appraiser, the question of value is legitimate; there should be guides that allow the worth of an object to be estimated, regardless of its age or historical importance. Over the period of a year, correspondence was sent to twenty-five museum curators and antiquities collectors requesting guidelines in assessing the value of ancient jewelry. From all parts of the world, the reply was strikingly similar: "Almost impossible to answer." Most museums declined to answer, some attempted to convey their own convoluted formulas, and a few individuals gave considerable attention to the questions and returned some reasonable, thoughtful, and practical answers.

René Brus, noted goldsmith, jewelry historian, and collector from the Netherlands, said that value depends partly on who the collector is. For Western collectors, Early European jewelry and items from the Middle Ages will be much more desirable than jewelry from Far Eastern and Asian countries, whereas Asian collectors search for objects from their own civilizations. When asked about royal jewelry, Brus said:

> Coronation objects are so rare, and in some countries so sacred, that almost none will be for sale and therefore no value can be fixed to them. I do know that the small crown of Empress Eugenie of France was valued by one of the leading auction houses for five million dollars, which was far beyond the value of the materials, which were gold, diamonds and emeralds.

From London, antiquities expert Richard Digby explains:

> [In] valuing medieval pieces, we must first start with the appearance, and then the quality of manufacture including design and the gems that are used. Also, a lot of early jewelry has ancient Roman or Greek cameos, intaglios, and other carvings, which in themselves can be valuable, so to value a piece for insurance is very much an educated guess. Moreover, if the item can be worn without being damaged or recognized by ordinary people as being ancient and possibly very valuable, this helps make the item expensive, because it doesn't look valuable.

Alfred M. Brown, a glyptic arts collector from California, has this to add:

> The monetary value of such things is rather arbitrary, depending mostly upon who has what and who wants it badly enough to pay for it. I have friends who have private collections of gems and seals and they are as savvy as any of the dealers. The false inflation of prices [in this field] has been brought about by unscrupulous dealers who will buy anything regardless of the price or quality. Who can say such masterpieces as an engraved scaraboid by Epimenes is worth X amount of dollars without knowing the market? More often than not, we are talking about a few carats of chalcedony, not infrequently of inferior quality or condition, engraved with obscure figures, letters, or symbols. Curiosity or treasure, investment or work of art—it all depends upon the personalities involved, the times and the place.

In short, supply and demand, authentication, and knowledge of the marketplace are essential factors in appraising jewelry antiquities. This is confirmed by a former California museum curator:

> Values for jewelry antiquities are established by the current market. The market is made up of private collectors and museums. Prices may vary greatly due to a number of factors: the rarity of the object in relation to others known of its kind, how long it has been on the market, the materials used in its fabrication, and the quality of craftsmanship.

At last! A curator has committed to value factors that we can write down on paper, understand, and follow. A former staff member of the J. Paul Getty Museum in Malibu, California, was also willing to assist in researching market data sources by offering the following suggestions:

> The museum curator can provide the names of individuals who make it their business to buy and sell such material and assist the appraiser in determining the culture and historical period to which the piece belongs. This description is essential in the valuation process. Major auction houses, such as Sotheby's and Christie's, include ancient jewelry in their special catalogs of antiquities art objects (ancient Near East, Egyptian, Greek, Roman, Byzantine, Medieval). Looking for comparatives in these catalogs is a good place to begin establishing current prices. Some dealers in the United States specialize in this sort of material and provide catalogs of their sales.

How can one prove the antiquity of a jewelry item? There is no lab analysis comparable to the Carbon-14 test used in archaeology. An ancient appearance can be deceptive: Corrosion of metals can be induced, as can accretions or patinas. Circa-dating these items is so difficult and requires so much specialized expertise that it is incumbent upon the appraiser to get as much help as possible. There is a lot of disagreement, even among experts in this field, on what constitutes proof of provenance, circa-dating, and identification. There are fakes and forgeries in jewelry antiquities. Some date to the eighteenth and nineteenth centuries, when the archaeological style was in vogue, and some can be traced to the Renaissance. As one museum curator warned: "Assume that anything can be and is copied or forged, with or without the intent to deceive." This curator appended a very interesting postscript to her letter: "As investments, [jewelry antiquities] are the least secure of any jewelry objects."

Use the following guidelines in judging jewelry antiquities:

1. The current market prices (for comparable items)
2. The rarity of the object, in relation to others known of its kind
3. The length of time it has been on the market
4. The materials used in construction
5. The quality of the craftsmanship
6. The supply and demand for this type of article
7. The condition of the object

For this market, the *correlation analysis* technique is used to help establish value. Simply put, in this technique, the similarities and differences of the item being appraised are measured against any and all comparables. The appraiser contrasts and collates comparable items until enough of a parallel exists for the appraiser to make a value determination.

Antique Jewelry

Valuing antique jewelry scares some appraisers, but this aspect of jewelry valuation is neither sacrosanct nor impossible to learn. Intense study of the specialized markets, acquisition of detailed references, concentrated research, good judgment, and common sense are all that is required.

Most of the jewelry your clients will call antique will not really be antique items, which must be at least one hundred years old. The jewelry will likely fall into one of these three categories: heirloom, collectible, and old junk. However, you must be able to distinguish among the three groups and translate their characteristics into value.

A few excellent books on antique, vintage, and collectible jewelry, which include price guides, are listed in the *Using Price Guides* section of this chapter. In addition, you can get valuable hands-on experience by attending antique jewelry seminars and trade shows.

To identify and assess the value of antique items, complete the following steps:

1. Determine the materials and construction technique.
2. Learn the styles typical of the period and evaluate the item's artistic merit.
3. Learn the hallmarks or maker's marks.
4. Become familiar with the types of gemstones and cuts used during specific periods.
5. Determine the desirability of the item.
6. Establish the condition of the item.

Gaining expertise takes time. Reading the following brief reviews of period jewelry will not, of course, make the appraiser an expert in these specialized fields of study. Rather, the discussion is intended to pique the interest of appraisers who may have shunned these areas of valuation, and to provide an overview of the subject. The periods of style discussed in this next section include:

- Georgian 1714–1830
- Victorian 1837–1901
- Edwardian 1901–1914
- Arts and Crafts 1890–1914
- Art Nouveau 1895–1915
- Art Deco 1920–1930
- Retro 1940–1950

Georgian Jewelry: 1714–1830

Antique jewelry cannot be separated from the social and economic trends of its time. During the eighteenth century, British jewelry was greatly influenced by foreign fashion, particularly that of Italy and France. England's political power was increasing throughout the world, and the country was prosperous: A middle class sprung up for the first time in history; greater numbers of people became interested in travel and art; and jewelry was much in demand.

Georgian jewelry was almost entirely made by hand, and is distinguished by its craftsmanship. The art of faceting gemstones was being developed at this time, and diamonds with twenty-four to fifty-six facets are characteristic of this period. Finely engraved metal work, mostly of 18K gold, was common, and *cannetille,* an intricate wirework, was also very popular. Jewelry styles were almost exclusively of flowers, leaves, and other natural subjects, and diamond jewelry was often decorated with such motifs as sprays of foliage, feather plumes, leaves, ribbons, flowers, and birds. Convertible jewelry, such as bracelets that joined to form a necklace, or a stomacher that could be disassembled to become several brooches and a pair of earrings, are also characteristic of the period. Georgian jewelry is also marked by *en tremblant* articles, which moved or trembled when worn, usually as hair ornaments. Necklaces from the early Georgian period were fitted with loops at either end to hold ribbons that were used to tie the necklace onto the wearer. Rings with stones set in silver with high-karat gold backings and gold shanks are also typical of the Georgian era. Most gems were set with closed backs. As the Georgian period progressed, engraved gemstones and intaglios became popular. And, during the last part of the eighteenth century, cabochon-cut gemstones were the rage.

Paste gemstones were common, and appraisers should be careful to verify the authenticity of all pink gemstones in Georgian jewelry. Developed in France, paste is a high-quality lead glass faceted and polished

5-1. This 18K Georgian necklace is enhanced by fine cannetille wirework and set with genuine pink topaz and natural pearls. *(Photograph courtesy of Lynette Proler Antique Jewellers, Houston)*

like a genuine gemstone. In 1766, a London craftsman named John Tassie came up with his own formula for making good-quality paste gemstones; some people still refer to these as *tassies*. Colored paste was a very popular substitute for such gemstones as ruby, emerald, sapphire, garnet, and pink topaz. Russian pink topaz was especially popular during this time, and pink glass was often used instead of the real thing. Paste opals were also manufactured, using colored foil to imitate the colors of opal. Figure 5-1 illustrates a late Georgian necklace in 18K gold with pink topaz and pearls.

From 1706 until about 1814, the ancient city of Pompeii was under excavation, and the discoveries made there captured the imagination of jewelry designers as well as of the public. Jewelry in the shape of ram's heads, pieces with mosaics of ancient temples, and other designs echoing the artifacts found at Pompeii became popular. Enamel jewelry was also stylish.

An important clue to dating these pieces is that only the front of enamel jewelry made during the Georgian epoch was fired; the backs are either plain or engraved.

Victorian Jewelry: 1837–1901

The Victorian period began with Queen Victoria's accession to the throne and ended with her death in 1901. Victoria adored jewelry and her influence over the development of styles was felt for more than seventy years. There are three discernable phases within the Victorian epoch: the Romantic period, which lasted until 1860; the Grand period, which continued until 1885; and the Late Victorian period, which ended in 1901.

The changes in jewelry style that mark the three periods reflect the British Empire's increasing prosperity and progress. However, there is no exact division separating one period from the next. Some styles continued to be popular in one region after the trend had faded in another area, and the styles tended to overlap. Appraisers should be aware that fully marked and stamped Victorian jewelry is rare, for the British government did not require jewelers to use markings during the nineteenth century. Firsthand knowledge and market research are necessary for the appraiser to be able to distinguish among jewelry of the different periods.

Romantic Period: 1837–1860

The fall of Napoleon and the inception of the Industrial Revolution set the stage for social change. More middle-class families were joining the professional class, and the taste in jewelry was toward naturalism and sentiment. As the necklace shown in figure 5-2 illustrates, jewelry love messages, often with natural themes, were taken seriously. Popular materials included jet, tortoise-shell, malachite, amber, agate, turquoise, and coral. Motifs were mostly stars, crosses, bursts of garnets, twigs, leaves, and branches. Around 1840, delicate seed-pearl jewelry came into vogue, and studying flower lore was fashionable.

Grand Period: 1860–1885

Archaeology affected jewelry design, especially the neo-Etruscan style that dominated jewelry fashion for many years. This jewelry was primarily the work of the Castellani family of Rome, and was shown in England in 1862 at the International Exhibition. The style, characterized by little gemsetting, high standards of goldsmithing, and small areas of enamelling, set a trend.

During this phase of Victorian jewelry, black glass began to be used as a substitute for jet, and the terms

5-2. Romantic-era Victorian necklace, circa 1860, is of old mine-cut diamonds and natural pearls in 15K yellow gold. *(Photograph courtesy of Lynette Proler Antique Jewellers, Houston)*

the same time, novelty jewelry—the reverse painted crystals—holiday souvenirs, hair jewelry, miniature portraits, and mourning jewelry were popular. Other jewelry items common in the Late Victorian period include stickpins, bar brooches, narrow bangles, open bangles, and star-shaped settings for gemstones. Popular gemstones were cabochon-cut moonstones, amethysts, opals, and emeralds.

There are some important maker's marks found on jewelry from the Victorian era. ACC and CC are both marks used by Fortunato Pio Castellani and his son, Alessandro Castellani. The CC is interlaced and back to back. Carlo and Arthur Giuliano used C & AG as their mark; Giacinto Melillo, an apprentice of Gialiano, signed his work GM. John Brogden's work is signed JB.

Edwardian Jewelry: 1901–1914

The Edwardian era was the short but sweet period before the beginning of World War I. Lavishness and ostentation mark the jewelry of this style. In 1903, the marquise-cut diamond was popular and the *lavalier*, a small, delicately styled pendant necklace, usually set with one or more gemstones and/or pearls, came into vogue along with the lighter, softer, post-Victorian clothing that was being worn. Platinum became the metal of choice, and jewelers were fashioning delicate patterns using the saw-piercing method of construction that distinguishes jewelry made between 1909 and 1914. Typical of the decoration is *milgraining*, a line of globular projections of metal applied by a tool around a setting holding a gem, or around the outer edges of a jewelry article (fig. 5-3).

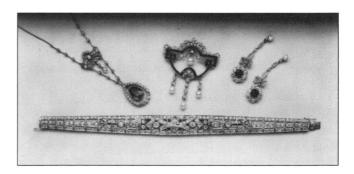

5-3. *Top left:* French Edwardian-era lavalier with violet pear-shaped sapphire and Oriental pearls set in platinum and milgrain bezel set with diamond. *Top center:* French brooch circa 1900–1925 with Oriental pearls and sapphires set in platinum. *Top right:* Late Victorian English pendant-style earrings of old European-cut and rose-cut diamonds with drop and bow platinum settings. *Bottom:* Platinum and diamond bracelet of very high quality. Total weight approximately 9 carats. *(Photograph courtesy of Lynette Proler Antique Jewellers, Houston)*

became interchanged. The most popular motifs were horses, dogs, birds, insects, horseshoes, and snakes (fig. 5-3).

From the jewelry of this era you may find items of bloomed gold, a type of matte finish produced by acid treatment. The gold discolors easily, so the trend was short lived. Lava and hardstone cameos as well as intaglios, with elaborate beadwork mountings and intricate metal decoration, were in style.

Gloria Lieberman, head of the antique jewelry department at Skinner Auction House in Boston, advises appraisers to consider whether the Victorian jewelry under appraisal can be worn in public today. If the answer is yes, then the piece has increased value.

Late Victorian Period: 1885–1901

There was a great difference between the commercial and aesthetic styles popular during this time. With the opening of the great diamond mines, diamonds became more widely available and were all the rage. At

Women wore their hair in the fashionable pompadour, decorating this hairstyle with diamond combs and *fourches,* large, tortoise-shell hairpins. Tiaras and large brooches were also in demand.

One of the favorite motifs of the era was the bow, but instead of being formal it was a relaxed, casual motif. King Edward, for whom the era is named, was married to one of the great beauties of the day, Alexandra. Because green stones were Edward's favorite, the demantoid garnet is seen in much of the jewelry of the time; Alexandra favored the amethyst, which was also used extensively in jewelry.

Arts and Crafts: 1890–1914

The Arts and Crafts movement was a brief period of revolt by artisans and craftspersons against mechanization. The academic backlash originated in England, where craftspersons organized around the principle that all jewelry should be made by hand. The movement was doomed because of the expense involved in the labor of handmade jewelry and because Arts and Crafts jewelry was never popular with the majority of the public.

A leading jeweler craftsman of the time was Charles Robert Ashbee. His mark turns up in jewelry of this period from time to time as CRA GOH Ltd. Other craftspersons whose marks you may find include Nelson and Edith Dawson (ND in an ivy leaf); Arthur Gaskin (AJG); Edgar Simpson (name in a circle); and Liberty & Co. (LY & Co. in a triple diamond).

Silver was the metal of choice. The most popular gemstones were turquoise, moonstone, fire opal, amethyst, and peridot. Most gemstones were cabochon cut and bezel set. The appraiser should use caution in judging this work because there is a tendency to overvalue handmade items. High standards of judgment should continue to be used, including assessing the quality of the materials and work.

Art Nouveau: 1895–1915

The Art Nouveau movement in art, architecture, and design began in the latter years of Queen Victoria's reign and lasted until World War I. Some of the jewelry motifs common in this era were popular both before and after Art Nouveau. The jewelry of the period followed three schools of design: new art, craft, and traditional. Each influenced the others and melded into some beautiful and unforgettable works. Sinuous lines are characteristic of this style, as is the use of natural images: motifs of graceful insects, maidens with long flowing tresses, sunbursts, crescents rendered in wavy whiplash curves, lizards, and snakes (figs. 5-4, 5-5, 5-6). Art Nouveau borrowed heavily from Japanese work, which was widely admired.

Nontraditional materials such as horn and glass were used in jewelry during this period, and designers mixed valuable gems with inexpensive ones, such as ivory with horn. Amber, garnet, and agate were used for lower-priced jewelry and silver jewelry was in demand. Enamel-work techniques were of special interest to designers, especially translucent plique-à-jour enamel, which was used to create the popular stained-glass effect (fig. 5-7). Jewelry took on an iridescent finish and dreamlike design fantasies were produced.

Cultured pearls made their first appearance in long necklaces and chokers during this era. Platinum jewelry became popular and settings were often chased or engraved. Although most of the fine work of the period was made by hand, it became more common to incorporate machine-made parts into jewelry as the century ended.

One of the most widely heralded goldsmiths of this era was Peter Carl Fabergé, court jeweler to the last czars of Russia. His legendary work was conducted until 1918. Be cautious about attributing jewelry to Fabergé or to his workshop unless you can authenticate the works positively. The Fabergé signature is shown in figure 5-8.

Art Deco: 1914–1935

Art Deco is the style of jewelry that predominated between the two World Wars. It was named after the great Paris Exhibition of 1925, *L'Exposition Internationale des Arts Décoratifs et Industriels Modernes.*

Art Deco is a bold, geometric style that emerged as a reaction against the pale color and fluid lines of the Art Nouveau period. The look is a straight, clean line with the curve of the previous period's jewelry replaced by the angle. Art Deco jewelers borrowed heavily from Asian, Islamic, Indian, African, and Egyptian motifs. The opening of King Tutankhamen's tomb in 1922 instituted a strong Egyptian trend in jewelry.

Art Deco jewelry was dramatic, bold, brassy, and exciting. The jewelry was finely crafted—even the costume pieces. Of particular note are platinum diamond clips (used in pairs), brooches, and jabot pins, which featured diamonds, sapphires, rubies, and emeralds in one piece of jewelry (figs. 5-9 and 5-10). Colorful and eclectic, these creations have become known as "fruit salad jewelry" in collector circles. Appraisers will find long, dangling jade earrings, straight-line bracelets (many with synthetic gemstones), carved emeralds, and lapel watches for both men and women to be representative of the era's jewelry. The jeweled "cocktail" wristwatch also became fashionable.

The principal theme during the period was movement. Common jewelry motifs include airplanes, cars, trains, ocean liners, and running greyhounds.

Table 5-1. Sample Antique Jewelry Appraisal Worksheet

Client_____ Date _____ Function: ❏ Insurance

❏ Other

Jewelry Type_____ Mfg.: ❏ Cast ❏ Die-Struck ❏ Handmade

Metal/Material_____ Karat_____ Weight _____

Measurements _____ Motif_____ Design/Style _____

Circa Date_____ Condition_____

Enamel_____Cannetille

Mounting Evaluation: ❏ Basket Mount ❏ Bright-cut ❏ Filigree ❏ Engine-turn

Other _____

Setting: ❏ Bead ❏ Bezel ❏ Channel set ❏ Claw set ❏ Belcher set ❏ Gypsy set

❏ Cluster set ❏ Crown/Coronet ❏ Illusion setting ❏ Pavé ❏ Invisible

❏ Star ❏ Prongs ❏ Other:_____

Craftsmanship: ❏ Excellent ❏ Good ❏ Average ❏ Poor

Describe Clasp _____ Karatage_____ ❏ Marked ❏ Tested

Embellishments on item _____

Repairs/Alterations visible _____

Repairs Needed_____

Wearability_____Fashion Collectible?

The item is: ❏ Genuine ❏ Reproduction ❏ Fake

Gemstones number and identity _____

Provenance _____

Item Description_____

Along with the precious jewelry came a surge in the use of nonprecious, less expensive stones and materials such as coral, onyx, and enamel. For the first time, costume jewelry became as important as fine jewelry and manmade materials were widely used. In 1908, a Belgian-American chemist, Leo Hendrik Baekeland, created a plastic intended for electrical installation purposes. He named it *Bakelite* and promoted it as "the material of a thousand uses." Bakelite molded nicely into bangle bracelets resembling ivory or wood and, by the early 1920s, an eclectic jewelry collection in horse, bird, small-animal, and fruit motifs was being produced from the polymer material.

Bakelite jewelry was popular from the 1920s through the early 1940s. Costume-jewelry designers used it for everything—from bangle bracelets to brightly colored jewelry ornaments shaped like animals, vegetables, and insects. Bangles were very popular and are among the most often found articles today. The colors of Bakelite jewelry are incredible—bright, cheerful, and bizarre yellows, reds, oranges, and greens. Polka-dot patterns and stripes predominated, and pastel-colored Bakelite is rare.

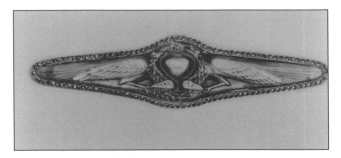

5-4. Rare Art Nouveau brooch signed by René Lalique. *(Photograph courtesy of Charterhouse & Co.)*

5-6. Enamel and seed-pearl pendant. *(Photograph courtesy of Charterhouse & Co.)*

5-5. Plique-à-jour enamel and diamond pendant by Masriera. *(Photograph courtesy of Charterhouse & Co.)*

Bakelite jewelry enjoyed a resurrection in the 1980s, and is now often priced at a hundred times its original cost, which ranged from a few cents to a few dollars.

The carved pieces of Bakelite jewelry generally will show some unpolished tool marks in the recesses of the item, while the new molded jewelry remains glossy all over and exhibits mold seams. Intricate floral and geometric motifs are common to the old Bakelite jewelry items, but the new plastics rarely have such a degree of craftsmanship. Appraiser beware that Bakelite jewelry is being faked—the original findings were screwed in place, but the new reproduction ones are glued!

In valuing fine Art Deco jewelry, look for the following factors:

1. Maker's name. Important jewelry pieces are always signed, as are important paintings and sculptures. The most famous and prolific jewelry designer of the Art Deco period was Louis Cartier; other distinguished designers and jewelry houses of the period include Van Cleef & Arpels, Mauboussin,

5-7. The 18K diamond and pearl Art Nouveau pendant is decorated with enamel and is in its original fitted box. *(Photograph courtesy of Lynette Proler Antique Jewellers, Houston)*

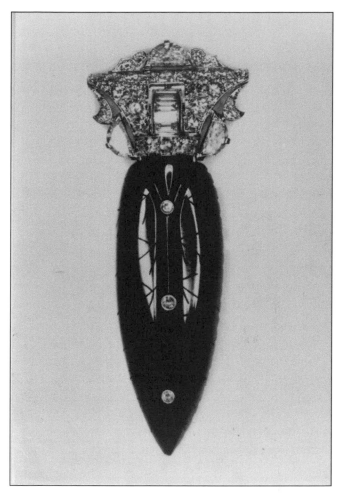

5-10. Art Deco diamond and onyx leaf brooch signed by Fougery. *(Photograph courtesy of Charterhouse & Co.)*

ФАБЕРЖЕ

5-8. The Fabergé signature.

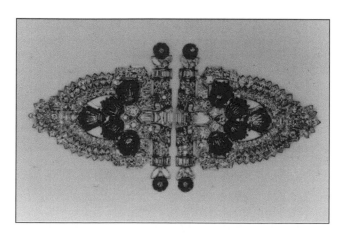

5-9. Art Deco ruby and diamond clips, circa 1925. *(Photograph courtesy of Charterhouse & Co.)*

Boucheron, Fouquet, Dusausoy, Chaumet, Sandoz, Marchak, and LaCloche (fig. 5-11).

2. Quality. Workmanship and materials play a significant role in determining value. Top designers always used first-class materials.

3. Condition. Check for damage and for signs of repair, such as fresh soldering, as well as for replacement or substitute materials.

4. Overall design. Not all pieces by the same designer are of the same caliber. Learn to distinguish good from fine, and fine from exceptional. The only way to gain this expertise is to do time-consuming research in this field, and to handle and examine as much of the jewelry as possible.

5. Motif. Floral-designed Art Deco jewelry is invariably of greater value than is jewelry with a geometric design.

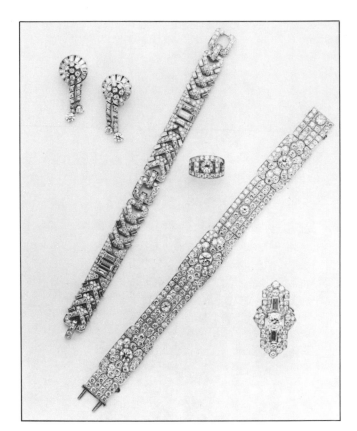

5-11. *Top left:* Trabert & Hoeffer, Mauboussin, platinum and diamond ear clips, circa 1930. Total weight, 4½ carats. *Center:* Platinum and diamond bracelet, circa 1930. Total weight, 12 carats. *Center right:* Diamond and sapphire platinum ring, circa 1920. Total weight of diamond, 2.2 carats. *Right:* Bracelet by J. E. Caldwell & Co., circa 1930. Total weight of diamond, 29.5 carats. *Far right:* Cartier platinum and diamond ring, circa 1930. Total weight of diamond, 5½ carats. *(Photograph ©1986 Sotheby's, Inc.)*

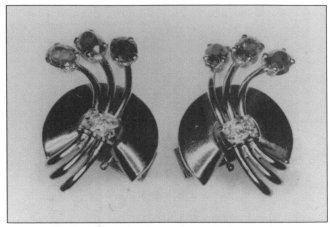

5-12. Retro modern gold ear clips with diamonds and multi-colored stones. *(Photograph courtesy of Charterhouse & Co.)*

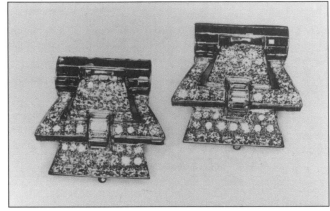

5-13. Retro modern ear clips. Mixtures of aquamarine, topaz, amethyst, and ruby were common in Retro jewelry. *(Photograph courtesy of Charterhouse & Co.)*

Retro Jewelry: 1940–1950

As recently as 1970, jewelry from the 1940s and 1950s was being sold for scrap value. Trends change, and jewelry from this period has now become collectible. Spokespersons from major auction houses say that the price of this jewelry is on an upward climb and it is believed that the trend will not peak for several more years. Intrinsically, this jewelry is not as valuable as Art Deco jewelry, which featured detailed workmanship and the use of more precious stones.

The drama and distinctiveness of the designs account, in part, for the popularity of Retro jewelry. The pieces are bold, oversized, and called gaudy by some. An almost three-dimensional look—left over from the popular Cubist movement in art—identifies the style. Rose gold with a high polish is typical, as is the heavy use of aquamarine, ruby, and citrine (figs. 5-12 and 5-13). Classic Retro motifs include ballerinas, bows, and large link chains and rings with dramatic, scrolled shanks.

Post-Retro Jewelry

According to dealers who buy hundreds of lots of estate and antique jewelry yearly, the newest trend, jewelry from the 1950s and 1960s, is already underway. Dubbed "Atomic Moderne" by some and "early Harry Winston" by others, the jewelry style is characterized by a multitude of diamond-and-platinum rings and brooches designed in a waterfall motif, as well as the popular irradiated diamond cluster pieces.

Consider that the furniture, pop-culture relics, and fashions from the 1950s and 1960s are enjoying renewed popularity and remember that jewelry follows fashion's lead.

To keep up with innovations in style, appraisers should be aware of what art and craft galleries and museums are exhibiting, and start now to build a reference library of jewelry styles, motifs, prices, and manufacturers of the era, while material is still readily available.

Appraising Revivalist Jewelry Using Market Data Comparison

Revivalist jewelry has been around a long time. To a jewelry appraiser without a good grasp on the peculiarities of the antiques and period jewelry market, identifying revivalist and reproduction jewelry can be confusing. In the same way designer and antique jewelry needs conscientious market research of comparable sales, valuing revivalist jewelry demands this, and more. The Market Data Comparison Method is used in the majority of appraisals. A piece identified as revivalist should be compared to an identical (or nearly so) one manufactured in the same period. When the manufacturer is known, the task is taken to an even higher level of research by comparing the manufacturer's past production with the jewel being appraised. First, of course, the piece must be identified as revivalist jewelry. Circa dating will help answer the question of "which" revival, since styles are cyclical therefore enjoy numerous returns.

Cyclical Style

Long before Liz Taylor played Cleopatra or King Tut's treasures were unveiled, things Egyptian were in demand. Before Napoleon Bonaparte marched into Egypt in 1798, objects from the land of pharaohs trickled into the hands of collectors in the Western world. Egyptomania—collecting things Egyptian—continues to be sparked from time to time by a movie or museum exhibit. The Egyptian influence is all around us, especially in jewelry reproductions and revival articles. Why is that? It can be answered with one word: *style*. Egypt had one of the most stable civilizations of antiquity, with skilled artists and artisans who produced a highly recognizable style. That everyone wore jewelry is confirmed by the poorest burial sites, which have yielded strings of shell, stone, and faience, a ceramic made of color-glazed quartz sand. In effect, the working classes wore costume jewelry.

The West first discovered the mysteries of Egyptian jewelry in 1798 after General Bonaparte launched his Egyptian campaign. It took off again in 1822 when Jean-Francois Champollion deciphered the Egyptian hieroglyphics on the Rosetta Stone, and again in 1831 when Egypt sent Louis XVIII an obelisk, which he erected in the Place de la Concorde in Paris. When the Suez Canal opened in 1869, it was attended by Empress Eugenie, wife of Louis Napoleon, who commissioned the court jeweler, Lemonnier, to create jewelry in Egyptian motifs.

Egyptian-inspired designs were on display at the Chicago World's Fair in 1893, and in 1910 Louis Cartier began to design fine jewelry using ancient Egyptian motifs. In the 1920s, Egyptian motifs were wed to the art deco style, and genuine small antiquities such as scarabs were used in the jewelry. In 1922, British Egyptologist Howard Carter announced discovery of the tomb of Tutankhamen, and it was the single most important factor in the interest for collecting things Egyptian. Egyptomania struck western collectors in the 1950s, 1960s, 1970s, 1980s, and 1990s. Why is this important to appraisers? With the style returning over many decades, it is clear there is more than *one* single period of Egyptian revivalist jewelry. Egyptian revivalist jewelry was produced extensively (but not exclusively) in the last half of the 19th century and most of the 20th century. Since most practitioners will either be issuing new appraisals or updating past appraisals, reaching a value conclusion will require doing a lot of homework. Where to research? Egyptian reproduction and revivalist jewelry are regularly sold by major auction houses; reproduction pieces are available at museum gift shops, especially when an Egyptian exhibition is touring. Numerous wholesale and retail jewelry dealers have found a market niche in Egyptian reproductions, and many sell at major gems and jewelry shows.

One of the first requirements of appraising an Egyptian style item is to determine if it is an antiquity (probably not), a revival, or a reproduction (no intent to defraud). The majority of *antiquities* are in museums or hidden away by wary collectors. *Revivalist* jewelry is produced to revive ancient or period styles and techniques with no intent to defraud. Egyptian revivalist jewelry is normally well made in gold and gemstones, and often signed by a famous designer whose aim is to "revive" the style. *Reproduction* jewelry is a copy of a genuine article. It might be a copy of an item made at a prior date with the same materials and design as the original, and sold legitimately with no intent to deceive, or it may have been made *with* every intention of deception. It may also be a reproduction made with inferior materials from the original, but without the fine craftsmanship seen in the originals.

The Egyptian design is one of the most enduring of the revival styles (returning frequently because of

5-14. Egyptian revival jewelry with rubies, diamonds, pearls, and enamel. Egyptian jewelry has cycles of demand that reach a peak when new exhibitions are mounted in national and regional museums. *(Photo by Gary L. Lester.)*

strong consumer demand). To illustrate handling a piece of Egyptian revivalist jewelry, an example of a brooch is pictured in fig. 5-14. A description of the article is shown in fig. 5-15. A timeline that may help with circa dating is found in fig. 5-16. During research the appraiser found an almost identical brooch sold one year earlier at Christie's East in New York City. In the auction catalog, the brooch is defined like this: "Revivalist ruby, diamond, pearl and enamel pendant of oval outline, depicting a varicolored enamel female figure with Egyptian headdress enhanced by rose-cut diamonds within a variously-cut ruby, rose-cut diamond, half pearl and engraved yellow gold frame, circa 1860." The pre-auction estimate was $3–4,000. The hammer price was $4,830.

Examining and Evaluating Period Jewelry

After you have circa-dated an item of antique jewelry to your satisfaction, follow these standards toward making final evaluation:

5-15. Certificate of Appraisal Sample Description

Enamel Brooch

One (1) lady's 18 karat (acid tested) yellow gold, oval shape, Egyptian Revival brooch, Circa 1860. The brooch is fashioned with an enameled portrait of a young woman in full Egyptian headdress enhanced with rose-cut diamonds, rubies, and pearls. The overall measurements of the brooch is 5.4 × 4.5cm. Total weight of the brooch including gemstones: 17.4 cwt. Overall condition: Excellent.

The portrait measures 3.1 × 2.3cm and displays enameling on the face in fair skin tones with large brown eyes. The lady is wearing drop earrings, each earring composed of three rose-cut diamonds; a necklace of nine rose-cut diamonds; and seven rose-cut diamonds across the bodice of her dress. All diamonds measure 0.6–1.5mm by Leveridge gauge for a combined estimated total weight of 0.33 carats.

The headdress is enameled in green, red, blue, white, and black in a traditional geometric design pattern. The crown is set with 10 rose-cut diamonds measuring 0.6–1.5mm. The portrait is framed in a spiral pattern of gold wire set with 39 round ruby cabochons. Rubies measure 1.5–1.7mm each with a combined approximate total weight of 1.00 carat. The rubies are medium dark slightly brownish Purple/Red (PR 6/3) graded by GIA GemSet color-grading system. The average clarity grade of the diamonds is SI1.

The outer top and bottom rim of the brooch is decorated with a textured finish and black enamel spiraling gold ribbon with a bow top and bottom. Three half-round pearls are set on each side of the brooch in tulip-head settings. The center pearls measure 4.5mm; side pearls measure 4.0mm each. Pearls are white with medium luster, slightly spotted. If original to the brooch they are natural; however, laboratory testing (x-ray analysis) is required for conclusive proof.

The brooch has a double white gold pin stem with safety catch modification and addition. There is also a hinged rabbit-ear bail using the original pin hinge as the ball hinge. Remnants of what appears to be a compartment cover hinge is visible.

Approximate Retail Replacement: $5000.00

5-16. Egyptomania Time Line

1700s	Frescoes discovered at Herculaneum and Pompeii hold references to the cult of Isis, fueling interest in ancient Egypt.
1798	Napoleon Bonaparte launches Egyptian campaign and encourages scholarly studies of the area.
1822	Jean-Francois Champollion deciphers hieroglyphics on the ancient Rosetta Stone as Egypt is opened to Westerners.
1831	French King Louis XVIII erects gift of Egyptian obelisk in Paris' Place de la Concorde.
1869	Opening of the Suez Canal
1871	Official celebration of the opening of the Suez Canal, with premiere of Verdi's *Aida* at Cairo Opera and visit by Empress Eugenie of France.
1910	Louis Cartier copies Egyptian ornamental motifs in fine jewelry
1911	Franco-Egyptian Exhibition at the Louvre opens with visit by Egypt's King Faud.
1917	Hollywood produces film *Cleopatra.*
1920	Egyptian motifs and inlay work are replicated in art deco designs.
1922	British Egyptologist Howard Carter and backer Lord Carnarvon announce the discovery of King Tutankhamen's tomb.
1923	Lord Carnarvon dies following an insect bite, fueling stories of the curse of King Tut's tomb.
1934	Cecil B. De Mille releases his version of *Cleopatra.*
1961–65	Objects from the tomb of King Tutankhamen on exhibition tour in the U.S. and Canada.
1963	Elizabeth Taylor stars in *Cleopatra.*
1976–79	Treasures of Tutankhamen tours U.S. museums
1985	Ramses tour of museums in the U.S.
1996–97	Splendors of Ancient Egypt tours U.S.

1. Examine the item under magnification and note any apparent wear, repairs, materials, construction, and design on your worksheet.

2. Acid-test the metal. Do not accept the markings at face value and remember that the karat fineness helps suggest a date of manufacture. (See the *Chronological Guide to Dating Period Jewelry* in this chapter.)

3. Note hallmarks, maker's marks, or touchmarks. Either draw them on your worksheet or photograph them if you have a macro lens on your camera.

4. Identify any gemstones, noting whether they are "right" for the period. Replacement stones lower the value of the piece.

5. Determine the weights of stones and note their quality.

6. Examine the workmanship again and make sure that the item is not a "married" piece of jewelry (two items of jewelry made into one).

7. Consider whether you can be sure it is not a reproduction. Carefully inspect the back of the item for important clues that signal reproduction, such as porosity or a wrinkled look in the metal. Both indicate the item was cast, typical of reproduction jewelry.

8. Check the findings and clasps. Are they "right" for the period? Have they been repaired or replaced? A pin back or earring wire dating from another period will reduce the value of the item by two-thirds. Figure 5-17 illustrates the findings commonly found in various antique and vintage jewelry. For example, pin backs vary during different periods, safety catches did not appear until 1910, and hinges can be significant—the earliest type of hinge consisted of three small pieces of tubing.

9. Does the item have enamel? If so, is the enamel in good condition?

10. Is it a micromosaic? If so, is it complete with no pieces missing?

11. If item is part of a set, are all the pieces present?

12. Should it be a pair of something? During the Victorian era, women commonly wore bracelets in pairs. A pair is more valuable than one; ditto earrings. Breaking up a set can destroy one-half to one-third of its value.

13. Are the prongs or bezel settings smooth? If they are rough or catch clothing or skin, they may have been changed.

14. Look at the chains. Are they smooth and supple when you run them through your fingers? Stiff chains signal section repairs. Also, inspect the links for wear, especially near the clasp; a worn-out chain is worth only intrinsic value. Look at the clasp; an original will frequently be hallmarked, which will give a higher value than a replaced one.

15. Are there any solder repairs? The presence of lead solder on antique jewelry reduces the value of the piece by 50 percent. Heat can destroy patina and cause irreparable damage to foil, cameos, and jet jewelry.

16. Do you have the original fitted box? This can add 20 percent to an item's value.

17. Look at the stones. Stones in a nineteenth-century piece will be well cut; those in a sixteenth-century piece will not. Modern stones such as tanzanite will not be found in antique jewelry unless the original stone has been replaced. Jewelry made before 1900 should have natural pearls; Mikimoto was sending cultured pearls into the marketplace

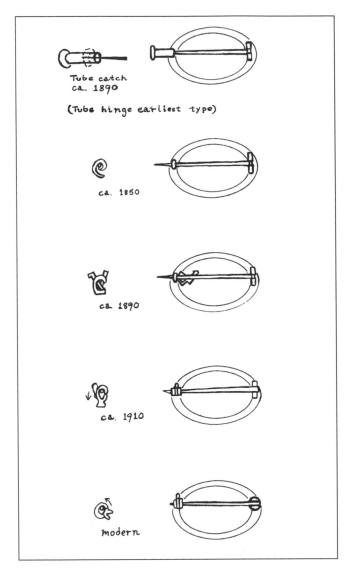

5-17. Findings commonly used on antique and vintage jewelry.

by the turn of the century and even won a medal for a pearl exhibition at the 1904 St. Louis Exposition.

18. Look at the safety chain. Victorian bracelets had a safety chain with a safety-pin attachment. Other antique bracelets had a small hook on the safety chain and no spring ring. Poorly soldered, especially lead-soldered, safety catches can reduce value up to 50 percent.

Alterations made to original articles are common. Pins or clips have often been turned into pendants. Look for the joining of two sections from different periods. As an appraiser, you are accustomed to judging quality in jewelry; use the same trained eye to detect changes such as these mentioned.

If the antique jewelry under appraisal needs repairs, advise your client that it takes a highly skilled specialist to do the job. Electric soldering is the best repair method. Enamel cannot be heated, and foiled stones will be charred and ruined by a sloppy repair job, which can devalue an item by as much as two-thirds.

When writing up the report, note any embellishment found on antique jewelry items, since any engraving on the item can add to or detract from the value, depending on the purpose of the report. For instance, if a bangle bracelet is appraised for insurance-replacement purposes, add the cost of any engraving and/or message inside the bracelet. If, however, the item is appraised at fair market value, the engraving would decrease the item's value. No one else would want a bracelet with this exact name or message.

Antique jewelry is correctly valued in relation to a comparable: the market-data approach. The cost of replacing the article with a comparable one may be higher or lower than the cost of remaking the item, but you cannot use the cost approach technique to appraise antique jewelry accurately. In addition to using comparables for replacement values, the appraiser needs a good current knowledge of supply and demand of like items within the appraiser's market region. This information can be collected only through personal research among antique jewelry dealers in the appraiser's local area. However, you should remember that almost all appraisers tend to *overprice* antique jewelry.

Provenance

Provenance is one of the most compelling reasons for your client to enter the world of antique jewelry collecting. Even before the great auction boom of the late 1970s, historic jewelry brought historical prices. Christie's auctioned two pearl-and-diamond earrings in Geneva in 1969. Although the quality of the pearls and the design were not especially noteworthy, the proof that the earrings were three hundred and fifty years old and once belonged to Henrietta Maria—daughter of Henry IV of France and Marie de Medici; sister of Louis XII; and wife of Charles I of England—attracted hordes of collectors, dealers, and museum directors. Three portraits, by Van der Helst, Netscher, and Voet, exist in which Henrietta Maria can be seen wearing the earrings.

If the client has any documentation of authenticity, or letters from previous owners claiming a pedigree on a piece of jewelry, append these to the appraisal report.

Telling a Reproduction from a Genuine Antique

Is it old or merely a reproduction? The answer has become tougher to resolve in the last few years because many companies are reproducing antique jewelry. Furthermore, once these items have been in the market for a few years, their genesis becomes even harder to determine. The field of antique jewelry reproduction has existed for centuries, with copies ranging from highly sophisticated works of skilled craftsmen to mass-produced examples that do not have the correct appearance of age, quality of design, or workmanship. Over the centuries, various techniques have been surreptitiously used to "age" jewelry. One method is to immerse gold metals in a weak acid or lye solution to impart an aged look; gemstones have been purposely chipped or scratched with emery or sand to give them the appearance of many years of use.

Fakes are a fact of life. There was a big trade in reproduction jewelry in ancient Rome—the Arabs rifled tombs and made copies of the engraved stones to sell to unsuspecting tourists. In England they tell the story of a find of so-called *fibulae* of Roman days dredged from the River Thames that turned out to be made only a few years before, and about jewelry from "Saxon graves" that forgers later confessed had been recently made and buried in the earth until a suitable patina was achieved. Through many centuries there has been no slackening in the production of fakes, copies, and reproductions of jewelry. As an appraiser you should approach every assignment of antique jewelry with skepticism. Authenticity is not proved by a presumed provenance, your client's circumstances of finding the item, or the price tag. A great story is told by a gemologist/appraiser who was on holiday in Paris and browsing at the Marche aux Puces (flea market). He was excited to spot a 16th-century ring in one of the showcases. The ring was very expensive but the appraiser was determined to have it. He negotiated all afternoon and just before the place closed for the night his offer was accepted, reluctantly. Back in London he took the ring to an expert in period jewelry. The expert took one look and said, "Oh, that! Isn't that from the Paris flea market? I keep seeing the same ring over and over."

The appraiser's primary defense against such pitfalls is in knowing as much as possible about the way authentic versions of the item were made:

1. What materials were used in certain periods
2. How the materials were used and held together
3. What finishes were used
4. The favored ornamentation (enamel, repoussé, etc.), and how it was applied.

Understanding the effects of aging on jewelry materials may help spot a fake, because knowing how an object was worn helps one draw conclusions about where it should show wear marks and patina. Although the ability to detect fakes, reproductions, and innocent misattributions will be improved by learning the old manufacturing techniques, if the reproductions have been made using the original old tools, dies, or casts, reproduction is almost undetectable, even by experts.

People who work in auction sales, especially those who handle lots of jewelry, are excellent resources for information on reproduction jewelry. They see a lot of it and they must be able to make a separation between the original and the replica. Gloria Lieberman of Skinner's Boston says that everything has been reproduced in the jewelry field. "At least 90% of the jewelry I see has been altered or is a reproduction," Lieberman says and adds, "The reproductions get better and better as time goes by." One of the reasons is that many manufacturing companies are now using the original old molds to turn out new copies. Lieberman made the following observations during an interview on the subject of reproduction jewelry: (1) Victorian bangle bracelets were reproduced in the 1950s; the florentine finish on the 1950s bracelets was not found on the original bracelets, thus giving away the copies. (2) Many lizard or salamander brooches were copied from the antique original motifs during the years 1978–1980. Carefully inspect the marks or hallmarks to help in separating reproductions. (3) Many reproduction brooches are without any galleys. Observe the backs, the metal, and the type of pin. Closed back brooches in 19K have been coming into the market from Portugal and they are only about 30 years old. The closed backs are made specifically so that the brooch will have an antique look. New silver over gold pieces are also being sent into the market as antique. Other characteristics to be alert for in the fakes coming from Portugal: buff top sapphires without any wear; heavy, thicker shanks on rings without wear; all diamonds full cut round brilliants.

Some additional suggestions for distinguishing between the genuine article and reproduction jewelry include the following:

1. Use a good loupe and a strong light source.
2. Look for porosity (surface pits and bubbles), which denote that the item was made from a mold—a common method of mass producing reproductions.
3. Note whether the prongs or shanks of rings show wear. Look at the links and clasps on bracelets and necklaces for signs of wear.
4. Reproduction jewelry, when new, has the fresh tone of new gold while antique jewelry has a slightly

warm tone consonant with the patina of gold antiquities.

5. A cast reproduction item will not have the finely detailed decoration or engraving of old jewelry as ornamentation will have been molded in with the casting.

6. Leftover pieces of gold from the casting procedure can often be found in the corners and edges of reproduction jewelry.

7. Examine gemstones for the following:

Cut: Is the cut incorrect for the period, i.e., modern brilliant in a Georgian piece?

Type: Is the gemstone incorrect for the period, i.e., tanzanite in a Victorian lavalier?

Wear: Look for abrasion on facet junctions, wear on the top of cabochons, nacre missing from pearls, the quality of carved stones or shell. While having stones in pristine condition may mean the object was well cared for, it can also mean that stones have been replaced.

Natural or Synthetic? The first synthetic rubies came onto the market in 1885. Emerald not until the early 1930s.

Settings: Are the gemstones mounted in bezel (also called collet) prongs? With some type of adhesive?

Enhancement: Are the gemstones dyed? Oiled? Polymer treated? Fracture filled? Polymer treatments are found in modern gemstones and suggest possible reproduction jewelry.

If you cannot tell for certain, get a second opinion from a knowledgeable colleague. Recognizing the limits of your knowledge and getting help when needed will keep you out of trouble.

Quality Factors of Enameled Jewelry

When writing your report on enameled jewelry, note the type—translucent or opaque—in your description. Color and technique are also important and can affect value.

The common enamelling techniques are *cloisonné, champlevé, basse-taillé, plique-à-jour, taille d'épargne, niello, grisaille,* and *guilloché.* Two other techniques encountered rarely are *en résille* and Limoges. *En résille* is a base glass or rock crystal upon which fine, hairlike lines are incised to form the design. The pattern is lined with gold, and the cells filled with soft, low-fire opaque or translucent enamel. Limoges enamelling is done without the aid of separate cells. Enamel is applied all over the metallic (usually copper) surface, one layer nearly drying before the next one is applied; the entire surface is then fused in one firing.

Note whether the enamel has strong and pure color and if care has been shown in the selection of the color combination. Mention whether the design is cleanly and clearly carried out and whether the metalwork is cleanly executed and free from excess solder or other evidence of careless workmanship. Note the polish; it should be a high luster. Fire-polished items can be recognized by the lack of a truly flat surface and betray an inferior piece. Mechanical polishing produces a comparatively flat and beautiful surface.

A few clues to age: If an enameled item purported to be Art Nouveau has concave cloisons, be suspicious. The enamel in the cloisons of old pieces is absolutely level. Furthermore, in old Italian and Portuguese pieces, each block of enamel in the cloisons is shaded in color; in newer items there is no shading.

Chronological Guide to Identifying Period Jewelry

1798: 18K gold standard introduced in English jewelry.

Before 1800s: The backs of stones in jewelry were closed because tools had not yet been developed for the proper faceting of stones. As cutting tools became available, the backs on stone settings began to be opened.

1835: First class rings (West Point).

1840: Gold electroplating process developed. The majority of necklaces had closures in front.

1854: 9, 12, and 15K gold jewelry introduced in England.

1868: Demantoid garnets discovered.

1870: Kidney wires first used in earrings. (These are still in use today.) Long chains and long pendants with no plain surfaces were common. All surfaces were ornately chased or engraved with trivial allover designs. Novelty jewelry includes birds, flowers, insects, moths, butterflies, and heads of females.

1880: Small stud and pearl earrings and choker necklaces popular.

1885: The first ruby synthetics came into use. Diamonds were used on nearly all articles.

1860–1880: Dangling, neo-Etruscan-style earrings in vogue.

1886: First Tiffany solitaire setting.

1890: Threaded stud earrings in style. Although still used today, they are smaller in diameter and the nut is lighter weight. Platinum first used in jewelry at this time. Platinum was first discovered in the fourteenth century, but a torch hot enough to work the metal comfortably was not developed until the 1870s.

1890–1915: Gold and platinum often used in the same item.

1880–1900: Colored golds popular: pink, yellow, and green gold combined in the same item.

1900: First cultured pearls appear in jewelry.

1903: Kunzite discovered by Dr. George Frederick Kunz in California.

1903: Marquise-cut diamonds and baguettes came into vogue.

1906: Law passed in U.S. that gold content must be stamped on jewelry.

1909: Screw-back earrings developed.

1910: First synthetic sapphires and spinels came into use.

1912: White gold developed.

1920s: "Invisible" settings popularized.

1938: Emerald synthetics developed by Chatham.

1940: Clip-back earrings in style (still used today).

Using Price Guides

There is a line from a song in the Broadway musical *The Music Man* about selling to the public: "You've got to know the territory." That applies to valuing antique jewelry, too.

You must know your own regional markets, as well as the national and—ideally—international markets of supply and demand. Price guides for antique jewelry should be used *only* as guides, not as fully accurate prices. Both Sotheby's and Christie's conduct auctions several times a year, and issue illustrated catalogs with realized prices.

Consult the following for identification and value guidance:

1. *Auction Market Resource for Gems and Jewelry,* by Gail B. Levine, P.O. Box 7683, Rego Park, New York 11374
2. *Official Price Guide to Antique Jewelry,* by Arthur Guy Kaplan
3. *Answers to Question About Old Jewelry, Fourth Edition,* by C. Jeanenne Bell, G.G.
4. *Warman's Jewelry,* by Christie Romero
5. Videos: *The Antique and Collectible Jewelry Video Series, Volume 1: Victorian Jewelry, Circa 1837–1901* and *Volume 2, Edwardian, Art Nouveau, & Art Deco Jewelry, Circa 1887–1930s.* Videos narrated by C. Jeanenne Bell.
6. *Hidden Treasures,* A collector's guide to antique and vintage jewelry of the 19th and 20th centuries, narrated by Christie Romero.

Cameos

Cameos are one of civilization's oldest art forms. Engraved gems—cameos and intaglios—evolved from the development of seals about 6500 B.C. in Mesopotamia, where they were used to authorize documents, seal goods, trademark, and tax products.

Egyptians wore scarab seals around their necks with their signature on the underside of the scarab. The Romans, however, are responsible for bringing cameos into their finest and most prolific epoch. They introduced designs of family portraits, erotic fantasies, animals, and gods. With the decline of the Roman Empire, the cameo's popularity also fell, and not until the Middle Ages were engraved gems revived as popular talismans.

During the fourteenth century, cameos and intaglios were revered, and the Medici family and other collectors made the importance of the gem soar. When banded agate was discovered in Germany in the sixteenth century, cameo production increased substantially and popularity continued until well into the early Victorian period, when Queen Victoria herself became an ardent shell cameo collector. The Italians, already exceptional carvers, were ready for the craze with mass production of locally available shells.

The word *cameo* literally means "raised above." This carving in relief is executed in a variety of shells and hardstones, coral, lava, glass, and jet.

Today, cameo production is carried out chiefly in Italy and Japan. The Italian cameos are generally found in coral, shell, and hardstones such as onyx and chalcedony. Many cameos are still crafted by hand, but automation has crept into the industry and ultrasonically carved cameos are now being mass produced. In Japan, most cameos for jewelry are machine carved from Brazilian agate. One machine can produce five pieces in one day, while it takes three or four days to carve one piece by hand.

The Japanese have been manufacturing well-defined hardstone cameos for pendants, brooches, earrings, rings, cuff links, belt buckles, and clasps for string ties for several decades. Further, they are using ultrasonic to increase production. The Japanese learned the ultrasonic method from the Germans, who pioneered it.

Learning to separate the ultrasonically carved cameo from the hand-carved one is not difficult, but it may take some practice. To learn this technique fully, practice with a cameo that you know is ultrasonically cut. Dealers are now able to distinguish between the cutting processes and are disclosing it to their customers. Under a strong light and 10× magnification, look carefully at the whitish area of the cameo (usually the top layer), especially in folds of hair and clothes for what is called a "fresh-fallen snow" appearance. This is also known by the proper name *cavitation* because of the microscopic indentations in the material. However, the look of fresh-fallen snow, a term coined by Anna M. Miller and Gerhard Becker during research for the book *Cameos Old and New,* is the most

5-18. The owner and model of the cameo shown in figure 5-19. *(Photograph courtesy of Timeless Gem Designs)*

5-19. This strikingly accurate chalcedony cameo portrait of the owner illustrates the quality of craftsmanship achieved by German master cameo carvers. *(Photograph courtesy of Timeless Gem Designs)*

striking evidence of ultrasonic cutting. Practice this technique with a *known* ultrasonically cut cameo, and with one that has been hand carved. They must both be of hardstone. At the time of this writing, shell cameos are still being carved by hand. Ultrasonic machinery will not work on shell because the surface is too bumpy. In order to work properly, the machine needs the smooth surface usually found in hardstone.

A few of the German carvers, including the notable Erwin Pauly, sign their work, which enhances the value of the gemstone. Idar Oberstein is still the hardstone carving capital of the world, where German cameos are produced in a variety of hardstone materials by a body of master carvers. By special commission, lifelike portraits such as the one pictured in figures 5-18 and 5-19 are being created. These pieces can cost from five hundred to over one thousand dollars wholesale, depending upon detail and size of the cameo.

Although there are slightly different rules for judg-

ing antique and contemporary cameos, all are examined under 10× magnification with a strong light to expose any cracks or breaks in the material. Since gemstone carving is an art form, it must be evaluated as one by judging composition, proportion, subject, detailing, finishing, and craftsmanship. Appraisers can use the following guide to estimate value of contemporary carved cameos:

1. Material. Identify the material used in the cameo and remember that hardstone is more valuable than shell. Examine the material to determine if the piece has been dyed or color enhanced. Is the cameo hand carved or machine made? Is it one piece or a composite?
2. Detail. Study the engraving. The composition, subject, and quality of craftsmanship should combine to point up the artistic quality of the cameo. Hair should have a hairlike texture; skin should look like skin.
3. Signature. On finer pieces, the artist's signature is almost always applied either to the front or the back. The signature may be prominently and boldly displayed, or hidden in clothing folds or locks of hair.

If you are unsure of your ability to judge the artistic merits of cameos, remember that the finest workmanship is generally used on top quality material by the most experienced engravers. Careful study of museum collections for comparison of craftsmanship and materials will enhance your ability to judge quality.

German master cutter Gerhard Becker has some firsthand knowledge about judging cameo quality: "In most cases craftsmanship is more important than the material used," he insists. "A fine craftsman can turn any rock into an art object, while an inexperienced carver may destroy the finest material. Carving quartz," he said, "is more difficult than carving agate, while lapis lazuli, topaz and corundum all require separate techniques."

Explaining further, Becker said an agate cameo carved in a layered flat-relief technique, such as the one shown in figure 5-20, is a much more difficult exercise than carving a cameo from thick layered material. He also stressed the importance of the surface finish and proportion of the carved motif to the stone as combining factors that point out the carver's expertise. The handsome cameo shown in figure 5-21 is a fine example of the cameo engraver's artistic abilities. In appraising antique cameos, all of the rules for appraising contemporary cameos apply as well as the three following:

1. Depth of carving. Deeply carved cameos are desirable and more valuable than shallowly carved ones. Lava particularly lends itself to this rare, fine, deep detailing. Examine the cameo for wear because this may indicate its age.
2. Period of origin. Examine the design theme as a possible clue to its time of production.
3. Subject. The subject or subjects may add value. Scenes, full-face and full-length figures, carvings of

5-21. A deeply carved shell cameo from an Italian workshop reflects the artist's interpretation of female beauty.

men and children, and identifiable portraits are all less common and thus more valuable.

When researching the price of antique cameos, consider current comparable item prices from antique dealers along with auction prices.

Class Rings, Fraternal Jewelry, and Religious Jewelry

Class Rings

Class rings made their debut in 1835 when the cadets of the U.S. Military Academy at West Point began wearing heavy gold signet class rings. The rings displayed a school insignia and the motto "Danger Brings Forth Friendship," as well as the graduation date. They were made to individual order and, as the story is told, one cadet set a pebble from West Point's old parade ground as a stone in his class ring. In the West Point class of 1837, the eight-dollar gold class ring was especially noteworthy because of the intaglio carnelian gemstone used. Later, other colleges, high schools, and West Point graduating classes agreed upon uniform rings struck from a standard die. The all-metal signet style ring was also changed to a purely ornamental gemstone-set ring.

Class rings then remained pretty much unchanged until the nonconformist period of the 1960s

5-20. A three layer carved agate shows detail achieved by 20th century German carvers.

and 1970s, when the military was scorned by so many young people and class rings changed dramatically. The uniform ring passed out of style and manufacturers started offering a variety of styles to the graduates. Fashion rings—a smaller, thinner class ring—have surged in popularity since they were first introduced in the mid-1970s. However, the traditional heavier ring is still sought by many teens, especially boys who insist on the traditional style with a square stone.

Class rings are made in a variety of metals: 10K, 14K, and 18K gold; or stainless steel, celestrium, trillium, yellow aurora, and white lustrium—all nonprecious metals. Some manufacturers of class rings are: ArtCarved Class Rings, Inc.; Balfour; Jostens, Inc.; and Jürgens. Their average retail price for a high school ring starts at one hundred dollars and escalates to over four hundred dollars for a college ring.

Price guides for replacements can be obtained from many class-ring manufacturers, and they should be consulted on a per item basis. Each one has slightly different charges and options.

Class rings and military-service rings are judged and valued according to the following standards:

1. Metal, fineness, and weight.
2. Identity and quality of gemstones, if any.
3. Optional features. These are important since they increase the costs. Optional features include enamelling, custom-made theme side panels, special gemstones, pierced shanks, and inscriptions. Options are numerous and at customer request; special dies can be made, which increase the price further.

Service Awards

In a separate but related category are service awards and corporate-incentive jewelry awards. Recognition jewelry is produced by all the manufacturers listed above, as well as such others as Bulova Watch and Seiko Time Corporation. These awards are sold through jewelers to businesses. Jewelry given your client as a sales incentive, service award, honor award, or retirement gift is often of precious metal and set with gemstones. For an appraisal, the item is handled as is any other fine jewelry; however, when figuring replacement price, consultation with the manufacturer or jeweler selling the item is highly recommended. Special dies, design, or handwork that add to the final price may have been used, and may not be readily apparent to the appraiser.

Fraternal Jewelry

The association ring is a symbol of the desire for mass companionship. Its use as a badge of fellowship has been going on for a very long time. You will find fraternal rings mentioned in the records of heraldry and ancient orders of knighthood, in which the ring played a stellar role as a symbol of membership. One of the first recorded accounts (quoted in Remington, 1945) refers to an English knight who was given a symbolic ring in 506 A.D. Rings have been used as heraldic emblems and in coats of arms throughout all kingdoms in Europe. In ancient days the ring was called an *amulet*.

Lodge and fraternal rings and pins are not so romantic today as in times past, but still symbolize people bound by religion or social, financial, or civic interest.

The following list, which is by no means comprehensive, is of major fraternal organizations and intended to be a useful starting point for appraisers seeking more information about such jewelry:

- The Loyal Order of Moose
- The Free and Accepted Masons
- The Benevolent and Protective Order of Elks
- The Knights of Malta
- The Knights of Pythias
- The Independent Order of Odd Fellows
- The Knights of the Maccabees
- The Improved Order of Red Men
- The Fraternal Order of Eagles
- The Woodmen of the World
- The Independent Order of Foresters
- The Knights of Columbus
- The Knights Templar of the United States and Canada
- The Royal Arcanum
- Phi Beta Kappa
- Alpha Delta Phi
- Alpha Sigma Phi
- Omega Delta
- Phi Gamma Delta

The rings for these organizations and their auxiliaries are varied in metal, manufacture, and style, but most are of gold. Many are set with diamonds and other precious stones or enameled in jewel-like colors. Some vary according to membership within the association. The Freemasons have at least two dozen types of Masonic rings, each representing a different degree of the main organization.

As with the class-ring manufacturers, complete listings of those who deal exclusively in fraternal jewelry can be found in the *Jewelers' Circular-Keystone Directory*. Some manufacturers have easily identifiable lodge and fraternal symbols in their catalogs, so you can make accurate identification of the lodge jewelry you may be appraising. The following are determining factors in valuing fraternal jewelry:

1. Metal fineness, weight, and type.
2. Precious stones, enamelling, or other applied decoration.
3. Condition. Has the jewelry been repaired, and if so, is the enamelling damaged? Reenamelling an item requires removing all existing enamel, recutting the areas to be reenamelled, and then applying the new enamel—a costly process.
4. Special designs, artwork, or logo. Custom work requires special dies, and is therefore more expensive.

Religious Jewelry

Interest in religion is reflected in gold and silver jewelry: it might be called faith on a chain. Religious jewelry is popular and fashionable, particularly among young adults. A metropolitan newspaper, quoting results of a survey of Christian and Jewish religious gift shops, declared that religious jewelry is finding a great niche market. For one Texas jewelry manufacturer,

5-23. Further examples of Christian crosses used in religious jewelry.

James Avery, it has become a 20-million-dollar-a-year business. Avery is regarded as one of the foremost religious jewelry designers and producers in the United States. A staff of five hundred and fifty employees keeps the jewelry moving to consumers all over the world. The jewelry is stamped with his three candle logo and JA. Prices range from ten dollars to two thousand dollars, with most items listed at less than one hundred dollars retail.

An appraiser needs to be familiar with the symbols used by all faiths and religions. With a working knowledge of the symbols and what they represent, you can interpret the religious jewelry and artifacts you may be called upon to value. These may include chalices, mezuzahs, Hanukkah lamps, menorahs, gem-set Torahs, gem-set croziers, scrolls, communion and ceremonial plates, Kiddush cups and beakers, crosses, rosaries, crucifixes, miraculous medals, seals and talismans, etc. Different styles of Christian crosses are illus-

5-22. Various styles of Christian crosses used in religious jewelry.

STAR OF DAVID

CHAI

TORAH

MEZUZAH

MAZEL

5-24. Jewish symbols used in religious jewelry.

trated in figures 5-22 and 5-23. Jewish symbols frequently used in jewelry and charms are identified in figure 5-24.

Patron Saints in the jewelry field:

Anastasius	Patron Saint of Goldsmiths
Andronicus	Patron Saint of Silversmiths
Dunstan	Patron Saint of Goldsmiths
Eligius	Patron Saint of Jewelers
Nicholas	Patron Saint of Pawnbrokers and Merchants

Judaica

The field of Judaica is a discipline unto itself. The determining value factors for jewelry or religious items in this category are:

1. Age of the item. Eighteenth-century and earlier European silver is in demand and given a higher value.
2. Hallmarks.
3. Condition.
4. Size.
5. Provenance.

Many modern mass-produced Jewish jewelry items such as chais and mazel tov charms are gem set. The items are valued in the normal way for precious metal content and gemstones. Chains should be weighed separately from the medals.

Comparable items of contemporary jewelry can be found in catalogs from manufacturers engaged almost exclusively in producing this jewelry. The annually updated *Jewelers' Circular-Keystone Directory* has complete listings of these manufacturers and their current addresses.

If an object of adoration such as a chalice, Torah, or icon falls to you for valuation, you can also conduct research in catalogs from the major auction houses. Companies handling religious goods, sacred vessels, and vestments also have catalogs. A catalog source: *The Complete Catalog of Religious Jewelry,* Lumin Jewelry Co., Inc., 12 Edgeboro Road, East Brunswick, New Jersey 08816.

Native American Jewelry

The commercial Native American jewelry craze began in the 1920s, when the Harvey House restaurant chain opened during the great days of rail travel in the United States. At first, Native American jewelry was simply sold as curios in the restaurants for patrons touring the West. Earrings and thin, small bracelets stamped with arrows and bows and containing oval pieces of turquoise were most in demand. Heavy Native American jewelry was not popular until about 1925, when the classic squash-blossom necklaces were first brought to the tourist market. The squash-blossom craze lasted until 1940, when they were discontinued by the Native artisans for requiring too much work and too much turquoise.

In the 1920s and 1930s, the concho belt changed from a simple silver belt to a belt with turquoise stones not only in the buckle but also turquoise in the *butterfly*—the spacer between the conchos. The tourist jewelry of that era is highly collectible today.

In the years following World War II, many Americans traveled across the country and, on their trips to the Southwest and other areas inhabited by Native Americans discovered that "traders" had rooms full of the Indians' old personal jewelry, which the "traders" called "pawn pieces." Most of these are jewelry items the Native peoples made for themselves and pawned for two reasons: they needed money, and it was a safe storage place.

As a result of the popularity of the pawn pieces, a host of "trading posts" sprang up in the Southwest. During this time, which extended to the early 1950s, turquoise was named, for sales purposes, after the mines in which it was found: Bisbee, Castle Dome,

Nevada Green, and others. The names have become so standardized over the years that they now have little to do with the mines or even the original color of the turquoise. For example, Bisbee turquoise originally had a brown matrix. The Bisbee that is mined today has no brown matrix, although the mine is still active; it has a high blue color. Your clients may ask you about their turquoise items that have changed from blue to green over the years. You can reply that natural, untreated turquoise will *always* turn green after a few years owing to the porous nature of the material. There is nothing available to bring back the original blue color.

Although some Native Americans continued to handcraft silver jewelry in the 1960s in the traditional way, their work was not widely popular until the late 1960s and early 1970s when there was a strong stimulus for appreciating value in silver and turquoise, the two main components of the jewelry. The incentive was *investment;* silver, gold, and gemstones were being touted as wise investments by several financial sources in the 1970s. People were also reminded of the speculation that followed recall of silver certificates in 1967. The social turmoil of the 60s also had an effect. As near as can be pinpointed, the craze for the jewelry started on the West Coast by film stars wearing an assortment of turquoise and silver Native American jewelry. About the same time, itinerant hippies began wearing handmade Native American jewelry as a symbol of protest against an increasingly mechanized society. When popular magazines and newspapers of the day began giving extensive coverage to the fad, the Indian look was established as in vogue.

The skyrocketing demand for this jewelry led to many changes in the Native American jewelry business. The request for the jewelry was so great that actual Native American craftsman could not keep up with the demand, and it was soon being produced as machine-made reproductions in Japan, Mexico, Taiwan, and the Philippines. At that time imported jewelry was seldom labeled with the country of origin and therefore difficult to distinguish from the authentic. While import laws today require that a label or indelible marking stating the country of origin be attached to import items, these labels may be lost or removed by the time the imported jewelry is placed into a jewelry showcase. As a result, many imports are sold—knowingly or unknowingly—as authentic in many outlets.

For appraisers the difference in pricing should be clear: imports sold as authentic are priced out of proportion to their true value. Most people unaware of differences between authentic and imitation, or differences in quality, bought Native American jewelry without concern for these factors. Those who bought reproductions have seen their purchases depreciate. The market for Native American jewelry became glutted, and by 1981 the supply was high but the demand was gone. The majority of customers for the jewelry was probably not aware that the largest percentage of turquoise used in Native American jewelry was not high-grade natural stone, but low-grade turquoise. As appraiser for this type of jewelry, you are expected to know and understand the disparity of prices between varieties of turquoise. Any form of treated, stabilized, or reconstituted turquoise is of less value than high-grade natural stone, and should sell for less. Top quality turquoise can be identified as coming from one particular mine, but there is so little variation in lower grades, their origins cannot be identified. Once a stone has been treated, stabilized, or reconstituted, the only way to identify the origin is by destructive chemical analysis.

The ways in which turquoise can be changed:

Treated Turquoise: Lower grades of turquoise are treated to change color and harden the stone. Two techniques used are: (1) Mineral oil or animal fats injected under low heat and pressure to fill pores and bring out color, most often a glossy or greasy blue. This treatment is considered unethical since oils can ooze out of the stone resulting in color change. (2) Petroleum paraffin injected under heat and pressure to fill the pores and enhance the green-blue color.

Stabilized Turquoise: Stabilization is used when turquoise has a good color and matrix. Stabilization is used to harden the stone and preserve natural color, *not change the color.* Turquoise is stabilized by injection of either a colorless polymer plastic or sodium silica gel into the pores of the stone. This process both seals and hardens the stone.

Reconstituted Turquoise: Turquoise fragments that are ground, mixed with resins, and shaped to form new stones are called *reconstituted.* This turquoise lacks the shine of natural turquoise.

There are four types of turquoise substitutes, used primarily in machine-made and low-quality handmade jewelry: (1) agates, quartz, howlite dyed to resemble turquoise; (2) chrysocolla, malachite, variscite, azurite, lapis lazuli; (3) artificial turquoise made with materials having the same chemical properties as natural turquoise; (4) dyed plastics.

Most authentic handmade Native American jewelry is produced by three Southwestern tribes, Navajo, Zuni, and Hopi silversmiths in northern Arizona and New Mexico. The Southwestern style of jewelry is unique to the Native Americans, since silverwork was introduced by Navajo Atsidi Saani, who learned blacksmithing at Fort Defiance, Arizona, in the 1850s.

Some good and fine artistic work has emerged. A

few of the exceptionally talented Native American silversmiths used their profits to develop new concepts and techniques in Native American jewelry design. The result is that now there are two kinds of jewelry for sale. The first category includes signed, handmade silver and gold jewelry, often set with turquoise, lapis lazuli, and even diamonds. These are contemporary in design, unlike the original Native American jewelry. The second category includes production-work Native American jewelry—Navajo, Hopi, and Zuni—which is characterized by new designs in silver and the use of more stones.

Navajo jewelry is distinguished by its simplicity and sparing use of turquoise or other stones. The Navajos are silversmiths. Their famous squash-blossom beads are not symbols of fertility—a romantic notion perpetuated by traders—but adaptations of Spanish ornaments, which were shaped like pomegranates. The dangling *najas*—crescent shapes—were also borrowed from the Spaniards, who in turn had adapted the shape from African charms used to ward off the evil eye.

The Zunis learned from the Navajos how to work silver, but their primary interest is lapidary. They are stonecutters and stoneworkers. In Zuni-designed jewelry, metal serves primarily as a support for colored stones. Designs are often so ornate that little silver is visible.

The Hopis used turquoise sparingly, and their contribution to jewelry and the most popular styles was developed after 1930. They use an overlay technique in which two sheets of silver are sweat-soldered together. The top or overlay has a cutout design, and the area directly beneath the design (on the bottom silver) is oxidized, creating a contrast between bright and dark silver. Traditional Hopi designs were drawn from pottery decoration.

The Santo Domingos are known for making fine beads called *hishi*. Turquoise, clam, and other shells are drilled, strung together, and rolled over to produce smooth and round edges. This tribe also includes silver in their necklaces.

Characteristics of value in old Native American jewelry, including old "pawn" jewelry:

1. Early Native American jewelry was made with melted silver slugs and coins fashioned into items by casting or hammering. By 1940, sheet silver was being used. The width of silver varies in old hammered items, and bracelets taper at the ends.
2. Old pieces are heavier and more massive. More silver was used in the early 1900s. Newer pieces are lightweight in comparison.
3. Hammer marks should be obvious on the inside of the older, heavier pieces.
4. While patina is not a positive indicator of age (because it can be induced by chemicals), old jewelry worn continually will exhibit a patina on the silver, from light to dark gray.
5. The old twisted wire bracelets were made with hand-hammered wire, which is distinguished by the irregular thickness and twist of the wire. The wire in the newer machine-drawn silver bracelets is perfectly even in diameter.
6. Old jewelry is usually found set with stones in their original shapes just as they came from the mines. In newer pieces, stones have been shaped to fit the design.
7. Some old stones originally used as earrings and pendants then reset into other pieces of jewelry may show a drill hole.
8. In old Native American jewelry, the stone was set flush with the bezel. After long use, the stone often wears down below the bezel.

The Indian Arts and Crafts Association, Albuquerque, New Mexico, gives these tips in evaluating *contemporary* Native American jewelry:

1. *Appearance:* Is the jewelry well crafted? Are images clear, lines unwavering? Are the stones well cut, uniform in size, and secure in their settings? If the design is stamped, is the design clear and even? Stamped designs that show on the inside of the jewelry are frequently mechanically stamped.
2. *Materials:* If jewelry is made of silver is it marked "Sterling"? If turquoise or other opaque stones are used, is the stone natural or has it been altered to change the color or hardness of the stone?
3. *Source:* By law, any item sold as Indian or Native American made, must be the creation of an individual who is a member of a state or federally recognized tribe or tribally certified as a Native American artisan. Ask the seller to certify that the item was Native made.

In your report, use the terms "like Zuni" or "like Navajo" to indicate style and design unless you can specifically classify the item by signature. Use correct nomenclature. The parts of a squash-blossom necklace are the beads, the trumpets (squash blossoms), and the *naja* (the U-shaped center dangle).

Some well-known signatures that increase the value of the jewelry include the following:

Navajo: Francis James, Helen Long, Jimmy Bedoni, Mary Morgan, Lee Yazzie, Andy Kirk, Eddie Begay, Sam Begay, John Hoxie, and Leroy Hill.

Zuni: Lambert Homer, Sherman Yuselu, Virgil Benn, Shirley Benn, Lucille Quam, Lon Jose, Kirk and Mary, Dennis Edaakie, Lee and Mary Weebothee.

Hopi: Charles Loloma, Lawrence Saufkie, Victor Coochwytewa, and Duane Maktima (who is of the Hopi and Laguna tribes both).

Santo Domingo: Charles Lovato, Paul Rosetta, Harold Lovato, and Sedelio F. Lovato.

Other signatures that you may see include David Tsikewa, Mary Tsikewa, Edna Leki, Veronica Nastacio, Larry Golsh, Charles Pratt, and Preston Monongye.

In the late 1970s, the price of Native American jewelry increased tenfold, only to drop dramatically some five years later. A bracelet that cost sixty dollars in 1968 cost six hundred dollars in 1978 and one hundred and fifty dollars in 1986. Large squash-blossom necklaces and fancy concho belts, selling for five thousand dollars in the 1970s, sold for twelve hundred dollars each at auction in 1986. Most concho belts, squash-blossom, coral, and turquoise necklaces currently sell in the five hundred to twenty-five hundred dollar retail range if they are signed items.

The 1930s thin silver bracelets stamped with arrows and similar motifs that originally sold for six to eight dollars each were worth sixty to one hundred dollars in 1986. They have become collectibles. These bracelets contain approximately two ounces of silver each and must be judged individually. The Indian Arts and Crafts Association has attempted over the last several years to require labeling on foreign counterfeit Native American style goods. In 1985, more than two hundred American Indian artisans, backed by two Congressmen, filed a request with the U.S. Customs requiring clear, indelible, and permanent labeling on the imitation jewelry. They would like all such imported items to be marked "imported."

According to an *Albuquerque Tribune* article published on July 10, 1987, the Senate passed an amendment designed to promote the export of Indian arts and crafts. The measure authorizes the Secretary of Commerce to make grants to pay for trade missions, promotional programs, surveys, and other market development activities for Indian jewelry, art, and crafts. The Senate also passed a second amendment that makes it illegal to import counterfeit Indian jewelry, art, and crafts unless the imports are indelibly marked with the country of origin.

To obtain prices of American Indian jewelry, one of the best resources is the *Southwestern/Indian Arts, Crafts and Jewelry* brochure offered by the Albuquerque, New Mexico, Convention and Visitors Bureau. For Internet users, a long listing of shops selling old and new Indian jewelry is accessible via the World Wide Web: http://www.abqcvb.org/shopping/swind.html.

The Indian Arts and Crafts Association, 122 La Veta NE, Albuquerque, New Mexico 87108, web address: http://www.iaca.com, offers help for your questions about Indian jewelry and a set of eleven educational brochures about Indian designs, jewelry, turquoise, etc., that can be ordered online.

Southwestern Association on Indian Affairs, Indian Market, P.O. Box 1964, Santa Fe, New Mexico 85704

Indian Arts & Crafts Board, U.S. Department of Interior, Room 4004, Washington, DC 20240

In addition, up-to-date auction catalogs of mixed-tribal merchandise can be purchased from Sotheby's, Christie's, and Butterfield and Butterfield.

Ethnic Jewelry

Each social culture has its own interpretations of fine jewelry, which may frequently be opposed to what Americans consider "fine." Appraisers often have complete collections and/or single items of ethnic jewelry to value as part of estates for probate, divorce, or insurance. How are these items handled and what criteria are used for value? Folk jewelry is an area in which the appraiser without experience in appraising jewelry of a particular culture may place too high or low a value on the article.

Although it is not necessary for you to attempt to be an expert on jewelry from all cultures, the better informed and the more widely read you are, the more accurate your valuation will be. Build a reference library of books on ethnic jewelry as well as of catalogs from major auction houses, museums, and rare-book dealers. Check the bibliographies of these reference works to find further sources of information.

In appraising ethnic jewelry, determine the following factors:

1. Culture of origin, such as Bedouin, Peruvian, Islamic, or Balinese, for example.
2. Purpose of the jewelry (other than decorative), if any.
3. Condition and age.
4. Material and fineness of metal if the piece contains metal. The material need not be a precious metal for the jewelry to be valuable in this category.
5. Craftsmanship and execution of design. The basic techniques of design are universal, only applications will differ. Recognize and list *repoussé, cloisonné,* embossing, and other techniques. These will often help to identify the country of origin.
6. Wearability of the item. Does the clasp work properly? Are there any broken or missing parts?

7. Provenance. Can it be authenticated?
8. Whether the item is a single piece or part of a collection.
9. Hallmarks, maker's marks, or other stampings.
10. Popularity of the item. Was it part of a fad or a trend? Trendy jewelry is almost always better made than fad items. The appraiser must be able to recognize particularly desirable objects.

It is important to be able to distinguish between the style of the jewelry and its actual country of origin. Many jewelry articles are produced in the style of another country or culture, and there are many reproductions of stylistic transitions. What the appraiser is concerned with are the actual items of jewelry produced in any particular country. Comparables in pricing Bedouin, Philippine, Moroccan, African, or other ethnic jewelry can be difficult to find. A creative approach is called for to obtain current prices and/or comparable item prices. The following market resources may be of help:

1. Catalogs, including those published by auction houses, museums, and various airports. In particular, try Sotheby's London catalogs, which cover jewelry from all cultures; catalogs published by the Metropolitan Museum of Art (New York) and the Smithsonian Institution; and catalogs from Saudi Arabian Airlines, Amsterdam Airport, and Shannon Airport. Some interesting and often information-rich web sites include:
Bedouin Jewelry: http://www.arab.net/photos/jewellery.html
Greek Jewelry: http://www.addgr.com/jewel/elka/
Hong Kong Jewelry Manufacturers' Association: http://www.jewelry.org.hk
Sonali: (22K gold) http://www.sonali.com
Egyptian: (18-22K) http://www.jewelofthelotus.com
2. Popular magazines and trade journals, including *Smithsonian, Ornament, Antique World,* and *Lapidary Journal,* under the headings "Finished Jewelry" and "Miscellaneous," for catalogs offered by dealers from Sri Lanka to Haiti, Mexico to Chile. Research your public library for other specialty publications.
3. Major metropolitan cities often have full-scale ethnic communities that can be fertile hunting grounds for the appraiser researching prices. Try ethnic church bazaars as well as crafts fairs. If there are no ethnic communities in your area, perhaps there is an import specialty store.
4. Trade/gem and mineral shows. Call foreign trade commissions and visit their trade shows as well to get the names and addresses of companies that publish catalogs. Art galleries, too, often have showings of jewelry as well as artwork from other cultures.
5. Retail and other stores. Don't overlook clothing boutiques that concentrate on foreign styles. They often hold trunk shows of jewelry, which are announced in local newspapers. Also, try canvassing local pawnshops for comparable items. If the jewelry you are appraising is trendy, try upscale department stores—they usually stock a few items in their "costume jewelry" department, where non-gold jewelry is sold.

Mexican Jewelry

If you believe all Mexican jewelry is made of heavy silver and decorated with Aztec motifs and green and black stones, you are wrong. That primitive style was developed for the tourist industry during the 1920s and has become the equivalent of American costume jewelry.

The contemporary silver and gold jewelry of major Mexican cities today is not very different from jewelry found in New York or Rome. The fine jewelry sold in the cities is international in scope and style and will offer few evaluation problems to the appraiser.

What may present a dilemma, however, is pricing the jewelry produced in small workshops all over Mexico and mostly made by hand. Such work is done with traditional and simple tools, ranging from crude silver work containing colored glass to finely wrought gold jewelry set with precious stones.

Mexicans are lovers of tradition. In many villages, ways of living have changed little over the generations. A woman may still wear the exact style of earrings her grandmother wore. These would be crafted by the village silversmith in the traditional designs the smith has used season after season. There are villages where the jewelry styles are the same as they were four hundred years ago. In Mexico, each village has its own style of decoration. Frequently the materials indigenous to the area and the primary means of earning will inspire the jewelry motifs, materials, and style used. For example, the village of Pátzcuaro is located on a lake and fishing is the main source of income. If you want the necklace with small silver fish that is famous in Pátzcuaro, you must go there, find the local artisan who makes the necklace, and buy it. Chances are he or she is the only one in Mexico who makes exactly that style.

Even more traditional are the earrings worn by the women in the six villages surrounding Pátzcuaro. Again, each village has its own design—and you can tell where a woman is from by the earrings she wears.

Mexico produces about a third of the world's silver and consequently has plenty of raw material to work. A large quantity of silver jewelry is still made today in and around the famous silver center of Taxco. Most Mexican silver items are stamped .925, sterling. These are required by law to be 925/1000 parts silver. Some Mexican silver jewelry is stamped as high as .980 because many craftspersons like to make their own alloys. The beauty of .980 silver is that it has a soft patina and is resistant to tarnish.

Mexican jewelry is typically characterized by simple forms; naturalistic motifs, such as flowers, vines, birds, and butterflies; religious motifs; and movement. Most pieces have separate parts that move, such as bells, pendants on chains, or have fringe decoration, as on dangling earrings.

The artistic merits of much of the silver jewelry crafted in Taxco during the 1920s and 1930s has resulted in the development of a small but serious collector's market. The heavy cuff bracelets, highly stylized with swirling or geometric designs, are currently priced at several hundred dollars in the U.S. market. Suites of silver jewelry, handmade and without stones, can be found priced at a thousand dollars and up. These escalating prices are the result of a combination of intrinsic value, artistry, and maker's marks. Maker's marks, some of which are listed below, contribute significantly to the value of a particular item:

Maker's Name	Mark
Frederick Davis	F inside a D
William Spratling	W joined to an S
Antonio Castillo, Jorge Castillo	Los Castillo Taxco, written in a circle around an eagle
Enrique Ledesma	Ledesma, written in two conjoined ovals
Antonio Pineda	Antonio Taxco, written in a crown design
Hector Aguilar	HA, joined in a circle
Felipe Martinez	Piedra y Plata
Ysidro Garcia	Maricela Mexico, in a circle
Margot de Taxco	Margot de Taxco, in a square
Bernice Goodspeed	Sterling B Taxco, in a circle
Salvador Teran	Salvador, cursive writing in a rectangle
Ricardo Salas Poulat	Matl Salas, cursive writing in a square

European Designer Jewelry

Jewelry crafted by European designers has a special appeal. Most of the people who purchase from the salons of Bulgari, Buccellati, Boucheron, Chaumet, Mauboussin, and others view the articles as investments in good taste as well as fine jewelry.

Some of the most beautiful styles come from the hands and minds of European designer jewelers. The mystique surrounding foreign designed and manufactured goods is somehow mixed with perception of superior quality and historical reputations. Putting a value on this jewelry presents a few extra problems to the appraiser.

The good news is that most European designer jewelry of high quality is signed by the maker; many pieces are also marked by numbers and letters on the mounting to indicate the city of manufacture and the total weight of the gemstones contained in the item. The appraiser should begin by making a careful survey of the inside, underside, and backside of each jewelry article, writing down all symbols, hallmarks, and numbers.

A Bulgari spokesperson in New York said that documenting the purchase of a designer article is like establishing a pedigree: "The jewelry is in the same category as a fine painting. If you have all the documentation surrounding its purchase, the item will be more valuable in the long run." It seems clear that the appraiser should ask the client immediately whether a sales receipt, appraisal report, or any other documentation given with the jewelry at time of purchase is available.

The most important point in evaluating European status jewelry is that an accurate replacement figure cannot be obtained by determining the cost of the components. The appraiser must research an item at its place of manufacture. One reason that the bricks-and-mortar approach will not provide an accurate replacement valuation is that some jewelry houses hire designers on contract basis. We cannot know if the designer charged a hundred dollars an hour to produce the jewelry or twice that amount.

To illustrate just how far off appraisers can be in determining price, a study of the replacement cost of an 18K yellow-gold necklace, set with diamonds and rubies by Bulgari, was conducted by the Association of Women Gemologists in 1986. The actual item was purchased in Paris for twenty-six thousand dollars in 1985, discounted from the asking price of thirty-five thousand dollars. The survey revealed that most appraisers used the cost approach for insurance replacement, and were thousands of dollars short of what the necklace actually sold for in France. Furthermore, these appraisers grossly underpriced the cost of replacing the item in this country. According to Bulgari spokespersons, replacing the item with an identical one in New York would cost forty-four thousand dollars.

The first rule in evaluating European designer jewelry for retail replacement is *call the company*. Speak with a knowledgeable individual, explain what you are appraising, and let the representative lead you

5-26. Bulgari 18K necklace with center bezel-set yellow diamond of 8.38 carats; 353 round diamonds with a total weight of 2.89 carats; and ten baguette diamonds with a total weight of .96 carats. *(Photograph courtesy of Bulgari, New York)*

5-25. Eighteen-carat gold, platinum, and diamond necklace signed by Van Cleef & Arpels is pavé set with 747 round and single-cut diamonds, with a total weight of approximately 20 carats. The 18K platinum-and-diamond ear clips signed by Van Cleef & Arpels have 140 round diamonds with a total weight of approximately 7 carats. The bangle bracelet of 18K gold, platinum, and diamond, with a total diamond weight of approximately 5 carats, is not attributed to any designer or jeweler. *(Photograph © 1986 Sotheby's, Inc.)*

5-27. Bulgari multistrand necklace set with sapphire beads (total weight, 6.2 carats); with bezel-set yellow sapphire in center (total weight, 94.63 carats); thirty-two baguette diamonds (total weight, 5.08 carats); and 224 round diamonds (total weight, 23.25 carats). Fittings are 18K. *(Photograph courtesy of Bulgari, New York)*

through the steps necessary for proper and documentable replacement price. The best-known firms all have salons in New York or Los Angeles. If you are searching for fair market value, catalogs of major auction houses are reservoirs of information for sales of similar European designer items (fig. 5-25).

Bulgari has salons in Rome, Geneva, Monte Carlo, Paris, Milan, Tokyo, and New York. Examples of Bulgari jewelry are illustrated in figures 5-26 and 5-27. One of the unique aspects of Bulgari is that everything sold by the firm is made by the firm; there are no outside commissions made by others and signed by Bulgari. Therefore, it is either Bulgari jewelry or it is not. In jewelry currently manufactured by the firm, you will find the letter C and four numbers stamped on items that are handmade in the New York workshop. Jewelry cast in one of the three Bulgari workshops in Rome is stamped with the letters BD followed by four numbers.

Write down each number and letter before you call Bulgari for consultation. Bulgari has been stamping its jewelry with serial numbers and their name for the past twenty-five years. Before that, they used the name only; prior to that, the jewelry was merely stamped .750. The Italian company has been in business for over a hundred years, and has maintained very careful records of clients and purchases. They will help you with a replacement price if you tell them when and where the jewelry was purchased, provide the name and address of the customer, give them the letters and numbers on the jewelry, and submit written authorization from the client to release information to you.

Extra care should be taken in researching and evaluating the work of these contemporary designers and jewelers: Cartier (Alfred Durante is the only Cartier designer whose individual initials have ever been allowed to appear next to the Cartier name on single pieces), Van Cleef & Arpels, Tiffany & Co. (Paloma Picasso and Jean Schlumberger), Travert & Hoeffer, Trabucco, Capello, and Ivo Misani.

Fakes and reproductions can be found in all markets, including that of fine European designer jewelry. Become familiar with the work of the individual jewelers. You must know how to identify quality to be able to tell a knock-off from the genuine article. Bulgari jewelry is widely copied, but fakes will be revealed by their incorrect proportions as well as by their relative crudity. A genuine Bulgari will be harmonious in every detail, with every stone precisely set. You will find this trait to be true of all fine designer jewelry.

Jewelry from Contemporary Designers

Jewelry is an exciting business. Each generation of designers and goldsmiths innovates new styles and trends, and the appraisers must be aware of these.

Perhaps the best way to keep up with new jewelry artists is to attend trade shows. Jewelers of America sets aside its New Designers room at its New York show to feature some of the latest pieces. What you will see may be a revelation: the designers are well trained in their craft, have imagination, and are daring in their use of materials and techniques. Some young designers already have their own lines of jewelry in galleries or stores around the country. Many have won national and international design awards. All instill a joyful and fresh look to jewelry design.

It is not easy to value this work, but standard guidelines do apply. Ask yourself the following questions. Is the item signed? Is the quality excellent? Is the finish in harmony with the style and does it help make the appearance complete? Is the material a precious metal or an exotic one? Are the stones natural or synthetic?

When you first examine the item, consider whether the artist has put any thought behind the design and/or gem material. You cannot use old ideas and methods to evaluate this designer jewelry. Instead, you should proceed more as an art appraiser. Compare the jewelry to similar works by the artist and check how well these items have been selling. The work must be marketable before the item can receive its full value potential.

For information about jewelry designers, contact the Society of North American Goldsmiths (SNAG), 6707 North Santa Monica Blvd., Milwaukee, Wisconsin 53217. This organization has the names of more than five thousand members on file and can offer insights into a particular designer's position in the market.

It is expected that art-as-jewelry will be a major trend for many years. One reason is the bold new use of three progressive, colorful elements, known as *refractory metals:* titanium, niobium, and tantalum. When the materials are heat treated or run through an electrical bath, they display a spectrum of colors—lush, tropical greens, blues, magentas, and purples. Because these metals can endure extremely high temperatures, they cannot be commonly soldered, and require more innovative techniques to hold gemstones and findings. Accents such as 14K gold, silver, and gemstones must be mechanically riveted or wrapped onto the exotic metals or must be suspended from holes pierced in the jewelry. It is this intricacy of craft that has attracted these media to many of the new designers. The ultimate cost of the item is based on the degree of craftsmanship required. A pair of titanium earrings can cost as little as ten dollars retail, whereas an intricate necklace incorporating silver and gold may retail for as much as five hundred dollars.

Even designers not attracted to the refractory metals are employing new and unusual finishes on their jewelry. Some are discovering and using interesting metal techniques from Asian and other cultures. A Japanese style called *mokume gane,* or layers of metal, has found followers among the new-wave designers.

Her Specialty: One-of-a-Kind Precious Adornments

Georgia jeweler Kathy Kinev works in gold and platinum crafting one-of-a-kind jewelry pieces in meticulous detail. Her prices vary: a pair of gold earrings can cost as little as $50; a gold mesh bracelet that took 1,000 hours of hand crafting over a three-year period is priced at $35,000. "When you make everything by hand, even pulling your own wire, the value goes up from an appraisal point of view, " Kinev (fig. 5-28) said.

Kinev, a Jewelry Design and Silversmithing graduate of Georgia State University, not only alloys her own metals, but draws her own gold wire, then weaves the gold mesh used in many of the unique gold jewelry articles. She is one of a handful of artists using the ancient granulation technique to embellish pendants, earrings, and rings. Granulation is the decorative process of applying minuscule gold spheres to jewelry surfaces. The technique, developed by the Minoans in 3000 B.C., fell out of use during Roman times and be-

5-28. Kathryn Kinev, owner of Jewel Creations, exercises great patience and skill in creating intricate jewelry designs.

5-29. Kinev is especially fond of the art of granulation and makes it her specialty. These exquisite creations are the results of hundreds of hours of handwork.

came lost to jewelers until the 19th century. The process is time consuming and requires patience and skill. Kinev makes the ancient art of granulation her specialty. Some of her pieces (fig. 5-29) are unique granulation items in 22K gold; some take as long as 900 hours to create. Kinev also teaches jewelry repair and manufacturing at various workshops around the Southeast part of the United States.

Jewelry Artistry with Minerals

Gary Dulac of Vero Beach, Florida, has been called a "maestro of minerals" and a gem of an artist. He started his career as a jewelry designer and handfabricator more than two decades ago by apprenticing with

a German-trained goldsmith. From his apprenticeship, he learned how to make jewelry into something very special—without solder joints or loose stones, and finished inside and out. Dulac works in the entire spectrum of colors of gemstones and crystals, rough and cut. And, he likes to mix unusual gems and minerals that are not normally seen in high end jewelry—such as druse quartz and uvorite—with high quality stones such as ruby, emerald, sapphire, and diamonds (figs. 5-30 and 5-31). Dulac enjoys creating one-of-a-kind jewelry in 14K gold (figs. 5-32 and 5-33) using high-karat techniques such as gold granulation and reticulation. He also likes working in a variety of gold colors—including red, green, and white—and in platinum. One of the reasons his jewelry is so unusual is that he likes to experiment with new techniques in goldwork. The technique called reticulation is a 35-step annealing process that creates vein-like patterns in gold. It is so time consuming, it is practiced by only a few goldsmiths in the United States. Dulac is especially interested in new techniques for finishes and makes all his own tools to accomplish his goal. "All my finishes are either hammer set or hand finishes," Dulac said. Finishes are important to him because he believes an interesting finish gives added value to a well-crafted piece. "My finishes are one thing that attracts people to my work," he says, "the character and finish are equal to the character and life of the jewelry." All his work is signed (fig. 5-34) with his own impressive logo-signature.

Costume Jewelry

Most appraisers won't touch it. "Junk" or "scrap" is their quick response when asked their opinion of cos-

5-30. Gary Dulac's hand-fabricated pendant in 14K yellow gold featuring uvorite garnet and diamonds. *(Photo by AZAD.)*

5-31. Dulac's hand-fabricated pendant made in 14K yellow gold and featuring tsavorite, blue chalcedony, boulder opal, and sugilite. *(Photo by AZAD.)*

5-33. Dulac's handmade earrings in 18K yellow gold and platinum with mabé pearls and diamonds. *(Photo by AZAD.)*

5-32. A crowd-pleasing handmade ring by Dulac in 14K yellow and white gold with green tourmaline, yellow sapphire, and diamonds. *(Photo by AZAD.)*

5-34. All Gary Dulac's work is signed with his logo-signature.

tume jewelry. Some, of course, are correct in their assessment because most costume jewelry has little or no intrinsic value.

Few owners of the flashy baubles will seek you out to make an insurance appraisal; if they do, they will often be dismayed to find that the cost of an appraisal is more than the item is worth. However, costume jewelry is one of the hottest fields of collectibles: one person's junk is another person's treasure.

Since the field of collecting costume jewelry is growing, you may well be called upon to assess the value of a collection for probate. Although you will not need many gemological skills, you will need to use your judgment and experience as an appraiser. If you do not understand that this is viable merchandise with its own market and set of value factors, your assessment will be inaccurate, perhaps by thousands of dollars.

Gloria Lieberman of the Skinner Auction House in Boston says that the work of a group of costume jewelry designers and manufacturers has become collectible to the point of a cult following. She cites Schiaparelli, Chanel, Coro, Trifari, Miriam Haskell, Krementz, Carnegie, Hobe, and Eisenberg. She states that prices for these items vary from one region of the country to the other, with collectors paying the highest prices in California. Two of the most sought after pieces are pins from the 1940s: One is an American flag decorated with colored glass or enamels and worn on the lapel, the other is a Scotty dog. The popularity of the American flag pins seems reasonable enough, since there was a war on at the time of its manufacture and many collectors are nostalgic. But Scotty dog pins? Lieberman explains that President Roosevelt had a Scotty dog at the White House during

the 1940s and that the antics of the little fellow were frequently reported in the press and enjoyed by the public. Scotty dogs were the favorite breed during that administration.

Retail prices for collectible costume jewelry range from ten dollars to more than one thousand dollars per item. A Trifari necklace made in 1943 with an original price of fifty-five dollars is now selling for approximately two hundred dollars. Rhinestones are a hot item, with most pieces hovering around the fifty-five to eighty-five-dollar mark—more than three times what they sold for when they were brand new!

Items retailing for two to three dollars during the 1940s will now be found marked twenty-five dollars and up. What makes the difference? It depends upon the item's visual appeal; whether the stones are hand set or glued into the mountings; whether the metal is sterling or base metal; and whether the piece is marked with the manufacturer's name. If the jewelry is in the original box, its value increases considerably.

Flea markets, thrift shops, house and garage sales, and, surprisingly, major antique shows are good places to research value. Dealers in antique shows, especially those held in shopping malls, are reporting increased sales in this category. Some auction houses handle the more desirable items. Of course, in advance of all trends are harbingers of the news, so a few cost guides are already on the market. For further help in identifying costume jewelry and learning more about this field, see *Collecting Rhinestone Jewelry* by Maryanne Dolan, *One Hundred Years of Collectible Jewelry* by Lillian Baker, *Collectible Costume Jewelry* by S. Sylvia Henzel, and *Fifty Years of Collectible Fashion Jewelry: 1925–1974* by Lillian Baker. All include price guides and are listed in the bibliography.

CHAPTER 6

VALUING WATCHES, COIN JEWELRY, CARVINGS, AND OTHER ARTICLES

Vintage and Contemporary Wristwatches

The difficulty in appraising antique and modern wristwatches is the time it takes to get information about the product. Some of the most important data in your personal price-and-research records will be the notes you accumulate on watches. To keep from spending an inordinate amount of time looking for comparable watches, set up some file folders marked with the names of major makers—Audemars Piquet, Baume & Mercier, and so on. In these folders, keep every scrap of price information you can find about individual watches from newspaper advertisements, jewelry trade journals, and upscale consumer magazines. Even though the prices become outdated, you will have a record of styles and the names of the stores carrying those particular brands so that you may more easily scout the market for comparable items and current retail prices.

Major auction houses issue catalogs of watches, but getting watch catalogs from manufacturers themselves is difficult. Why this should be such a problem is unclear, but unless you are a retail jeweler who has business with a specific watch manufacturer, it will be difficult, if not impossible, to get a current catalog for your reference library. If you are doing appraising in a jeweler's store, the jeweler will usually not be averse to letting you browse through the watch catalogs he or she receives.

Some companies have catalogs that you can obtain for a small fee, and you can also order special fliers with style and retail-price information from some watch manufacturers. Look for these flier advertisements in fine magazines such as *Vogue* or *Town and Country*.

Modern Wristwatches

Some of the most popular and sought-after wristwatches for both men and women are by Patek Philippe, as illustrated in figures 6-1 and 6-2. The 18K watches are all individually handcrafted works of art. Other status names are Audemars Piquet, Baume & Mercier, Brequet, Cartier, Concord, Corum, Piaget, Rolex, Tiffany, Universal Genevé, and Vacheron & Constantin. Become familiar with the trademarks and hallmarks of the various important watchmakers— their names raise the value of the watches. There are those who advocate opening the backs of watches to count jewels and to remove the movement to weigh the case. This is a mistake and entirely unnecessary in normal appraisal practice. Unless you are a qualified watchmaker, you can seriously damage the watch by attempting to open the back. The most important value factors include:

- Name on the dial
- Condition of the case and movement
- Metal and metal fineness
- Case style
- Features (day/date, moon phase, etc.)
- Precious or synthetic stones
- Movement: jeweled, quartz, or other
- Bracelet attachment

A complete appraisal of a modern watch should include all the following information as well as a photograph of the timepiece:

1. Description of the case style and a record of the case serial numbers. (Case styles are illustrated in figure 6-3.)
2. A description of the hour and minute-hand style (fig. 6-4).

6-1. Modern woman's wristwatch, 18K yellow gold quartz Ellipse by Patek Philippe. *(Photograph courtesy of Henri Stern, New York)*

6-2. Modern man's watch by Patek Philippe: quartz Ellipse, 18K gold, and leather band attachment. *(Photograph courtesy of Henri Stern, New York)*

3. Movement serial number, if it can be obtained from the client's records, not by opening the back.
4. A description of the gemstones, colored lacquer, or other decoration on the dial and case.
5. The weight of the watch (including movement) in pennyweights or grams.
6. A note of any engraving on the case.
7. A description of the attachment.
8. Check and note whether the watch is in running condition; this is often overlooked.

Vintage Wristwatches

Researching value for vintage wristwatches could become your life's work, as it seems there is a market with well-defined standards. In actual practice, however, much depends upon trends, fads, and collectors. The following factors determine value in vintage watches:

Style. Fads and trends determine the style at any particular time and that affects value. Figure 6-5 illustrates the great appeal of the men's flared, cushion, and tank style wristwatches.

Utility. Because a wristwatch is useful and enjoyable to wear, it is a top item to collect. Watches that were expensive originally will always be in demand. Junk watches will always be junk.

Metal. All materials, from platinum to stainless and plastic, have been used in watch cases. The intrinsic value of the case metal is the *only* value of some watches, but watches with top brand names and platinum and/or gold cases are worth more than the weight of the metal.

When you are assessing value of older watches, look at the dial first. Does it need to be refinished? Refinishing can cost a hundred dollars or more. Does the dial have any missing or damaged figures, scratches, or dents?

Examine the case for signs of wear. Is it bent, dented, or worn? Are the spring-bar holes worn? On gold-filled watches, inspect the high edges of the case to see if the brass shows through. In addition, look for engraved initials or a dedication on the watch case; engraving lowers fair market value.

Old watches that you have to appraise may have been recased but it is very difficult to tell a recased movement from the original. Watch experts believe

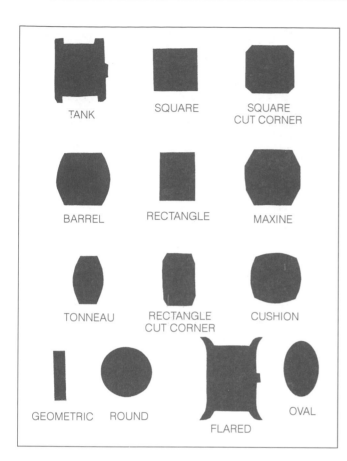

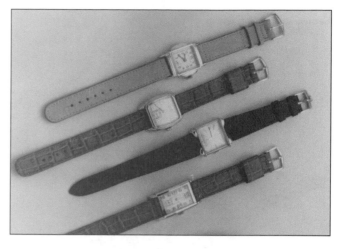

6-5. Four watches dating from 1925 to 1940. (*Photograph courtesy of Lynette Proler Antique Jewellers, Houston*)

that if you can establish that a movement has been recased, the value of the watch will drop dramatically.

In vintage watches, the original winding crown should be in place. This is especially important on Patek or Rolex watches. Deduct value if the crown has been replaced. Add value for hinged lugs, curved or enameled cases, two-tone gold cases, numerals on the bezels, numerals on an enamel bezel, and Art Deco-style numerals on the dial (fig. 6-6).

The watch bands or bracelets of most old watches are usually worth only a small premium over the intrinsic value of any precious-metal content. Added value is given *only* if the bracelet or attachment is in pristine condition (fig. 6-7). Exceptions are made for

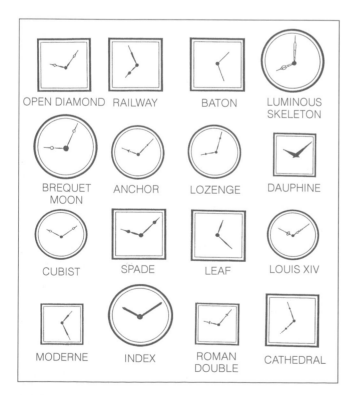

6-3. Wristwatch case styles.

6-6. Woman's wristwatch from the 1940s with unusual chameleon bracelet and case in 18K gold with silvered metal dial. The Patek Philippe signature on the dial, unusual design, and pristine condition add value to the watch.

6-4. Wristwatch hand and minute styles.

6-7. Early 1900s woman's wristwatch of 18K gold, chased and inlaid with rose-cut diamonds, with a white enamel dial and blued steel hands. The wristwatch's rare design, perfect condition, and Patek Philippe logo on dial add value to its appraised price.

exotic-skin bands on original and signed Patek, Rolex, or Cartier watches.

Comic characters watches, alarm watches, chronographs, repeaters, and calendar watches are valued slightly above liquidation. The original box and guarantees greatly enhance the value of a wristwatch. The more valuable the watch, the greater the value of the box and papers.

Private label or contract wristwatches are found with the jeweler's name on the dial, movement, or case. These watches were used primarily for advertising.

When writing insurance appraisals for vintage watches, do not price them as new replacements. True classics such as Gruen Curvex, 1920–30s Rolex models, old Patek Philippe watches, 1950s electric Hamilton venture, and LeCoultre Moonphase all have trackable secondhand markets, much like old-cut diamonds.

Since many vintage watches are collectibles in today's market, they are sold regularly by major auction houses. Antiquorum, an auction house based in Geneva, says that the most ever paid at auction for a perpetual calendar wristwatch was a 1953 Patek Philippe, platinum perpetual calendar model that fetched $754,839 in Hong Kong in June 1997. The watch had outstanding provenance because it was the *only platinum* version of the 179 watches the company made in this series from 1952 to 1963. In 1995, Sotheby's broke records with the sale of a rare gold cushion-form minute repeating wristwatch by Patek Philippe & Co. It sold to the Patek Philippe firm for $519,500, the highest price ever paid for a Patek Philippe timepiece in the United States. If either of these watches would have landed on the desk of the *average* American appraiser for insurance replacement, it is questionable whether they would have been correctly valued. Clearly, for appraisers working in the watch market, expertise in European and American watches is needed. For those not willing to invest time in acquiring special instructions, bring in an expert to consult, or decline the assignment.

Determining fair market value or insurance replacement value of a vintage watch requires the appraiser to do focused research. Survey prices from antique dealers and auction catalogs. To receive a catalog of a complete selection of books on watches and clocks, contact Scanlon American Reprints Co., P.O. Box 379, Modesto, California 95353; (800) 854-8639, e-mail: discanlon@aol.com. Also on the Internet: WATCH NET, http://www.watchnet.com and SwissWatches, http://www.fhusa.com

Gray Market Watches

Some "gray market" watches—trademarked watches imported into the United States by channels other than the manufacturer's authorized U.S. distributors—have no valid warranty in this country. Many, in fact, cannot be repaired because no compatible replacement parts or accessories are available.

Gray market watches *can* be legitimate items that are obtained outside of regular channels. But not all gray market watches are legitimate—they can be fakes or made from various parts to look like the genuine item. When a jeweler who is not an authorized dealer for a major watch line obtains a line by some unknown method and sells it in his store at a highly discounted price, he is said to be participating in a "gray" market. If the jeweler/seller is not an authorized dealer of the watch brand, customers who may later need repairs on the watch are out of luck. All well-known brands are found in the gray market, but especially Rolex. There are many modified and gray market Rolex watches on the market; therefore, careful identification is required when this item is being appraised. Modified watches can sometimes be identified from the band replacement, particularly when the band is a stainless and gold Jubilee model. To identify, look at the model number (four figures at 12 o'clock position on the watch case, between the top lugs, under the band). If the model number is for a stainless steel watch and the watch is a stainless and gold, this is proof of a modification. Regarding phony Rolex Presidential bands: use magnification to observe the screws in the band. If the screws are milled and threaded the band is genuine Rolex. A *threaded wire screw* signals a phony band. If you have a gray market wristwatch for appraisal, and you can determine it without doubt, state it on the appraisal report.

Spotting Imitation and Counterfeit Wristwatches

Imitation and counterfeit luxury watches can be a serious problem for the appraiser. Unless you are an experienced watchmaker, you do not want to open the back of a wristwatch to see the movement, and yet this is where it is easiest to detect whether a watch is genuine. If the watch is of a brand that is often counterfeited and you have any grounds to suspect the item's authenticity, it may be smart to have the movement inspected by a watchmaker before you complete your report. If you fail to do so and remain skeptical about a watch's authenticity, indicate in your appraisal that you did not confirm the movement, the reasons you did not confirm, and why you are suspicious.

A lecturer at a Gemological Institute of America Gemfest offered the following tips on detecting counterfeit watches. The spelling of the trade name is often a giveaway. Genova for Genevé, Omeca for Omega, 3enrus for Benrus; Longine for Longines. Look closely at the style of the script of the brand name. Become familiar with the styles of maker signatures. Genuine Rolexes are illustrated in figures 6-8 and 6-9. Check the logo and make sure it is correct. You will find fake Rolexes without crowns or crowns that are the wrong size. The Rolex crown on the Italian gold band is a different size from the crown on the Swiss gold band. The Greek-letter logo that dignifies Omega is not recognizable on the counterfeits.

Check the metal. Do not trust karat stampings. Gold-filled and gold-plated watches are common in bogus watches. Acid testing is the only reliable means of authenticating metal. Genuine stainless steel and gold Rolex bands have a number on the underside of the band; the last two digits indicate whether the gold is 14K or 18K mixed with stainless steel. Also, the gold finish is not very good on some of the imitation 18K

6-8. One of the most frequently counterfeited watches is the Rolex brand. Pay attention to the weight of the watch; check the logo for correct spelling and type style; check crown design for correct size. Look at the finish on the bezel and watch attachments. Be certain the dial has all the information it is supposed to contain, such as Rolex Oyster Perpetual Datejust.

gold bands. Look especially near the lugs and at the end of the rows of metal for poor finishing.

Heft is another clue to fake watches, but you must have handled a lot of genuine watches of the brand to be able to detect the difference. The Rolex man's Presidential model, for instance, has a certain heaviness that is not present in a counterfeit. Phony stainless steel and gold Rolex models are much lighter in weight than the genuine; this lightness will be immediately apparent upon inspection. Stainless steel snap-on backs also reveal fake Patek Philippe and Piaget tank-type watches; the movements of these imitation brand

6-9. The old way to spot a counterfeit Rolex was to check the second hand closely. A genuine Rolex Oyster Perpetual second hand moves four times per second, while the imitation moves once per second. This is viable on the old counterfeits—it does not apply to the new gold fakes.

watches are quartz, and only selected watches in the Patek line are quartz.

Check any gemstones that mark hours on the dial. Frequently, a diamond on a genuine watch dial will be prong set; counterfeit watches often have glued-in stones.

Rolex is one of the most popular brand names in the United States, therefore one of the most often counterfeited. The Rolex company was founded in London in 1905 by Hans Wilsdorf, when he was 22 years old. Wilsdorf, born in south Germany, was backed by the wealthy Alfred Davies and together they imported Swiss watch parts to London to be assembled and distributed throughout Britain and the Empire. In spite of a large market for pocket watches, Wilsdorf believed wristwatches could be popular. The First World War proved him right when the wristwatch proved much more practical than the pocket watch.

Wilsdorf named the watch *Rolex* in 1908, and although the name had no particular significance, it was easy to pronounce in any language. When the war began Wilsdorf reregistered his company in 1915 as The Rolex Watch Company Ltd. After the war, production moved to Geneva, with headquarters in London. The first waterproof watch, the "Oyster," was offered for sale in 1927, and Rolex has continued to be the market leader to the present day. Being market leader means being counterfeited. The fake Rolex watch has gone from being a cheap flea-market knock-off with easily distinguishable fake marks and features, to sophisticated 14K/18K watches that can only be authenticated by an expert. In Rolex watches, the appraiser will also find "modified" and gray market watches. Modified watches are those that may begin life with a stainless steel band, but adapted by using a gold band—sometimes genuine, often not. Modified watches can sometimes be identified from the band replacement, particularly when the band is a stainless and gold Jubilee model. To identify, look at the model number (four figures at 12 o'clock positioned between the top lugs, under the band). If the model number is for a stainless steel watch and the watch is a stainless and gold, this is proof of a modification. The watch bought from a gray market seller will not have a factory warranty. The Rolex one-year warranty states that it is valid only in the store of an authorized Rolex distributor. Some gray market watches cannot be repaired because no compatible replacement parts or accessories are available.

Separating the Fakes

1. On the *older models* of Rolex Presidential bands and early counterfeits, use magnification to observe the screws in the band. If the screws are milled and threaded the band is genuine Rolex. A *threaded wire screw* signals a phony band.
2. The latest model counterfeits are very skillfully made. Know how to read the model and serial numbers and how to verify them.
3. According to one watch expert you need to look at the watch *movement*. If you are not a watchmaker, consult with one who can open the watch back so that you may observe the movement. Write down any numbers you see, then *have the watchmaker* close the case. Research the dates when the numbers you found on the movement were used. Although the Rolex company does not publish a list of dates to correlate movements and serial numbers, some have been compiled independently by watch experts. These may be available through

various appraisal associations. You must be very familiar with Rolex model numbers, and all the attachments and special functions of each model to separate the fake from the genuine.

4. Carefully observe the Rolex hallmarks in the band. Is the profile clear? Are there any indentations over the hallmarks? Are the hallmarks blurred in any way? On the stainless steel model, does the Rolex Crown symbol go all the way through the clasp with a slightly raised crown on the outside of the clasp; indented crown on the inside?

In the final analysis—unless it is one's own special area of expertise—appraisers should research diligently and consult with a watch expert before estimating value on watches.

Writing an Appraisal on a Wristwatch

A new, currently available wristwatch will provide few problems for the appraiser. You may have to do some research as to who carries a particular brand, or call the company for information. But, the appraised value will be contingent upon prices (sales) of identical watches in the local market. If the watch is lost, it will be replaced with a brand new watch by the client's insurer.

How to Appraise a Used Watch

Appraisers see a lot of used watches. They are often confused about replacement because the watch the client wants to insure may be twenty years old. While most insurance companies will replace "new for old" in case of loss, this approach could change with the insurance company replacing the lost watch with another of similar age and condition. In this scenario the appraiser must know the value of a new model (identical to one being appraised) watch in the *new retail market,* along with the value of a similar watch on the *"used"* market. Most insurance policies include a statement that reads like this: "The Insurance Company will pay the full amount of *our cost* to replace the item with one substantially identical to the item lost or damaged." So the option to replace in kind with a used model is a possibility or, if the client rejects the insurance replacement, they must cash out *at the insurance company's cost to replace.* This begs the question, what value should be put on the appraisal document—new or used? One appraiser says he solves this dilemma by providing two estimates of value to his customer: one value covering a new identical replacement watch and value of an equivalent model available in the second-hand retail market. With two values in separate markets, the insured and insurance company can make a sensible decision on the amount of insurance to carry on the watch, and how it is to be replaced.

Pocket Watches

The appraiser must have experience and expertise in handling pocket watches before attempting an evaluation. A knowledgeable jeweler can quickly learn to differentiate among poor, medium, and high quality pocket watches, but it takes actual hands-on experience to understand how value standards operate for pocket watches.

Although the subject is both antique and modern pocket watches, "modern" in this context refers to pocket watches made until 1960. Makers of luxury Swiss watches, such as Patek Philippe, who are still in business have their own set of value standards and guides. These watches must be individually researched for value with like brands and styles.

To appraise the majority of pocket watches, follow these procedures:

1. Note whether the item is a man's pocket watch or a woman's pendant watch.
2. Write whether the watch is a hunting case, or covered dial, model; an open-faced style; a pair case (two cases); or a form case in the design of a flower, cross, shell, ladybug, fan, or so on (figs. 6-10 and 6-11).
3. Determine whether the watch is working and if the functions (the repeater mechanism, moon phase, calendar, and so on) are working. The more functions the watch has, the greater its value.
4. Establish which metal was used to manufacture the case. Some watches, even though gold filled, chrome, nickle, or silver, may be valuable if the case and movement are original.
5. Determine the case condition. A case of 14K or 18K gold in mint condition will be of higher value than a case that shows wear. What is the condition of the case—pristine, mint, extra fine, average, fair, or scrap? On a hunting-case watch, note the condition of the hinge—is it worn? Can you determine whether the case is original? Note how the case is decorated: *repoussé,* engine turned, enameled, or any other technique. List any initials or dedications engraved on the case. Engraved words or letters reduce value if the appraisal is for fair market value. If the appraisal is for insurance replacement value, describe any fancy engraving or dedications and

add this cost to the estimate. Hand engraving is expensive.

6. Size. A couple of systems are used to gauge size. The Lancashire Gauge is the most commonly used system; you can buy it at your local watchmaker's supply house. The gauge has two sides. The American watches use size 8, 12, 16, and 18. European watches are measured in *lignes;* that is 2, 3, and 4 lignes. The size of a watch is determined by measuring the outside diameter of the face. Most books about watches print reference gauges for easy judgment of watch sizes, which you can use if you do not have a proper gauge.

7. Look at the dial and note the condition. Is it chipped or does it have any hairline cracks? Both will reduce value. Is the dial porcelain? Note the style of the hour and minute hands, as shown in figure 6-12, and whether the numerals are arabic or roman. Is there color on the dial? Are there photographs on the dial? Is it single or double sunk? Does it have subsidiary second hand? Is the crystal pristine, broken, or missing?

8. Movement. This is as important to a pocket watch as color is to colored gemstones. From the movement you can determine the type of plates used (three-quarters, full, or bridge), the type of balance, the winding type (stem wind, key wind, or lever set), the number of adjustments, the number of jewels, the presence of *damaskeening* (the process of applying ornate designs on metal by etching—this adds value to the watch), and the serial number of the movement. Note on your report every number and word you see on the movement of American-made watches. The serial number is used to determine the year it was made; manufacturers' serial numbers correspond with the years of production. Low serial numbers are more valuable than high ones.

You can usually date European and English pocket watches by referring to the signature of the maker on the movement and using either Britten's *Old Clocks, Watches and Their Makers* or the G. H. Baillie work *Watchmakers and Clockmakers of the World* as reference sources for dates during which various manufacturers were in business. If you encounter a name that you cannot find listed in any reference, chances are that the name is either the importer or the jeweler, not the manufacturer. Studying the characteristics of the movement will also help you determine the date of the watch.

Provenance is a difficult area to establish on many pocket watches. One exception is those made by Patek Philippe. This company, which was founded one hun-

6-10. Open-faced railroad watches were very accurate timekeepers. Many can still be found in estate appraisals. *(Photograph courtesy of Charterhouse & Co.)*

dred and fifty years ago by French watchmaker Adrien Philippe and Polish nobleman Count Antoine de Patek, maintains detailed records of its timepieces. If you can provide the movement number, case number, and description of the watch, the company will send you the history of the piece, including its date of manufacture, date sold (and to whom), and any repairs conducted through the company. In short, you will receive everything you need to make a positive provenance record, which adds value to the object.

Stampings

The hallmarks of foreign gold cases will usually be legitimate indications of the karat quality, but beware of foreign cases that are stamped 18, especially if this is the only mark you can find on the watch. Acid tests may confirm that the karatage is actually only 8K to 10K. Similarly, American cases stamped with the manufacturer's hallmark, with the mark of the U.S. Assay Office, or the marks 14K and 18K will usually be correct, although in some cases, the mark 14K refers only to the gold-filled part of the case. Test the case to be sure.

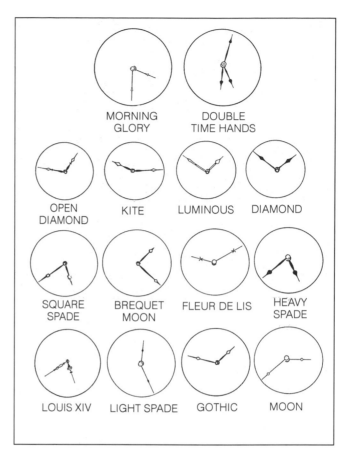

6-12. Hour- and minute-hand styles for pocket watches.

6-11. Hunting-case pocket watch in pristine condition with ornamental cover. Very desirable to collectors. *(Photograph courtesy of Charterhouse & Co.)*

In 1924, the U.S. government prohibited the use of the guarantee terms on watch cases. If you see the guarantee terms 5, 10, 15, 20, 25, and 30, or the word *permanent*, you are looking at gold-filled material, not solid gold. Case companies began to use the markings 14KGF or 10KRGP to indicate the actual qualities of case metals.

Silver-color cases may be marked *silveroid, silverine, silverode,* or *silverore.* These are trademarks for white metal cases that are not silver but a combination of copper and manganese. Sometimes these are marked "guaranteed for 100 years."

Dating American Pocket Watches
1870s: Damaskeening appeared on pocket watches in the late 1870s.

1879: First appearance of 14K and 18K multicolor gold cases.

1910: Multicolor gold cases no longer made in the 16 and 18 sizes; smaller sizes continue to be produced.

1924: Government prohibits further use of the guarantee terms 5, 10, 15, 20, 25, 30 years. After 1924, manufacturers marked cases 10K, 14K gold filled, and 10K rolled gold plate.

Dating European Pocket Watches
1635: Enamel dials used

1640: Pair cases used

1687: Minute hands used

1697: Hallmarks used

1700: Jewels used in movements

1774: Dust caps used

1820: Keyless winding instituted. Widely popular after 1860.

Two examples of the modern watchmaker's art are the Patek Philippe skeleton pocket watches shown in figures 6-13 and 6-14. These extraordinary timepieces are destined to become the heirlooms of tomorrow. How will the twenty-first-century appraiser value these items? By the same standards we use today: Beauty, rarity, demand, supply, condition, and age. At a recent

6-13. Contemporary Patek Philippe pavé-set diamond skeleton pocket watch. This commissioned watch took fifteen months to create.

auction in Geneva, a blue enamel and diamond pocket watch, dated 1650, decorated with figures and flowers by watchmaker Jehan Cremsdorff of Paris, sold for more than 2 million dollars. Only four or five comparables exist.

6-14. Contemporary 18K skeleton model Patek Philippe pocket watch.

Handling a Hunting Case Pocket Watch

Do not embarrass yourself as an appraiser by failing to learn the correct way to handle a pocket watch.

Collectors who have such watches know instantly if you are abusing their property by careless or incorrect handling. It brands you as an amateur.

Hold the watch in the right hand with the bow or swing ring between the index finger and thumb. Press on the crown with the right thumb to release the cover over the face. Never snap the cover or push in the middle of the cover to close the watch. Instead, hold the watch in the palm of your hand, press the crown to move the catch in, close the cover, and then release the crown. This will reduce wear on the soft gold rim and catch and keep from damaging the cover.

For watches with a screw-on front and back, such as the railroad models, hold the watch in the left hand and, with the right hand, turn the bezel counterclockwise. While removing the bezel, hold carefully to the stem and swing ring so you do not drop the watch. Lay the bezel down and check the dial for cracks and other signs of damage. Look at the lever to see that it will allow the hands to be set. After examination, replace the bezel and turn the watch over. While holding the stem between the left thumb and index finger, remove the back cover. If it is a screw-on back cover, turn it counterclockwise. For a snap-on cover, look for a lip on the back and use a pocket watch knife to lift the back off. Do *not* attempt any of these moves unless you have been personally shown how to proceed by a watchmaker.

Appraising pocket watches is a subspecialty of the gems and jewelry discipline. If you feel you are not qualified in this area, turn the item over to a colleague who has the necessary expertise. Even antique pocket watches have their fakes and counterfeits.

For identification and price guides, the following publications may be helpful: *The Complete Guide to American Pocket Watches* by Cooksey Shugart and Tom Engle and *American Pocket Watch Identification and Price Guide* by Roy Ehrhardt. Both are listed in the bibliography. By joining the National Association of Watch and Clock Collectors (513 Poplar Street, Columbia, Pennsylvania 17512), members receive a bulletin with historical information about watches and clocks and a periodic newsletter devoted to buying and selling announcements.

Known as the standard text for American vintage wristwatches, *American Wristwatches* by Edward Faber and Stewart Unger should be in every appraiser's library. This book covers five decades of watches and includes all of the important makers, watch illustrations, descriptions, and a price guide. Another good choice for appraisers is *Wristwatches, Second Edition,* by Kahlert, Muhe, and Brunner.

Aaron Faber of Aaron Faber Gallery, 666 Fifth Avenue, New York, New York 10103, publishes a small but illustration-rich brochure of wristwatches (old and new) that are for sale in his gallery. Faber calls this brochure "Watch Word."

A subscription to *Specht Sheet,* a monthly wristwatch pricing sheet, is helpful to the appraiser. An annual subscription is $150: Specht Sheet, (305) 371-6827. On the cover of the Specht Sheet it says: "We will pay our published prices listed." This may be of help in estimating value.

Coin Jewelry

Many appraisals of coin jewelry that you will be asked to do will concern retail replacement for insurance. You can get the current prices of many foreign and United States coins from the daily newspaper market listings. Internationally known foreign and domestic coin dealers such as Manfra, Tordella & Brookes, have buy-and-sell price sheets based on current gold prices; many domestic and foreign coins of contemporary vintage are listed. Silver coins in well-circulated condition are considered bulk coinage and sold as silver scrap.

The Internet is a valuable source of information for London spot prices: http://www.kitco.com.

Three factors combine to determine the value of any coin: rarity, demand, and condition. Coins of numismatic quality are occasionally found in jewelry. Collectors of numismatic coins are generally sophisticated enough to realize that once a coin is mounted in jewelry, it loses value based on its wear and exposure to damage; however, some place expensive numismatic coins in jewelry because they are family heirlooms, or have sentimental value. Additionally, the current trend in coin jewelry is to place Spanish treasure coins and expensive Roman and Greek coins in fancy, custom-made coin frames. Age alone has little effect on the value of a coin, and many appraisers make the mistake of conferring special value on old coins. Table 6-1 covers coin gradings as publicized by the American Numismatic Association.

When you have coin jewelry to appraise, one of your first impulses may be to clean the jewelry. Do not do it! Coins should be left in their existing condition and no attempt should be made to alter their appearance by cleaning or polishing. Never test the metal content of gold coins—the rub on a touchstone or gel from an electronic tester could reduce the value of a collectible coin.

To appraise numismatic items, you need a working knowledge of world coin values, or have a good

Table 6-1. Coin Gradings as Publicized by the American Numismatic Association

AU-55 (Choice About Uncirculated)	Only a small trace of wear is visible on the highest points of the coin.
AU-50 (About Uncirculated)	With traces of wear on nearly all of the highest areas. At least half of the original mint luster is present.
EF-45 (Choice Extremely Fine)	With light overall wear on the coin's highest points. All design details are very sharp. Mint luster is usually seen only in protected areas of the coin's surfaces, such as between the star points and in the letter spaces.
EF-40 (Extremely Fine)	With only slight wear but more extensive than the proceeding, still with excellent overall sharpness. Traces of mint luster may still show.
VF-30 (Choice Very Fine)	With light, even wear on the surface; design details on the highest points slightly worn, but with all lettering and major features sharp.
VF-20 (Very Fine)	As preceding but with moderate wear on highest parts.
F-12 (Fine)	Moderate to considerable even wear. Entire design is bold. All lettering, including the word "Liberty" (on coins with this feature on the shield or headband), is visible but with some weakness.
VG-8 (Very Good)	Well worn. Most fine details such as hair strands, leaf details, and so on are worn nearly smooth. The word "Liberty," if on a shield or headband, is only partially visible.
G-4 (Good)	Heavily worn. Major designs visible, but with faintness in areas. Head of Liberty, wreath, and other major features visible in outline form without center detail.
AG-3 (About Good)	Very heavily worn with portions of the lettering, date, and legends worn smooth. The date barely readable.

working relationship with a local, knowledgeable coin dealer. It might take an appraiser hours of research to determine the value of a coin, but a simple phone call to a numismatist would provide the same information in minutes. Most contemporary coin dealers are anxious to help appraisers, as it gets them an occasional referral. Modern coin shops often deal in gems and will sometimes reciprocate by seeking advice from the appraiser. If there is no local coin shop, it would be helpful to peruse a copy of *The Standard Catalog of World Coins* by Krause. This book lists the weight, fineness, and numismatic value of every coin minted in the world since about 1600. For American coins only, *The Handbook of United States Coins: Dealer Buying Prices* by R. S. Yeoman is recommended. A subscription to *Coin World* magazine or *Numismatic News* would provide very helpful information. One of the finest magazines of numismatic art of antiquity, *The Celator*, is available by subscription. Author David R. Sear's three books, *Roman Coins and Their Values*, *Greek Coins and Their Values*, and *Byzantine Coins and Their Values*, are must-have books for valuers who write appraisals in the coin market. Attending coin shows is also an excellent way to get information and meet coin dealers.

What are the criteria for appraising coins? According to Art Arbutine, Belleair Coins, Inc., in Belleair Bluffs, Florida, *rarity* is the most important element. "Rarity is the most important factor in determining coin value since without rarity the other two criteria are of minor significance," Arbutine says. "A rare coin is one that may be struck in a limited quantity for a certain period; struck in only one year; one of the few surviving coins of a large number originally struck; or a rare coin that may have been uncirculated and is now considered scarce." *Demand* is the indicator of the coin's place in the market because no matter how rare, it cannot be sold for a price matching its rarity unless a demand exists for the item. *Condition* is the state of preservation of the coin. As gemstones are desirable without chips, nicks, or cracks, coins in the finest condition—those that show mint luster and no signs of wear—are most desired by collectors. "Modern bullion coins and commemorative medals incorporated in jewelry are generally worth bullion value plus about 5 percent.

Follow these standard steps when appraising coins:

1. Establish country of origin, metal, denomination, and date.
2. Determine whether the coin jewelry is authentic or counterfeit.
3. Note condition of the coin.
4. Note the weight of the coin (alone if possible, or in the mounting as part of the total weight).
5. Provide coin measurement in millimeters
6. Describe the mounting and appraise as you would normally appraise any precious metal jewelry.

Coin Gradings

These are the general characteristics defining the various coin grades:

Fair: Designs and lettering identifiable. Quite worn.

Good: Legends, design, and date are clear.

Very Good: Features clearer and bolder, better than good.

Fine: Circulated coins with little wear. All legends should be clear.

Very Fine: All details and relief are sharp, only the highest surfaces show wear.

Uncirculated: Never circulated, regular minting. Toning or tarnish may show on older issues.

Proof: Coins struck especially for collectors. These usually have a mirrorlike surface, although sandblasted and matte finishes are produced for some proof series.

The American Numismatic Association has a certification service for the authentication of coins. Appraisers uncertain about the authenticity or potential numismatic value of any coin of any metal can get help from the ANA. Coins need not be removed from frames for authentication. A photo certificate of the coin in the frame will be returned with the coin, if it is authentic. If the coin is counterfeit or suspect, it will still be returned intact, but without a certificate.

The American coin jewelry trend accelerated when the Gold Bullion Act of 1985 authorized the minting of the first general-circulation U.S. gold coins since 1933, and is expected to continue. The series of four gold coins contains the following amounts of pure gold: one ounce for the $50 coin; one-half ounce for the $25 coin; one-quarter ounce for the $10 coin; and one-tenth ounce for the $5 coin. Jewelers can expect to pay about 5–12% above spot gold prices; the smaller the coin the larger the percentage.

If the appraiser has no expertise in coins, the logical next step is to get help from a coin expert. For information and help: American Numismatic Association Authentication Bureau, 818 N. Cascade Avenue, Colorado Springs, Colorado 80903, (719) 623-2646; *Coin World*, P.O. Box 150, Sidney, Ohio 45365, (937) 498-0800; *Numismatic News*, 700 E. State Street, Iola, Wisconsin 54990, (800) 258-0929.

Appraising Ancient Coin Jewelry

In the last decade there has been a big increase in the amount of ancient coin jewelry seen in the marketplace. The traditional manufacturers such as Bulgari, and designers such as Stephen Lagos, have been joined by coin jewelry manufacturers to produce and market ancient coin jewelry.

The coins used in the jewelry are usually from the Greek and Roman empires, although coins from other civilizations such as Persian, Hebrew, Celtic, and Byzantine are common. Mint dates of the coins range from the 6th century B.C. to the 15th century A.D. depending upon the civilization of origin. The designs of the coins range from portraits of various Caesars, Alexander the Great, Byzantine emperors, mythological figures such as Herakles, gods and goddesses such as Zeus and Athene, and animals or mythological creatures like Pegasus. The coin pictured in figs. 6-15 and 6-16 has been authenticated by David R. Sear, Professional Numismatist, as a Roman Imperial silver denarius, 196–217 A.D. Obverse: Caracalla. Reverse: Felicitas.

Andrew Lucas, G.G., G.J., C.G., Registered Master Valuer, has been buying and selling ancient coins for several years and says that many factors contribute to the value of the coins. "There is a small but strong collector market in the U.S. and in Europe," Lucas says. "Investors and jewelers are also involved in this market. Contributing factors to the value of the coins includes *rarity, condition, quality of the striking, metal type, denomination, artistic quality, age, period, civilization, issuing ruler,* and *demand* in the market." Lucas advises that the common metals used for ancient coins are bronze, bronze with a silver wash, silver, electrum, and gold. "Many of the coins used in jewelry are inexpensive Roman bronze coins that often range from under $10

6-16. The reverse of the coin: Felicitas, the goddess of good fortune.

to $200 per coin," he said, and added, "The Greek and Roman silver coins used commonly range from $30 to $800. Gold and electrum coins from the Greek, Roman, Celtic, and Byzantine range from $250 to several thousand dollars." In some cases, the value of the coins does not comprise a large percentage of the retail value for the piece of jewelry. And, Lucas counsels, "the values of the different metal types will overlap. The value of a rare Roman silver coin in very fine condition and in demand may be higher than that of some Roman gold coins. Some ancient coin jewelry contains coins that are magnificent examples and are much higher in value than the common ranges listed, although this is not the norm."

Lucas gives the following list as a grading scale of the state of preservation for ancient coins:

FDC   Mint state, fleur-de-coin
EF   Extremely fine
VF   Very fine
F   Fine
M   Mediocre
P   Poor

Authenticity?

How can the authenticity be established? Lucas explains, "The coin jewelry may come with a certificate of authenticity, a description of the coin, and sometimes a grade, which is highly subjective. Often, the certificate of authenticity is a paper written by a coin

6-15. Certified by David Sear, a Roman Imperial silver denarius 196–217 A.D. with Caracalla on the obverse.

dealer handed down to manufacturer, retailer, customer.

"Although there are some reproductions of ancient coins that are very deceptive, most reproduction coins used in jewelry are easy to recognize providing the appraiser has done diligent research and understands the subject. Appraiser be aware that some ancient coins have been altered by filing or soldering to make setting them easier. Of course, any alteration dramatically lowers the numismatic value."

Appraisers who need to identify, grade, and place a value on ancient coins used in jewelry are urged to develop a working relationship with a coin dealer specializing in ancient coins. These dealers often advertise in *The Celator,* a publication devoted to ancient coins. Also to be found in *The Celator* are references to literature and price guides on ancient coins and organizations. *The Celator* can be accessed via the Internet: http://www.celator.com or by telephone: (608) 592-4684.

Atocha Coins

Appraising coins from treasure ships demands lots of questions and diligent research. Some of the most beautiful and important gold and silver coins have come from the treasure ship *Atocha.* Most Americans are familiar with the story of the *Atocha* from movies, books, and television. The *Atocha* was a 17th-century Spanish Guard galleon in a fleet of 28 ships that set sail from Havana, bound for Spain in 1622. A hurricane sank the *Atocha* and seven other ships laden with treasure exceeding $500 million. The *Atocha* was found in 1985 off Key West, Florida, after many years of persistent searching by Mel Fisher, his crew, and family. The 103 gold coins and the finished gold jewelry pulled from the wreck were still shiny and beautiful, and Mel Fisher was established as the "source" for genuine gold coins of the 17th century. Although Spanish gold coins of the 19th century are available to collectors, gold coins from the 17th and 18th centuries are scarce. Gold coins from the Bogota, Colombia mint recovered from 1715 shipwreck sites are among the rarest issued in the New World, and in fact, their very existence was hotly debated before the discovery. This type of coin is still very rare.

The *Atocha* treasure being offered for sale today includes silver pieces-of-eight minted in Peru for Spain, some finished jewelry set with emeralds, loose Colombian emeralds, and re-creations of some of the other artifacts found on the ship. The recreations claim 3%–5% of the total metal content (gold and silver) of a coin from the actual *Atocha* treasure. This allows a buyer to get a fragment of history.

The question arises: What will an appraiser do when a client asks for an appraisal on, for instance, a coin from the *Atocha* hoard? Where will we research? How do we document value? How will we know if the coin is authentic or a re-creation? The Mel Fisher Museums in Key West and Sebastian, Florida, and their touring exhibitions sell both the original artifacts and re-creations, and every piece of the *Atocha* treasure sold is accompanied by a *Certificate of Authenticity.* Without the Certificate, the origin of the piece as an authentic "Mel Fisher Atocha Treasure" is not defensible. Most of the identification, provenance, and value questions are especially pertinent because Spanish coins from the same *period* as the *Atocha* are available in quantity from American coin dealers. However, although the coins may be purchased for as little as 1/3 of the price of the *Atocha* coins offered by Fisher, they are *not* the *Atocha* treasure coins. Therefore, lacking the provenance of the *Atocha,* value is affected. In all cases one of the first questions to ask the client when a gold treasure coin is involved is, "Where was this coin purchased?" followed by, "Is there a Certificate of Authenticity?"

The *Atocha* treasures have their own demand, market niche, and limited supply. Therefore, the insurance replacement value of a gold or silver *Atocha* coin—or piece of treasure jewelry—originally purchased from Mel Fisher Company with Certificate of Authenticity attached, is determined by tracking actual comparable sales transactions from the *primary source,* the Mel Fisher Company. Unfortunately, tracking comparable sales from Fisher may be a lot more difficult in the future because of decreasing supply of treasure. At some future date, however, appraisers may be able to research a viable secondary market for the coins—for instance auction or coin dealers—as privately owned items are resold.

When writing an insurance replacement document for an *Atocha* coin, carefully photograph and record all information possible, especially mint marks. Documentation and diligent research will justify the value. Verify both coin and Certificate of Authentication by a call to the Mel Fisher Company. Make clear on the appraisal report that the *only* replacement possible is by the same primary source. If the client wants assurances that the insurance company will not go to a secondary market (coin dealer, auction) in case of replacement, suggest they ask their insurance agent about an "Agreed Value" policy. Although the premiums are higher, this type of policy assures the client of getting the full appraised value. See table 6-2 for a list of the coins jewelers sell.

Love Tokens

Love tokens, interesting articles of jewelry and a popular art form, are currency coins that have been

Table 6-2. The Coins Jewelers Sell: Cost to Retailer from Dealer*

Coin	Country	Fineness	Gold Weight	Diameter	Price
$20 St. Gauden	USA	.900	.97 oz.	34mm	$455
$20 Liberty	USA	.900	.97	34	445
$10 Indian	USA	.900	.48	27	350
$10 Liberty	USA	.900	.48	27	235
$5 Indian	USA	.900	.24	21	185
$5 Liberty	USA	.900	.24	21	150
$2.50 Indian	USA	.900	.12	17	155
$2.50 Liberty	USA	.900	.12	17	155
50 peso	Mexico	.900	1.20	37	431
20 peso	Mexico	.900	.48	27	175.90
10 peso	Mexico	.900	.24	22.5	90.50
100 corona	Austria	.900	.98	37	339
4 ducat	Austria	.968	.44	39	165.80
1 ducat	Austria	.968	.11	19.6	42.90
Maple leaf	Canada	.999	1.00	33	358
Panda	People's Republic of China	.999	1.00	32	368.20
Panda	People's Republic of China	.999	.50	27	190.40

* Based on gold at $344.50 per ounce. Prices change daily based on spot gold prices.

erased and especially engraved on one side. Their history goes back, reportedly, as far as the Middle Ages, and they were quite popular in Europe in the sixteenth century. Also popular in the United States for about forty years, beginning in 1870, they went into a decline after the federal government made it illegal to deface currency in 1909.

Love tokens were commonly engraved with initials, monograms, scenes, or messages. Messages can be charming: *Baby, 5-9-86;* sentimental, *Annie 6-29-88;* or to the point, *Jeweler,* as on those used for advertising purposes. Many of the coins you will see are dated 1876, the year of the U.S. Centennial celebration. Many engravers were present at the New York World's Fair, plying their trade to the mass of souvenir hunters.

Engravers, however, were not the only ones to produce love tokens. This ancient art is ascribed to lonely sailors, soldiers, and prisoners. Amateur craftsmen and artists began carving messages, names, or initials and pictures of houses, boats, and birds. Some crude, primitively scratched coins are called *pin hole* or *punchwork* tokens. More artistically finished love tokens were usually by jeweler engravers who ground one side of the coin flat for engraving (sometimes both sides) and used enamel, glass, gemstones, and often an overlay effect to enhance their designs.

Gold coins with initials cut out of other gold coins (often a different color gold), intertwined and soldered onto the base coin are beautiful and have the look of finely engraved initials. Jewelry love tokens include brooches, necklaces, bracelets, stickpins, and cufflinks. Young women of the Victorian era liked to collect as many love tokens as possible from their sweethearts; it was a visual display of a young woman's popularity. Gail B. Levine, a graduate gemologist and collector of love tokens, recommends the following factors to help appraisers determine prices for the coins:

- Condition of the coin and date
- Craftsmanship of the engraving
- Message or scene on the coin

Dual sided pieces bring the highest prices. Special scenic coins command a greater premium, and messages that relate to historical events add value. Levine gives this list of love tokens rating from commonly found (less valuable) to most desirable (more expensive):

- *Initials*—plain, fancy, elaborate, combination with scene or date: seven dollars and up.
- *Monograms*—plain, fancy, elaborate, combination with scene or date: ten to twelve dollars and up.
- *Names*—plain, fancy, elaborate, combination with scene or date: fifteen to eighteen dollars and up.
- *Scenes*—flowers, birds, animals, landscapes, seascapes, people, trains, ships, guns, religious emblems: twenty dollars and up.
- *Dual pieces*—both sides smoothed off with monograms or initials with combination sayings, date, or scenic: twenty-five to thirty-five dollars and up.
- *Historical*—Centennial, World's Fair, patriotic, political: fifty dollars and up.

6-17. A love token brooch made from dimes with fancy lettering. *(Photograph courtesy of Gail Levine)*

6-18. Love token bangle bracelet—a memento made from dimes. *(From the Gail Levine collection)*

Add value to the coins if they have any of the following: enamel, cutout designs, gemstones, relief-carved designs, or any combination of these.

Coins with love messages command the top price, followed in value by pornographic/erotica, historic, Masonic, funeral remembrances, contest awards, identification tags, anniversary, birth, and wedding coins. Belt buckles are the most expensive of jewelry love tokens, followed by shirt studs, hat pins, earrings, spoons, buttons, cufflinks, watch fobs, brooches, necklaces, stick pins, bracelets, pendants, pocket pieces, and charms. Figures 6-17 and 6-18 illustrate two pieces of love token jewelry.

Coins that are most *desired* (making a love token most expensive) descending to least expensive are: the twenty-dollar gold piece, copper and nickel pieces, large cents, twenty-cent pieces, five-dollar gold pieces, Morgan and trade dollars, the 2.25 dollar gold piece, three-cent silver coins, the dollar gold piece, silver dollar, half-dollar, half-dime, quarter, and the dime. A dollar gold piece with one side planed off and the name "Ella" engraved was recently quoted for one hundred and fifty dollars retail in a coin shop.

If you have love token jewelry to appraise, research coin shops, coin shows, flea markets, antique shops, and antique shows; occasionally, one will turn up at an exhibition in a gem and mineral show. Local coin clubs can inform you about coin auctions, which may be of assistance in comparable pricing.

Erotica

Erotica has always been a part of the arts, from exquisitely executed tomb paintings to contemporary vulgar jewelry and *objets d'art*. Today's gemstone and jewelry dealers say there is a solid group of collectors for these items. There are antique items in this category but they seldom reach the public market because they sell briskly among collectors.

Objects of erotica are found in Oriental ivory netsukes and East Indian jewelry, Ashanti gold weights, pre-Columbian jewelry and art, love token jewelry, and among the gold and silver jewelry of the "flower children" movement of the 1960s.

In ancient Egyptian and Roman jewelry, many articles were decorated with erotic motifs, with a phallus used on amulets, rings, and brooches. In *An Illustrated Dictionary of Jewelry,* Harold Newman reports that erotic motifs were carved on cameos of the Hellenistic era and the Renaissance period. Erotica is also found in the jewelry of Peru, Japan, and Germany. Pornographic buttons were made in eighteenth-century France, Japan, and India. Also, erotic automatons—watches with a mechanism that cause figures on the dial or under the cover to move or rotate—were produced for the East Indian market.

Much of the jewelry is or was created for ritualistic charm use, for religious rites, as love charms, and so on, but the purpose of some was simply to please or excite. Consequently, some are only obscene novelties.

Ivory is a favorite medium for carvers of erotica. A complete collection of antique carved netsukes can be measured in value only by what the last collector actually paid for them. They are rare. The new netsukes, explicitly sexual, are priced at retail about 50 percent higher than their plain counterparts of similar size. Many of the new ones are in color and it should be noted this is a twentieth-century variation. The value factors in determining price are the same as in carvings:

• Material
• Depth of carving and craftsmanship
• Intricacy of detail
• Polish and finish

The appraiser can figure that a three-inch-high ivory netsuke (without color) new, but nicely carved and finished, will be valued at approximately one hundred dollars wholesale.

Ashanti weights, which were used to weigh gold dust, can still be found in the market and will often be presented for appraisal. The originals sold for up to one hundred dollars retail. Ashanti reproductions now on the market retail for about five dollars each. They are crudely made and finished. Even if you have never seen any of the original weights with their primitive kind of beauty, you cannot mistake the overwhelming ugliness and vulgarity of the new reproductions.

At the height of the hippie era in the United States, cast silver and gold erotic jewelry was plentiful. Most of the jewelry was mass produced, poorly cast, and cheaply finished. To value it, apply the same standards used to appraise other metal items: fineness of metal, weight of metal, workmanship, method of manufacture, and finish.

Love tokens with erotic scenes are still around, but collectors buy them so quickly at coin shows that you may not have time to catalog current prices. Silver coin erotic love tokens are priced at thirty-five dollars and up; gold coin prices begin at about one hundred and fifty dollars and go as high as the market will bear.

To antique erotica jewelry and carvings, add these additional value factors:

• Rarity
• Market demand
• Circa date
• Signature (some Japanese and Chinese netsukes were signed)
• Partial or complete collection (value is added for a complete over a partially assembled collection)

Carvings

Many of the carvings you will be asked to appraise will be part of a classification known as tourist trade or air-

port art. These are popular hardstone carvings of jade and its imitations—serpentine, quartz, and agate—representing likenesses of Kwan Yin, phoenix birds, eggs, frogs, and snuff bottles. Most will have been purchased from gem and mineral dealers, gift shops, boutiques, or Asian markets. These items retail from ten dollars for a more-or-less oval malachite egg to three hundred dollars for a 6¼-inch-high green serpentine jar with lid on a wooden stand. The serpentine jar is masquerading as a fine carving, but the discerning eye will appreciate that it is nothing special. The hallmarks of these commercial carved objects are their crude shaping, lack of detail, and glasslike polish. The dazzling polish is intended to divert your attention from the obvious poor quality of the carving.

Mass-produced carvings from Hong Kong, Taiwan, and China arrived in the wake of the introduction of power tools and crass commercialism to Asia. Where an apprentice in China used to spend ten years learning his craft, he or she now spends four or less. It was estimated recently that new factories in Beijing employ up to ten thousand men and women in this industry. Given the ocean of goods spilling onto the market, how does the appraiser tell the fantastic from the feeble? These are some standard guidelines:

1. Look at the carving in the same way you look at colored gemstones and judge its hue, tone, and color saturation.
2. Judge the appropriateness of the material to the subject.
3. Evaluate the luster or polish.
4. Look for an absence of undercutting, chips, and cracks.
5. Check the detailing. An excellent and expensive carving is finely detailed and finished on the front, back, and even on the base.
6. Look at the stand. Fine carvings deserve well-made and -fitted stands.

These are the basic criteria used to judge all hardstone carvings with additional value factors varying according to specific materials.

Jade Carvings

It is difficult to date jade. An authentic ancient piece would have come from a scientifically excavated tomb, but few jades on the market today have such provenance. Nevertheless, you will have clients bring you jade carvings they believe are ancient and ask your assessment and authentication.

If the item is said to be Chinese pre-1784 jadeite, be suspicious. The year 1784 marked the resumption of trade between China and Burma and the time when jadeite was introduced to China. The Chinese used only nephrite imported from Turkestan for carving until jadeite was introduced. Not until after 1880 did Chinese craftsmen start using jadeite for large ornamental pieces, and green jadeite censers, bowls, and vases were neither produced nor on the market until the turn of the twentieth century. Graduated necklaces of jadeite were not crafted in China earlier than 1900, and then they were made for Westerners, stylistic copies of the pearl necklaces popular at the time.

If you firmly believe that the jade carving you are appraising is antique, carefully examine it to see if raw edges or uneven texture is present, or if the engraved designs have loose ends. Since many antique jades were carved as ritual objects for divine forces, it was believed that each object must be absolutely perfect. The cutting of such objects was not rushed; each design was a model of perfection. Not all old jade is good jade, however, so do not be misled just because an object is old, or by the fact that compared to latter-day mass-market carvings, the old designs look less faulty and less crude. Chinese antique jade carvings purported to be from the Ch'ien Lung period (1736–1795) will have no sharp corners and no raw edges, no matter what the subject executed by the carver, for during this period the art of gemstone carving reached its zenith in China.

These are general standards for judging jade carvings. First, examine all carvings under 10× magnification for quality, the main consideration. The better the jade quality, the higher the price of the carving. The toughness of jade makes it the ideal carving medium, with the finest quality jade generally used for cabochons or small carvings used in jewelry, and less costly grades of jade used for larger ornamental items. For carvings and cabochons of the same color and quality, the cabochon will command the higher price because of its higher luster. An exception is a one-of-a-kind carving.

Next, consider the following basic factors:

1. Is it jadeite or nephrite?
2. Color.
3. Translucency, texture, and finish.
4. Size of the finished object.
5. Is there effective use of shading and different colors in the host material to highlight the subject of the carving?
6. Look for uniformity of color versus pattern. Patterns may be multicolored, swirled, speckled, or mottled. A combination of colors and markings determines the desirability of patterned jade.
7. Have all the scratches been worked out? Is the carving clean and distinct?

8. Is the polish uniform? Be aware that there is a waxing process used by Asian craftspersons that involves soaking the item in molten wax and then buffing. This results in a very high polish.
9. Are fractures or other undesirable inclusions present? Both metallic and crystalline inclusions affect the price and lower the value.
10. Oxidation of the material lowers the value.
11. Does the piece have aesthetic appeal? Even if a piece is technically perfect, if it looks like a monstrosity, it may have little marketability.
12. Is the material treated or enhanced?

If the jade carving you are appraising scores 100 in all the mentioned positive factors, consider whether its country of origin can be established beyond all reasonable doubt. If so, then value should be added.

Some jade experts believe that there is another, intangible factor that must be considered in valuing jade carvings. They think that an object should evoke some emotion from the beholder, even if it is just admiration of the coloration. In the *Standard Catalog of Gems*, author John Sinkankas says that sophisticated collectors frequently judge gemstone carvings on the basis of "message, or appeal to the sensibilities. . . . If the message is weak, trivial, or nonexistent, artistic value declines to the point an object is judged only on ornamental or utilitarian value" (Sinkankas, 1968, 220).

After considering all the quality factors and various points of view on judging jade carvings, the use of comparables may still be the only accurate method of determining value. When collecting jade market prices, the appraiser should note the prices of both commercial-quality and fine-quality carvings at art exhibitions, gem and mineral shows, and antique shows. The more references to identical or similar pieces found and documented, the more clearly it will justify the estimated value. The magazine *Arts of Asia* lists important jade pieces sold at international auctions, and includes color photographs of the items, the auctioneer's estimates, and the final hammer prices.

Antique Ivory

The Walters Art Gallery houses one of the world's great collections of antique ivory objects. The Baltimore gallery has over eleven hundred ivory articles carved in the round and in relief and ranging in date from 4500 B.C. to 1900 A.D. The collection is extraordinary, comprising more than four hundred Far Eastern ivory netsukes as well as ancient Egyptian, Hellenistic, Roman, Minoan, Greek, and Etruscan period masterpieces.

In the Middle Ages, ivory was a favorite carving medium for important liturgical objects, many of which have survived. Ivory carvings from the Gothic period include mirrorback articles and jewelry boxes as well as diptychs and triptychs. Ivory was also a favorite material for carving and jewelry during the Art Nouveau period.

While it is true that few antique ivory carvings may be seen outside of museums, you need to know these do exist and avail yourself of any opportunities for viewing. In seeing antique ivory at its finest and in observing genuine patina, you will not as easily be fooled by artificially aged ivory.

Color does not prove age nor does it identify ivory. While some ivories remain white, others age and darken to a color ranging from brown to mahogany. However, because it is commonly believed that all antique ivories darken, it has become standard practice in many countries to "age" ivories artificially by darkening them. Favorite methods used to age ivory include heating it under fire and burning incense on it, or soaking the ivory in coffee, tea, tobacco juice, or other substances that stain. One way to age ivory prematurely is with potassium permanganate. It will not fade and remains brown until it is sanded off. Similarly, because most old ivory develops cracks, new ivory frequently is heated to a high temperature and then plunged in cold water until it begins to crack and supposedly resembles aged ivory.

As a gemologist, you know that crosshatch markings identify elephant ivory. However, if the markings are absent, this does not necessarily mean the material is not ivory. Since many substitutes for ivory are on the market, positive identification of the material is the first order of business. Bone is the material most often confused with ivory and at first they do look similar. Bone, however, has some major differences. First, bone is hollow along its entire length and is a hard, white material without the soft, warm touch of ivory. Also, bone has tiny dots (capillary openings) that make it easy to distinguish from ivory. Horn, another ivory substitute, can be identified by its fibers. Artificial ivories include *ivoryite,* made of ivory or bone chips mixed with a resin and molded; *galolith,* a molded curd product known as *casein;* and celluloid, an early plastic invented in France about 1860 (and sometimes called French ivory) and popular in the 1930s. A clue to distinguishing celluloid is its lines, which wrap around the object, whereas lines in genuine elephant ivory cross. When valuing an item you believe is elephant ivory, consider that the elephant tusk is solid only along one-third of its length (fig. 6-19). The most expensive items are carved from the solid part. Turn the item over and inspect the bottom. If it is hollow, has a hole, or has a hole that is capped, this is an indication of a lesser-priced item. Larger items are more expensive in general because they must be carved from

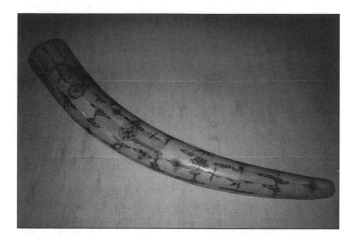

6-19. Elephant tusk ivory is solid for one-third of the length and the most expensive carvings come from the solid portion. Although this looks like a regular elephant tusk, this is a new assembled bone on wood tusk. *(Collection of Bobby Mann.)*

larger tusks that cost more per kilo. Each increase in the size and weight of a carving raises its value. An analogy might be made to a 2-carat diamond that is worth more per carat than a 1-carat diamond of the same quality.

In today's market, the most valuable carvings are Japanese, if they can be authenticated. Next on the value scale are Chinese carvings (fig. 6-20), followed by Hong Kong copies of finely carved Japanese ivory carvings, if proven as Japanese copies. Standard Hong Kong mass-produced carvings are at the very bottom of the price list, joined by ivory carvings from India and Africa (fig. 6-21).

What about damage—does a damaged carving have no value? If the damage does not detract from the overall carving, value it as you normally would and discount it 50 percent. If damage to the carving is too extensive to be repaired, the item is worth only 5 percent of its normal value, or roughly the intrinsic value of the ivory.

Ivory chess sets are common items for valuation. Solid chess sets are priced 20 to 25 percent higher than are hollow ivory chess sets. Hollow sets have a cap on the bottom of each playing piece. Chess sets were commonly underpriced in terms of their fine ivory material until 1970, so if you are appraising a set that is several generations old, you may wish to take the former undervaluation into account when assessing current retail replacement. Explain the big price jump to your client.

Factors to be considered when valuing ivory carvings include the following:

6-20. This 15″, circa 1900 elephant ivory carving of a Chinese man holding a spear is part of the ivory collection of Robert Weisblut, cofounder of The International Ivory Society. *(Photo by Bobby Mann)*

6-21. African elephant ivory warrior, 9½ ″, circa 1950. Collection of Robert Weisblut. Value $450. *(Photo by Bobby Mann)*

1. What is the grade of the ivory: clean, cracked, damaged, or rotten?
2. Can you find crosshatch markings or nerve endings? (Nerve endings, large or small, are revealed as black dots.)
3. Is the item well carved, with details on both front and back?
4. Is this a rare subject or antique item?
5. Is the item signed? Netsukes are frequently signed, but signatures are reproduced for the mass market and should be authenticated by experts.

Importing Ivory and CITES

There is misinformation circulating throughout the appraisal community regarding owning, possessing, and selling ivory. (figs. 6-22 through 6-25.) Some appraisers decline to value ivory, pleading lack of expertise, or ignorance of import laws. For those who do accept an ivory assignment, finding comparable sales and pricing information is very difficult. Elephant ivory was banned from importation into the United States June 9, 1989, as part of an agreement signed at the Convention of International Trade in Endangered Species (CITES). The African Elephant is also protected under several specific U.S. laws: the Endangered Species Act 16 USC 1531–1544, and the African Elephant Conservation Act 16 US 4201–4244, which bans the import of raw ivory. Twenty-six states in the United States have enacted endangered species legislation in addition to the federal laws. Appraiser, check your state laws before beginning an ivory assignment.

Noncommercial African elephant ivory, and pre-act ivory acquired prior to February 4, 1977, is allowed for sale in the U.S. accompanied by CITES Pre-Convention certificates. Antique pieces, defined as items over

6-24. Chinese elephant ivory Flower Garden Group, circa 1900, 14″ × 5 ½″. Value $2,500. Collection of Robert Weisblut. *(Photo by Bobby Mann)*

6-22. Chun Kuei, a Chinese one-piece elephant ivory carving dated 18th century or earlier, 17½″ high, 5″ wide. Value $35,000. Collection of Robert Weisblut. *(Photo by Bobby Mann)*

100 years old, composed in whole or in part of any endangered species or threatened species, that have not been repaired or modified with any part of any such species on or after December 28, 1973, are allowable. Because the appraiser is dealing with a commodity potentially comprised of a highly protected wildlife species, it is suggested to obtain as much information as possible regarding the item.

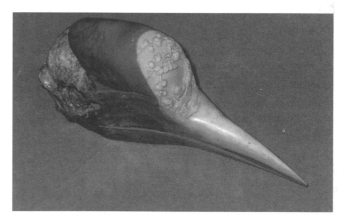

6-25. A rare carved Hornbill ivory. Value $2,500. *(Photo by Bobby Mann)*

This should include information—and any documentary proof—of the age of the item, the animal species the ivory is from, where and when it was acquired, import information, receipts of sale, or preexisting appraisals. African elephant ivory in the U.S. market before 1989 *can legally be sold interstate.* Auctions used to do business in ivory artifacts, carvings, and jewelry and were good pricing resources; however, there are few ivory auctions in the U.S. today. Since most ivory merchants did not plan ahead for the ban, they did not get or give documents on circa date or country-of-origin in sales transactions. Customers who bought items before 1989 may be without documentation of any kind, frequently not even a bill of sale. Appraisals without any documentation, receipts, or bill of sale require the most diligent inquiry and research in an attempt to estimate value. A spokesperson for the

6-23. A Chinese elephant ivory Dragon Boat, circa 1900, 33″ long × 10″ high. Value $13,000. Collection of Robert Weisblut. *(Photo by Bobby Mann)*

U.S. Fish and Wildlife Service said, "Post-1989 ivory articles without documentation may cause problems for appraisers trying to establish a value." Despite the stringent law, African elephant ivory is still being legally sold, held, and traded in *interstate commerce* in the United States by suppliers who have met all import fees, fish and wildlife inspections, and adhered to the following criteria promulgated by the U.S. Fish and Wildlife Service:

What Can Be Imported:

1. Commercial import is allowed for antique worked ivory with CITES Pre-Convention certificates.
2. Noncommercial import of pre-act ivory acquired prior to February 4, 1977, or antiques, with CITES Pre-Convention certificates.
3. Noncommercial import of sport-hunted elephant trophies with CITES export or reexport certificates from the foreign country and potentially U.S. CITES import permits depending upon the country of origin, with any subsequent activity regarding the imported tusks dependent upon permit conditions.

Intrastate/Interstate Sales: Allowed if the ivory was legally imported and/or acquired; check on individual state laws. Special permit condition for imported sport-hunted trophies may not allow their sale.

Possession: Allowed if ivory was legally imported and/or acquired.

Interstate Transport: Allowed if the ivory was legally imported and/or acquired.

Limited Trade in Ivory Approved: In the summer 1997, resumption of ivory trade was the topic at a CITES meeting. The official U.S. position was against resumption of trade; however, the rest of the world favored it, and a *limited* trade was approved by close to 75% of the CITES delegates. The African countries (all with good conservation programs) viewed the downgrading of the level of protection in three countries in Southern Africa—Zimbabwe, Namibia, and Botswana—as a victory for African sovereignty. These three countries will be allowed to sell an annual quota from their collective stockpile of 120 tons. The sales, at $250 per pound, will be to Japan *only* and the Japanese have promised that all of the ivory will remain in Japan.

Hong Kong, once the world's primary customer for raw elephant ivory tusks, has felt effects of the CITES ban. Elephant ivory is still being carved but on a smaller scale.

Currently, most of the Hong Kong production stays in Asia, although some is sold in tourist markets throughout the Far East. American tourists who buy a few carvings in Asia and hand carry them into the U.S.

risk seizure of the articles by U.S. Customs. "If a protected piece is brought into the United States and identified by U.S. Customs inspectors, it will be confiscated," a spokesman for U.S. Customs said. There is a legal export ivory choice for Hong Kong carvers: fossilized ivory. Mammoth ivory is identified by subtle color changes from white to tan, dark brown, or blue-green (iron phosphate—vivanite) and by the Schreger Lines (cross hatching). Fossil walrus (fig. 6-26) is another choice. Mammoth ivory is available in a limited supply to Hong Kong carvers, who try to keep up with demand. Fossil mammoth ivory shows the distinctive "crosshatching" pattern also seen in African elephant ivory. Some current substitutions for elephant ivory used by Asian carvers include hippopotamus, cattle bone, and ox bone. Cattle and ox bone are easily identified with their areas of black, pepper-like spots, pits, scratch-like irregularities, and hollow lengths when used in larger items. The carvings have an assembled look and, indeed, many carvings are created by using pieces of bone cleverly assembled and glued to a wooden form to resemble one large piece. This is done in the imitation of both tusks and carvings. Cattle and ox bone are often smoked to produce an aged dark brown color the same as elephant ivory, or bleached to produce a bright white color. Hippo ivory can be identified by the unusual shape of the tusk. Viewing the base, there is a "V" shape that is not seen in other forms of ivory. Hippo (fig. 6-27) ivory has a smooth, even texture, and takes a high polish. The hippo ivory is generally new ivory. Dealers import it into the United States with a license issued in compliance with the CITES convention regulations mentioned earlier.

Asian Elephant Ivory

The Asian elephant is listed as an endangered species under the U.S. Endangered Species Act and Appendix I under CITES. However, the rules of its ivory sale and use are slightly different according to the U.S. Fish and Wildlife Service Laws and Regulations.

Import: Commercial import is allowed for antiques with CITES Pre-Convention certificates. Noncommercial import only allowed for pre-act ivory acquired before July 1, 1975, according to CITES, with CITES Pre-Convention certificates.

Intrastate sales are allowed if the ivory has been legally imported and/or acquired, i.e., antiques and pre-act. Interstate sale is allowed *only* for antique ivory articles. The possession of such articles are allowed if they have been legally imported and/or acquired.

Testing Ivory

Robert Mann of the International Ivory Society says that ivory with little or no patina should fluoresce

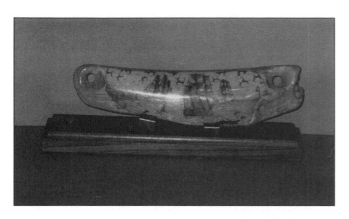

6-26. Scrimshaw fossil walrus sleigh runner, 20th century. Value $750. Collection of Robert Weisblut. *(Photo by Bobby Mann)*

white with longwave ultraviolet. "Other fluorescent colors can eliminate artificial materials." He emphasized, "Study the shape and size of the unknown item.

The finished form is usually dictated by the naturally occurring shape with some modifications. Study surface features for remains of natural outer surface. And he warned, "If the item is supposed to be one piece construction, then remember, the larger the carving the fewer the possibilities. Locate the straight grain pattern and be wary if none exists. Look at the top and bottom of any item for the crosshatching

diagnostic of elephant ivory. Use reflected light and low magnification." In manufactured ivory substitutes (polyester resin, celluloid) look for mold lines, mold marks, air bubbles, and lack of a grain. Commonly found in the substitutes are simulated grain lines that run the length of the piece, usually even and regular, but no crosshatching. Appraising ivory means becoming familiar with a highly complicated market. Consultation with an ivory expert may be needed. The specialist should be conversant in international, federal, and local state laws covering ivory use, possession, and resale. For general and specialized ivory information contact either cofounder of the International Ivory Society, Robert Mann, G.G., International Ivory Society, 4111 Rocky Mt. Drive, Temple Hills, Maryland 20748; or Robert E. Weisblut, International Ivory Society, 11109 Nicholas Drive, Wheaton, Maryland 20902. Another resource is Bill Egleston, 509-A Brentwood Road, Marshalltown, Iowa 50158, a specialist in the mail order sale of fine Oriental art (including ivory and bone) for over 25 years.

The International Ivory Society—Ivory in Other Languages:

Assyrian	Habba
Bulgarian	Slonova Kost
Coptic	Eboy
Greek	Elephas
Hebrew	Shen
Hindi	Basta

6-27. Hippo ivory of a Village Scene Bridge, 15½″ long, 8½″ high, 20th century. Value $1200. Collection of Robert Weisblut. *(Photo by Bobby Mann)*

Hungarian	Elefantsont
Japanese	Zoge
Korean	Sang-A
Latin	Ebur
Lithuanian	Slanio Kaulas
Rumanian	Fides
Scandinavian	Elpenben
Serbian	Phildish
Siamese	Nga Chang
Swedish	Elpenben
Welsh	Asgwyn Eliffent

This glossary of ivory terms was supplied by the *International Ivory Society*. The list is not comprehensive but defines general ivory terms used by collectors and appraisers.

Alabrite	Imitation ivory made from a mixture of alabaster and matrix.
Celluloid	Imitation ivory made from plastic.
Dolphin Teeth	Another term for hippopotamus teeth.
Extant	In existence; not destroyed or lost.
Extinct	No longer in existence, died out.
Fictile Ivory	Plaster of Paris copy cast from genuine ivory carving.
French Ivory	A term for false ivory or ivory substitute.
Galolith	Imitation ivory made from a curd product called casein.
Golden Jade	A term for Hornbill ivory.
Ho-Ting	A term for Hornbill ivory.
Ivorite	Imitation ivory made from ivory sawdust and resin.
Kung Pu	The Chinese Imperial Board of Works.
Mammoth	An elephant ancestor extinct for 10,000 years.
Mastodon	An elephant ancestor extinct for 50,000 years.
Medicine Lady	Another term for a Doctor's Lady.
Micarta	Imitation ivory—compressed layers of cloth and Bakelite.
Odontolite	Turquoise-colored fossil ivory.
Pa Hsien	The Eight Immortals.
Seahorse Tusks	A term for hippopotamus tusks.
Veneer	Thin slices of ivory used to cover items such as wood.

Hardstone Carvings and Gemstone Sculptures

Some of the most collectible and therefore most expensive carvings come from the German carvers of Idar-Oberstein, Germany. Cameo engraving and carving was first introduced to Idar from Paris in the first half of the nineteenth century. Given the concurrent development and growth of the gemcutting industry, it was inevitable that the creation of sculptures from gem materials should also develop. The Idar-Oberstein craftsmen's artistic expression, skills, and use of state-of-the-art tools have proved them masters of all lapidary activities.

Noted German cutter Gerhard Becker says that the carving field has become extremely popular with an "astonishing trend of using more and more valuable rough for gem carving." This is true for sculpture as well as cameos, he believes. Becker considers movement and creativity important factors in estimating carving value. In addition, he believes that appraisers should be prepared to judge the artistic merits of gem sculptures. Of great importance is the harmony between a sculpture and the base upon which it is mounted. Becker innovated the use of bases made from finely carved rock crystal, smoky quartz, and agate (figs. 6-28 and 6-29). He instituted this practice partly to avoid the common way in which minerals and gems were combined.

Little attention is paid to the risk run by the carver who takes on the challenge of a new work, and Becker thinks that appraisers should make this a consideration: "There is a large investment of time by the sculptor with materials lost because of breakage or other problems that do not surface until the end of a carving project." Becker believes that the time required for the sculptor to consider the design, search for the correct material, and create the gem sculpture should be factored into final evaluation. Overall, Becker advises, "Take craftsmanship first and then materials into consideration" (figs. 6-30 and 6-31).

6-28. Rock crystal elephant group on red jasper stand. *(Photograph courtesy of Gerhard Becker)*

6-29. Agate mallard duck alighting gracefully on a wave of rock crystal. *(Photograph courtesy of Gerhard Becker)*

6-30. A masterpiece of carving in quartz and amethyst. *(Photograph courtesy of Gerhard Becker)*

In determining value on gemstone carvings, consider the following factors:

1. Craftsmanship. How well did the artist render the subject or convey a discernible message?
2. Suitability of the material for the subject. How do the form and pattern of the material relate to the subject?
3. Color.
4. Luster. Evaluate the final polish and finish.
5. Signature. Signed pieces are more valuable.
6. Desirability.
7. Function. Does it have a use besides decoration?
8. Provenance. If proven, it adds value.

When writing up the appraisal report for a hardstone carving, do not fail to note the following particulars:

1. Size of item in inches, giving height before width.
2. Subject matter, written description, and photograph.
3. If signature is present, indicate where it is positioned. Also, note if the signature has been authenticated.
4. Condition: new, old, repaired, old and not repaired, etc.
5. If the carving has been repaired, indicate the quality and extent of the repairs.

Repairs

The cautious appraiser will scan all carvings under ultraviolet light. Repairs will usually appear as yellowish, whitish, or very pale bluish blotches or lines, depending on the bonding or cement used to mend any break or crack in the piece. Use longwave first and then shortwave ultraviolet light to conduct the examination, taking care that you are seeing actual former cracks, not the section where two pieces may have been joined together to form the carving. Fine and expensive items that have been repaired by a skilled

6-31. Frosted rock crystal ducks on a pedestal of rough black obsidian. *(Photograph courtesy of Gerhard Becker)*

restorer may resist UV detection and require examination under high magnification.

Diagram the damage, repair, or loss on a separate sheet of paper and attach it to your report (as a plot of a gemstone would be attached to a gem report). Some still believe that a broken or repaired carving is valueless, but that is incorrect. If a carving has been restored in a proper and expert manner, it is once again marketable and therefore has value. The exceptions are carving and statues that cannot be repaired by the work of a good conservator, and items that have been allowed to chip and crack, or on which details and features have eroded owing to neglect and carelessness. These items are worth only the intrinsic value of the material.

Silver Flatware and Holloware

Appraisers of residential contents consistently claim jurisdiction over appraisals in this category. Rightly so, since the field of silver appraisals is vast and marked by many subspecialties. Some appraisers work a lifetime to earn expertise in a small part of the world of silver articles. A few are willing to tackle the field from antique English sterling to contemporary American; these are the colleagues to whom you turn for advice when you have an unknown and very precious item to value.

In the real world of everyday commerce and trade, however, you are far more likely to be given a set of Reed & Barton silver flatware, a pair of Towle candlesticks, or a Gorham tray to evaluate than you are to see great sterling antiquities. All your client will want from you is a correct answer to the question, What's it worth? Before you can give an answer, you will need to identify the item and evaluate the metal content. Most homes have two kinds of silver, sterling and silverplate. You will need the following tools to identify and appraise common silver articles, just as you need proper tools to appraise gems and jewelry:

1. A 10× loupe or a strong hand lens.
2. Scales. You will need a troy ounce spring scale for small objects and a balance scale for large ones.
3. Supply of plastic bags to hold small objects that are weighed on a spring scale by tying a loop at the top of the bag and hanging it onto the scale.
4. Tape measure.
5. Dropcloth for photographic background.
6. Camera and film.
7. Acid-test kit.

Silver is weighed in the troy system. One troy ounce of silver equals twenty pennyweight, and there are twelve ounces to the troy pound. See the appendix for weight tables on the troy system, pennyweight-to-gram, and troy-to-avoirdupois conversion. Also see *Analyzing Metal Fineness* in chapter 3 for more information on silver and silver fineness.

Sterling or solid silver flatware is produced in varying weights, but there is no legal weight standard imposed on their manufacture. By trade custom, silverware is made in weights known as trade, medium, heavy, and extra heavy, with the difference in weight between each grade, on sterling forks, being about two ounces per dozen forks. Silverplated ware is made by electroplating silver onto a base metal. The thickness of the silverplate may be only about 1/100,000 of an inch. The weight of each silverplated flatware piece means nothing to an appraiser, since there are no legal standards regulating the minimum amount of silver on silverplated tableware and the plating may be extremely light.

Any flatware items marked A1 or Standard, A1 Plus or A1X, AA, Double or XX, Triple or XXX, or Quadruple or XXXX have been silverplated. Sterling-silver articles should be stamped *sterling*. The key below explains other common markings:

- EPNS: Electroplate on nickel silver
- EPWM: Electroplate on white metal
- EPBM: Electroplate on Britannia metal

- EPC: Electroplate on copper
- EPB: Electroplate on brass

It is sometimes extremely difficult to read marks on silver holloware and flatware. For silver holloware, you need a strong light reflected off the back or rim of the item, preferably angled so that you can see the markings, which may be very faintly or lightly inscribed. On flatware knives, look at the junction of the blade and handle for marks. Other utensils should be stamped on the back of each handle.

Identifying the manufacturer is important; you will want to become familiar with the marks of the most common American makers. An excellent reference source is Dorothy Rainwater's *Encyclopedia of American Silver Manufacturers* (see the bibliography).

To keep from overlooking essential details in evaluating silver articles, use the silver flatware and holloware worksheets illustrated in figures 6-32 and 6-33. On your worksheet, complete the following steps:

1. Identify the metal (sterling, silverplate, etc.).
2. Note trademarks or their absence.
3. List the weight of sterling items in troy ounces.
4. List the measurements of the item if it is holloware.
5. Note the approximate age or period of manufacture.
6. Note the pattern of silver flatware.
7. Note the decoration or motif on silver holloware.
8. Note the style and shape of holloware.
9. List any surface decoration, such as any engraving, inscription, or monogram.
10. Note any breaks, cracks, chips, and damage as well as any repairs that have been made.
11. Describe the mounts (i.e., ivory finials, ivory handles, etc.).
12. Photograph the items. If the items are flatware, photograph an entire place setting, making sure that the utensil ends showing the pattern are in the photo.

Some appraisers draw the flatware pattern onto their worksheet, which is nice but unnecessary if you can obtain a good closeup photograph. The photograph is a better aid to pattern identification and keeps the appraiser from having to rely upon memory for details in writing the description. Several indexes to pattern identification are available. One of the best known is the *Sterling Flatware Pattern Index*, published by the *Jewelers' Circular-Keystone* book club.

When evaluating silver, keep in mind that all items stamped and identified as sterling must be weighed. Some holloware and flatware can differ in price per ounce within the same style period. Bullion or spot silver prices do not affect antique silver because its value lies in its age, quality, and design. Silverplate does not need to be weighed. In addition, weight has no bearing on the value of silver articles like religious artifacts, souvenir spoons, or wine and tobacco collections.

In her work *Early American Silver for the Cautious Collector,* Martha Gandy Fales offers practical and valuable help in dating silver holloware through the finials, thumbpieces, spouts, handles, feet, lids, and bodies used. By familiarizing yourself with styles, you will be able to recognize if you have something extraordinary to appraise. Some silver terms, motifs, and styles are illustrated in figures 6-34 and 6-35. Fales reminds us that "sterling" was not stamped on American silver until about 1850 and the word "coin" was used on silver from about 1830 to 1860.

The majority of these appraisals, however, will concern the current replacement price of contemporary American-made sterling silver flatware and holloware. To find this figure, the appraiser needs to use proven market-research methods: obtaining the manufacturer's suggested retail prices from individual silver companies and department stores; finding privately published silver price guides; and consulting trade journals, auction catalogs, antique stores, and flea markets, and prices from estate sales. Auction hammer price is *one* useful reference that can be used to determine fair market value.

In an estate liquidation, used sterling flatware is commonly valued at either the scrap value of the silver, when sold to dealers in bulk according to the New York price quote for silver per troy ounce on that day, or the price a dealer of used silver will pay for a particular pattern as of the date of the appraisal. One of the largest nationally known dealers of used silver is the Walter Drake Company, which buys silver with a published price list guaranteed for thirty days. The company is located in the Drake Building, Colorado Springs, Colorado 80940.

The prices of sterling silver and silverplated flatware have fallen dramatically since their highs in 1980–1981. In 1981, some sterling silver flatware was valued at over five hundred dollars per place setting. Now the same flatware is worth about ninety-nine to one hundred and twenty dollars per place setting. Holloware has also plunged in price.

More Pattern and Price References

The Book of Silver by Scott and June Martin has plenty of identification information on American sterling flatware and is available from SM Publications, 353 W. 56th St., MS7A, New York, New York 10019. Annual informational updates are mailed to purchasers

SILVER FLATWARE APPRAISAL WORKSHEET

Appraisal for: _____ Date: _____

Purpose: _____ for _____

PATTERN: _____

Sterling _____ Silverplate _____ Other _____

No. Pcs.:

_____	Knives Dinner_____Place_____	@$_____	_____
_____	Forks Dinner_____Place_____	@$_____	_____
_____	Salad Forks	@$_____	_____
_____	Teaspoons	@$_____	_____
_____	Soup, Cream	@$_____	_____
_____	Soup, Boullion	@$_____	_____
_____	Butter Spreaders HH_____FH_____	@$_____	_____
_____	Cocktail Forks	@$_____	_____
_____	Iced Beverage	@$_____	_____
_____	Demitasse Spoon	@$_____	_____
_____	Fish Fork	@$_____	_____
_____	Fish Knife	@$_____	_____
_____	Fruit Knife	@$_____	_____
_____	Grapefruit/Melon Spoon	@$_____	_____
_____	Ice Cream Fork	@$_____	_____
_____	Salt Spoon, Individual	@$_____	_____
_____	Steak Knife	@$_____	_____
_____	Infant Feeding Spoon	@$_____	_____
_____	Baby Fork	@$_____	_____
_____	Baby Spoon	@$_____	_____
_____	Child's Fork	@$_____	_____
_____	Child's Knife	@$_____	_____
_____	Child's Spoon	@$_____	_____

TOTAL: _____

SERVING PIECES

_____	Berry, Casserole, Salad Spoon	@$_____	_____
_____	Butter Serving Knife	@$_____	_____
_____	Cake Knife	@$_____	_____
_____	Cheese Serving Knife	@$_____	_____
_____	Cold Meat or Buffet Fork	@$_____	_____
_____	Cream Sauce Ladle	@$_____	_____
_____	Flat Server	@$_____	_____
_____	Gravy Ladle	@$_____	_____
_____	Jelly Server	@$_____	_____
_____	Lemon Fork	@$_____	_____
_____	Olive, Pickle, Butter Fork	@$_____	_____
_____	Pie Server	@$_____	_____
_____	Salad or Serving Fork	@$_____	_____
_____	Salad or Serving Spoon	@$_____	_____
_____	Soup Ladle	@$_____	_____
_____	Sugar Spoon or Sugar Tongs	@$_____	_____
_____	Tablespoon	@$_____	_____
_____	Tablespoon, Pierced	@$_____	_____

TOTAL: _____

6-32. Silver flatware appraisal worksheet.

SILVER HOLLOWARE WORKSHEET

Appraisal for: _____ Date: _____

Purpose of Appraisal: _____ for _____

No. _____ Item: _____ Manufacturer: _____

    Pattern: _____ Hallmarks or Stampings: _____

    Weight: _____ Sterling Silver_____ Silverplate_____ Other_____

    Height: _____ Width: _____ Diameter: _____ Depth: _____

    Body Shape: _____ Handle: _____ Finial: _____ Spouts: _____ Base/Feet: _____

    Decorative Motif: _____

    Repairs: _____

    Description of Object:

                                      Estimated Value:

No. _____ Item: _____ Manufacturer: _____

    Pattern: _____ Hallmarks or Stampings: _____

    Weight: _____ Sterling Silver_____ Silverplate_____ Other_____

    Height: _____ Width: _____ Diameter: _____ Depth: _____

    Body Shape: _____ Handle: _____ Finial: _____ Spouts: _____ Base/Feet: _____

    Decorative Motif: _____

    Repairs: _____

    Description of Object:

                                      Estimated Value:

    Resources and References of Value:

6-33. Silver holloware appraisal worksheet.

of the book. In addition, Scott Martin's *Guide to Evaluating Gold & Silver Objects* is full of advice on inspecting, testing, and evaluating gold and silver objects. This data filled book will be useful to every silver appraiser.

The Silver Update is a quarterly guide to sterling flatware prices that no appraiser of silver should be without. Available by subscription: *The Silver Update,* P.O. Box 2157, Ellicott City, Maryland 21041. Publisher Nannette Monmonier prints companies' suggested retail prices for American sterling flatware and holloware in a three-times per year format. Also available: annual price publications for both silverplate flatware and silverplate holloware.

Silverplate

If you are evaluating silverplated goods, the quality of the article is determined by these points:

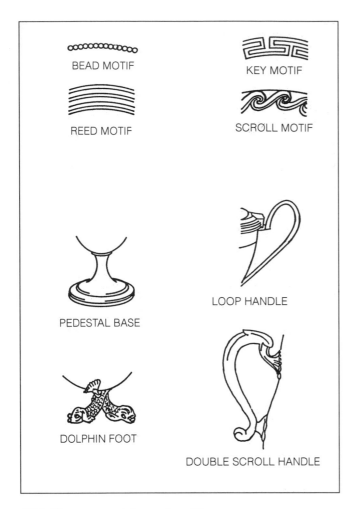

6-34. Silver terms, styles, and motifs.

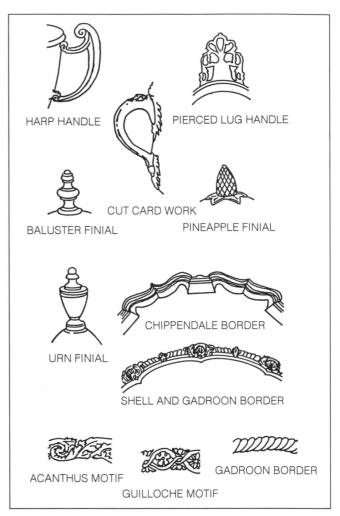

6-35. Further examples of silver terms, styles, and motifs.

manufacturer, base metal, and quality of the design in terms of aesthetics and technique.

The most important factor, the manufacturer, adds value to the piece if the company is one collectors are interested in or is known for style and quality. Look at and note the metal. Silverplating on copper is better and more expensive than silverplating on white metal. Is the design pleasing and well executed, with the border (usually cast and applied) cleanly detailed? Silverplate is inexpensive compared to sterling, but silverplate will have added value if the quality is extraordinary, or if the article has historical or collectible value.

When the examination of the silverplated items is finished, your client will nearly always ask: "Should I have my silver replated?" Read that: Will replating enhance the value? Your reply is that copper showing through silverplate is called "bleeding" and is commonly considered very attractive and desirable. If the client dislikes this look and wants the item to look new, he or she should consider whether the piece is worth the expense of replating. Check with a silver replater to compare the price of replating against the price of a comparable new piece.

If your clients are getting an appraisal of flatware for insurance, counsel them to ask their insurance agent what value the insurance company will accept. Explain that major silver manufacturers have normal retail prices as well as frequent sales of their flatware, with standard discounts of up to 70 percent off the list prices. The client and agent should agree on the price to be used for replacement and in so doing keep you clear of any future settlement discord.

Silver Appraisers' Words of Advice

Anthony C. Clark, G.G., silver historian and valuer with Fuller & Associates, Washington, D.C., has some words of advice for appraisers of silver flatware and holloware. "Be careful with what you are appraising. Silver objects are now being looked upon as fine art, and many pieces are being appraised for historical value. One good example might be individual, national, regional, or prominent trophies with engravings. While they used to be melted down, many are now resold because of their provenance." Clark also adds this reminder checklist for appraisers:

1. Determine date of manufacture, if possible.
2. Determine if the pattern is active, made to order, obsolete.
3. In all appraisals include the dimensions of items along with weights.
4. If the item is made to order, include die preparation charges in value estimate.
5. The types of blades on knives should be noted: blunt, Old French, New French, modern. Also, identify the blade material.
6. For all appraisals state the market on which the item was valued: Manufacturer's Suggested Retail Price for active and made to order, Comparable, Secondary.

7. For insurance, put a value on monograms or other engravings because for replacement, this is an added expense.
8. In the initial interview with the client, establish in case of loss as to whether he or she would replace the silver with new, comparable, or secondary, and stipulate the fact in both the cover letter and appraisal report.
9. On older silver—both flatware and holloware—state the construction method: handmade versus machine made. State quality of workmanship.
10. Note the condition of all items on the appraisal.
11. If a piece has been discontinued by the manufacturer, note it on the appraisal.

Finally, Clark advises silver appraisers to be careful in using any sale or discounted prices. "These prices may be *very* temporary and are usually inconsistent." Along that same thought, Nannette Monmonier of *The Silver Guide* reminds appraisers that many manufacturer's suggested retail prices are regional; therefore, careful regional pricing should be researched.

CHAPTER 7

LEGAL AND ETHICAL ASPECTS OF APPRAISING

Appraisers have both a legal and an ethical responsibility toward their clients. The relationship between an appraiser and a client is not based on the principle of *caveat emptor* (let the buyer beware), but instead is founded on confidence and trust. It is as important to the appraiser as it is to the client that the appraiser holds a reputation for being professional and scrupulous.

In developing a code of ethics and principles of appraisal practice, the American Society of Appraisers has defined the relationship between the appraiser and client as follows:

> As the vocation of property appraisals has developed during past decades from a business occupation into a profession, certain concepts have emerged and become clear. . . .
>
> Because of the specialized knowledge and abilities required of the appraiser which are not possessed by the layman, there has now come to be established a fiduciary relationship between him and those who rely upon his findings (ASA, 1968, foreword).

A fiduciary relationship is one that is based on trust. For the appraiser, it connotes serious obligations, both spoken and written, to clients, third parties, and to the public. Moreover, a fiduciary responsibility is a duty imposed by law, one that a trustee owes to a beneficiary of the trust; an officer or director of a corporation owes to the corporation and its stockholders; a lawyer owes to the client; an employee owes to the employer; and an appraiser owes to his or her client. Fiduciary duties are not limited to these situations, but are present in every relationship founded on faith and trust.

One fiduciary obligation for the appraiser is keeping the nature of an appraisal assignment, as well as the client's name, confidential. Ethics deem it improper to disclose either of these, unless the client approves of disclosure, clearly has no interest in keeping the fact of appraisal confidential, or unless the appraiser is required by law to disclose the fact of the engagement to make an appraisal. It is also improper for an appraiser to reveal the amount of valuation of a property without the client's permission, unless required to do so by law. All of the major appraisal societies and gemological organizations, and many industry trade groups have a code of ethics.

In paragraph 3.6 in the booklet *The Principles of Appraisal Practice and Code of Ethics of the American Society of Appraisers,* the paragraph entitled "Appraiser's Responsibility to Third Parties" clearly outlines the duties of the appraiser:

> Under certain specific circumstances an appraisal report may be given by a client to a third party for their use. If the purpose of the appraisal includes a specific use by a third party, the third party has a right to rely on the validity and objectivity of the appraiser's findings as regards the specific stated purpose and intended use for which the appraisal was originally made. Members of the Society (ASA) recognize their responsibility to those parties, other than the client, who may be specifically entitled to make use of their reports (American Society of Appraisers, Revised January 1994).

An appraisal report may be given by the client to a third party for use, such as to an attorney to proceed with settlement of common property. The third party may or may not be known to the appraiser, but has a right to rely on the validity and objectivity of the appraiser's findings. Another example of third-party usage is an appraisal report completed for insurance replacement, when the insurance company as the third party will rely on the appraisal report as accurate.

When the welfare of the general public is involved in the final value judgment of an item, the appraiser has obligations and responsibilities to the general public that supersede the obligation to the client. This position of trust is broad and ranges from assignments involving depositors in financial institutions—such as appraisals used to make collateral loans—to publicly displayed values of personal property offered for sale to the general public, as in appraisals for independent auction houses and for auctions of federal, state, and city surplus property.

In agreeing to this position of trust by accepting the assignment, the appraiser has acceded to a personal and professional incumbency. The concomitant legal and moral liabilities must be grasped completely, especially by jewelers and appraisers who continue to appraise in any old way. They are prime targets for a lawsuit.

The Appraiser's Role in Gemstone Barter

There is a tradition of bartering in this country that stretches back to colonial New England. By definition, *bartering* is exchanging goods or services in return for other goods or services; in other words, trading. Implicit in this definition is that the goods or services traded be of equal value. A bold use of the idea can be traced to Peter Minuit, who successfully completed an incredible exchange when he bought Manhattan Island for trinkets valued at twenty-four dollars. Although the use of gemstones and jewelry has a long tradition as a medium of barter, such trading was given new emphasis a few years ago during a real-estate-for-jewelry barter era. While encountered by the appraiser less frequently today than in the early 1980s, gemstone barters are still around. Appraisers called in to estimate value in this market must research prices diligently.

The concept of gemstone exchange for other property is valid only if certain criteria are met. The gemstones must be of a specific minimum quality (in recent years, the full range of qualities has been used in gemstone exchanges, from gems to junk), and all parties involved must be aware that the market is highly competitive and that the sale of gemstones can be difficult and time consuming.

While it is true that some high-quality gemstones appreciate rapidly, chances are that the gemstones involved will be of commercial grade or less and may be difficult to liquidate. Even good gems may have a very small liquid market—if they are very large and not suitable for use in jewelry, their resale potential will be limited. And, although medium to low-medium quality gems that can be used in jewelry are generally easier to liquidate, resale of the gems may nonetheless be difficult because most of these stones are used in the manufacture of jewelry, a very competitive market. At the bottom of the barrel are barter gemstones of such poor quality that they can only be used in the hobby market. These are frequently compared to "fishbowl gravel" and are sold by the kilo (one kilogram equals 5,000 carats). Unfortunately, most of the barter material comes from this latter group of stones.

The responsible appraiser will make every effort to inform and educate his client about the possibilities for sale or best use of the property. The client will look to the appraiser for an explanation of all applicable markets.

If you are called upon to perform an appraisal for barter, observe the following precautions:

1. Suggest that your client obtain an appraisal from at least two independent gemological laboratories or independent gemologists.
2. Counsel your client not to accept an appraisal from a source connected in any way with the party attempting to trade the gems.
3. Do not put a dollar figure on the gems based on projected appreciation of the gems in a vague future market. No one can predict their future value; the gemstone market is too volatile.

If your client cannot be dissuaded from participating in an exchange of property for gemstones (usually your client will be the party with the real estate), try to match the levels of the appraisals for all parties involved. The most common event is for either party to the exchange to submit a grossly overinflated appraisal, obtained from an unethical appraiser, and then offer his or her part of the deal at a fraction of the appraised value. This kind of offer is calculated to make other parties believe that they are getting more in exchange than they are trading. Any appraiser who is involved in this kind of transaction is unethical. The ethical appraiser will expose the true nature of the deal to the client and recommend that both properties be revalued to represent actual values to be traded for actual values.

It takes great skill as an appraiser and diplomat to make sure that the client receives a correct interpretation of the marketability of any gemstones offered in trade. If parcels of stones are involved, each gemstone must be appraised; the price of one stone multiplied by the number of stones in the parcel is *not* a true or representative lot valuation. This kind of appraisal requires deep and careful research.

Many stones will arrive for your evaluation encased in plastic or sealed containers. You cannot evaluate gemstones unless they are removed from these containers. Advise your clients immediately of this fact and do not be a party to any appraisal in which you cannot personally handle and examine the gemstones to evaluate them in your prescribed manner. You are courting litigation if you do otherwise. If your client gives you permission to remove the gems from their containers, carry out the appraisal as you would normally, but make sure that you remove and examine the gemstones in front of the client and before another witness, if possible, so there will be no question later of whether the stones are the same ones the client originally brought into your office. Plot the stones (colored gems, too) in front of the client and give him or her a copy of the plot if the stones are left in your hands while you prepare the complete report. When the client returns to retrieve the stone(s), reverse the procedure by comparing the plot he has to the stone you are showing him in the microscope. You want no future cries of "stone switching" from a client.

Investment Gems—Real or Racket?

Plenty of unfortunate people suffered serious financial loss during the investment-gems craze of the early 1980s. Many did not want to believe the bad news when told that their "investments" were of poor quality and most thought themselves too smart to be conned in such a manner. All were victims of the maxim "You can't beat a man at his own game," because they accepted the seller's valuation of quality and failed to have the gemstones appraised *before* money changed hands. Of course, each victim was hopeful that this investment—which sounded too good to be true—was true. Being an educated individual was no guarantee of invincibility to the hype; the list of those taken in included doctors, lawyers, and members of all professions. A business valuation appraiser confided that he, too, was once relieved of several thousand dollars by a gemstone investment firm. The gemstones he bought later turned out to be worth a fraction of their stated "value."

The gemstone investment firms were, for the most part, boiler-room operations run by individuals who knew nothing about gems and jewelry business but a lot about high-pressure selling. They played upon the desires of collectors and others who wanted to take advantage of the huge increases in gem and precious-metal valuations and touted gemstones as a buffer against the rampant inflation of the time. High-pressure sellers made convincing arguments by pointing to such events as Sotheby's April 1983 New York jewelry sale, which brought a world record for a jewelry auction with such lots as a Cartier Art Deco sapphire and diamond bracelet and matching clip that sold for over half a million dollars—eighty thousand dollars beyond its high estimate. It is no wonder that everyone wanted to jump onto this fast-moving gravy train. This included financial consultants who advised their clients to use gems and jewelry as tax shelters. Unfortunately, only a small percentage of players came out winners.

With the hysteria over, little apparent gemstone investment market is left. Financial advisors have reversed direction and now agree that pieces should be purchased for love of the workmanship and style because should markets collapse, tastes change, precious metals tumble, or disaster strike, the beauty of the jewelry will be the only consolation left to the purchaser. Responsible jewelers and professional appraisers, of course, have always advised their clients to take this course.

How can an appraiser help the client turn purchases into cash? Liquidity has always been a major obstacle for gemstone investors. Liquidating gems requires market exposure, price, and time. If your clients have patience, you may be able to assist them by acting as their broker. One route is to send the loose gemstones or finished jewelry to a major auction house such as Sotheby's or Christie's, whose worldwide locations will give your client the advantage of selling in a foreign market. The best option for appraisers who work at home is to use the services of the Internet. By using a network of this kind, you can list your client's articles for review by hundreds of network subscribers all over the United States. Most of those who have used the Internet have only praise for electronic buying and selling.

The effects of the investment gemstone craze were not lost on the jewelry industry, which has reacted, through the Jewelers Vigilance Committee, by preparing and submitting new *Guides for the Jewelry Industry* to the Federal Trade Commission for publication in the Federal Registry (see bibliography). The guides represent the industry's wish to impose restrictions on those who sell gemstones for investment purposes and those who appraise and certify them.

Major changes in the investment section of the *Guides* state that it is an "unfair trade practice to use the words *investment gems, investment grade, investment quality* [italics added], or similar terms when such words or terms imply that specific gemstones merit a classification or grade superior to, more desirable than, or essentially different from the grades of gemstones marketed for use in jewelry."

It is also considered unfair trade practice to sell or offer to sell an industry product as a financial investment unless the seller discloses, among other facts, "that appreciation or profit cannot be assured," and "no organized market exists for the resale of industry products by private owners" (Federal Trade Commission, 1986, 23.1 (d), 2).

The *Guides* also prohibit, for obvious reasons, the use of sealed containers in the sale of gemstones for investment. One section that deals with the sub rosa links of certain appraisers to sellers of gemstones, states:

> It is an unfair trade practice to describe, identify, or refer to an industry product as "certified" or use any other word or words of similar meaning or import, unless:
>
> The identity of the certifier and the specific manners of qualities certified are clearly disclosed; and
>
> The certifier is qualified to certify as to such matters and qualities, has examined the specific product, and has made such certification; and
>
> Full disclosure is made of any existing business relationship, association or affiliation of the certifier with the firm selling or offering for sale the industry product; and
>
> There is available to the purchaser a certificate setting forth clearly and nondeceptively the name of the certifier and the matters and qualities certified (Federal Trade Commission, 1986, 23. 1 (c), 2).

Survival Techniques for Expert Witnesses

The title of professional jewelry appraiser involves you in more than researching values, and signals additional fiduciary responsibilities and obligations. You are presumed to be expert in your field by the public, and as such can be called into court to give testimony on valuation.

Take a course in business law from your local community college. You will gain a market advantage if you do, because it is no longer enough for an appraiser to be an expert in art or jewelry valuation. In addition to knowing current prices and values, you are expected to be familiar with laws regulating taxes, insurance, and divorce. While it is unpleasant to get caught in any legal crossfire, you can mentally prepare for court by understanding that the nature of your business exposes you to litigation, which is burgeoning in this country. Most appraisers are called to the witness stand at some point in their career, either as expert in

defense of their own reports, or to disprove someone else's valuation.

Courts have ruled that qualified experts can be compelled to testify when they have knowledge pertinent to the case. Therefore, if you refuse to appear voluntarily when summoned, you can be subpoenaed. Do not let this happen—depending upon local statutes, being subpoenaed may mean that you receive little or no fee. Employment as expert, however, either in court or in giving a disposition, entitles you to compensation. The common practice is to charge either a half-day or full day's regular fee for your services.

If you are rendering appraisals for divorce cases, you will find substantial court work generated. One and sometimes both parties involved may have a grossly exaggerated idea of what used jewelry in the average estate is worth. The wife in the case will usually view the jewelry as separate property. The husband will generally remember only that thousands of dollars were spent on jewelry during the marriage and, as he recalls the occasions, that they were not intended as gifts but as family investments. He calculates the inflated price of other goods and services and assumes that the jewelry must be worth a bundle. Or, if he fancies himself to be educated about market values and jewelry sold in a secondary market, he will probably believe the jewelry is worth at least half of its original purchase price. This can hardly be the case when your appraisal provides the fair market value of the goods. If the total value of the items you examine is lower than the principals in the case expected, you will be called to justify, validate, and substantiate your numbers—in an atmosphere of hostility. Understanding that such situations will probably result in litigation should make a difference in how you appraise. This knowledge should not make a difference in your bottom-line number, but it should make a difference in the thoroughness of your research and documentation. Since most divorces take six to nine months to come to trial after filing, you will need to review all the market circumstances that affected the valuation before you appear as an expert witness.

Of course, divorce cases are not the only ones that involve angry and hostile clients. You could be called as witness for a jeweler suing another jeweler; a customer suing a jeweler; to identify jewelry in damage claims, stone-switching or theft charges; and to value items in an inheritance case. Almost any transaction of gems and jewelry could involve you with the judicial system.

The event usually starts with a call from an attorney's secretary telling you your testimony is needed (for a mutual client) on a document you supplied weeks, months, even years ago. Moreover, you are expected to appear in court at 9:00 A.M. the next morning. In some circumstances, you will be asked to give a deposition—the testimony of a witness taken out of court before a person authorized to administer oaths. But in most cases you will have to appear in court at the appointed day and time with little advance warning. Ask your attorney (the one for whom you are testifying) for a pretrial conference. To do your job properly, you must be acquainted with what is expected of you. You need to know what credentials will qualify you as an expert witness in the eyes of the court. You need information from the attorney on what you should expect in both direct and cross-examination. Of course, it is absolutely essential that you know the purpose and function of the appraisal so that you can explain the values given and be able to anticipate questions that will probably be presented by the adversary. Make sure you can spell and accurately define the technical terms you will use during your testimony. Be certain that your definition is consistent with technical dictionaries, and that you have read these definitions. Cross-examiners sometimes attempt to embarrass experts on these points.

If you have never testified or been in a trial before, and have a few days to prepare before you testify, it is worthwhile to visit a courthouse and familiarize yourself with the courtroom. Find out where each party sits and observe courtroom protocol so that you will know what will be expected of you. You will learn that you should stand when the judge arrives or leaves the bench; that you should not leave the witness stand without asking the judge's permission or being excused; and that if you wish to leave the courtroom after you have given testimony, that you should have your attorney ask the court's permission.

Prepare a list of questions that your attorney will ask you during the questioning to establish your qualifications as an expert. A list might include the following:

1. What is your name?
2. What is your present occupation?
3. How long have you been an appraiser?
4. What experience do you have in valuing the particular types of items?
5. How many times have you previously testified as expert witness?
6. To which professional appraisal organizations do you belong?
7. How did you value the articles?
8. What steps did you take to arrive at your valuation?
9. How would you define fair market value?

Also see the *Witness Testimony* section of this chapter for an example of typical questioning. You also need to take a copy of your qualifications to court. Regardless of the number of times you may have testified for a particular attorney, or how well he or she knows you personally, it is wise to have an extra list of your qualifications with you. Often the attorney will need to review your expertise quickly, or the attorney may show the list to the opposing counsel before handing it to the court stenographer to enter into record.

William F. Causey, litigation lawyer and adjunct professor of trial practice at Georgetown University, recommends that you advise your attorney to refuse to allow an opposing attorney to prevent your qualifications and background from being heard in court. He is referring to a technique in which the opposing counsel will offer to the judge to "concede" your qualifications as soon as you take the witness stand. In doing so, opposing counsel will keep the jury from hearing about your background and expertise.

"A jury rarely knows much about art, antiques or jewelry," Causey says, "and your judgment may be accepted more on the strength of expert opinion." He adds: "Your credentials are your power, your influence."

In a paper prepared by Houston attorney Robert M. Welch, Jr., for Southern Methodist University, emphasis is given to methods used to disqualify or discredit witnesses:

Cross-examination of the opponent's expert should begin with an inquiry into his or her qualifications. However, where the opponent's expert is obviously qualified, it is best to minimize the expert's qualifications and offer to stipulate that the expert is qualified. (By the same token, it is better to reject the opponent's offer to stipulate if one's own expert has credentials that will impress the trier of fact.) The attorney should probe into the expert's background and experience in order to find weaknesses that will disqualify the expert or at least show that his or her credentials are inferior to those of the attorney's own expert, or that bias exists (Welch, 1980).

A trial is a battle with you as one of the targets. Opposing counsel will search for any flaw in your valuation that can be used against you. Welch adds that the attorney should challenge an expert's testimony for accuracy if any apparent errors in the appraisal are found, or if an analysis of the property is incomplete or faulty in any manner.

If you believe that your answers will be too cautious for the opposition to make you look unqualified or make the jurors doubt your expertise, think about this: A lot depends on the line of questioning the opposing attorney takes, as well as his or her tone of voice and any innuendo the counsel tries to make about your age or character. Some attorneys have a gift for this and will try to discredit you by drawing the court's attention to any aspect about you that could be a common basis for prejudice.

Stephen A. Blass, a counselor-at-law based in Miami, was making this very point to a group of appraisers when one woman commented that she did not believe or understand how an attorney could make it difficult for her to testify as an expert witness. Blass pointed out that an attorney could draw the jury's attention to the appraiser's youth and beauty by asking such questions as "How did a pretty young lady like you get involved in such a business?" or by commenting on how attractive she looked in court. Moreover, in using a condescending tone of voice or in appearing amused by the witness's answers, the opposing counsel can give a jury the message that the witness's testimony is not to be taken seriously. The games are not just for women witnesses. Female attorneys can be as ruthless as their male counterparts. A young jewelry appraiser followed Blass's comments with tales of his own court adventures. He recounted how a shrewd woman lawyer tried to discredit him as witness and cast doubts about his ability by asking questions about his age ("Aren't you awfully young to be in such a position of trust?"), and about his Italian heritage.

Can you stop this as a witness? Yes. If your attorney does not stop the harassment, you can turn to the judge and say: "Your Honor, is this pertinent to my testimony?" Or, you can recognize the game for the high courtroom drama it is, stay calm, and answer the questions with a yes or no.

Twenty Rules for Expert Witnesses:

1. Listen carefully. You cannot answer what you have not heard.
2. Understand. If you do not understand, ask for the question to be repeated or rephrased.
3. Pause. Reflect before answering. A pause conveys a sense of thoughtfulness and thoroughness.
4. Never guess. If you do not know, say so.
5. Do not volunteer information. Answer only the questions that are asked.
6. If interrupted, stop and wait. Attorneys will use the interruption to divert attention from your answer, but sometimes judges may ask questions.
7. Answer loudly and clearly. Address the courtroom. Speaking clearly shows confidence.
8. Beware of mental math. While you are calculating—often erroneously—you will look indecisive. Carry a pocket calculator.
9. Stay calm. Opposing attorneys will try to rattle you.
10. Be independent. State your professional opinion, even if it is not what the attorney wants to hear.
11. Speak to the jury. The final decision rests with them.
12. Admit you have prepared your testimony. This shows your professionalism to the jury and also shows the opposing attorney that you are prepared.
13. Admit that you are being paid. This is your professional prerogative. But be sure it is not a contingency fee.
14. Be confident. Relay information in a positive manner.
15. Know all documents and evidence. Fumbling with notes or documents can make you appear indecisive and unprofessional.
16. Keep it simple. The jury must understand what you are saying. Avoid obscure and esoteric terms.
17. Define terms accurately. If you are talking about a pavilion on a diamond, explain that this is the bottom portion of the stone.
18. Ask to be allowed to answer questions. Remember this when the opposing attorney interrupts you, or when you feel you need to explain your answer. However, do not ramble when given the opportunity to speak.
19. Be thorough. Make sure the attorney on your side knows what is important to ask you so that you provide a complete explanation.
20. Give definitive, thoughtful, and concrete answers so that you appear to be the expert you are (Causey, 1986, personal interview).

Witness Testimony

The following is an excerpt from actual testimony given by an expert witness during a divorce trial by jury. The testimony illustrates a typical line of questioning and successful answering by the witness—clear, brief, and to the point.

Q. State your name and occupation.

A. Jane Jeweler, gems and jewelry appraiser.

Q. How long have you been appraising?

A. About eighteen years.

Q. What are your qualifications?

A. I am a graduate gemologist of the Gemological Institute of America, former wholesaler and retailer of gems and jewelry with a full-time jewelry appraising business for the past ten years.

Q. Do you belong to any appraisal organizations?

A. Yes. I am a senior member of the American Society of Appraisers, a member of the National Association of Jewelry Appraisers, a Registered Master Valuer, and a member of the Appraisers Association of America. I am a member of numerous other appraisal-related organizations, in which I hold either a local or national office.

Q. Is this a fair and accurate description of your qualifications which is appended to this appraisal report?

A. Yes.

Q. Were you paid $X as a fee for the appraisal?

A. Yes.

Q. Is this a reasonable fee?

A. Yes.

Q. Pass the witness.

Q. How did you go about obtaining these values you have listed on this report?

A. These items have been researched for fair market value. Each item was examined, identified, and researched for comparable items in the most appropriate market for the goods.

Q. What is fair market value?

A. The price an item will bring between a willing buyer and a willing seller, neither under compulsion to buy or sell and both having all relevant information.

Q. Do you mean that you appraised *each* object?

A. Yes. Each individual object.

Q. How many items is that?

A. A total of six hundred items.

Q. How long did it take you to appraise each object?

A. That depended upon the item.

Q. Isn't a diamond just a diamond?

A. No. It is not.

Q. What makes a difference?

A. Diamonds, like colored gemstones, have quality grades and fine-quality diamonds and colored gemstones are more expensive than commercial or lesser-quality material. Fine designer quality jewelry is more desirable than commercial quality jewelry, etc.

Q. But after you look at each piece, isn't that all you do, just go back to your office and write it down?

A. No. It is not.

Q. Well, tell us what you do next.

A. First, each item with gemstones has gemstones identified, graded, and measured; metal fineness is confirmed through acid testing; weights of metals are confirmed through individual weighing of items; any extraordinary jewelry is confirmed through markings or stampings, or hallmarks of manufacturer. All items are individually researched as to their value in the appropriate secondary market.

Q. Didn't you appraise these items in the aggregate and take them into consideration as a total unit?

A. No.

Q. Well, did you take into consideration any fees involved in selling these items; is there any overhead or profit margin in your evaluation?

A. That, sir, would be covered by mark-ups in a new jewelry market and jewelry that would be resold by a retailer. It is usually not a factor in estates such as this. However, on the jewelry which might be sold at auction, fees have been taken into account, where it is appropriate to do so.

Q. How much are you being paid for your testimony today?

A. I'm not being paid for my testimony.

Q. What do you mean? Do you mean you are not being paid?

A. I'm being paid my regular fee for my time spent in court. My testimony is not for sale.

Total time on the witness stand in this case was over an hour. When the opposing attorney repeats or rephrases the same question over and over, he or she is attempting to confuse or anger the witness. The witness must be patient and cooperative under the scrutiny of the jury, who may decide the case partly on the basis of the appraiser's professionalism and credibility. The witness must remain in control of the situation even when confronted by an aggressive and belligerent adversary.

If you make a mistake in answering, admit it immediately. If the opposing lawyer traps you into agreeing to a statement that you know is not true, correct the mistake immediately, before you become enmeshed in confusing and embarrassing explanations that can compromise your credibility.

Brent L. Burg, a former judge, gives this advice to expert witnesses:

> If you are asked on the stand about the work you did not do because the client refused to pay for it, all you can answer is: "I was not asked to provide that information, only the information that I have provided."
>
> Jurors draw upon their own experiences when they make a decision. They don't hear everything that is said and only one thing usually sticks in their mind. They will make up their mind about you as an expert witness and your personality will sell your testimony. But, give an *opinion*, don't be an advocate.
>
> If you have to give testimony against another expert witness and the opposing attorney says to you, "How do you account for the difference in prices?" Your answer could be: "This is my opinion."
>
> Do not malign the other expert witnesses. Some jurors develop a liking for, and may identify with,

the other witness, therefore they may take it personally if you besmirch him or her.

Never lie. If you don't know something, say so.

Do not get angry or lose your temper. If you do, you lose credibility (Burg, 1986, personal interview).

Opponent Experts

If there are experts on the opponent's side, the attorney should apprise you of this fact as soon as their names are known. Interrogatories (questions asked in writing) will be sent to the opposing side asking the name and addresses of the experts who will be used at trial and whether they have prepared any written appraisal reports. Sometimes appraisal reports are not prepared until just before trial, to avoid discovery.

When you know who the opposing expert is and can find out about his or her background and qualifications, you will be able to offer pertinent questions for the attorney to use in drawing attention to any weaknesses of the other's valuation or expertise. In this way, you can help your attorney gain a psychological advantage.

Opportunities for Witnesses

If you have qualified as an expert witness and given testimony in trials enough to know whether you can tolerate (even enjoy) the experience, be aware that there is a growing need for expert witnesses in this country. You may be able to parlay witnessing into a lucrative part of your appraisal business. In today's litigious society, specialists who testify for a fee make up an expanding industry. Fees for trial preparation range from an hourly low of twenty dollars for arboriculture experts to two hundred and fifty dollars for physicians. Daily fees for court testimonies can add up to two thousand dollars and more. Gems and jewelry experts can earn from five hundred to fifteen hundred dollars per day depending upon geographical area, level of experience, profile in the industry, and ability to handle the job. Being a paid witness is ideal for retirees who have expertise to market. You can build a clientele by advertising in legal trade papers, which may have a special classified advertisements section. The IRS also hires experts to testify, and according to those who have worked for them, the pay ranges from seven hundred to over a thousand dollars per day.

A group of people called jury selection specialists investigate prospective jurors for attorneys to find those best suited for a jury panel. Usually trained psychologists, the investigators observe how prospective jurors respond to questions to ascertain the truthfulness of the answers. These clues can be applied to expert witnesses as well and are helpful to review whether you will be a one-time witness or plan to make it a sideline of your business: The clues to truthfulness include the juror's choice of words, the immediacy of response, and how well eye contact is maintained. Anxiety is revealed through unfinished sentences, deep breathing, and blocked or disjointed thoughts. A loud voice indicates a tendency to be domineering.

If you wish to read or purchase a copy of your testimony, tell the court reporter that you want a copy of the transcript. The usual charge is approximately five dollars per page. The reporter can look back at the records and estimate how many pages of testimony you have given. It is interesting to review your own testimony and especially helpful to recognize where your answers to cross-examination could have been more succinct. This review leads to more careful and professional responses next time.

Dressing for Court Appearances

Although it is irrational, people judge you by the way you dress. Before you are to appear in court, consider whether what you plan to wear will give you a professional image—it is important to do so. Tailored, conservative dress will give you maximum credibility with the jury and judge. Wear a dark business suit, a white shirt or blouse, conservative shoes, a dark tie, and dark belt, and be as neat and well groomed as possible. Do not wear loud clothing or white shoes. Many psychological studies have been conducted on how the different kinds of clothing people wear in court affect the jury. Lawyers say that brightly colored clothing may distract juries so that they focus on what the witness is wearing, not saying. Similarly, do not wear a sports jacket and slacks; wear a business suit. Dressing appropriately will help your credibility, your appeal, and will make the jury think more highly of you. You are an expert and a professional—look like one.

Attorneys from coast to coast agree that witnesses should leave their expensive jewelry at home. If you appear in court wearing diamond rings and an eight-thousand-dollar Rolex wristwatch, you may unintentionally antagonize a juror who holds a minimum-wage job. Jurors may become prejudiced and resentful if they see you sitting in the witness stand wearing obviously expensive jewelry while discussing your fee schedule.

One counselor, ever mindful of public and peer scrutiny, tells about the time he was going to the Texas State Capitol to talk with some people about running for state office. His own advisors told him not to wear any rings and to make sure he wore a plain watch with a leather band. He was puzzled. "Why?" he asked. "Because Republicans don't trust flashy jewelry," was the carefully considered reply. Neither do jurors.

Avoiding Fee Collection Problems

The golden rule for appraisers has become "get your money up front." If that is impossible, at least get a retainer. Few of us can afford to work without being paid—as one Houston attorney so eloquently expressed it: "We are not in this for the art form."

Getting paid can be a problem. Depending upon the individual case and the economic conditions in your area, obtaining your fee can become almost a full-time exercise in persuasive diplomacy. Prevent this aggravation by getting contracts signed before you begin work. Then reiterate your fee structure (retainer now, balance upon delivery of completed document) before you leave the premises. It is important to have the attorney you are working for sign a contract exactly as you would any other client. Many will balk, as they do not like signing contracts. If you do not wish to lose the job over their refusal to sign, or if the attorney is not present to do the actual signing before you begin work on the project, write a letter asking for full payment before you relinquish the report (fig. 7-1).

The form shown in figure 7-2 is an example of a contract that can be used between appraiser and attorney. Like all the forms in this text, this contract is meant to serve as an example only, and should be carefully examined by the appraiser's legal advisor before adoption. Contract laws differ throughout the United States; be sure the forms you use are legal in your area.

All appraisers generate the written report. This document represents the appraiser's methodology, analytical acumen, efforts, values, and business ethics. It is your leverage; once it passes into the hands of attorney or client, you have lost the advantage. If you still have trouble collecting your fee, one Texas judge suggests that a call or letter to the state Bar Association might get results. "Anytime a complaint is filed against a member, the grievance committee reviews the charge and duly notes it in the attorney's record. The attorney can be suspended, disbarred, or reprimanded in some other way." "And," he added, "you might get paid."

If you have been called to court by an attorney who is notoriously slow to pay, you have explained that you need your fee before testifying, and the attorney fails to bring it—what do you do?

"It is within your right to say, 'I'm sorry, the deal was I'd get paid before I took the stand. I'll be glad to go to the judge and tell him our arrangement, but until I get my fee, I won't testify,'" a Texas judge counseled.

What if you are subsequently subpoenaed?

"Then," the judge said, "you will have to testify. But I think a subpoena in this instance unlikely because the attorney will realize that by this type of action the witness may become hostile or very forgetful."

Collecting Fees for Bankruptcy Appraisals

Be sure of your legal rights as appraiser before you become involved in valuing property for a bankruptcy appraisal. There may be situations in which you cannot collect your fee if the appraisal contract was signed after the client started bankruptcy proceedings. Or, if you have collected a fee, you may be subject to suit by the creditors for return of the fee. Bankruptcy laws are complex and frequently attended by lengthy court procedures. The court-appointed trustee may wish to have you appointed by the court as appraiser. This will necessitate three forms: an application for appointment of appraiser; an oath of appraiser; an order appointing you as appraiser. In this instance, your fee will be stipulated and recorded, but it still does not guarantee that you will receive payment for services rendered.

The operative word in this arena is "caution." Proceed thoughtfully and find out all the ramifications before involving yourself in this type of appraisal job.

7-1. Sample form letter for requesting payment for services rendered.

Dear Counselor:

    According to your instructions, we have completed the appraisal of jewelry and gemstones for Mr. I. Stone, 1010 Main Street, City and State.

    The inventory was extensive and two days were required for the summary. Each item was individually examined, photographed, and recorded, noting gold content and metal weight, identification of gemstones and their estimated weights. Fair market values have been established for the dissolution of common property.

    A statement of appraisal services is enclosed. Please be advised that the original document, with photographs and four copies of the report, will be delivered to your office upon receipt of the full payment.

Sincerely,

Appraiser

7-2. Sample court appearance or deposition agreement.

THIS MEMORANDUM OF AGREEMENT this day made and entered into by and between _____ hereinafter referred to as Appraiser and _____ hereinafter referred to as Client.

That, in consideration of the mutual covenants herein contained and of the payment hereinafter provided to be made by Client to the Appraiser, the parties hereto agree as follows:

1. *SCOPE:* The Appraiser agrees to appear in court or through deposition, if requested, and serve as an Expert Witness providing true and objective testimony based upon appraisal and or expertise.
2. *FEE:* As full consideration for such services performed by Appraiser, the Client agrees to pay Appraiser therefore as follows:
   Upon completion of testimony by Appraiser, in court or through deposition, the sum of $ _____ per day or a minimum of $ _____ per half day or less. Time includes portal to portal travel. In the event services extend beyond one day, the same rate schedule continues whether testifying or waiting.
3. *REIMBURSEMENTS:* It is agreed that all out-of-pocket expenses including, but not limited by, travel, transportation, lodging, and meals associated with this requested service shall be promptly reimbursed Appraiser by Client.
4. *RETAINER:* Client shall provide a retainer prior to any testimony by Appraiser to cover such rate schedule and reimburseables as cited in articles 2 and 3. Such fee and expense shall be due and payable upon completion of the Appraiser's testimony. If payment is not received within five (5) days, then a late payment penalty of one (1%) percent per month compounded shall occur.
5. *ATTORNEY'S FEE:* In the event action is commenced to enforce or interpret the provisions of this agreement, the Appraiser shall be entitled in addition to such other relief as the court may award to a reasonable sum as and for attorney's fees and costs.
6. *ASSIGNMENTS:* This agreement shall be binding on the successors and assigns of the party hereto, but the same shall not be assigned by the Appraiser without written consent of the Client.
7. *GOVERNING LAW:* This agreement shall be governed by the law of the State of _____

This agreement is executed on the _____ day of _____ , 20 _____

APPRAISER: _____   CLIENT: _____

Printed Name: _____   Printed Name: _____

Address: _____   Address: _____

_____

CHAPTER 8

PREPARING THE APPRAISAL DOCUMENT

The Appraisal Report

Just as we judge and are judged by first impressions, so will your appraisal report—and the way it is presented—reflect upon your professionalism. An appraisal report is a legal document that should be effective and useful to the client and easy to read and understand.

The report includes the appraiser's opinion of value and the evidence that supports this opinion. The report itself is the single most significant product of the appraisal, since it is the appraiser's professional opinion, and it is the only physical evidence by which the client can judge the work.

Reports should be submitted on well-designed forms and typed on bond paper—handwritten appraisals are completely unacceptable. Reports should be closely reviewed before being delivered to the client to make sure no errors in math or spelling are present. Sloppy reports brand you as an amateur, or as lazy or incompetent. Insurance appraisals should be stapled into their own folders or covers to convey the importance of the document to the client. At the time of presentation, the client should be counseled to keep the document in a safe place, preferably a bank safe-deposit box. Reports validating data for fair market value generate a multipage document that looks best when presented to the client either velo or spiral bound, with front and back covers. If you are not familiar with this type of binding, contact your local print shop to see if it offers this service (most do and at reasonable rates.) Velo binding is a clean-looking soft plastic strip that uses a heat-sealing system to ensure a tight binding along the spine. Spiral bindings utilizes a plastic retaining material on the spine, joining prepunched holes through the printed matter.

Every appraisal report should include the following items:

A. Letter of transmittal (fig. 8-2).
  1. Introduction and table of contents.
  2. Client's name and address and location of the property being appraised.
  3. Date of the appraisal.
  4. Statement of the value.
  5. Limiting conditions that affect the final value.
  6. Purpose of the appraisal.
  7. Statement of confidentiality.
  8. A reference that the letter of transmittal is not the appraisal but rather a letter transmitting the appraisal that follows in the report.

B. Cover and cover sheet (fig. 8-1).
  1. A cover gives a professional look to the appraisal and supports your image as a responsible valuer.
  2. The cover sheet should:
    • Identify the report as jewelry appraisal.
    • Include the name of the client for whom the appraisal was executed and the date.
    • Include the name and address of the appraiser.

C. Cover letter (fig. 8-3).
  1. The purpose of the cover letter is to contain a statement of the purpose and function of the appraisal.
  2. The cover letter includes a definition and explanation of the value and includes basis of the value conclusions.
  3. The cover letter also contains a statement on the status of the market; notes any additional fees or taxes that may affect the final value figure; and details any restrictions on the use and/or publication of whole or part of the appraisal report.

4. The cover letter also defines and explains any future responsibilities of the appraiser for legal proceedings based upon the appraisal report.

5. Clear statement on the disinterestedness of the appraiser.

D. Appraisal preface (fig. 8-4).

The appraisal preface is an overview of the valuation process applied to different marketplaces. The preface contains explanations, definitions, and limitations of various markets. To include it as part of the report will help your client understand the different markets and prevent possible misunderstandings as to the extent of the services rendered.

E. Body of the appraisal report, or the certificate of appraisal (fig. 8-5).

1. Definitions and complete descriptions of the property. The description includes both written and photographic pictures of the item(s) to include all physical characteristics (i.e., material, size, construction, etc.), as well as information on style, hallmarks, signatures, etc. Gemstone plots and terms.

F. Signatures: (1) The principal appraiser; (2) consultants, collaborators, or associate appraisers; (3) dissenting appraisers and opinion(s).

G. Reference source page (fig. 8-6). Validate provenance here. Some appraisers consider the reference page to be unnecessary paperwork. However, if you are faced with the need to back up your statements and verify the prices that you used, the reference page may prove invaluable. A reference page can also reveal your strengths and weaknesses of research.

H. Statement of limiting conditions (fig. 8-7).

I. Appraiser's certification statement (fig. 8-8).

J. Qualifications of appraiser (fig. 8-9).

K. Dissenting opinions (if any) with signatures.

Every page of the certificate of appraisal should be numbered, with a total number of pages listed on the first page. All items should be individually numbered on the appraisal pages and photographed items should be numbered to match with the appropriately described article. Photograph captions should state the scale at which the items were shot, such as 1:1 ratio.

Every page of the certificate of appraisal should have the client's name and date along with the purpose of the appraisal. The total number of pages in the report should be reiterated on the last page.

The illustrations of the various sections of a sample appraisal are provided as a framework or point of departure for your own reports. Of course, you may vary in style or approach to suit the needs of your appraisals. Figures 8-10 through 8-13 illustrate a sample explanation of diamond terminology that might be included in an appraisal report as well as several sample cover letters sent to various individuals: an insurance claim adjuster, clients receiving an insurance appraisal, and an executor receiving an estate, or probate, appraisal.

Developing a Professional Brochure

If you want a profitable sales tool, take the time to create a professional and informative brochure. Once placed in a prospective client's hands, either by you or by mail, it will have his or her undivided attention. The brochure is capable of establishing a bond between you and the customer; it is almost as if you were talking directly to him or her, presenting the service.

A well-designed brochure is an important communication tool. If your budget does not permit you to hire a public relations firm to create a folder for you, you can go to a creative copywriter for assistance in

8-1. Sample appraisal report, showing a few of the essential elements.

8-2. Sample letter of transmittal for an estate, or probate, appraisal.

Date

Mr. John Doe, Attorney
First Bank of Houston
P.O. Box 1000
Houston, Texas 77024

Dear Mr. Doe:

In accordance with your request, I have conducted an investigation of the personal jewelry property of Mr. Andrew Scott, 2000 Opal Avenue, Houston, Texas, on December 20, 1999, in order to form an opinion of current Fair Market Value for dissolution of common property.

Based on the inspection of the items, the research and analysis undertaken, and subject to the assumptions and limiting conditions contained herein, it is my conclusion that the current Fair Market Value is $175,000.

The document that is attached to this letter of transmittal includes the following sections:

> 1) Summation of Conclusions
> 2) Appraisal Preface with Definitions
> 3) Description and Valuation of the Property
> 4) Photographs of the Property
> 5) Limiting and Qualifying Conditions
> 6) Qualifications of the Appraiser

All information concerning this appraisal is regarded as confidential. We retain a copy of the document, together with our original notes, and do not permit access to them by anyone without your authorization.

Thank you for this opportunity to be of service.

Cordially,

---

writing the text, to a desktop publishing service for help in designing and preparing the brochure, and finally to a local printing service to have the brochures printed. These are the basic steps in the process:

1. Decide what size you want the brochure to be. It should be large enough to contain all the information you wish to disseminate about your business, but small enough to fit into a standard business envelope. Although there is no one "correct" size, there are standard sizes which are much more economical to print; consult with your desktop publishing service or your local printing service to decide on your best option.

2. If you want to have photographs printed in the brochure, have them developed immediately. If you are going to include a picture of yourself, make it a studio portrait for a professional look. In printing parlance, the photographs that will go into your brochure are called *halftones*.

3. Gather the text, photos, logo, and any other elements you will be including.

The front cover should tell who the appraiser is and the nature of the business. Inside, the reader should see the type of appraisals performed, qualifications of the appraiser, location of the service, and the fee arrangement. On the back page are discussed quality standards used to grade diamonds and the gemological instruments used in identification.

If you appraise items other than jewelry (silver, coins, and so on), you will wish to list those areas of expertise. You may also want to add that you are available for lectures and workshops.

If you can provide gemprints and/or laminated reports, be certain to state this in the brochure.

4. Measure a piece of paper and fold it to the size you would like the brochure to be. Now create a "mock-up" of your brochure, indicating generally which information goes on which panel/area of the brochure. Decide on any especially important elements that should receive visual emphasis. By discussing this mock-up with the desktop publishing service, you will be able to clearly communi-

8-3. Sample cover letter for an estate, or probate, appraisal.

A. Appraiser
Date

FOR: John Doe, Attorney
RE: Andrew Scott Estate
Cause #0000

In accordance with the instructions of John Doe, Attorney, I have made an inventory of items identified to me as being the jewelry property of Mr. Andrew Scott, 2000 Opal Avenue, Houston, Texas, and investigated and researched each item to determine Fair Market Value. The purpose of the appraisal is to estimate the Fair Market Value of the jewelry common property for divorce settlement.

As used in this report, the term Fair Market Value represents the mode of prices that could be realized in an orderly sale of the various items in the most common and appropriate market to that item. Fair Market Value of any item of property is not to be determined by the sale price of an item in a market other than that in which such item is most commonly sold to the public taking into account the location of the item wherever it is appropriate. Further, Fair Market Value as provided in this report takes into consideration items of like kind and quality by the greatest number of reasonably knowledgeable willing buyers and willing sellers, neither being under any compulsion to buy or sell, in the market in which these items were most commonly sold to the public—to an ultimate consumer who is buying for a purpose other than for resale in the purchased form.

All diamonds and colored gemstones in the jewelry were examined, identified, and graded for the qualitative and quantitative properties defined separately in this report, and are in accordance with the standards of the jewelry appraisal profession and trade.

The market analysis and values provided are based upon my eighteen years of experience as a wholesale gemstone dealer, retail jewelry store owner and appraiser, during which time I have sold and appraised large quantities of like items. Market data approach was used to obtain FMV. Values in this report are based on the most common and appropriate markets: auction and retail. I have made no investigation as to the title or ownership of the property appraised. Information given me concerning origin or acquisition of certain items has been accepted as fact when this information was not contradicted by my findings. Let it be stated that I do not have a present or contemplated interest in the purchase and/or resale of the property appraised and the fee for this appraisal is not contingent upon values submitted.

My instructions for this assignment were to provide my best impartial opinion as to the appropriate markets for the jewelry and their Fair Market Value in those markets. In my opinion the property described herein is fairly stated as being $175,000.

ONE HUNDRED SEVENTY-FIVE THOUSAND DOLLARS

This report has been prepared in accordance with the principles and procedures for the evaluation of personal property as prescribed by the American Society of Appraisers. This appraisal report is only to be used and interpreted in its entirety.

A. APPRAISER (Signature) _____

cate what you want the finished brochure to achieve.

5. Work with the desktop publishing service until you are pleased with the results of the layout. Read it over for typographical errors. Would you pick it up and read it if you were John Q. Public? Put it away overnight and then take a good look at it the next day. If it still looks good, take it to the printer.

6. Most towns have a printing service. Take your finalized brochure (usually supplied as a computer disk) to the printing service and select a stock for your brochure. The desktop publishing service or the printing service can suggest stocks which will work best for your project.

7. There is usually a great variety of colors and types, from leatherlike to pebble finish. Putting color combinations together can be a challenge. Look at samples of brochures and letterheads and pick out color and stock combinations that appeal to you. You will want to put some thought into the correct look for this venture, because your brochure will speak for you in many situations and may be your only opportunity to make a good impression.

8-4. Sample appraisal preface.

I. WHAT IS AN APPRAISAL?
    An appraisal is an informed opinion as to the authenticity, quality, design and value of a gem or jewelry article. The opinion is backed by appraiser training, market experience, and gemological equipment.

II. FAIR MARKET VALUE
    Fair market value is defined as "the most probable price in cash, or in other precisely revealed terms, for which the appraised property will sell in a competitive market under all conditions requisite to fair sale, with the buyer and seller each acting prudently, knowledgeably, and for self-interest, and assuming that neither is under undue duress."

    Implicit in this definition is the presumed consummation of the sale at a specified date and the passing of title from seller to buyer under conditions whereby:

    1. The buyer and seller are typically motivated.
    2. Both parties are well informed, and/or advised, each acting in what he or she considers his or her own best interest.
    3. A reasonable time has been allowed for exposure to the open market.
    4. Payment is made in cash or its equivalent.
    5. The price represents a normal consideration for the property sold unaffected by special financing amounts and/or terms, services, fees, costs, or credits incurred in the transaction.

III. RETAIL REPLACEMENT VALUE FOR INSURANCE
    The retail replacement (new) value is required by an insurance company before it will insure jewelry beyond a certain dollar amount or schedule it separately on one's homeowner policy. This appraisal is the record consulted by the insurance firm to determine the insured amount for jewelry that is lost, damaged, or stolen, depending upon the terms of the actual insurance policy.

    This type of value is determined by using either a Market Data Comparison or a Cost Approach depending upon individual circumstances and market conditions prevailing at time of appraisal. The Market Data Comparison approach compares the qualities of the subject item to an article with similar or identical qualities, and researches and records current verifiable sales of such merchandise. The Cost Approach establishes value of an item by breaking down the item (hypothetically) into its component parts such as precious metal content, gemstone weights and qualities, labor for setting, and any other fees that would impact on the final value. The sum total of value also includes the appropriate retail markup according to the norms of jewelers in the locale, supply and demand, and the current state of the marketplace.

IV ANTIQUE JEWELRY APPRAISAL
    Antique, heirloom, and collectible jewelry is always valued using the Market Data Comparison approach. Cost approach and revenue approaches are not applicable to this market.

V. JEWELRY INSURANCE Homeowner's and Apartment Tenant's insurance policies commonly include coverage for personal property with the value of jewelry included up to a certain limit. Most policies restrict jewelry coverage for theft, burglary, or robbery to $500 aggregate, with a few companies providing coverage to $1,000 aggregate. Such insurance usually will not cover the property owner for "loss" of an item or for loss of a single stone from the item. In order to obtain coverage for the full value of the item(s), an appraisal for each item will be required and the coverage scheduled on your policy, with a specific description of the article and a replacement value on each item. For full and proper value coverage, a detailed professional appraisal is paramount.

VI. IN CASE OF LOSS
    Most insurance policies contain a clause that permits the company to replace the jewelry in like kind with a comparable replacement rather than make cash payment for the loss. If so, use your appraisal to verify that the quality of the replacement is similar to the lost item. The original appraiser of the insured item should be consulted for verification of the quality and value of the proposed replacement.

VII. APPRAISAL UPDATE
    We recommend that your appraisal is updated periodically. Check annually with us about the necessity of updating your appraisal.

VIII. NOTICE
    This appraisal is not an offer to buy unless specifically stated.

8-5. Sample certificate of appraisal form, initial page only.

Date:

Expiry Date:

The Name of
Your Company

FOR:

Address:

City:

State:

Appraisal Purpose:

Appraisal Function:

Precious Metal Base Price:

Certificate of Appraisal

Page _____ of _____ Pages

Description of Article

Estimate of Value

Signature of Appraiser

8-6. Sample reference source page.

The subject jewelry property has been researched in numerous reference books, price guides, auction catalogs and from personal calls upon retail jewelers who sell comparable or identical merchandise in this geographical region. Research for appropriate pricing has also been conducted by telecommunications network.

Among the materials used for research are:

Rapaport Diamond Index (Date)

Johnson Matthey Precious Metal Price Reports (Date)

The Guide, Gemworld International, Inc. (Date)

8. Once you have chosen your stock, the printing service can give you a price quotation for the job. If you wish to have matching envelopes in which to mail the brochures, this is the time to make inquiry.

9. The last step is the most satisfying. Pick up the finished brochures and distribute them to prospective clients.

While you are working with the printing service, you may wish to inquire about a matching business and Rolodex card. These are good additions to the brochure and can be mailed in the same envelope. A Rolodex card is an excellent way to maintain high visibility with insurance agents, attorneys, bank loan officers, other clients, and their secretaries.

8-7. Typical limiting conditions clause.

It is understood and agreed that fees paid for this appraisal do not include the services of the appraiser for any other matter whatsoever. In particular, fees paid to date do not include any of the appraiser's time or services in connection with any statement, testimony, or other matters before an insurance company, its agents, employees, or any court or other body in connection with the property herein described.

It is understood and agreed that if the appraiser is required to so testify or to make any such statements to any third party concerning the described property appraisal, applicant shall pay appraiser for all of such time and services so rendered at appraiser's then current rates for such services with half of the estimated fee paid in advance to appraiser before any testimony.

Unless otherwise stated, all colored stones listed on this appraisal report have probably been subjected to a stable and possibly undetectable color enhancement process. Prevailing market values are based on these universally practiced and accepted processes by the gems and jewelry trade.

8-8. Sample appraiser's certification statement.

(___Appraiser's name___) deposes and says: That the statements contained in this report and upon which the opinions expressed herein are based are true and correct to the best of (his/her) knowledge and belief.

That no direct or indirect personal interest exists; that the appraisal fee is not contingent upon values stated herein.

Valuations stated are based on items of comparable or identical equal and condition, available in the wholesale or retail marketplace depending upon the purpose and function of the valuation.

This report has been made in conformity with the requirements of the code of professional ethics and standards of professional conduct of _____ (professional appraisal organization).

(Appraiser's name)

Date

8-9. Statement of the appraiser's qualifications.

THE QUALIFICATIONS OF ___(___Appraiser___)___ FOR THIS SERVICE ARE:

Graduate Gemologist of the Gemological Institute of America, New York, New York. Senior Member of the American Society of Appraisers; Senior Member of the National Association of Jewelry Appraisers; Registered Master Valuer, University of South Florida.

(Appraiser's name) is engaged as an independent appraiser of gems and jewelry for private clientele, banks, insurance companies, law firms, and museums. She/he is a guest speaker for colleges, civic groups and seminars. She/he instructs appraisal classes for the American Society of Appraisers and has been instructor for gemological classes at numerous community colleges.

(Appraiser's name) is qualified as expert witness in the State of _____, Civil and County Courts, and in United States Federal Court.

(Appraiser's company name) maintains a fully accredited gemological laboratory certified by the Accredited Gemologists Association.

IDEAL BRILLANT-CUT PROPORTIONS

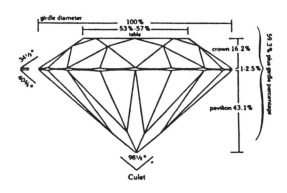

QUALITY STANDARDS

GIA CLARITY GRADING SCALE

Flawless

| VVS1 | VVS2 | VS1 | VS2 | SI1 | SI2 | I1 | I2 | I3 |

Flawless

Imperfect

GIA COLOR GRADING SCALE

| D | E | F | G | H | I | J | K | L | M | N | O | P | Q | R | S | T | U | V | W | X | Y | Z |

Colorless — Very Light Yellow — Light Yellow — Yellow — Fancy Yellow

Mounted Stones Appear Colorless
Mounted Stones Appear Increasingly Tinted
Mounted Stones Appear Yellow
Small Mounted Stones Appear Colorless

DIAMOND PROPORTIONS

RANGE OF ACCEPTABLE PROPORTIONS

Table Percentage	54%	to	66%
Depth Percentage	57.5%	to	62.5%
Crown Height	11.0%	to	16.0%
Pavilion Depth	41.5%	to	45.5%
Crown Angles	30.0°	to	35.0°
Pavilion Angles	39.7°	to	42.4°
Girdle Thickness	Thin, Medium, Slightly Thick		
Culet Size	Small, Medium		

THE ABOVE RANGES APPLY FOR ROUND BRILLIANT-CUT STONES. FANCY SHAPES VARY CONSIDERABLY FROM ABOVE RANGES.

INSTRUMENTS USED

- ☐ Master Stones
- ☐ Gemolite (Binocular Dark Field Illum.)
- ☐ Leveridge Gauge (Micrometer)
- ☐ Diamondlite (Color Grading)
- ☐ Proportionscope
- ☐ Diamond Balance
- ☐ Long/Short Wave Ultra Violet
- ☐ Illuminator Polarscope
- ☐ Colormaster
- ☐ Refractormeter
- ☐ Thermal Reaction Tester
- ☐ Pen Light
- ☐ Emerald Filter
- ☐ Dichroscope
- ☐ Heavy Liquids
- ☐ Spectroscope
- ☐ Photographic Equipment
- ☐ Metal Tester
- ☐ Gemprint
- ☐ Dwt. Scale

INTERNAL CHARACTERISTICS

- —Feather
- —Included Crystal
- —Cloud
- —Knot
- —Bruise
- —Pinpoint
- —Internal Graining
- —Bearded or Feathered Girdle
- —Laser Drill Hole
- —Indented Natural

EXTERNAL CHARACTERISTICS

- —Pit
- —Cavity (Now shown in red)
- —Natural
- —Scratch and Wheel Marks
- —Extra Facet (Shown in Black)
- —Surface Grain Lines
- —Nick (Now shown in Red)
- —Chip (Now shown in Red)
- —Abraded facet junction

RED SYMBOLS DENOTE INTERNAL CHARACTERISTICS. GREEN SYMBOLS DENOTE EXTERNAL CHARACTERISTICS. SYMBOLS INDICATE THE NATURE AND POSITION OF CHARACTERISTICS, NOT NECESSARILY THEIR SIZE.

8-10. An explanation of diamond-grading terminology that would be included in an appraisal of diamonds.

8-11. Sample transmittal letter sent to an insurance claims adjuster.

Date

Mr. Matthew Goodboy
The Hartford Company
1212 Emerald Avenue
Houston, TX 77001

Re: Claim #66/B/O—Jewelry

Dear Mr. Goodboy:

Enclosed is our appraisal for insurance purposes of the items indicated to have been stolen in the above claim. A copy of this document is enclosed for your convenience.

The values given represent, in my opinion, the current replacement value of the items in the appropriate market based upon recent available sales information for items of comparable quality and kind. They do not include any costs or fees that may be incurred in replacing the items, such as sales tax.

The named appraiser has never personally examined the jewelry items that were stolen. The insured was interviewed to obtain descriptions of the pieces and I examined some photographs provided by the insured. All values were researched based upon this information.

Information regarding this appraisal is regarded as confidential. A copy of the document is retained by my office, with our working notes. Access to them is not permitted without your authorization.

I hope this information is helpful to all parties concerned. If I can be of further service, please do not hesitate to call.

Cordially,

8-12. Sample transmittal letter sent to the recipients of an insurance appraisal.

Date

Mr. and Mrs. John Doe
123 Ruby Street
Los Angeles, CA 92100

Dear Mr. and Mrs. Doe:

Enclosed you will find our appraisal for insurance purposes of your jewelry located at the above address, and examined by me on —————— . A copy of this document is enclosed for the convenience of your insurance agent.

These items have been examined, researched to the best of our ability, and identified for the purpose of retail replacement valuation. In our opinion the values given represent the current retail replacement (new) based upon recent available sales information for items of identical or comparable quality and kind. The figures represent the average retail replacement in the most appropriate market in the regional area. Averages are based upon appropriate markets for individual items. These figures, however, do not include sales tax or any other charges that might be payable, and you may wish to take this factor into consideration when calculating your insurance needs.

We recommend all items in this report be covered from breakage as well as theft and mysterious disappearance. The total replacement cost of the items listed is $ —————— . The photographs are included in this report and are ready for reference in the event of a claim under any insurance policy.

All information regarding this appraisal is confidential. We retain a copy of the document, together with our original notes, and do not permit access to them by anyone without your authorization.

It was a pleasure to be of service to you.

Cordially,

8-13. Sample transmittal letter sent to the executor of an estate, the recipient of a probate appraisal.

Date

Mr. J. Jones, Executor
3000 Diamond Drive
Los Angeles, CA 90000

Re: Estate of Jane Doe: Appraisal of Personal Property located at 456 Garnet Avenue, Oceanside, California

Dear Mr. Jones:

Enclosed you will find our appraisal for jewelry personal property at the above address, indicated to be part of the estate of Jane Doe, deceased. The items were examined by me on January 20, 1998. A copy of this document is enclosed for your convenience.

These pieces have been examined, researched to the best of our ability, and identified for the purpose of valuation. The values given reflect the current Fair Market Value of these or comparable pieces, on or about the date of death, December 20, 1997. The current Fair Market Value is defined as the price agreed upon by a willing buyer and a willing seller, both knowledgeable of relevant facts, neither under any compulsion to buy or sell, and given a reasonable amount of time to complete the transaction. The values do not, however, include any costs that may be incurred in the sale of the items, such as advertising, commissions, fees, etc.

Each item has been itemized individually on the appraisal and photographed. Our working notes are available if you should require them.

All information regarding this appraisal is regarded as confidential. We retain a copy of the document, together with our original notes, and do not permit access to them by anyone without your authorization.

We appreciate this opportunity to be of service.

Cordially,

8-14. A custom-designed logo adds a professional look to your reports and brochures.

APPENDIX

ILLUSTRATIONS OF CUTTING STYLES

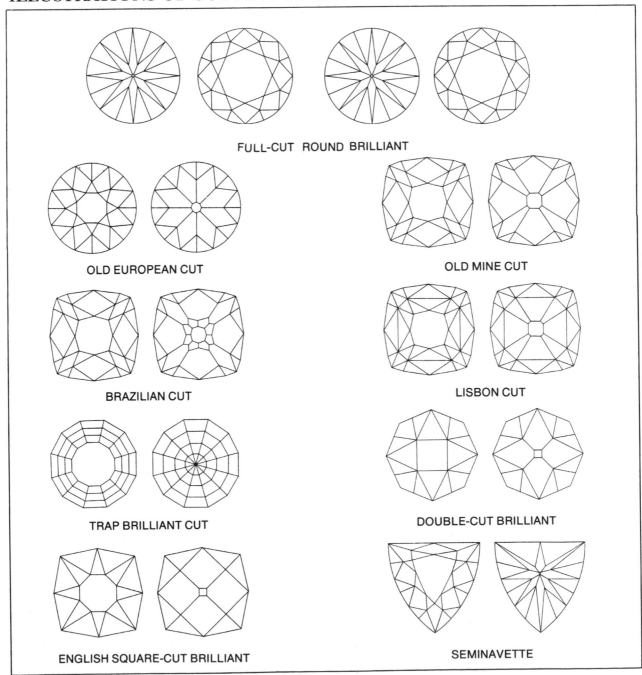

FULL-CUT ROUND BRILLIANT

OLD EUROPEAN CUT

OLD MINE CUT

BRAZILIAN CUT

LISBON CUT

TRAP BRILLIANT CUT

DOUBLE-CUT BRILLIANT

ENGLISH SQUARE-CUT BRILLIANT

SEMINAVETTE

Source: GIA

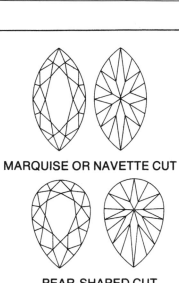

MARQUISE OR NAVETTE CUT

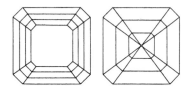

PEAR-SHAPED CUT

SQUARE EMERALD CUT

EMERALD CUT

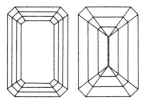

HEART-SHAPED CUT

SINGLE CUT

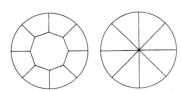

SWISS CUT

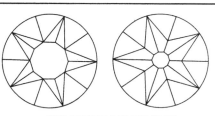

SPLIT BRILLIANT CUT

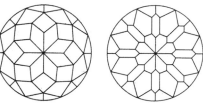

TWENTIETH-CENTURY CUT

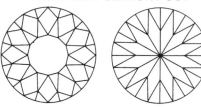

KING CUT

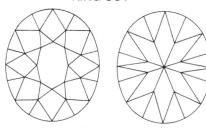

OVAL CUT

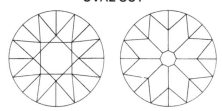

ENGLISH ROUND-CUT BRILLIANT

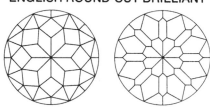

JUBILEE CUT

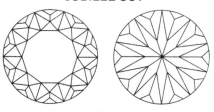

MAGNA CUT

Source: GIA

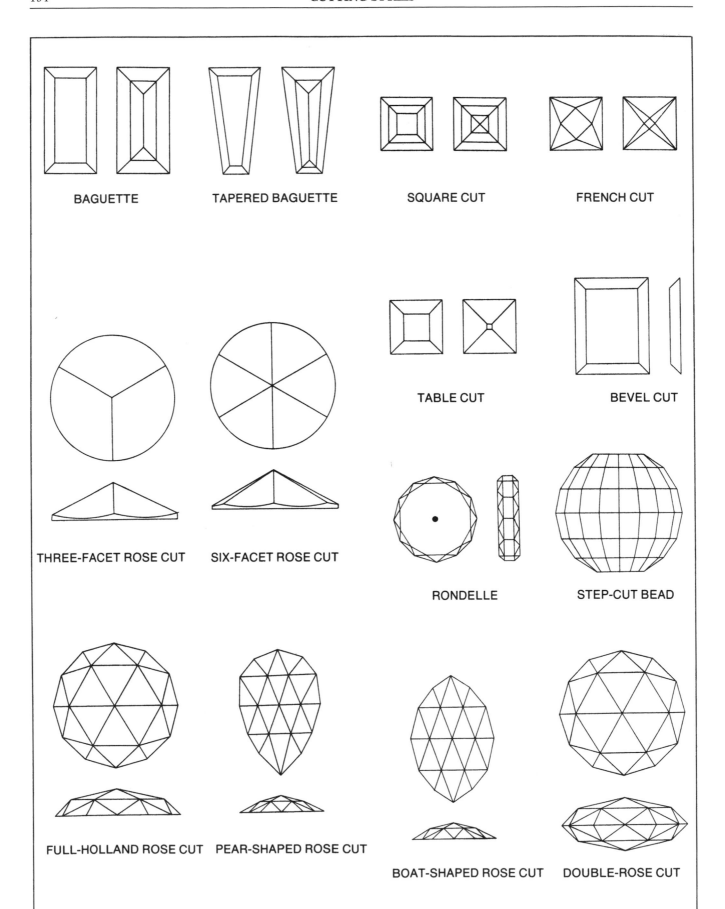

BAGUETTE   TAPERED BAGUETTE   SQUARE CUT   FRENCH CUT

TABLE CUT   BEVEL CUT

THREE-FACET ROSE CUT   SIX-FACET ROSE CUT   RONDELLE   STEP-CUT BEAD

FULL-HOLLAND ROSE CUT   PEAR-SHAPED ROSE CUT   BOAT-SHAPED ROSE CUT   DOUBLE-ROSE CUT

Source: GIA

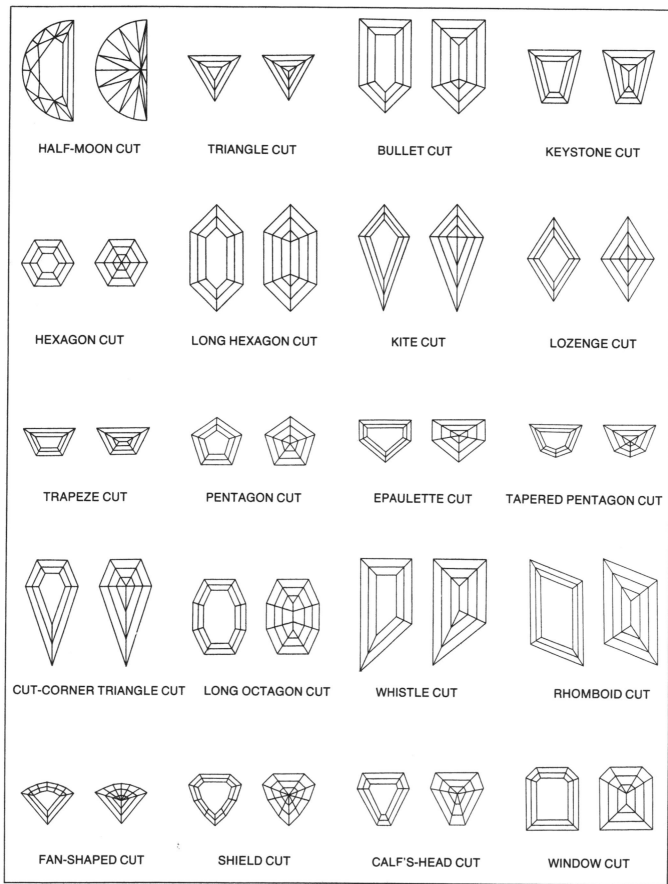

HALF-MOON CUT   TRIANGLE CUT   BULLET CUT   KEYSTONE CUT

HEXAGON CUT   LONG HEXAGON CUT   KITE CUT   LOZENGE CUT

TRAPEZE CUT   PENTAGON CUT   EPAULETTE CUT   TAPERED PENTAGON CUT

CUT-CORNER TRIANGLE CUT   LONG OCTAGON CUT   WHISTLE CUT   RHOMBOID CUT

FAN-SHAPED CUT   SHIELD CUT   CALF'S-HEAD CUT   WINDOW CUT

Source: GIA

Size-to-Weight Conversion Chart: Standard-Size Cabochon Gems

Type of Stone	8/6	10/8	12/10	14/10	16/12	8	10	12
				Millimeter Size				
Ruby and Sapphire	1.9	4.1	6.9	8.7	4.5	3.1	5.8	10.6
Emerald	1.3	2.8	4.7	5.9	9.9	2.1	4.0	7.2
Amethyst	1.3	2.7	4.6	5.8	9.7	2.0	3.4	7.1
Tourmaline	1.4	3.1	5.3	6.7	11.1	2.3	4.5	8.1
Peridot	1.6	3.4	5.8	7.3	12.1	2.6	4.9	8.9
Rhodolite Carnet	1.8	3.9	6.6	8.4	14.0	2.9	5.6	10.2
Lapis Lazuli	1.3	2.8	4.7	6.0	10.0	2.1	4.0	7.3
Coral	1.3	2.7	4.6	5.8	9.7	2.0	3.9	7.0
Black Onyx	1.2	2.6	4.5	5.7	9.5	2.0	3.8	6.9
Chrysoprase	1.3	2.7	4.6	5.8	9.7	2.0	3.9	7.1
Jade (Nephrite)	1.4	3.0	5.1	6.4	10.7	2.2	4.3	7.8
Hematite	2.5	5.3	9.0	11.3	18.9	4.0	7.6	13.8
Ivory	.9	2.0	3.5	4.4	7.2	1.5	2.9	5.3
Turquoise	1.3	2.8	4.8	6.0	10.0	2.1	4.0	7.3

This chart is meant to be used as a weight conversion and comparison guide. For example, this chart shows that a properly proportioned medium size 14/10mm ruby cabochon will convert into a weight of approximately 8.7 carats, which, comparatively speaking, is 1 ½ times the weight of the same size emerald cabochon.

Source: Seymour Amstein, Walter Amstein Inc., New York City. Reprinted courtesy of *Modern Jeweler.*

Size-to-Weight Conversion Chart: Opal Cabochons

Round Cabochons		Oval Cabochons		Pear Shaped		Marquise	
MM	CTS	MM	CTS	MM	CTS	MM	CTS
2¼	0.054	5 × 3	0.16	5 × 3	0.13	6 × 3	0.15
2½	0.066	5 × 3½	0.25	6 × 4	0.25	8 × 4	0.40
2¾	0.078	6 × 4	0.30	7 × 5	0.35	10 × 5	0.70
3	0.090	7 × 5	0.45	8 × 5	0.45	12 × 6	1.00
3¼	0.114	8 × 6	0.70	8 × 6	0.60	15 × 7	2.00
3½	0.135	9 × 7	1.00	9 × 6	0.70		
3¾	0.16	10 × 8	1.50	10 × 7	1.00		
4	0.175	11 × 9	2.00	12 × 8	1.50		
4¼	0.20	12 × 10	2.50	13 × 8	1.70		
4½	0.25	14 × 10	3.00	14 × 9	2.10		
4¾	0.28	14 × 12	4.00	15 × 10	2.90		
5	0.33	16 × 12	4.50				
5¼	0.36	18 × 13	5.20				
5½	0.40	20 × 15	8.00				
5¾	0.50						
6	0.60						
6¼	0.65						
6½	0.70						
6¾	0.75						
7	0.80						

Size-to-Weight Conversion Chart: Caliber-Cut Gemstones

mm.	1	2	3	4	5	6	7	8
				Round Stones				
2.0	.03	.04	.04	.04	.04	.04	.04	.04
2.5	.05	.06	.06	.08	.08	.08	.08	.09
3.0	.10	.11	.11	.13	.13	.14	.14	.16
3.5	.16	.18	.20	.20	.21	.22	.23	.24
4.0	.24	.27	.29	.30	.31	.33	.34	.36
4.5	.34	.39	.40	.43	.46	.46	.48	.51
5.0	.47	.53	.56	.59	.62	.64	.66	.70
5.5	.62	.72	.74	.78	.83	.85	.88	.94
6.0	.82	.92	.96	1.00	1.07	1.09	1.14	1.21
6.5	1.04	1.17	1.22	1.27	1.37	1.39	1.46	1.55
7.0	1.30	1.47	1.53	1.60	1.70	1.73	1.82	1.92
7.5	1.60	1.78	1.84	1.95	2.07	2.13	2.25	2.37
8.0	1.94	2.16	2.23	2.37	2.51	2.59	2.73	2.88
				Oval Stones				
5 × 3	.20	.23	.23	.24	.26	.27	.29	.30
6 × 4	.42	.48	.49	.52	.55	.56	.59	.62
7 × 5	.75	.86	.90	.94	.99	1.01	1.07	1.12
8 × 6	1.24	1.40	1.46	1.52	1.63	1.65	1.73	1.83
9 × 7	1.89	2.13	2.22	2.31	2.47	2.52	2.64	2.80
10 × 8	2.72	3.08	3.21	3.35	3.56	3.64	3.82	4.04
				Pear-Shaped Stones				
5 × 3	.17	.18	.20	.21	.22	.22	.23	.24
6 × 4	.35	.40	.42	.43	.47	.47	.49	.52
7 × 5	.64	.73	.75	.79	.85	.86	.90	.96
8 × 6	1.05	1.20	1.25	1.30	1.39	1.42	1.48	1.57
9 × 7	1.63	1.83	1.91	2.00	2.12	2.17	2.28	2.41
10 × 8	2.35	2.67	2.78	2.90	3.08	3.15	3.30	3.50
				Rectangular Stones				
4 × 2	.09	.10	.10	.10	.11	.11	.12	.13
5 × 3	.24	.27	.29	.30	.33	.33	.35	.36
6 × 4	.52	.60	.62	.65	.69	.70	.74	.78
7 × 5	.95	1.08	1.13	1.18	1.25	1.27	1.34	1.42
8 × 6	1.57	1.78	1.86	1.94	2.07	2.11	2.21	2.34
9 × 7	2.41	2.73	2.85	2.96	3.16	3.22	3.38	3.58
10 × 8	3.50	3.96	4.12	4.30	4.58	4.67	4.90	5.19
				Square Stones				
3 × 3	.13	.14	.15	.16	.17	.17	.18	.19
4 × 4	.31	.35	.36	.38	.40	.42	.43	.46
5 × 5	.60	.69	.72	.74	.79	.81	.85	.90
6 × 6	1.04	1.18	1.24	1.29	1.37	1.39	1.47	1.55
7 × 7	1.65	1.87	1.96	2.04	2.17	2.21	2.33	2.46
				Marquise Stones				
4 × 2	.05	.06	.07	.07	.07	.08	.08	.08
5 × 2½	.10	.11	.13	.13	.14	.14	.15	.16
6 × 3	.18	.20	.21	.22	.23	.24	.26	.27
7 × 3½	.29	.33	.34	.35	.38	.39	.40	.43
8 × 4	.43	.48	.51	.53	.56	.57	.60	.64
9 × 4½	.61	.69	.73	.75	.81	.82	.86	.91
10 × 5	.85	.95	.99	1.04	1.10	1.12	1.18	1.25

Size-to-Weight Conversion Chart: Caliber-Cut Gemstones (Continued)

				Heart-Shaped Stones				
mm.	1	2	3	4	5	6	7	8
4 × 4	.18	.20	.21	.23	.24	.25	.26	.27
5 × 5	.40	.44	.46	.49	.52	.53	.56	.59
6 × 6	.63	.70	.73	.77	.82	.84	.89	.94
7 × 7	.95	1.06	1.09	1.16	1.23	1.27	1.34	1.41
8 × 8	1.35	1.50	1.55	1.65	1.75	1.80	1.90	2.00

Chart gives average weights in millimeters for more than fifty varieties of gemstones. Calculations are based on gems with no bulge factor and a depth of 60 percent of the narrow diameter. Weights are rounded to the nearest point ($\frac{1}{100}$ of a carat), and all weights are approximate.

The list is intended only as a guide; most stones will vary from these ideal-cut gemstone weights. Observe the cut of the stone. Gemstones with high crowns and/or heavy pavilions may weigh as much as 20 percent more than chart weights. Deep stones may weigh as much as 20 percent more than chart weights; shallow stones may weigh up to 20 percent less than chart weights.

Key: Gemstones categorized according to specific gravity.
1. Quartz (amethyst, citrine, etc.) and beryl (emerald, aquamarine, etc.)
2. Tourmaline (green, pink, etc.)
3. Andalusite and spodumene (kunzite)
4. Peridot and zoisite (tanzanite)
5. Topaz (Imperial, blue, etc.)
6. Spinel (all colors) and grossular garnet (tsavorite, etc.)
7. Chrysoberyl (alexandrite, etc.) and rhodolite/pyrope garnets
8. Corundum (ruby, all sapphires), zircon, and almandite garnet

Pennyweight-to-Gram Conversion

DWT.	GRAMS	DWT.	GRAMS	DWT.	GRAMS
0.20	0.31	7.00	10.89	13.80	21.46
0.40	0.62	7.20	11.20	14.00	21.77
0.60	0.93	7.40	11.51	14.20	22.08
0.80	1.24	7.60	11.82	14.40	22.39
1.00	1.56	7.80	12.13	14.60	22.71
1.20	1.87	8.00	12.44	14.80	23.02
1.40	2.18	8.20	12.75	15.00	23.33
1.60	2.49	8.40	13.06	15.20	23.64
1.80	2.80	8.60	13.37	15.40	23.95
2.00	3.11	8.80	13.68	15.60	24.26
2.20	3.42	9.00	14.00	15.80	24.57
2.40	3.73	9.20	14.31	16.00	24.88
2.60	4.04	9.40	14.62	16.20	25.19
2.80	4.35	9.60	14.93	16.40	25.51
3.00	4.67	9.80	15.24	16.60	25.82
3.20	4.98	10.00	15.56	16.80	26.13
3.40	5.29	10.20	15.87	17.00	26.44
3.60	5.60	10.40	16.17	17.20	26.75
3.80	5.91	10.60	16.48	17.40	27.06
4.00	6.22	10.80	16.80	17.60	27.37
4.20	6.53	11.00	17.11	17.80	27.68
4.40	6.84	11.20	17.42	18.00	27.99
4.60	7.15	11.40	17.73	18.20	28.30
4.80	7.46	11.60	18.04	18.40	28.62
5.00	7.78	11.80	18.35	18.60	28.93
5.20	8.09	12.00	18.66	18.80	29.24
5.40	8.40	12.20	18.97	19.00	29.55
5.60	8.71	12.40	19.28	19.20	29.86
5.80	9.02	12.60	19.60	19.40	30.17
6.00	9.33	12.80	19.91	19.60	30.48
6.20	9.64	13.00	20.22	19.80	30.79
6.40	9.95	13.20	20.53	20.00	31.30
6.60	10.26	13.40	20.84		
6.80	10.58	13.60	21.15		

To convert pennyweights to grams: Dwts. x 1.552 = Grams.
To convert grams to pennyweights: Grams x 0.6430 = Dwts.

The Troy System

1 gram	=	15,4324 grains
1 gram	=	.643 pennyweights
1 gram	=	.03215 troy ounce
1.5517 grams	=	1 pennyweight
31.10348 grams	=	1 troy ounce
1000 grams	=	1 kilogram
1 kilo	=	32.15076 troy ounces
1 pennyweight	=	24 grains
1 pennyweight	=	.05 ounces troy
20 pennyweights	=	480 grains
20 pennyweights	=	1 troy ounce
14.583 troy ounces	=	1 pound avoir
16 avoir ounces (7000 grains)	=	1 avoir pound
avoir weight x .911	=	1 troy weight

To convert troy ounces to grams:
Oz.(t) × 31.1035 = Grams.
To convert grams to troy ounces:
Grams × 0.0322 = Oz.(t).

Avoir and Troy Weights

Troy Oz.	Adv. Lbs.	Troy Oz.	Adv. Lbs.
.91 oz.	1 oz.	12.74 oz.	14 oz.
1.82 oz.	2 oz.	13.65 oz.	15 oz.
2.73 oz.	3 oz.	14.58 oz.	1 lb.
3.64 oz.	4 oz.	29.16 oz.	2 lb.
4.55 oz.	5 oz.	43.74 oz.	3 lb.
5.46 oz.	6 oz.	58.32 oz.	4 lb.
6.37 oz.	7 oz.	72.90 oz.	5 lb.
7.28 oz.	8 oz.	87.48 oz.	6 lb.
8.19 oz.	9 oz.	102.06 oz.	7 lb.
9.10 oz.	10 oz.	116.64 oz	8 lb.
10.01 oz.	11 oz.	131.22 oz.	9 lb.
10.92 oz.	12 oz.	145.80 oz.	10 lb.
11.83 oz.	13 oz.		

The Carat System

1 carat = ⅕ gram
1 carat = 100 points
1 carat = 4 pearl grains
1 pearl grain = ¼ carat
1 point = 1/100 carat
To convert carats to grams: Carats x 0.2 = Grams.

Historic Gold Prices from 1833–1997

1833	18.93	1861	18.93	1889	18.93	1917	18.99	1945	34.71	1973	97.32
1834	18.93	1862	18.93	1890	18.94	1918	18.99	1946	34.71	1974	159.26
1835	18.93	1863	18.93	1891	18.96	1919	19.95	1947	34.71	1975	161.02
1836	18.93	1864	18.93	1892	18.96	1920	20.68	1948	34.71	1976	124.84
1837	18.93	1865	18.93	1893	18.96	1921	20.58	1949	31.69	1977	147.71
1838	18.93	1866	18.93	1894	18.94	1922	20.66	1950	34.72	1978	193.22
1839	18.93	1867	18.93	1895	18.93	1923	21.32	1951	34.72	1979	306.68
1840	18.93	1868	18.93	1896	18.98	1924	20.69	1952	34.60	1980	612.56
1841	18.93	1869	18.93	1897	18.98	1925	20.64	1953	34.84	1981	460.03
1842	18.93	1870	18.93	1898	18.98	1926	20.63	1954	35.04	1982	375.67
1843	18.93	1871	18.93	1899	18.94	1927	20.64	1955	35.03	1983	424.30
1844	18.93	1872	18.94	1900	18.96	1928	20.66	1956	34.99	1984	360.48
1845	18.93	1873	18.94	1901	18.98	1929	20.63	1957	34.95	1985	317.26
1846	18.93	1874	18.94	1902	18.97	1930	20.65	1958	35.10	1986	367.66
1847	18.93	1875	18.94	1903	18.95	1931	17.06	1959	35.10	1987	446.46
1848	18.93	1876	18.94	1904	18.96	1932	20.69	1960	35.27	1988	436.94
1849	18.93	1877	18.94	1905	18.92	1933	26.33	1961	35.25	1989	381.44
1850	18.93	1878	18.94	1906	18.90	1934	34.69	1962	35.23	1990	383.51
1851	18.93	1879	18.93	1907	18.94	1935	34.84	1963	35.09	1991	362.11
1852	18.93	1880	18.94	1908	18.95	1936	34.87	1964	35.10	1992	343.82
1853	18.93	1881	18.94	1909	18.96	1937	34.79	1965	35.12	1993	359.77
1854	18.93	1882	18.94	1910	18.92	1938	34.85	1966	35.13	1994	384.00
1855	18.93	1883	18.94	1911	18.92	1939	34.42	1967	34.95	1995	384.17
1856	18.93	1884	18.94	1912	18.93	1940	33.85	1968	38.69	1996	387.77
1857	18.93	1885	18.94	1913	18.92	1941	33.85	1969	41.09		
1858	18.93	1886	18.93	1914	18.99	1942	33.85	1970	35.94		
1859	18.93	1887	18.93	1915	18.99	1943	33.85	1971	40.80		
1860	18.93	1888	18.94	1916	18.99	1944	33.85	1972	58.16		

Diamond Valuation Chart
(1949 base price $100)

Date of Increase	Percent Increase	Cumulative Percent Increase	Dollar Value	Cumulative Percent Increase to July 1996
Jan. 1949	----	----	$ 100.00	1,918.31
Sept. 1949	25.00	25.00	125.00	1,514.65
March 1951	15.00	43.75	143.75	1,304.04
Sept. 1951	2.50	47.34	147.34	1,269.80
Jan. 1954	2.00	50.29	150.29	1,242.94
Jan. 1955	2.50	54.05	154.05	1,210.18
Jan. 1957	5.70	62.83	162.83	1,139.53
May 1960	2.50	66.90	166.90	1,109.30
March 1963	5.00	75.24	175.24	1,051.71
Feb. 1964	10.00	92.77	192.77	947.01
Nov. 1967	16.60	124.77	224.77	797.95
Sept. 1968	2.50	130.39	230.39	776.05
July 1969	4.00	139.60	239.60	742.36
Nov. 1971	5.00	151.58	251.58	702.24
Jan. 1972	5.40	165.17	265.17	661.14
Sept. 1972	6.00	181.08	281.08	618.06
Feb. 1973	11.00	212.00	312.00	546.90
March 1973	7.00	233.84	333.84	504.58
May 1973	10.00	267.22	367.22	449.62
Aug. 1973	10.20	304.68	404.68	398.75
Dec. 1974	1.50	310.75	410.75	391.38
Jan. 1975	3.00	323.07	423.07	377.06
Oct. 1976	5.75	347.40	447.40	351.12
March 1977	15.00	414.51	514.51	292.28
Dec. 1977	17.00	501.97	601.97	235.28
Aug. 1978	30.00	682.56	782.56	157.91
Sept. 1979	13.00	784.30	884.30	128.24
Feb. 1980	12.00	890.41	990.41	103.78
Oct. 1982	2.50	915.17	1,015.17	98.81
April 1983	3.50	950.70	1,050.70	92.09
May 1986	7.50	1,029.51	1,129.51	78.69
Nov. 1986	7.00	1,108.57	1,208.57	67.00
Oct. 1987	10.00	1,229.43	1,329.43	51.82
May 1988	13.50	1,408.91	1,508.91	33.76
March 1989	15.50	1,642.78	1,742.78	15.81
March 1990	5.50	1,738.63	1,838.63	9.77
Feb. 1993	1.50	1,766.21	1,866.21	8.15
Nov. 1995	5.00	1,859.52	1,959.52	3.00
July 1996	3.00	1,918.31	2,018.31	------

Courtesy Richard Drucker, *The Guide*

Weight Estimation Formulas: Diamonds

ROUND BRILLIANT:	Diameter^2 × Depth × .0061.
OVAL BRILLIANT:	Average the length and width to determine diameter. Apply formula: Diameter^2 × Depth × .0062.

The conversion factor used in the following formulas is based on the length-to-width ratio of the diamond. For example, a stone with a length of 9mm and a width of 6mm would have a length-to-width ratio of 1.5:1.

EMERALD CUT:	
Length × Width × Depth ×	.008 (1:1 ratio)
	.0092 (1.5:1 ratio)
	.010 (2:1 ratio)
	.0106 (2.5:1 ratio)
MARQUISE CUT:	
Length × Width × Depth ×	.00565 (1.5:1 ratio)
	.0058 (2:1 ratio)
	.00585 (2.5:1 ratio)
	.00595 (3:1 ratio)
PEAR SHAPED:	
Length × Width × Depth ×	.00615 (1.25:1 ratio)
	.0060 (1.5:1 ratio)
	.0059 (1.66:1 ratio)
	.00575 (2:1 ratio)

All formulas are based on stones with thin-to-medium girdles. Adjust weight as follows for stones with thicker girdles: medium up to slightly thick, add two to four points per carat; thick to very thick, add five to ten points per carat. All measurements should be taken in millimeters.

Source: Gemological Institute of America

Weight Estimation Formulas: Colored Stones

Round Faceted Stones:
Diameter^2 × depth × S.G. × .0018 = carat weight.

Oval Faceted Stones:
(Average the length and width to obtain diameter.) Diameter^2 × depth × S.G. × .0020 = carat weight.

Emerald-Cut Faceted Stones:
Length × width × depth × S.G. × .0025 = carat weight.

Rectangular Faceted Stones:
Length × width × depth × S.G. × .0026 = carat weight.

Square Faceted Stones:
Length × width × depth × S.G. × .0023 = carat weight.

Navette or Boat-shaped Stones:
Length × width × depth × S.G. × .0016 = carat weight.

Pear-shaped or Teardrop-shaped Stones:
Length × width × depth × S.G. × .00175 = caret weight.

Cabochons:
Length × width × depth × S.G. × .0026
(.0029 for very flat or shallow domed stones.)

Check for bulge factor, usually present; depending upon bulge factor, add 2 to 6 percent. All measurements should be taken in millimeters. To ensure accuracy, measurements should be made to 1/10 millimeter.

Source: Gemological Institute of America

Formula to Calculate Weight of Diamonds

BRILLIANT	W × W × D × 0.0061 = cts.
PEAR-SHAPED	L × W × D × 0.0062 = cts.
SQUARE	(L-1/3W) × W × D × 0.013 = cts.
OVAL	(L-1/3W) × W × D × 0.011 = cts.
MARQUISE	(L-1/3W) × W xD × 0.0077 = cts.

For old brilliant-cut diamonds, probably cut pre-1920, use the formula:
W × W × D × 0.0065 = cts.

Source: National Association of Goldsmiths, UK

Formula to Calculate Weight of Colored Gemstones

L=length W=width D=depth SG=specific gravity

Measurements should be accurate to 1/10th millimeter

OVAL	(L - 1/3W) × W × D × SG × 0.0031 = cts.
SQUARE	(L - 1/3W) × W × D × SG × 0.0037 = cts.
MARQUISE	(L - 1/3W) × W × D × SG × 0.0022 = cts.
PEAR	L × W × D × SG × 0.002 = cts.
CABOCHON	L × W × D × SG × 0.0026 (if shallow use 0.0029) = cts.
ROUND FACETED	W × W × D × SG × 0.0021 = cts.

Source: National Association of Goldsmiths, UK

Gem Identification Report*

Date_____

Client_____   Item #_____

Address_____

_____

_____

Refractive Index_____; Birefringence_____(_____)_____

Comments_____

Polariscope Reaction: DR ☐   SR ☐   AGG ☐

Optic Character: Uniaxial ☐   Biaxial ☐   Indeterminable ☐

Optic Sign: Positive ☐   Negative ☐   Indeterminable ☐

Pleochroism: Weak   ☐   Dichroic Colors_____

                 Medium   ☐   Trichroic Colors_____

                 Strong   ☐   _____

Specific Gravity:_____Determined by: Liquids ☐   Hydrostatic ☐   Indeterminable ☐

Fluorescence: Longwave_____Shortwave_____

Microscopic Examination:_____

_____

_____

Luster: Polish_____Fracture_____

Absorption Spectra:

4000				5000		6000		7000
VIOLET	VIOLET BLUE	BLUE		BLUE GREEN	GREEN	YELLOW GREEN	YELLOW ORANGE	RED

Ancillary Tests:_____

_____

Comments:_____

Weight:_____   Actual ☐   Estimated ☐

Consistent with the observations indicated above, I believe this gem to be:

Variety_____

Species_____

Prepared by_____

Quality Analysis: Colored Stones

Date_____

Client_____

Address_____

_____

_____

Item #_____

Measurements:_____mm X_____mm X_____mm Deep

Shape and Cut: Round ☐   Oval ☐   Marquise ☐   Emerald ☐   Pear ☐

Heart ☐   Cabochon ☐   Other_____Comments_____

Hue:

Red-Violet ☐	Reddish Orange ☐	Yellow ☐	Bluish Green ☐	Blue-Violet ☐
Violetish Red ☐	Orange ☐	Greenish Yellow ☐	Blue-Green ☐	Bluish Violet ☐
Red ☐	Yellowish Orange ☐	Yellow-Green ☐	Greenish Blue ☐	Violet ☐
Orangish Red ☐	Yellow-Orange ☐	Yellowish Green ☐	Blue ☐	Reddish Violet ☐
Red-Orange ☐	Orangish Yellow ☐	Green ☐	Violetish Blue ☐	

Tone:

VERY LIGHT | LIGHT | SLIGHTLY LIGHT | ME-DIUM | SLIGHTLY DARK | DARK | VERY DARK | EX-TREMELY DARK

Comments:_____

Intensity:

DULL | SLIGHTLY DULL | MEDIUM | SLIGHTLY INTENSE | INTENSE | VIVID

Comments:_____

Clarity:

FLAWLESS | LIGHTLY INCLUDED | MODERATELY INCLUDED | HEAVILY INCLUDED | EXTREMELY INCLUDED

Comments:_____

Proportions:

POOR | FAIR | GOOD | VERY GOOD | EXCELLENT

Comments:_____

Brilliancy:

POOR | FAIR | GOOD | VERY GOOD | EXCELLENT

Comments:_____

Finish:

POOR | FAIR | GOOD | VERY GOOD | EXCELLENT

Comments:_____

Additional Comments:_____

_____

_____

Prepared by_____

Quality Analysis: Opals

Date _____

Client _____

Address _____

_____

_____

Item # _____

Measurements: _____ mm X _____ mm X _____ .

Shape and Cut: Round ☐   Oval ☐   Marquise ☐   Emerald ☐

              Pear ☐   Heart ☐   Cabochon ☐   Other _____

              Comments _____

Body Color: ☐ White   ☐ Black   Other _____

            Comments _____

Transparency of Body: ☐ Transparent   ☐ Semi-Transparent

                          ☐ Translucent   ☐ Semi-Translucent   ☐ Opaque

Predominant Spectral Hue: ☐ Red   ☐ Orange   ☐ Yellow   ☐ Green   ☐ Blue   ☐ Violet

Secondary Spectral Hue: ☐ Red   ☐ Orange   ☐ Yellow   ☐ Green   ☐ Blue   ☐ Violet

Hue Intensity:

POOR	FAIR	GOOD	EXCELLENT

Phenomena Saturation:

POOR	FAIR	GOOD	EXCELLENT

Additional Hues Present: ☐ Red   ☐ Orange   ☐ Yellow   ☐ Green   ☐ Blue   ☐ Violet

Hue Pattern: ☐ Mosaic   ☐ Pinfire   ☐ Flash

         Other _____

Comments: _____

_____

Prepared by _____

* Reprinted with permission of the National Association of Jewelry Appraisers.

Quality Analysis: Change-of-Color Stones

Measurements: _____ mm X _____ mm X _____ mm.

Shape and Cut: ☐ Round ☐ Oval ☐ Marquise ☐ Emerald ☐ Pear
☐ Heart ☐ Cabochon ☐ Other _____

INCANDESCENT LIGHT SOURCE

Hue:
☐ Red-Violet   ☐ Yellow-Orange   ☐ Blue-Green
☐ Violetish Red   ☐ Orangish Yellow ☐ Greenish Blue
☐ Red   ☐ Yellow   ☐ Blue
☐ Orangish Red   ☐ Greenish Yellow ☐ Violetish Blue
☐ Red-Orange   ☐ Yellow-Green   ☐ Blue-Violet
☐ Reddish Orange ☐ Yellowish Green ☐ Bluish Violet
☐ Orange   ☐ Green   ☐ Violet
☐ Yellowish Orange ☐ Bluish Green   ☐ Reddish Violet

Other _____

Tone:
☐ Very Light   ☐ Slightly Dark
☐ Light   ☐ Dark
☐ Slightly Light ☐ Very dark
☐ Medium   ☐ Extremely Dark

Intensity:

DULL   SLIGHTLY   MEDIUM   SLIGHTLY   INTENSE   VIVID
       DULL   INTENSE

FLUORESCENT LIGHT SOURCE

Hue:
☐ Red-Violet   ☐ Yellow-Orange   ☐ Blue-Green
☐ Violetish Red   ☐ Orangish Yellow ☐ Greenish Blue
☐ Red   ☐ Yellow   ☐ Blue
☐ Orangish Red   ☐ Greenish Yellow ☐ Violetish Blue
☐ Red-Orange   ☐ Yellow-Green   ☐ Blue-Violet
☐ Reddish Orange   ☐ Yellowish Green ☐ Bluish Violet
☐ Orange   ☐ Green   ☐ Violet
☐ Yellowish Orange ☐ Bluish Green   ☐ Reddish Violet

Other _____

Tone:
☐ Very Light   ☐ Slightly Dark
☐ Light   ☐ Dark
☐ Slightly Light ☐ Very Dark
☐ Medium   ☐ Extremely Dark

Intensity:

DULL   SLIGHTLY   MEDIUM   SLIGHTLY   INTENSE   VIVID
       DULL   INTENSE

Clarity:

FLAWLESS LIGHTLY   MODERATELY HEAVILY   EXTREMELY
          INCLUDED   INCLUDED   INCLUDED   INCLUDED

Finish:

POOR   FAIR   GOOD   VERY GOOD   EXCELLENT

Proportions:

POOR   FAIR   GOOD   VERY GOOD   EXCELLENT

Brilliancy:

POOR   FAIR   GOOD   VERY GOOD   EXCELLENT

Comments: _____
_____
_____
_____

Prepared by _____

* Reprinted with permission of the National Association of Jewelry Appraisers.

Quality Analysis: Cultured Pearls

Date _____

Client _____

Address _____

_____

_____

Item # _____

Body Color:
- ☐ Pink Rosé
- ☐ Pale Pink
- ☐ White Rosé
- ☐ Very Light Cream Rosé
- ☐ Very Slight Green White Rosé
- ☐ Greenish White Rosé
- ☐ White Without Rosé
- ☐ Cream Rosé
- ☐ Greenish Cream Rosé
- ☐ Cream
- ☐ Green-White
- ☐ Green-Cream
- ☐ Dark Cream Rosé
- ☐ Dark Cream
- ☐ Gold Rosé
- ☐ Blue
- ☐ Gray, Silver
- ☐ Yellow, Gold

(decreasing desirability)
↓

Sphericity:
- ☐ Round in All
- ☐ Round in Most
- ☐ Slightly Off-Round
- ☐ Off-Round
- ☐ Semibaroque
- ☐ Baroque

Luster:

VERY BRIGHT	BRIGHT	HIGH	MEDIUM	SLIGHTLY DULL	DULL

Nacre Thickness:

VERY THICK	THICK	MEDIUM	THIN	VERY THIN

Continuity:

POOR	FAIR	MEDIUM	GOOD	EXCELLENT

Blemishes:

SPOTLESS	LIGHTLY SPOTTED	SPOTTED	HEAVILY SPOTTED

Comments: _____

_____

_____

Measurements: _____

_____

NOTE: The information contained in this report represents the earnest and considered opinion of this appraiser and/or its parent company with regard to the numerous existing characteristics of the submitted gem(s). The conclusions expressed herein are a result of the interpretation of data gathered from gemological instruments and accepted appraisal/grading procedures and techniques. In that conclusions may vary due to the subjective nature of gemstone analysis, neither this appraiser, its parent company, nor any of its employees and officers can be responsible for any action that may be taken on the basis of this report. This report is not a guarantee or warranty of the quality or value of the submitted stone(s).

Prepared by _____

* Reprinted with permission of the National Association of Jewelry Appraisers.

Quality Analysis: Cat's-Eye and Star Stones

Measurements: _____ mm X _____ mm X _____ mm.

Shape: ☐ Round ☐ Oval ☐ Navette ☐ Emerald ☐ Pear

☐ Heart ☐ Other_____

Hue:

☐ Red-Violet	☐ Yellow-Orange	☐ Blue-Green
☐ Violetish Red	☐ Orangish Yellow	☐ Greenish Blue
☐ Red	☐ Yellow	☐ Blue
☐ Orangish Red	☐ Greenish Yellow	☐ Violetish Blue
☐ Red-Orange	☐ Yellow-Green	☐ Blue-Violet
☐ Reddish Orange	☐ Yellowish Green	☐ Bluish Violet
☐ Orange	☐ Green	☐ Violet
☐ Yellowish Orange	☐ Bluish Green	☐ Reddish Violet

Other: _____

Tone: ☐ Very Light ☐ Slightly Light ☐ Slightly Dark ☐ Very Dark

☐ Light ☐ Medium ☐ Dark ☐ Extremely Dark

Intensity:

| DULL | SLIGHTLY DULL | MEDIUM | SLIGHTLY INTENSE | INTENSE | VIVID |

Ray Centering:

| POOR | FAIR | GOOD | VERY GOOD | EXCELLENT |

Ray Intensity:

| VERY WEAK | WEAK | MEDIUM | STRONG | VERY STRONG |

Ray Movement:

| POOR | FAIR | GOOD | VERY GOOD | EXCELLENT |

Phenomena Completeness:

| POOR | FAIR | GOOD | VERY GOOD | EXCELLENT |

Comments: _____

_____

_____

_____

Prepared by _____

Jewelry Appraisal Update

Date of Original Appraisal _____

Appraisal Type _____

Addenda Number _____

Addenda Date _____

Client's Name _____

Address _____

_____

_____

Precious Metal Base Price _____

NOTE: I have personally examined the following described article(s) and have found (it) them in good condition unless otherwise noted and it (they) does (do) not require any repairs at this time with the values and description as listed in this appraisal being correct to the best of our knowledge and belief based on present day market values and accepted appraisal procedures in accordance with the standards and ethics of the National Association of Jewelry Appraisers. In that mountings prohibit full and accurate observation of gem quality and weight, it must be understood that all data pertaining to mounted gems can only be considered as provisional. Additionally, because jewelry appraisal and evaluation is not a pure science but rather a subjective professional viewpoint, estimates of value and quality may vary from one appraiser to another with such variances not necessarily constituting error on the part of the appraiser. Therefore, due to the very subjective nature of appraisals and evaluation, statements and data contained herein cannot be construed as a guarantee or warranty. We assume no liability with respect to any action that may be taken on the basis of this appraisal or for any error in or omission from this report (except for fraud, willful misconduct, or gross negligence). Unless specifically noted otherwise, this report does not represent an offer to buy and shall be for the exclusive use of the above mentioned client.

ITEM'S APPRAISAL LOCATION	ITEM'S VALUE ON ORIGINAL APPRAISAL OR PREVIOUS ADDENDA	UPDATE VALUE

Prepared by _____

Watch Worksheet

Client _____ Date _____

Brand of Watch _____ Metal content & weight _____

Type of Band (wristwatch) _____

Any gemstones? _____

Case Condition   Excellent   Fine   Good   Worn   Badly Worn

Engraving Front _____

        Back _____

        Inside _____

Comments:

Name on dial _____

Dial type _____

Dial color _____

Dial Condition   Excellent   Fine   Good   Worn   Badly Worn

Comments:

Case manufacturer _____

Case serial number _____

Case quality _____

Comments:

Movement manufacturer _____

Movement size (Pocket watch) _____

Movement serial number _____

Movement manufacture date _____

Movement type _____

Jewels _____

Movement Condition   Excellent   Fine   Good   Poor   Scrap

Appraisal for IRS Tax Deduction (Donation). Chrysoberyl Var. Alexandrite: Sales Information and Data Sheet

Date	Size (in carats)	Information/ Source	Sale	Lot	Price (in dollars)	Per-carat Price	Color Change	Clarity	Country of Origin
July 1985	75.00				900,000.	12,000.	Good	Good	Sri Lanka
	66.00	Smithsonian Inst.							
	57.08	British Museum							
	48.20	Smithsonian Inst.			See Appraisal				
Oct. 1977	35.40	Sotheby's	4028	39	*140,000.	3,944.	Brownish green Deep wine red		Sri Lanka
Oct. 1977	34.50	Sotheby's	4028	246	125,000. 150,000.	4,000.	Fair to good		Sri Lanka
1985	30.78				52,170. 92,340.	**1,500. 3,000.	15%	Clean	Sri Lanka
Oct. 1980	26.35	Sotheby's		592	50,000. 60,000.	2,277.			
1985	24.00 to 27.00				*275,000.	10,784.	Good		Sri Lanka
Oct. 1978	22.30	Sotheby's	4163	299	*145,000.	6,500.	Fairly good	Good	Sri Lanka
1976	19.95				*250,000.	12,531.	80%	LI1,	Sri Lanka
1985	19.76				*118,560.	6,000.	50% to 80%		Sri Lanka
1986	17.00				*90,000.	5,294.	Good	Clean	Sri Lanka
1985	13.00				*90,000.	6,923.	Good	Clean	Sri Lanka
Apr. 1980	12.12	Sotheby's	4364	180	*95,000.	7,838.	75% Dark murky green Burgundy red		Sri Lanka
1984	12.00	Christie's			*36,000.	3,000.	Average		
Feb. 1979	11.60	Sotheby's		149	22,000. 25,000.	2,155.			Sri Lanka
1986	9.71				70,833. 116,520.	**7,300. 12,000.	75%	Clean	Sri Lanka
1976	6.13				*160,000.	26,101.	100%	LI	U.S.S.R.
1986	26.00				* 182,000. 312,000.	** 7,000. 12,000.	70%	Clean	

* Indicates actual sale.

** Indicates dealer selling price. Second price is adjusted fair market value.

Source: This data was compiled by Bill Sufian, IRS Valuation Engineer, New York, and Joseph W. Tenhagen, Appraiser, Miami.

GLOSSARY

Metal Finishes

Appliqué. One color of gold soldered onto another.

Basse taillé'. Enameling technique in which design is carved into metal recess and translucent to semitransparent enamel is applied.

Bloomed gold. Matte surface formed by acid treatment. Popular in the mid- to late-nineteenth century, bloomed gold jewelry discolors easily.

Braun email. Dark reddish enamel effect achieved by firing linseed oil in engraved lines.

Bright cut. Deep, sharply cut engraving, typically used from 1810–1830.

Burnishing. Luster added to metal finish.

Champlevé. Technique in which etched design is filled with enamel. Resembles cloisonné work but more surface metal is left exposed.

Chasing. Accent technique used to punch detail onto repoussé-finished work.

Cloisonné. Technique in which cells to hold the enamel are created by soldering wire to a base.

Diamond cutting. A process of decorating metal jewelry, especially chains, with a pattern of sharp cuts in the metal. The designs have bright finishes and patterns ranging from symmetrical straight lines to curved lines.

Embossing. Relief ornamentation applied to the front of a metal surface with engraved dies or plates used to drive down the surface mechanically and leave a relief design.

Enamelling. Colored powdered glass fused onto metal surface with heat.

Engine turning. Machine engraver used to produce a brilliant surface, which often serves as a base for enamel.

Engraving. Metal surfaces decorated from the front with incised lines and patterns, using chisels called *gravers*. Differs from carving in that pattern depth is only suggested with shaded lines.

Etching. Chemical engraving.

Filigree. Gold wire twisted and soldered into intricate patterns.

Florentine. Metal surface textured in crosshatching pattern with liner tool.

Gilding/gilt. Metal dipped in gold or electroplated with gold.

Granulation. Tiny round balls fastened to surface by heating process. Typical of the Etruscan styles popular from 1850–1880.

Grisaille. Layers of enamel applied over a gray ground, producing a monochromatic effect. Technique popular since the sixteenth century.

Guilloché. Translucent enamel fired over engine-turned or hand-engraved gold surface. Enameling is sometimes fired five or six times.

Hammering. Indentations pounded into metal.

High polish. Mirrorlike finish.

Matte. Soft, dull finish.

Oxidized. Blackened finish caused by immersion in potassium sulfide.

Parcel gilt. Partially gilded.

Pliqué-à-jour. Enamel confined within unbacked metal frames to give stained-glass effect. Popular from 1890–1910.

Repoussé. Raised, modeled designs that are hammered and punched from the back of a metal plate to raise the design on the front. The work is done with hand punches and hammers, or is mechanically imposed with metal dies.

Roman gold. Surface that has been matted and then gold-electroplated.

Satin. Finish with the grained texture of satin cloth.

Taille d'epargne. Blue, black, or white enamel set in deeply engraved line designs. Popular mid-nineteenth-century technique.

Opal Terms

Black opal. Opal that has an opalescent play of color against a gray or black background.

Cachalong. Porous, opaque opal that absorbs water quickly.

Cherry opal. Opal with a cherry-red ground color that occasionally has a play of color.

Common opal. Nontranslucent opal with no play of color.

Some of this variety is not so common at all—colors may be sky blue, lemon yellow, orange, red, or green.

Contra luz. Opal, usually from Mexico, that shows its best colors against the light.

Fire opal. Translucent Mexican opal with red or orange overall color and no play of color. Not synonymous with precious opal. Red opal with a play of color is called *precious fire opal.*

Flame opal. Precious opal with elongated streaks of prismatic flamelike colors.

Flash opal. Precious opal with a broad-flashing play of color.

Girasol opal. Water-clear opal with broad floating colors.

Harlequin. Precious opal with play of color similar to a checkerboard mosaic.

Hyalite. Pure, transparent, colorless opal that has formed as crusts.

Honey opal. Pale, amber-colored opal, usually with a play of fire.

Hydrophane. A variety of cachalong that becomes almost transparent in water except for its prismatic colors.

Jelly opal. Translucent, colorless opal with a play of fire—a variety of precious opal.

Lechosos or *milk opal.* Opal with play of color against a pure white ground color.

Matrix opal. Host rock that is impregnated with tiny flecks and veinlets of natural opal, which cannot easily be separated from the matrix.

Pinfi re opal. Iridescent opal with small, closely spaced pinpoints.

Play of color. Optical phenomenon of several prismatic flashing colors seen within or near the surface of an opal as the gem is moved.

Play of fire. A degree of colored flame that can be seen within transparent precious opal ranging from amber colored to red.

Precious opal. Opal that has the prismatic play of color for which this gem is noted. If it does not change color, it is not precious opal.

Seam opal. Narrow rows of precious opal that have formed in the fissures and cracks of a host rock.

Wood opal. Opal pseudomorph formed on wood, found in many countries as well as in the United States. Commonly colored in shades of beige, gray, cream, white, brown, and black.

Source: June Culp Zeitner, *Lapidary Journal,* 1986

Antique and Period Jewelry Terms

Albert. Man's vest watch chain, single or double width, popularized by Prince Albert of England.

Antique. Item judged to have been made at least one hundred years ago.

Argentan. French term for nickel silver, German silver, or other nonprecious imitation.

Art Deco. Design style of the 1920s through 1935, characterized by geometric forms and motifs, fine handicraft, and the use of precious materials.

Art Nouveau. Japanese-influenced design style popular from 1890 through 1910, characterized by curves, flowing lines, asymmetry, and the use of natural forms and motifs.

Arts & Crafts movement. Late Victorian/Edwardian (1860–1910) design style characterized by handmade silver and enamel pieces set with rough or flawed stones.

Asterism. Optical phenomenon of a rayed figure, such as a star, seen in a cabochon-cut stone.

Baguette. Rectangular cut used mainly for small diamonds.

Bail. Suspension loop on pendants, lockets, and similar articles.

Baroque pearl. Pearl of irregular shape, more common than spherical pearls. May be natural or cultured.

Base metal. Any nonprecious metal.

Basket mount. Ring head with openwork sides and shank sections.

Bead set. Stone set flush with the mount and secured with metal beads, as in paved pieces.

Belcher link. Simple round links common in Georgian and Victorian chains.

Belcher mount. Ring mounting with the setting claws, or prongs, formed in the shank of the ring or brooch.

Bezel set. Collar burnished over the girdle of a gemstone. Also called *collet set.*

Blister pearl. Pearl formed naturally on the inside shell of a mollusk. Usually hollow.

Blue white. FTC-regulated industry term that may be used to describe only diamonds that have a blue or bluish body color. The term has been so widely misused that it has become nearly meaningless.

Bohemian garnet. Dark red rose-cut garnet, widely used in nineteenth-century jewelry.

Bombé mount. Convex mount often used in period jewelry, especially in bracelets and brooches.

Briolette. Oval or teardrop-shaped stone covered with small triangular facets.

Buff top. Stone cut with cabochon crown and a faceted pavilion.

Cabochon. Round or oval domed stone, polished but not faceted. Commonly used in cutting cat's-eye or star stones.

Caliber cut. Gemstones cut to a special or exact size and used to highlight or outline a jewelry item. Commonly used from the 1920s to the 1930s.

Cameo. One-piece gemstone material carved to leave a raised design and show the design and background in different colors. Commonly used materials include carnelian, chalcedony, and sardonyx.

Cannetille. Open-coiled wirework technique popular during the first half of the nineteenth century.

Cartouche. Shield or scroll motif.

Cast. Piece formed by pouring molten metal into a hollow mold.

Cat's eye. Well-defined streak of light the length of a cabochon. The optical phenomenon is termed *chatoyancy.*

C clasp. Simple, C-shaped clasp found on antique brooches.

Channel set. Rows of gems secured by metal flanges. No claws or beads are used.

Clawed collet. Gemstone ring setting characterized by integral triangular, flat claws or prongs. Typically used in early nineteenth-century jewelry.

Closed back. Setting in which the pavilion of a stone is completely enclosed; may be foiled.

Collar. Metal band encircling a gemstone.

Collet set. See Bezel set.

Composition. Plastics, including celluloid, Bakelite, and similar varieties. Earliest examples date to the 1850s.

Crown. Portion of the gemstone above the girdle.

Cruciform. Cross-shaped article or jewelry section.

Culet. Small facet polished across the pavilion point of a faceted stone.

Cultured pearl. Pearl created by artificial introduction of a nucleus into a mollusk, which stimulates accumulation of nacre and forms the pearl. Cultured pearls take approximately three years to form in salt water; less in fresh water or the South Seas.

Curb chain. Chain characterized by flattened links.

Cushion cut. Square or rectangular stone with rounded corners, as in old mine-cut stones.

Demi-parure. Small ensemble of jewelry, usually brooches and earrings or a necklace and earrings.

Doublet. Two-part assembled stone, frequently a garnet crown over glass pavilion. May imitate any stone.

Emerald cut. Rectangular step-cut or trap-cut stone with a 45-degree corner angle.

En esclavage. Plaques joined by two or more parallel chains. Necklace style popular in the early nineteenth century.

Estate jewelry. Previously owned jewelry, not necessarily antique items.

Faceting. Process of polishing a gemstone into a series of planes for maximum beauty and brilliance.

Fancy color. In sapphires, any color other than blue; in diamonds, gold, blue, pink, green, and deep brown.

Filigree. Fine wire bent and soldered to create a design. May be backed or open.

Fob. Seal or other decorative item suspended from a man's watch chain.

Foiling. The practice of backing a stone in thin metal foil in a closed-back setting to add color and/or brilliance to the stone. Common in antique jewelry, even in diamonds.

Fracture. Break of any sort other than cleavage; may occur in any stone.

French ivory. Celluloid made to resemble ivory. Popular in twentieth-century jewelry.

French jet. Black glass used to simulate jet. Popular in late nineteenth- to twentieth-century jewelry.

Gallery. Area below the setting in a ring. May be pierced, carved, or otherwise designed.

Girandole. Brooch or earrings with swinging pear-shaped drops. Popular in the eighteenth and nineteenth centuries.

Girdle. The extreme edge of a fashioned gemstone that divides the crown and pavilion.

Gold filled. Base metal joined with layers of gold, similar to rolled gold. A stamped fraction may indicate the ratio of gold content to total metal weight.

Green beryl. Green gemstone not intense enough to be called emerald.

Gypsy setting. Setting style in which the stone is set with table flush to the surface of the shank.

Habillé. Cameos "dressed" with gems and/or metal jewelry.

Hair compartment. Glazed recess on the reverse side of a jewelry article that holds the hair of the owner's friend, lover, or relative. Not necessarily memorial items, hair compartments were common in jewelry made during the 1840s.

Hair jewelry. Braided human hair made into watch chains, earrings, and other jewelry items, as mementos or memorial pieces.

Hallmark. British system of marking precious metals, used since 1300 to signify metal fineness, maker, and town in which the item was assayed.

Holbeinesque. Nineteenth-century Renaissance-style jewelry named after Hans Holbein *fils,* the German painter.

Hololith ring. Finger ring cut from one piece of gemstone material.

Illusion setting. Stone surrounded by metal, making it appear larger than it is.

Imperial jade. Translucent, evenly colored, emerald green jadeite. The finest jadeite, Imperial jade is extremely rare.

Incrustation. Overlay of gemstones, gold, and the like on the surface of another substance.

Intaglio. Design incised on a hardstone carving material; the opposite of a cameo.

Lavaliere. Delicate pendant worn on or attached to the neck chain and dating to approximately 1900.

Mabe pearl. Cultured blister pearl, usually filled and backed with mother-of-pearl bead; used for earrings, rings, and other jewelry articles.

Maker's mark. Initials or trademark stamped or engraved on jewelry.

Marquise. Stone or jewelry item that is essentially oval but has pointed ends.

Matrix. Parent rock supporting the growth of a gem or mineral, usually turquoise or opal.

Mazarin cut. See Single cut.

Micromosaic. Small pieces of *tesserae,* or glass, grouted to form a design, usually in jewelry from Rome.

Mosaic. Pieces of glass or gems set in grouting to form a pattern.

Mourning or *memorial jewelry.* Common remembrances of relatives or acquaintances. May be engraved with details or have hair compartments. If enameled, these items are usually black or blue. White enamel, indicating purity or innocence, was used only for memorials of children and unmarried women.

Native cut. Cutting style characterized by facet irregularities. Common in pre-twentieth-century jewelry, items made in India, and in synthetic gemstones.

Natural pearl. Pearl formed naturally in the mollusk, probably as a reaction to a virus and not because of irritation caused by grains of sand, as previously thought. X-radiography is sometimes used to prove natural origin.

Nickel silver. An alloy of 65 percent copper, 5 to 25 percent nickel, and 10 to 30 percent zinc.

Niello. A mixture of silver, lead, and sulphur used like enamel.

Old European cut. Diamond cut with circular shape and large culet; table diameter is usually 50 percent or less than that of the girdle. The cutting style was commonly used between 1885 and 1915.

Old mine cut. Diamond cut with a cushion shape, large culet, and the girdle placed nearly halfway between the table and culet. Table diameter is usually 50 percent or less than that of the girdle. The cutting style was commonly used in the last half of the nineteenth century.

Open back. Setting that allows interplay of light within the set stone.

Parure. Suite of antique (usually late-eighteenth to nineteenth century) jewelry that may include a necklace, pendant, brooch, earrings, and bracelets.

Paste. Glass that has been molded, faceted, carved, or otherwise made to resemble gem material.

Paved. Bead-set jewelry whose surface has been "paved" with small stones.

Pavilion. Portion of the gemstone below the girdle.

Pietra dura. Pieces of polished gem material set in a ground of slate, lapis lazuli, or similar material. It is produced primarily in Florence, and is also called Florentine mosaic work.

Pink sapphire. Corundum not red enough to be called ruby.

Piqué. Gold and silver worked into tortoiseshell in patterns of lines, scallops, or geometrical designs. Styles include flowers (*piqué posé*), stars and dots (*piqué point*), and larger points (*piqué clouté*). Also, European clarity grade of diamonds in the imperfect range.

Provenance. Documented history of an item, including origin and important owners.

Rebus. Words represented by pictures of objects or by symbols, the names of which, when sounded in sequence, reveal a message. Often used in intaglios for seal purposes.

Reconstituted amber. Fragments of amber compressed under heat and pressure to form beads.

Registration mark. Mark or symbol indicating the registration date of a design, not commonly used on jewelry. When present, it confirms British manufacture and the approximate production date. Also called *kite mark.*

Reverse intaglio. Incised carving on the base of a rock-crystal cabochon that is then colored and backed by mother-of-pearl. Popular technique from the late-nineteenth through the first half of the twentieth century. Sometimes called *Essex crystal.*

Revivalist jewelry. Jewelry pieces reviving ancient or period styles and techniques, produced throughout the last half of the nineteenth century.

Rococo. Early to mid-nineteenth-century design style featuring curved lines and shell, scroll, and foliage motifs.

Rose cut. Cutting style in which a stone is cut with a flat base, a pointed, faceted top, and at least three regularly placed triangular facets. The style originated in India, was a common early diamond cutting style, and is still often used for garnets.

Rose gold. Gold of any karat alloyed with copper or with copper and silver.

Round brilliant cut. Standard modern cutting style for round diamonds and most colored stones, featuring fifty-eight facets, thirty-three above the girdle and twenty-five below. Not all round brilliant-cut gemstones will have a faceted culet.

Sautoir. Long rope of beads or chain, continuous or open-ended, popular from the early nineteenth century onward. Modern versions are often completed with tassels.

Seal. Intaglio carving with design reversed so that it is readable when impressed in wax.

Senaille. Cutting style similar to rose cut but characterized by irregular facet shapes and arrangement.

Silk. Microscopic needlelike inclusions found in ruby, sapphire, chrysoberyl, and similar materials. Responsible for producing the cat's-eye or star effect.

Single cut. Round brilliant cutting style featuring eighteen facets. Used for smaller stones.

Soudé emerald. Fused emerald doublet. The term is commonly misapplied to nonfused emerald doublets.

Split ring. Ring that will hold suspended lockets, fobs, and so on, similar to the modern key ring.

Star set. Star engraved into the metal surface of a jewelry item, with the stone bead set in the center. Sometimes confused with gypsy settings.

Step cut. Cutting style with horizontal, layered facets, as in emerald cut. Also called *trap cut.*

Style. Refers to jewelry article with the appearance of being made in a designated period but actually made at a later date.

Sugar loaf. Highly domed, even-ridged cabochon popular from 1910–1930.

Swiss cut. Old diamond cutting style halfway between a single and a full cut. Usually has thirty-two facets.

Synthetic. Manmade material with essentially the same optical, chemical, and physical properties as its natural counterparts.

Table. Flat top facet of a gemstone.

Target brooch. Round brooch often paved with turquoise. Popular from the mid- to late-nineteenth century.

Tesserae. Tiny pieces of glass tubing used to produce Roman mosaics.

Tested. Metal that has been acid tested to ascertain type and fineness.

Tiffany setting. Head for setting stones with four or six long, slender prongs and a round, flared base.

Trap cut. See Step cut.

Tremblant. Jewelry item with sections mounted on tiny springs to allow movement.

Triplet. Three-part assembled stone that is intended to resemble a fine gemstone, such as a crown of garnet, layer of colored cement, and glass pavilion that looks like a fine emerald.

Vegetable ivory. Palm tree nut (tagua nut) that can be carved and polished.

Vermeil. Gold plated on a sterling-silver base.

(Prepared by Waller Antiques, Ltd., Victoria, British Columbia)

BIBLIOGRAPHY

Adair, John. 1945. *The Navajo and Pueblo silversmiths.* Norman, OK: University of Oklahoma Press.

American Indian Art Magazine. 1986. Great Lakes Issue 11, no. 3 (Summer).

American Institute of Real Estate Appraisers and the Society of Real Estate Appraisers. 1981. *Real estate appraisal terminology.* Rev. ed. Ed. Byrl N. Boyce. Cambridge, MA: Ballinger Publishing Co.

American Society of Appraisers. 1968. *The principles of appraisal practice and code of ethics.* Rev. ed., July 1986, reprint series #33. Pamphlet. Rev. ed. 1994.

Anderson, Ronald A., and Walter A. Kumpf. 1976. *Business law.* Cincinnati: South-Western Publishing Co.

Appraisers Guild. 1985. *The jewelry appraiser's manual.* Garden Grove, CA: Appraisers Guild.

Babcock, Frederick M. 1976. A look at valuation science. In *Commentary on personal property appraising.* ASA Monograph #7. Washington, DC: Corporate Press.

Babcock, Henry A. 1980. *Appraisal principles and procedures.* Washington, DC: American Society of Appraisers.

Baker, Lillian. 1978. *One hundred years of collectible jewelry.* Paducah, KY: Schroeder Publishing Co.

———. 1986. *Fifty years of collectible fashion jewelry: 1925–1975.* Paducah, KY: Collector Books.

Barlow, Ronald S. 1979. *How to be successful in the antique business.* El Cajon, CA: Windmill Publishing Co.

Becker, Vivienne. 1982. *Antique and twentieth-century jewelry.* New York: Van Nostrand Reinhold.

Bell, Jeanenne. 1985. *Answers to questions about old jewelry: 1840–1950.* Florence, AL: Books Americana.

Berk, Merle. 1986. Deborah Aguado. *Lapidary Journal* 39, no. 12 (March): 36.

Biddle, Julia. 1981. Appraising an appraiser. *Colored Gem Digest 2,* no. 3 (Fall): 18.

Blakemore, Kenneth. 1971. *The book of gold.* New York: Stein and Day.

Brugger, George A. 1981. A short course in survival techniques for expert witnesses. *ASA Valuation* 27, no. 1 (November): 11–20.

Brunner, Herbert. 1971. *Kronen und herrschaftszeichen in der schatzkammer der residenz München.* Münich: Verlag Schnell & Steiner.

Burack, Benjamin. 1984. *Ivory and its uses.* Rutland, VT: Charles E. Tuttle Co.

Canadian Jeweller 1986 Trade Mark Index. Ed. Simon Hally. 107, no. 7 (July). Annual publication.

Changing Times. 1985. Your jewelry: What it's worth. *Changing Times* 39, no. 2 (February).

Chu, Arthur, and Grace Chu. 1978. *The collector's book of jade.* New York: Crown Publishers.

Clair, Bernard E., and Anthony R. Daniels. 1982. *Consultation with a divorce lawyer.* New York: Simon & Schuster.

Covington, Margaret. 1985. Use of expert assistance in jury selection. *Case & Comment 90,* no. 4 (July/August): 20–26.

Davenport, Cyril. 1904. Cameos. Extract from *The Smithsonian Report,* reproduced in facsimile, 1967. Seattle: Shorey Book Store.

David, Mary L., and Greta Pack. 1982. *Mexican jewelry.* Austin: University of Texas Press.

Dolan, Maryanne. 1984. *Collecting rhinestone jewelry.* Florence, AL: Books Americana.

Drucker, Edward. 1980. Appraiser's fees: The other side of the coin. *The Appraiser's Information Exchange.* Newsletter of the International Society of Appraisers. (October): 8.

Ehrhardt, Roy. 1974. *American pocket watch identification*

and price guide. Bk. 2, rev. ed. Kansas City, MO: Heart of America Press.

Ehrhardt, Sherry, and Peter Plane. 1984. *Vintage American and European wristwatch price guide.* Kansas City, MO: Heart of America Press.

Fales, Martha Gandy. 1970. *Early American silver for the cautious collector.* New York: Funk & Wagnalls.

Farrell, Eileen, and Marie E. Thomas. 1983. The search for a perfect language. *The Goldsmith* 163, no. 6 (October): 33–39, 87.

Farrell, Eileen. 1985. The pros and cons of price lists, part two: The appraiser—friend or foe? *The Goldsmith* 166, no. 6 (March): 83–86.

Federal Trade Commission. *Guides for the jewelry industry.* Rev. April 15, 1986. 16 Code of Federal Regulations, part 23. Washington, DC: U.S. Government Printing Office.

Gemological Institute of America. 1967. *The jeweler's manual.* Los Angeles: Gemological Institute of America.

Gill, Spencer. 1975. *Turquoise treasures.* Portland, OR: Graphic Arts Center Publishing Co.

Gump, Richard. 1962. *Jade, stone of heaven.* Garden City, NY: Doubleday & Co.

Harris, Ian. 1979. *The price guide to antique silver.* Suffolk, Great Britain: Baron Publishing.

Hemrich, Gerald I. 1966. *The handbook of jade.* Mentone, CA: Gembooks.

Henzel, S. Sylvia. 1982. *Collectible costume jewelry with prices.* Lombard, IL: Wallace-Homestead Book Co.

Herzberg, Carol. 1983. Experts' clues aid in evaluating antique jewelry. *National Jeweler* 27, no. 14 (July 16): 28.

Holland, Margaret. 1978. *Phaidon guide to silver.* Oxford, Great Britain: Phaidon Press Ltd.

Huffer, Helene. 1983a. Gem identification, treatment, appraisals, antiques: Conference tackles industry issues. *Jeweler's Circular-Keystone* 154, no. 8 (August): 11–20.

_____. 1983b. Appraisal groups test and title. *Jeweler's Circular-Keystone* 154, no. 11 (November): 53–54.

_____. 1983c. How much markup is enough? *Jeweler's Circular-Keystone* 154, no. 12 (December): 60–61.

_____. 1985. Which appraisal system is best? *Jeweler's Circular-Keystone* 156, no. 3 (February): 146–54.

Jenkins, Emyl. 1982a. *Why you're richer than you think.* New York: Rawson, Wade Publishers.

_____. 1982b. Your day in court. *The Appraiser's Information Exchange.* Newsletter of the International Society of Appraisers (May/June): 6–7.

_____. 1986. It's no big deal—Form 8282: To sign or not to sign. *ASA Valuation* 31, no. 1 (June): 37–39.

Jensen, Shelle S. 1986. Tapping the corporate jewelry market. *Modern Jeweler* 85, no. 2 (February): 91–92.

Jeweler's Circular-Keystone. 1970. *Sterling flatware pattern index.* 2nd ed. Radnor, PA: Chilton Co.

_____. *Brand name and trade mark index.* 11th ed. Ed. Helena Matlack and Arlene Robinson. Radnor, PA: Chilton Co. Updated periodically.

_____. *Jeweler's Circular-Keystone Directory.* Radnor, PA: Chilton Co. Updated annually.

Kaplan, Arthur Guy. 1985. *The official price guide to antique jewelry.* Orlando, FL: House of Collectibles.

Kovel, Ralph M., and Terry Kovel. *A directory of American silver, pewter, and silver plate.* New York: Crown Publishers.

Kramer, Bobbie. 1983. History of class rings. *Southern Jeweler* 58, no. 6 (April): 9.

Kremkow, Cheryl. 1985. Bernd Munsteiner: Gem sculptor. *The Goldsmith* 168, no. 1 (October): 37–38.

Laure, Ettagale. 1983. Bulgari: Simply a sense of style. *Modern Jeweler* 82, no. 12 (December): 26–31.

Legrand, Jacques. 1980. *Diamonds: Myth, magic, and reality.* New York: Bonanza Books.

Leithe-Jasper, Manfred, and Rudolf Distelberger. 1982. *The Kunsthistorische Museum Vienna.* London: Philip Wilson Publishers and Summerfield Press.

Liddicoat, Richard T., Jr. 1975. *Handbook of gem identification.* Los Angeles: Gemological Institute of America.

Lipshy, Bruce. 1985. Customer service: The first core value at Zale Corporation. *Texas Retailer* 12, no. 4 (Winter): 16.

Lorene, Karen. 1984. *Jewelry Newsletter* 3, no. 2 (Fall).

MacBride, Dexter D. 1976. Personal property appraisal guidelines. In *Appraisal Monograph #7.* Washington, DC: American Society of Appraisers.

Matlins, Antoinette L., and Antonio C. Bonanno. 1998. *Jewelry & gems: The buying guide, 4th ed.: How to buy diamonds, pearls, colored gemstones, gold & jewelry with confidence and knowledge.* Woodstock, VT: Gem-Stone Press.

McCarthy, James Remington. 1945. *Rings through the ages.* New York: Harper & Brothers.

Medoff, Rosalind S. 1986. Value added, selecting organic gemstone material. *Lapidary Journal* 40, no. 2 (May): 42–49

Meilach, Dona Z. 1981. *Ethnic jewelry.* New York: Crown Publishers.

Moss, Barbara. 1981. Pearls: What to tell the customer. *The Goldsmith:* 70–71.

Muller, Helen, 1980. *Jet jewellery and ornaments.* Ayesbury, Great Britain: Shire Publications.

Naas-Kemper, Roberta. 1985. The story behind the names. *National Jeweler* 29, no. 16 (August): 63.

Ng, John Y., and Edmond Root. 1984. *Jade for you: Value guide to fine jewelry jade.* Los Angeles: Jade N Gem Corporation of America.

Newman, Harold. 1981. *An illustrated dictionary of jewelry.* London: Thames and Hudson.

Northrup, C. Van. 1986. Professionalism and the International Society of Appraisers. *The Appraisers Information Exchange.* Newsletter of the International Society of Appraisers.

Pliny the Elder (Gaius Plinius Secondus). N.d. *Historia Naturalis.* Book 37, *A Roman book on precious stones,* trans. Sydney H. Ball. 1950. Los Angeles: Gemological Institute of America.

Poynder, Michael. 1976. *The price guide to jewellery.* Suffolk, Great Britain: Baron Publishers.

Purtell, Joseph. 1971. *The Tiffany touch.* New York: Random House.

Rainwater, Dorothy T. 1979. *Encyclopedia of American silver manufacturers.* New York: Crown Publishers.

Retail Jewelers of America. 1979. *Appraisal guidelines.* New York: Retail Jewelers of America.

Rice, Patty. *Amber: Golden gem of the ages.* New York: Van Nostrand Reinhold Co.

Ring, Alfred A. 1972. *Real estate principles and practices.* 7th ed. Englewood Cliffs, NJ: Prentice-Hall.

Robinson, Larry. 1986. What to do about discount competition. *Jeweler's Circular-Keystone* 156, no. 3 (March): 76.

Ruppenthal, A. N.d. *Die edelstein gravierkunst/The art of gemstone engraving.* (Three-language edition.) Idar-Oberstein, West Germany: Ruppenthal Co.

_____. N.d. *Edle steine und mineralien/Precious gemstones and minerals.* (Three-language edition.) Idar-Oberstein, West Germany: Ruppenthal Co.

Ruskis, John J. 1981. Random suggestions for those working with gold and silver. *The Appraiser's Information Exchange.* Newsletter of the International Society of Appraisers: 13.

Sataloff, Joseph. 1984. *Art Nouveau jewelry.* Bryn Mawr, PA: Dorrance & Co.

Scarisbrick, Diana. 1984. *Il valore dei gioielli e degli orologi da collezione/Antique jewellery and watch values.* (Dual-language edition.) Turin, Italy: Umberto Allemandi & Co.

Schabilion, Shirl. 1983. *All in a nutshell.* Flora, MS: Keystone Comedy.

Shugart, Cooksey, and Tom Engle. 1985. *The complete guide to American pocket watches.* 5th ed. Cleveland, TN: Overstreet Publications.

Shuster, William G. 1983. How to buy or sell a store. *Jeweler's Circular-Keystone* 156, no. 10 (October): 140–41.

Sinkankas, John. *Van Nostrand's standard catalog of gems.* New York: Van Nostrand Reinhold Co.

Sitwell, H.D.W. *The crown jewels and other regalia in the Tower of London.* London: The Dropmore Press, Ltd.

Smith, Len Y., and G. Gale Roberson. 1960. *Business law.* St. Paul: West Publishing.

Snell, Doris. 1980. *American silverplated flatware patterns.* Des Moines: Wallace-Homestead Book Co.

Tardy. 1942. *Poincons d'or et de platine.* Paris: Tardy International Hallmark.

_____. 1981. *International Hallmarks on silver.* Paris: Tardy International Hallmark.

Tavernier, Jean-Baptiste. 1676. *Travels in India.* Reprint. Trans. Valentine Ball, ed. William Cooke. New Delhi: Oriental Books Reprint Co. 1977.

Thomas, Sally A., and Hing Wa Lee. 1986. Gemstone carving in China: Winds of change. *Gems & Gemology* 22, no. 1 (Spring): 32–34.

Valant, Francine. 1973. The care and cleaning of gems and jewelry. *Rocks and Minerals.* Official journal of the Rocks and Minerals Association. 48, no. 6: 423–24.

Victorian Silverplated Holloware. 1972. Des Moines: Wallace Homestead Book Co.

Walker, Marguerite P. 1982. The cost, income and market approaches to valuation as utilized by personal property appraisers. *ASA Valuation* 28, no. 1 (November).

Welch, Robert M., Jr. 1980. *The closely-held business in divorce division: Discovery and valuation.* Paper read at Southern Methodist University Center for Advanced Professional Development, March 28.

Wertz, Edward, and Leola Wertz. 1968. *The handbook of gemstone carving.* Mentone, CA: Gembooks.

Westropp, Hodder M. 1874. *A manual of precious stones and antique gems.* London: Sampson Low, Marston, Low & Searle.

Zeitner, June Culp. 1986. Netsukes. *Keystone Marketing Catalogue:* 70.

_____. 1986. Opal in the United States. *Lapidary Journal* 40, no. 3 (June): 44.

SOURCES OF ADDITIONAL INFORMATION

American Gem Trade Association
P.O. Box 420643
Dallas, TX 75342-0643
A nonprofit organization formed to represent and promote the colored-stone industry. More than 465 members; sponsors annual gem fair in Tucson each February; offers a code of ethics for the industry.

American Society of Appraisers
P.O. Box 17265
Washington, DC 20041-0265
Founded in 1936 and represented by over five thousand members. ASA is the only multidiscipline appraisal testing/certifying society in the nation. ASA has eighty chapters in the United States and abroad.

American Watch Association, Inc.
P.O. Box 464
Washington, DC 20044-0464
AWA is open to members of the industry and has fifty full and associate members, including firms that manufacture, assemble, and import watches, and firms that supply components to the industry. AWA represents its members at federal and state governmental levels on all foreign-trade issues; participates in trademark integrity activities and consumer product warranty regulations.

Appraisers Association of America Inc.
386 Park Ave. South, Ste. 2000
New York, NY 10016
A group of over twelve hundred appraisers in a variety of fields, who establish and maintain ethical standards, improve appraisal skills, and publicize the profession.

The Canadian Gemmological Association
1767 Avenue Road
North York, Ontario M5M 3Y8 Canada

Canadian Jewellers Association
27 Queen St. East, Ste. 600
Toronto, Ontario M5C 2M6 Canada
Founded in 1918, with more than two thousand retail, wholesale, and manufacturing members.

Canadian Jewellers Institute
27 Queen St. East, Ste. 600
Toronto, Ontario M5C 2M6 Canada

The CJI offers a training course to retail jewelers that leads to the Graduate Jeweler and Accredited Appraiser certification.

Indian Arts & Crafts Association Inc.
122 La Veta Dr. NE
Albuquerque, NM 87108-1613

International Society of Appraisers
16040 Christensen Rd. Ste. 320
Seattle, WA 98188-2929

Jewelers of America, Inc.
1185 Avenue of the Americas
New York, NY 10036-2601
JA is the national trade association dedicated to promoting the welfare of all retail jewelers. The association offers benefits, services, and educational programs designed to aid its twelve thousand members in their retail operations.

Master Valuer International
P.O. Box 1844
Pearland, TX 77588
Comprehensive correspondence course and practical workshop for gems and jewelry appraising. No prerequisites. Course is accredited by University of South Florida and earns Professional Development Credits from ASA and ISA. Students who are gemologists can earn the Registered Master Valuer diploma.

The National Association of Goldsmiths of Great Britain and Ireland—Retail Jewellers' Silversmiths' & Horologists' Organization—Registered Valuers
78a Luke Street
London EC2A 4PY England

The National Association of Jewelry Appraisers
P.O. Box 6558
Annapolis, MD 21401-0558
Founded in 1981, NAJA is a professional association of individuals with an interest in the valuation and appraising of gems and jewelry.

The Silver Institute
1112 16th St. NW
Washington, DC 20036-4823
Worldwide association of miners, refiners, fabricators, and manufacturers.

INDEX

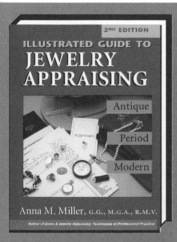

Buy Your "TOOLS OF THE TRADE . . ."
Gem Identification Instruments
directly from GEMSTONE PRESS

Whatever instrument you need, GemStone Press can help. Use the convenient order form (see over), or contact us directly for assistance.

ITEM / QUANTITY	PRICE EA.*	TOTAL $
Loupes—Professional Jeweler's 10X Triplet Loupes		
_____ Bausch & Lomb 10X Triplet Loupe	$44.00	$ _____
_____ Standard 10X Triplet Loupe	$29.00	_____
_____ The FillFinder ™ Darkfield Loupe (RosGem)	$174.95	_____
—Spot filled diamonds, other enhancements and zoning instantly. Operates with large maglite (optional—see over)		

Complete Pocket Instrument Set
SPECIAL SAVINGS!
BUY THIS ESSENTIAL TRIO AND SAVE 12%
Used together, you can identify 85% of all gems with these three portable, pocket-sized instruments—the essential trio.

• 10X Triplet Loupe • Chelsea Filter • Calcite Dichroscope

Pocket Instrument Set:
Standard: With Standard 10X Loupe • OPL Dichroscope • Chelsea Filter **only $144.95**
Deluxe: With Bausch & Lomb 10X Loupe • RosGem Dichroscope • Chelsea Filter **only $179.95**

	PRICE EA.*	TOTAL $
Color Filters		
_____ Chelsea Filter	$44.95	_____
_____ Synthetic Emerald Filter Set	$32.00	_____
_____ Bead Buyer's & Parcel Picker's Filter Set	$24.00	_____
Pocket Instrument Sets		
_____ **Standard:** With Standard 10X Loupe • OPL Dichroscope • Chelsea Filter	$144.95	_____
_____ **Deluxe:** With Bausch & Lomb 10X Loupe • RosGem Dichroscope • Chelsea Filter	$179.95	_____
Calcite Dichroscopes		
_____ Dichroscope (RosGem)	$115.00	_____
_____ Dichroscope (OPL)	$89.95	_____
Diamond Testers and Tweezers		
_____ Diamond Star I Diamond Tester	$99.95	_____
_____ Diamond Beam II Diamond Tester	$169.00	_____
_____ Moissketeer 2000 SD	$269.00	_____
_____ Diamond Tweezers/Locking	$10.65	_____
_____ Diamond Tweezers/Non-Locking	$7.80	_____
Gem Analyzer		
_____ Combines Darkfield Loupe, Polariscope and Immersion Cell in "pocket size" unit (RosGem)	$275.00	_____
Jewelry Cleaners		
_____ Ionic Cleaner—Home size model	$59.95	_____
_____ Ionic Cleaner—Professional large size model	$125.00	_____
_____ Ionic Solution—16 oz. bottle	$20.00	_____
Polariscope		
_____ Portable Polariscope	$90.00	_____

See Over for More Instruments & Order Form

* Prices, manufacturing specifications, and terms subject to change without notice. Orders accepted subject to availability.

Cut along dotted line

Buy Your "TOOLS OF THE TRADE . . ."
Gem Identification Instruments
directly from GEMSTONE PRESS

Whatever instrument you need, GemStone Press can help. Use the
convenient order form (below), or contact us directly for assistance.

ITEM / QUANTITY	PRICE EA.*	TOTAL $
Refractometer		
_____ Portable Refractometer (RosGem RFA 322)	$470.00	_____
—operates with small maglite (optional - see below)		
_____ Refractive Index Liquid—10 gram	$42.50	_____
Spectroscopes		
_____ Spectroscope—Pocket size model (OPL)	$89.00	_____
_____ Spectroscope—Desk Model w/stand (OPL)	$225.00	_____
Ultraviolet Lamps		
_____ Small LW/SW	$69.00	_____
_____ Large LW/SW	$189.00	_____
_____ Viewing Cabinet (for Large Lamp)	$147.00	_____
_____ **Purchase Large Lamp & Cabinet together**	$299.00	_____
for $299 and save $37.00		
Maglites		
_____ Large Maglite	$15.00	_____
_____ Small Maglite	$11.00	_____

Shipping/Insurance per order in the U.S.: $4.95 1st item,
$3.00 each add'l item; $7.95 total for pocket instrument set.   SHIPPING/INS. $_____

Outside the U.S.A.: Please specify _insured_ shipping method you prefer and
provide a credit card number for payment.

                                TOTAL $_____*

Prices, manufacturing specifications, and terms subject to change without notice. Orders accepted subject to availability.

Check enclosed for $_____ (Payable to: GEMSTONE Press)

Charge my credit card: ❏ Visa ❏ MasterCard

Name on card _____

Cardholder Address: Street _____

City/State/Zip _____

Credit   Card   # _____ Exp.   Date

_ _ _ _ _ _ _ _ _ _ _ _ _ _ _ _ _

Signature _____ Phone (_____)_____

Please send to: ❏ Same as Above ❏ Address Below

Name _____

Street _____

City/State/Zip _____ Phone (_____)_____

Phone, mail, or fax orders to:
GEMSTONE Press, P.O. Box 237, Woodstock, VT 05091
Tel **(802) 457-4000** • _Fax_ **(802) 457-4004** • _Credit card orders_ **(800) 962-4544**
www.gemstonepress.com

TOTAL SATISFACTION GUARANTEE
If for any reason you're not completely delighted with
your purchase, return it in resellable condition within
30 days for a full refund.

*All orders must be prepaid by
credit card, money order or check
in U.S. funds drawn on a U.S. bank.

010

See Over for More Instruments

Cut along dotted line

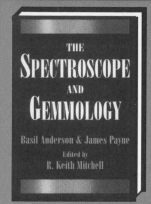

THE SPECTROSCOPE AND GEMMOLOGY
Ed. by R. Keith Mitchell, F.G.A.

"Well written and illustrated. An invaluable work for anyone involved in gemstone identification."
—*Choice, Science & Technology*

The first book devoted exclusively to the spectroscope and its use in gemstone identification, this comprehensive reference includes the history and development of spectroscopy; discussion of the nature of absorption spectra and the absorption spectra of solids and gem minerals; the many uses of the spectroscope and the spectrophotometer; light sources and the causes of color; absorption in synthetic gemstones; and more.
Indispensable for professional and amateur gemologists and students of gemology.

6" x 9", 288 pp., over 75 b/w illustrations; index
Hardcover, ISBN 0-943763-18-5 **$60.00**

THE PEARL BOOK:
THE DEFINITIVE BUYING GUIDE
How to Select, Buy, Care for & Enjoy Pearls
COMPREHENSIVE • EASY TO READ • PRACTICAL

The Pearl Book by Antoinette L. Matlins, P.G. is a timely addition to her other internationally acclaimed best-sellers on buying gems and jewelry. This comprehensive, authoritative guide tells readers everything they need to know about pearls to fully understand and appreciate them, and avoid any unexpected—and costly—disappointments, now and in future generations.

- A journey into the rich history and romance surrounding pearls.
- Differences between natural, cultured and imitation pearls, and ways to separate them.
- The five factors that determine pearl value.
- How to judge pearl quality, including tips on how to see differences with the naked eye.
- How to wear and care for pearls.
- Magnificent pearl creations from the world's leading jewelers.
- Comparisons of all types of pearls, in every size and color, from every pearl-producing country in the world.
- What to look for, what to look out for: How to spot fakes.
- Treatments: Good and bad.
- Important resource information, including pearl glossary, size charts, sample lab reports and more...

6" x 9", 232 pp., 16 full-color pages & over 250 color and b/w illus./photos
Quality Paperback, ISBN 0-943763-15-0 **$19.95**

FOR CREDIT CARD ORDERS CALL 800-962-4544
Available from your bookstore or directly from the publisher. TRY YOUR BOOKSTORE FIRST.

Please send me _____ copies of *The Pearl Book: The Definitive Buying Guide*
    at $19.95 plus $3.50 s/h for 1st book, $2.00 each add'l book in the U.S.*
Please send me _____ copies of *The Spectroscope and Gemmology*
    at $60.00 plus $3.50 s/h for 1st book, $2.00 each add'l book in the U.S.*
Check enclosed for $_____ (Payable to: GEMSTONE Press)
Charge my credit card: ❑ Visa ❑ MasterCard
Name on card _____
Cardholder Address: Street _____
City/State/Zip _____
Credit Card # _____ Exp. Date _____
Signature _____ Phone (_____)_____
Please send to: ❑ Same as Above ❑ Address Below
Name _____
Street _____
City/State/Zip _____ Phone (_____)_____

TOTAL SATISFACTION GUARANTEE
If for any reason you're not completely delighted with your purchase, return it in resellable condition within 30 days for a full refund.

Phone, mail, or fax orders to: **GEMSTONE Press**, P.O. Box 237, Woodstock, VT 05091 • www.gemstonepress.com
Tel (802) 457-4000 • Fax (802) 457-4004 • Credit Card Orders (800) 962-4544
Generous Discounts on Quantity Orders

Prices subject to change

*(Outside U.S.: Specify shipping method (insured) and provide a credit card number for payment.)

010

Please send me, at no charge, a *FREE* copy of *After You Buy:*
Tips on Gem & Jewelry Care & Protection and a *FREE* GEMSTONE Press Catalog.

I am particularly interested in the following subjects (check all that apply):
❏ Diamonds ❏ Colored Stones ❏ Pearls ❏ Jewelry Design
❏ Antique Jewelry ❏ Seminars/Workshops
❏ Costume Jewelry ❏ Periodic Price Guides
❏ Gemstone Cutting ❏ Videotapes ❏ Jewelry Appraising
❏ Gem Identification Equipment ❏ Other _____

My name _____

Street _____

City/State _____ ZIP _____

For additional copies of *After You Buy: Tips on Gem & Jewelry Care & Protection*
Send $5.00 and a *large* stamped, self addressed envelope for each copy to:

GEMSTONE Press
P.O. Box 237, Woodstock, VT 05091 | 009 |

- -

Please send **CAMEOS OLD & NEW, 2ND EDITION**
_____ copies at $19.95 (Quality Paperback) *plus s/h**

Please send **ENGAGEMENT & WEDDING RINGS, 2ND EDITION:**
THE DEFINITIVE BUYING GUIDE FOR PEOPLE IN LOVE
_____ copies at $16.95 (Quality Paperback) *plus s/h**

Please send **GEM IDENTIFICATION MADE EASY, 2ND EDITION:**
A HANDS-ON GUIDE TO MORE CONFIDENT BUYING & SELLING
_____ copies at $34.95 (Hardcover) *plus s/h**

Please send **GEMS & JEWELRY APPRAISING, 2ND EDITION**
_____ copies at $39.95 (Hardcover) *plus s/h**

Please send **THE ILLUSTRATED GUIDE TO JEWELRY APPRAISING, 2ND EDITION**
_____ copies at $39.95 (Hardcover) *plus s/h**

Please send **JEWELRY & GEMS: THE BUYING GUIDE, 4TH EDITION**
_____ copies at $17.95 (Quality Paperback) _____ copies at $24.95 (Hardcover) *plus s/h**

Please send **THE PEARL BOOK: THE DEFINITIVE BUYING GUIDE**
_____ copies at $19.95 (Quality Paperback) *plus s/h**

Please send **THE SPECTROSCOPE AND GEMMOLOGY**
_____ copies at $60.00 (Hardcover) *plus s/h**

Please send **THE TREASURE HUNTER'S GEM & MINERAL GUIDES TO THE U.S.A.: WHERE**
& HOW TO DIG, PAN AND MINE YOUR OWN GEMS & MINERALS—IN 4 REGIONAL VOLUMES
(Circle the volume(s) desired: NE States   SE States   NW States   SW States)
_____ copies at $14.95 per volume (Quality Paperback) *plus s/h**

Check enclosed for $_____ (Payable to: GEMSTONE Press)
Charge my credit card: ❏ Visa ❏ MasterCard
Name on card _____
Cardholder Address: Street _____
City/State/Zip _____
Credit   Card   # _____ Exp.   Date

Signature _____ Phone (_____)_____
Please send to: ❏ Same as Above ❏ Address Below
Name _____
Street _____
City/State/Zip _____ Phone (_____)_____

Phone, fax or mail orders to: **GEMSTONE Press, P.O. Box 237, Woodstock, VT 05091** • **www.gemstonepress.com**
Tel (802) 457-4000 • *Fax* (802) 457-4004 • *Credit card orders* (800) 962-4544
Generous Discounts on Quantity Orders

Prices subject to change | 010 |
* Shipping/Handling in U.S.: $3.50 for 1st book, $2.00 each additional book. Outside U.S.: Specify shipping method (insured) and provide a credit card number for payment.